North Carolina

A Guide to Backcountry Travel & Adventure

North Carolina

A Guide to Backcountry Travel & Adventure

James Bannon

Maps by

Jennifer G. Treeger
&
James Bannon

out there press
post office box 62092 • durham, nc 27715

North Carolina:
A Guide to Backcountry Travel & Adventure

Copyright © 1996 James Bannon

Library of Congress Catalog Card Number: 95–71155
ISBN   0–9648584–0–1

Although the author and publisher have made every attempt to insure the accuracy of the information provided herein, they accept no responsibility for any loss, damage, injury, or inconvenience sustained by any person using this book. Users of this book should be aware that wilderness travel carries certain inherent risks and can be dangerous or even fatal.

Cover photograph and design: James Bannon
Back cover photograph: Robert Jakubik

Manufactured in the United States of America

10 9 8 7 6 5 4 3 2 1

For My Grandparents

...when vegetation rioted on the earth and the big trees were kings.

– Joseph Conrad

Contents

Maps

Map Legend

••••••• .... Hiking Trail
ooooooo .... Mountain Bike Trail

⟨W⟩ .... Wild Trout Waters

⟨H⟩ .... Hatchery Supported Waters

⟨CR⟩ .... Catch & Release Waters

▲ .... Developed Campground

△ .... Primitive Campground

△ .... Backcountry Camping Area

▲▲ .... Group Campground

⟨shelter⟩ .... Shelter

⟨canoe⟩ .... Boat Ramp

⟨40⟩ .... Interstate

⟨64⟩ .... U.S. Highway

⟨70⟩ .... State Highway

⟨3651⟩ .... State Road

⟨411⟩ .... Forest Service Road

⟨ranger⟩ .... Ranger Station/Park Office

⟨building⟩ .... Other Building

— — — — — .... State Border
— — — — — .... Forest/Park Boundary

⟨bald⟩ .... Bald

Acknowledgments

The author gratefully acknowledges the assistance of the following people, who supplied information, answered questions, checked facts, and even corrected typos: Doug Oliver at the Tusquitee RD; Frank Findley and Dave Gustafson at the Cheoah RD; Sally Browning and Joe Nicholson at the Wayah RD; Chad Boniface and Judy Green at the Highlands RD; Sue Elderkin and Michael Gryson at the Pisgah RD; Tanya Henderson at the French Broad RD; Phil Kromer at the Grandfather RD; Lee Thompson at the Toecane RD; Kathy Ludlow at the Uwharrie NF; Holly Jenkins at the Croatan NF; at the NF headquarters in Asheville, Pat Momich for graciously volunteering to coordinate a review of the manuscript and Melinda McWilliams for supplying an inventory of trails; Dave Cook at Eno River SP; Beth Highley at West Point on the Eno Park; Mark Evan at the Piedmont Environmental Center; Steve Branson at Hagan-Stone Park; James Sessoms at Lumber River SP; George Carter at North Mills River Rec Area; Susan Reese and Michael Woody at Tuttle Educational SF; Ida Lynch and Linda Gintoli at The Nature Conservancy; at the Division of Coastal Management, John Taggart for sending me a ton of invaluable information on the estuarine reserves; Margaret Hassell at the DEHNR in Raleigh; Harry Le Grand and Inge Smith at the Natural Heritage Program; and Tanja Vujic at Duke Forest. Thanks are also owed to the NC Travel & Tourism Division, the NC Wildlife Resources Commission and the NC Division of Marine Fisheries for supplying information that undoubtedly made this a better book.

Also, for their generosity, good humor and tolerance of my frequent distractions while in their employ, thanks to the Honorable Patricia S. Love (retired), Edward E. Lawson, M.D. and Roberta G. Williams, M.D. And to Patricia Krebs of the Princeton Review, for her willingness to accommodate my busy schedule while I researched this book.

Personal thanks to Jennie and Jake for their contributions. And or course, to my family, for their encouragement and support.

Preface

I wrote this book because I wanted to use it and it didn't already exist. I live in North Carolina, in Durham, and spend a fair amount of my free time (and now also my work time) pursuing the activities covered in this book. On a typical outing, I combine several activities. My tastes in outdoor adventure run to long backpacking trips, fly-fishing for trout, and canoeing and kayaking on both white water and flat water. I wanted a guide book that would describe all the designated backcountry areas in the state and the possibilities for five major activities—hiking, camping, paddling, fishing and mountain biking. I wanted that book to be heavy on facts and light on subjective descriptions. In other words a book that would give me all the information I needed to plan a trip and to get started once I did. And nothing more. I think this guide book does that.

Of course in putting so much into one book, other stuff inevitably got left out. The descriptions of flora and fauna, for instance, have been kept to a bare minimum. Within each section, I rarely mention more than the major plant communities found at each area. Short sketches of these communities are included in the introductions to each of the state's three regions. If you're interested in fuller descriptions or in identifying specific species of flora and fauna, I recommend using one of the field guides available in bookstores. The Audubon Society and Peterson's both publish a complete series of nature guides with color photos.

A question I'm often asked when people learn that I've written this book is "Did you visit all of the areas?" The answer is yes, although the amount of time I spent in different areas varied greatly. Many I visited with the sole purpose of gathering information for this book. Others I spent several days at, with little else in mind beside hiking, fly-fishing, paddling and generally having a good time. The information contained herein is first-hand, supplemented by the generous help of the staff members of the various agencies that manage the state's natural resources.

One other thing. The information in this book is accurate as of the fall of 1995. Inevitably, things change. Prices will rise. Permitted uses on trails will change. An entrance fee to Great Smoky Mountains National Park seems to be just over the horizon. A marine fishing license is being discussed. In other words, the information in the book is reliable—to a point. If you're uncertain about something, use the addresses and phone numbers provided in each section to get current information.

I hope that you find this guidebook useful. I spent the better part of a very enjoyable year and a half researching and writing it. And now that it's done, I plan on spending some serious time putting it to use. See ya out there.

James Bannon
1995

Abbreviations

4WD	four wheel drive
approx	approximately
BRP	Blue Ridge Parkway
CCC	Civilian Conservation Corps
DEHNR	Department of Environment, Health, and Natural Resources
E	east
ERR	estuarine research reserve
ft	foot/feet
FS	Forest Service
GSMNP	Great Smoky Mountains National Park
hr	hour
jct	junction
I	interstate
L	left
mi	mile/s
mp	milepost
mtn	mountain
N	north
NC	North Carolina (state highway)
NF	national forest
NP	national park
NPS	National Park Service
NS	national seashore
NERR	national estuarine research reserve
NWR	national wildlife refuge
ORV	off road vehicle
R	right
RD	ranger district
rec	recreation
RS	ranger station
S	south
SF	state forest
SP	state park
SR	state road
SRA	state recreation area
USFS	United States Forest Service
USGS	United States Geological Survey
W	west
WRC	Wildlife Resources Commission

Introduction

From the Smoky Mountains to the Outer Banks, North Carolina is blessed with an astonishing variety of natural habitats and geographic features. The state is divided into three distinct regions—the mountains, the Piedmont and the coastal plain. In the mountains, you'll find the highest peaks east of the Rockies; on the rolling piedmont plateau are many of the states major rivers and recreational lakes; and on the coast are a string of famed barrier islands that stretch almost the entire length of the state. For the backcountry traveller and outdoor enthusiast, this diversity translates into a windfall of possibilities. You can kayak for weeks around pristine beaches and salt marshes in the sounds and ocean that surround the Outer Banks; fly-fish for wary brook, rainbow and brown trout on more than 2,000 miles of public trout waters in the mountains; hike to the highest peak on the East Coast, on a 50-mile stretch of deserted beach, or along more than 300 miles of the *Appalachian Trail*; mountain bike dozens of miles of roads on a national forest or refuge; and make camp at one of more than 100 developed campgrounds or backpack into the backcountry and camp with only the stars for company. With so much diversity, it would take years to exhaust all the options that the state offers the outdoor recreationalist.

North Carolina is a big state. On a straight line, it covers more than 500 miles from the Outer Banks to Tennessee. North to south at the state's widest point is nearly 200 miles. The coastal plain occupies the eastern half of the state, extending west almost as far as Raleigh, the state capital. The Piedmont is a rolling plateau that occupies a slightly smaller area. It extends from the fall line west to the Blue Ridge Escarpment. The mountains occupy a relatively small land area—less than one-tenth of the state's total area.

Agriculture once formed the backbone of the economy. Although it still plays a major role, in the past fifty years the state has become increasingly urban and high-tech. Most agricultural products—tobacco, cotton and peanuts are the primary crops—are produced on the Piedmont and coastal plain, where hog farming is also common. Major urban centers are located on the Piedmont, where they form a crescent defined by Charlotte, Winston-Salem, Greensboro, Durham and Raleigh. Asheville is the largest city in the mountains; Wilmington is the largest coastal city. Total population in the state is approximately six million.

Climate & Weather

North Carolina's climate is generally mild, with short winters in all parts of the state except the mountains, where the seasons are more clearly distinguished and winter is accompanied by freezing temperatures and substantial snowfall. Temperatures in most of the state range between an average high of about 87° in July and 50° in January, with temperatures in the mountain region about 10° lower at all times of year. Record lows below -30° have been recorded at the highest elevations. The Piedmont and coastal region experience snow not more than a handful of times each year; some years there's no snow at all. Spring and fall (and summer in the mountains) are typically the most comfortable seasons for strenuous outdoor activity. Summer can be hot and humid across most of the state, with temperatures in the 90s not uncommon. Late afternoon is often the hottest time of day. Severe storms are rare, except on the coast during hurricane season in late summer and fall. Afternoon thunderstorms in late spring and summer are common across much of the state. These storms are often accompanied by dramatic displays of lightening. If you're outdoors during one of these electrical storms, you should take necessary measures to reduce the risk of being struck by lightening. More people are struck by lightening in North Carolina than in almost any other state.

The Backcountry

Almost two million acres of publicly-owned land—an area the size of Delaware and Rhode Island combined—are covered in this book. Included in these holdings are a national park, two national seashores, ten national wildlife refuges, four national forests, twenty-seven state parks, four state recreation areas, four national estuarine research reserves and six state forests. Each category is administered with slightly different goals, providing for the outdoor enthusiast a diversity of environments and opportunities for hiking, paddling, camping, fishing, mountain biking and other recreational pursuits.

The national park, national seashores and national forests have the most extensive backcountry. Recreation is a major focus of all three and it's here that you'll find the most primitive conditions—each is a place where you can meet nature on its own terms. Facilities and conveniences are kept to a minimum, and these areas provide the best opportunities for extended backcountry expeditions.

The national wildlife refuges and estuarine research reserves are similarly undeveloped, though their primary mission is wildlife preservation and study, with recreation of relatively minor importance. The wildlife refuges and estuarine reserves are open to visitors only during daylight hours; camping is not allowed.

The state parks and state recreation areas, on the other hand, are geared toward heavy recreational use. The parks and rec areas are smaller than the national forests or national park, and the limited backcountry is less demanding on the visitor and more suitable to short, casual visits that don't require the same level of preparation as extended trips. These areas provide the majority of recreational opportunities in the Piedmont. While most of the parks and rec areas have camping facilities, they all close at night. State parks and rec areas all open at 8 am daily. Closing time is according to the following schedule: Nov–Feb 6 pm; Mar, Oct 7 pm; Apr, May, Sep 8 pm; Jun–Aug 9 pm. The rec areas are all located on bodies of water—three lakes and an ocean.

In the state forests, the primary goal is educational. These are good places to go to brush up on your knowledge of plants and trees. Covering not more than several hundred acres, they're best suited to day-trips.

The Blue Ridge Parkway, a 469–mile scenic highway administered by the National Park Service that runs between Great Smoky Mountain National Park and Shenandoah National Park in Virginia. 7 rec areas—up to 6,000 acres in size—are located along the parkway in North Carolina.

Private preserves and county and city parks round out the categories of backcountry areas described in this book.

Backcountry Travel

In the last century and a half, America has become a nation of city-dwellers. As we've moved from the farms and fields to apartment complexes and suburban developments, the undeveloped parts of the country have again become a *terra incognita*—a land unknown, or at least less familiar. When we visit mountain forests, isolated rivers, or deserted islands, it is often as strangers in a strange land. We encounter plants we cannot name, hear noises we do not recognize, fear animals whose habits we do not know. Often, both we and the wilderness suffer from this ignorance.

Travelling in the backcountry requires precautions to protect both the traveller and the backcountry. Although each of the five activities featured in this book requires at least some specialized knowledge and preparation unique to it, what follows is a basic outline of helpful information and potential hazards common to all backcountry pursuits.

The 10 Essentials

Topographic Map	Compass
Warm Clothing	Adequate Food
Flashlight	Fire Starter & Matches
First Aid Kit	Water
Knife	Whistle

10 More Essentials

Insect Repellent	Sunscreen
Sunglasses	Rain Gear
Hat	Hiking Boots
A Book	Camera
Backpack or Daypack	Tent

Clothing

Outfitting the well-appointed hiker, mountain biker, paddler, etc has become a major industry. One reason is the revolution in outdoor clothing that has occurred with the invention of water-proof-breathable materials such as Gore-Tex and synthetic fabrics that wick moisture away from the skin. Utilizing these technologies, clothing is now made for every conceivable activity and atmospheric condition, from kayaking in Patagonia during an ice storm to bushwhacking in the jungles of Borneo. In outfitting yourself for the outdoors, there are two points to keep in mind: 1) Hiking boots are the single most important piece of equipment; and 2) Clothing should keep you comfortable and dry under the worst conditions you're likely to encounter. In general, avoid wearing cotton, except during the hottest months. Cotton retains moisture and is extremely slow to dry, which means that if you're wearing jeans and a sweatshirt and get caught out in a rainstorm, you can expect to stay wet until you change clothes. If you don't have a change of clothes and the temperature is under 70°, hypothermia becomes a danger. Winter travel requires greater care in selecting equipment, as survival is more directly a factor of your clothing and other gear. A list of outdoor supply stores can be found at the back of this book.

Water

It's no longer safe to assume that water taken from rivers, lakes and streams is safe to drink. Regardless of how crystal clear the water of a cool mountain creek may look, odds are good that it contains bacteria and viruses. Giardia, a microscopic organism, has become the number one culprit in illnesses resulting from drinking untreated water. If you're going to drink surface water, you'll need to treat it first. There are currently three main methods of treatment. The oldest, and probably safest, is to boil the water for several minutes (some sources recommend 10 minutes). This is the method usually recommended in national park and national forest literature. Another method, increasingly popular with backpackers, is to filter the water through a portable water filter. Many different models are available; most cost between $50 and $150 and weigh less than 20 ounces. If you choose this method, be sure to buy a filter that eliminates organisms as small as 0.5 microns. One that also eliminates bacteria is preferable to one that doesn't. The third method is to treat the water with iodine tablets. The tablets impart a taste to the water that many find unpleasant. This is probably the least effective method, particularly if the water is very cold.

Hypothermia

Hypothermia is the condition that results when the body's core temperature drops below normal. If untreated, it is fatal. Symptoms include disorientation, lack of coordination, slurred speech, shivering and fatigue. To treat a victim, change him into warm, dry clothes, give him warm drinks, and put him in a sleeping bag. Building a fire can also help. In most cases of hypothermia, a combination of cold temperatures and wet clothes are responsible. The best way to prevent the condition is to be prepared. Bring clothes that will keep you dry and warm during the worst weather you might encounter.

Snakes and Insects

North Carolina is home to a number of species of poisonous snake, among them the cottonmouth, timber rattlesnake, copperhead, pigmy rattlesnake, eastern coral snake and eastern diamondback rattlesnake. Of these, the most commonly seen are the timber rattlesnake and the cottonmouth. The cottonmouth's range is limited to the coastal region, where it lives in habitats that provide fresh water. Its bite is dangerous, and has even been fatal in some cases. The eastern diamondback rattler, found only in the southeast corner of the state, is also to be avoided, as its bite is extremely dangerous. The best precaution is to be aware of where you're stepping and putting your hands. Snakes are usually only dangerous if threatened or startled. A snakebite kit, available at most outdoor stores, should be part of your first-aid kit.

Insects are more of a nuisance than a health hazard. Still, they can turn an otherwise enjoyable outing into an unpleasant exercise in swatting and itching. Mosquitoes, gnats, ticks, flies and chiggers all inhabit North Carolina. Biting insects are most prevalent in the coastal region between the months of May and October.

Getting Lost

If you become lost while in the backcountry, the most important thing to do is to avoid panicking. Sit down. Relax. Try to remember how you got where you are. If you're on a trail, backtrack and try to recognize familiar landmarks. If it's getting dark or you're injured or exhausted, don't move. The universal distress signal is three of anything—shouts, whistles, flashes of light (a mirror works for this). As a last resort, follow a creek or drainage downstream. Eventually it will lead to a road or trail. The best way to avoid getting lost is always to carry a topo map and compass and to know how to use them.

Hunting

White-tailed deer, black bear, wild turkey, ruffed grouse, quail, ducks and geese are all hunted in North Carolina. Hunting seasons vary considerably across the state. In general, the season runs from fall through winter, with typically much shorter seasons for individual species. Because seasons vary from county to county and region to region, it's impossible here to provide exact dates. A complete list of open season dates and hunting regulations is available from the N.C. Wildlife Resources Commission, 512 N. Salisbury St., Raleigh, NC 27604-1188; 919/715-4091. A state hunting license is required to hunt in North Carolina. Hunting is allowed on the national forests, national wildlife refuges and designated game lands. If you visit one of these areas during hunting season, be sure to wear at least one article of blaze orange clothing.

The No-Trace Ethic

The no-trace ethic is neatly summarized in the oft-quoted phrase, "Leave only footprints, take only photographs." Where once the untraveled portions of the country were true wildernesses, unvisited regions where the principal dangers were to the traveler, today the situation is reversed. When we speak of wilderness now, we mean a designated area protected by law from development and set aside for natural resource protection and backcountry recreation. The greatest dangers are to the wilderness, not to those who visit. Far from the mysteries and dangers that the word wilderness conjures, these places too often show abundant signs of human presence. Littering is of course inexcusable anywhere. But other, less obtrusive signs of human impact can also diminish the quality of a trip into the backcountry—and of the backcountry itself.

Campfires are first among these unsightly blemishes. Although the appeal of an open fire is undeniable, so too is its impact. Fire rings and the tramped-down, scarred earth that inevitably spreads around them remind us that we are not in the wilds, but are merely following in the footsteps of many others. Burning firewood deprives the soil and forest floor of important nutrients. Whenever possible, a portable camp stove is preferable. It may lack the visceral, romantic appeal of an open fire, but it preserves resources that are unfortunately jeopardized by our numbers. If you do build a campfire, keep it small and contained within an already existing fire ring. If no fire ring exists, build your fire on soil cleared of vegetation; a fire ring is not necessary. When you break camp, make sure the fire is extinguished; scatter the fire ring and any remaining wood and return the surrounding area to a natural state.

In choosing a campsite, it's best to select a site that already exists, but has not deteriorated into an obviously overused state. Minimize impact in making camp. Do not alter the site by digging trenches or creating log benches. When you break camp, return the area to a natural state by scattering leaves, twigs and other forest debris over the area.

To dispose of human waste, dig a hole six inches deep at least 100 feet from trails, campsites and water sources. After use, fill the hole in with soil and lightly tramp it down. Toilet paper should be burned or packed out.

Anything you bring with you into the backcountry should be packed out. When hiking, avoid using shortcuts on switchbacks.

Using this Book

This guidebook has two main purposes: 1) To catalog and describe all of the major backcountry areas in the state open to the public for recreation; and 2) To provide all the information you need to decide where to go, to get there once you do decide, and to know what to expect when you arrive. The book is divided into approximately 150 different backcountry areas covered in three main sections—The Mountains, The Piedmont and The Coast. Within each section the areas are arranged geographically, from west to east and from south to north, with a few minor exceptions.

This layout is intended to let you know which areas are close to one another and so help you plan trips where you visit more than one area.

Each listing begins with a brief description of the backcountry area. Information such as size, location, history, major natural features and open dates is included here. The main purpose of these descriptions, however, is to convey a general sense of the area—whether it's isolated, roadless wilderness; an easily accessible park frequently crowded on weekends; a busy recreational lake; or a remote region of the Outer Banks where water is scarce and mosquitoes abundant. Also included is the nearest town or city and the direction in which it lies.

A number of the areas have accompanying maps. These maps are intended to give a sense of the layout and most prominent features of an area. They are for illustration purposes only and should not be used for navigation or backcountry travel.

contact: Each entry includes the address and phone number of the administrative office that manages the area. This is your best source for additional information. If you have questions about local conditions or are uncertain about opening dates or times, this is the number to call. For all areas where there's a main listing followed by sublistings (i.e. national parks, national forests, state recreation areas, etc.) the address and phone number are only given once, under the main listing.

getting there: Directions to each area are from either a nearby town or city or from a major highway. I measured all distances in my car. Because odometer readers vary, it's a good idea to start looking for turns several tenths of a mile before where they're supposed to be.

A good road map is necessary to locate the starting point of the directions. You can buy one at any service station or get one free from the Department of Transportation, P.O. Box 25201, Raleigh, NC 27611; 919/733-7600 or 800/VISIT NC from outside the state. If you're going to be doing a lot of travelling in North Carolina, a good investment is DeLorme's *North Carolina Atlas & Gazetteer*.™ It's an 88-page atlas with large-scale maps that are particularly useful for finding and navigating back roads.

topography: This section will give you a rough idea of the type of terrain you can expect to encounter. Major geographical features—rivers, lakes, mountains, forest cover—are described, and high and low elevations are given where they have an impact on backcountry travel or are of interest. Hikers will find this section useful in determining the level of difficulty to expect on the trails. Elevations on the coastal plain are between sea level and 150 feet; on the Piedmont they range between 150 and 2,000 feet, with most elevations under 1,000 feet; in the mountains, most elevations are between 2,000 and 6,000 feet, with 43 peaks above 6,000 feet. Keep in mind that as altitude increases, oxygen supply decreases. **maps:** A good topographic map should be considered essential equipment for backcountry travel. Maps listed under this heading are only those that have a large enough scale to be useable as topo maps. There are 3 major types of topo maps that cover the backcountry areas described in this book: The 7.5 minute series published by the United States Geologic Survey, maps published by the Forest Service that cover the most extensive backcountry areas on National Forest Land, and maps published by private companies that cover Great Smoky Mountains National Park. USGS topo maps are listed for every area covered in the book. Maps listed as USGS-FS are USGS topo maps modified for Forest Service use. For areas where other maps are available, those are also listed. The list of outdoor stores at the back of this book indicates which stores sell the USGS topo maps. They're also available from the N.C. Geological Survey, P.O. Box 27687, Raleigh, NC 27611-7687; 919/733-2423. USGS-FS maps are available at each of the district ranger stations or from the NF headquarters in Asheville.

starting out: The primary purpose of this section is to indicate what you can or must do, once at an area, before heading out into the backcountry. Facilities, such as restrooms, water, pay phones, picnic areas, etc., that are located in the area are always mentioned here. Also included is any on-site source of information, such as a ranger station or park office. If you need to obtain a permit or pay a fee, that's indicated as well. Where possible, I've tried to determine where crowds tend to congregate and suggest where you can go to get away from them.

The last paragraph of the section lists some of the more important restrictions, such as rules against alcohol use and pet regulations. Don't assume that because something isn't included here it's allowed. Complete lists of restrictions are available from the various administrative contacts.

activities: This guidebook describes the North Carolina backcountry from the point of view of five major activities: hiking, camping, canoeing & kayaking, fishing and mountain biking. I've attempted to list these activities in order, beginning with the one that's the major attraction of any area. Although most areas are suitable for other outdoor activities, such as horseback riding, rock climbing, cross-country skiing, nature study and photography, only those five are listed under this heading. If one or more of the other activities is a significant attraction, it's typically mentioned as part of the main description or under *starting out*.

hiking: There are more than 2,000 miles of hiking trails in North Carolina. The large majority of these are located in the state's mountain region, with a substantially smaller number in the eastern half of the state. Descriptions under this heading are intended to give a general idea of hiking opportunities and conditions at each of the areas. Mention of individual trails is fairly uncommon. An attempt has been made to indicate trail mileage, conditions, allowed uses, location of trailheads, level of difficulty and any improvements, particularly bridges across rivers or streams. Mileages have been taken from administrative sources. In many instances I've rounded them to the nearest half-mile. The location of trailheads and trail markings and improvements have all been verified first-hand.

Trails on National Forest land have been assigned a number by the USFS. This number is shown on the maps in this book and in parentheses following the name of the trail the first time it's mentioned under this heading. These numbers are printed on the USFS wilderness and backcountry maps as well as on the USGS-FS topo maps. An exception to this numbering scheme is found on the Pisgah Ranger District, where the district has assigned its own trail numbers. These different numbers are reflected on the Pisgah District Trail Map and on some of the maps in this book.

If you want fuller descriptions of individual trails than is given here, I recommend *North Carolina Hiking Trails* by Allen de Hart. It describes all of the hiking trails in the state.

camping: Camping facilities have been divided into three main categories: developed campgrounds (usually referred to here as car campgrounds), primitive campgrounds that are accessible to autos, and backcountry camping. The last category can be further divided into two sub-categories: designated sites, such as those at Great Smoky Mountains National Park and at some of the state parks, and undesignated sites, often referred to elsewhere as wilderness sites. Dates for campground openings and closings should be considered estimates, as they vary from year to year depending on the weather.

canoeing/kayaking: Opportunities for paddling in North Carolina fall under three broad categories: flat water on enclosed bodies of water such as lakes and coastal rivers, whitewater on the rivers of the mountains and piedmont, and open water, encountered on the ocean, sounds and major tidal rivers. The intention of this section is to make you aware of the general conditions you can expect to encounter on a body of water and to indicate where access points are. Whitewater classifications, where given, are subjective. They are based on first-hand experience and official sources. This section is not intended as a primer on paddling techniques. If you are inexperienced or uncertain of whether conditions on a particular body of water are within your capabilities, you should seek instruction or advice from a reputable paddling school. Every year canoeists and kayakers become stranded or are seriously injured or killed because they put themselves in dangerous situations. The inevitable rescues cost money, risk lives and give the sport a bad name.

For paddlers wanting fuller descriptions of the state's rivers, two volumes are recommended. *A Paddler's Guide to Eastern North Carolina* by Bob Benner and Tom McCloud covers the rivers of the Piedmont and coastal plain. *Carolina Whitewater: A Paddler's Guide to the Western Carolinas* by Bob and David Benner describes all of the runnable whitwater rivers in North and South Carolina.

fishing: There are three major types of fishing in North Carolina. In the mountains, brook, rainbow and brown trout are the primary species of game fish. Approximately 4,000 miles of creeks and rivers contain trout, with 2,100 of those designated as Public Mountain Trout Waters. Only the brook trout is native to North Carolina. Browns and rainbows were introduced from Europe in the 19th century. Other species sought by anglers in the mountains are smallmouth bass, walleye and the very large, elusive muskellunge. On the freshwater rivers and lakes of the Piedmont and coastal plain, largemouth bass is the major game fish. Other species include striped bass, hybrid bass, crappie, bluegill, perch, chain pickerel and several species of catfish. The tidal rivers, sounds and Atlantic Ocean surf offer renowned fishing for species such as bluefish, Spanish and king mackerel, seatrout, pompano, flounder, red and black drum, cobia and tarpon. A state fishing license is required to fish the freshwater lakes, creeks and rivers of North Carolina. You can get one from an authorized seller or from the N.C. Wildlife Resources Commission, 512 N. Salisbury St., Raleigh, NC 27604-1188;

919/715-4091. As of this writing, no license is required for salt water fishing. The marine fishery is managed by the N.C. Division of Marine Fisheries, P.O. Box 769, Morehead City, NC 28557; 800/682-2632 (inside NC) or 919/726-7021 (outside NC).

This section is intended primarily to list most of the major game species found in a particular body of water; to describe the most appropriate angling methods, whether from a boat, bank or by wading; and to describe access.

mountain biking: This section should be used in conjunction with information included under *hiking*, where most trail information is given. Supplemental information found under this heading includes type of trail, whether single track, ORV trail, gated forest road or road open to autos; permitted dates of use; traffic level; typical conditions; and difficulty level. Most opportunities for mountain biking are on the national forests and at several of the national wildlife refuges.

A Last Word

There is something inherently appealing about parking your car, walking, paddling or pedaling into a remote region and being self-sufficient for a weekend, a week, or longer. It restores a sense of accomplishment and belonging. Although much is made of the risks of backcountry travel—both to the traveller and to the wilderness—in truth it takes little to insure a successful outing that minimizes both risk and impact: common sense, preparation, and respect for the land and its resources.

The Mountains

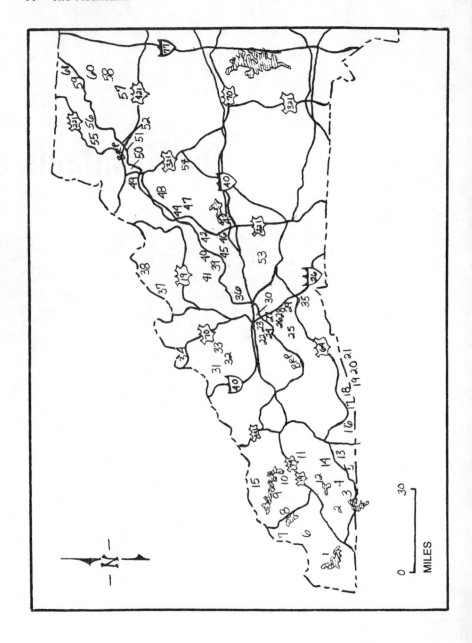

Mountains Region Key Map

1. Hiwassee Lake
2. Fires Creek Area
3. Chatuge Lake
4. Chunky Gal Mountain Area
5. Southern Nantahala Wilderness
6. Snowbird Mountain Area
7. Kilmer-Slickrock Wilderness
8. Lake Santeetlah
9. Fontana Lake Area
10. Tsali Rec Area
11. Nantahala River Gorge
12. Nantahala Lake
13. Standing Indian Area
14. Wayah Bald
15. Great Smoky Mountains NP
16. Cullasaja Gorge Area
17. Glen Falls Scenic Area
18. Blue Valley Area
19. Chattooga Wild & Scenic River
20. Ellicott Rock Wilderness
21. Whitewater Falls Scenic Area
22. Middle Prong Wilderness
23. Shining Rock Wilderness
24. Black Balsam Knob Area
25. Davidson River Area
26. Pink Beds Area
27. South Fork Mills River Area
28. North Fork Mills River Area
29. Lake Powhatan Rec Area
30. Mt Pisgah Rec Area
31. Harmon Den Area
32. Rocky Bluff Rec Area
33. French Broad River Area
34. Camp Creek Bald Area
35. Holmes Educational SF
36. Craggy Gardens Rec Area
37. Nolichucky River
38. Roan Mountain Area
39. Black Mountains Rec Area
40. Carolina Hemlocks Rec Area
41. Mt Mitchell SP
42. Crabtree Meadows Rec Area
43. Lake James SP
44. Linville Falls Rec Area
45. Old Fort Picnic Area
46. Curtis Creek Area
47. Linville Gorge Wilderness
48. Wilson Creek Area
49. Grandfather Mountain
50. Tanawha Trail
51. Julian Price Memorial Park
52. Moses H. Cone Memorial Park
53. South Mountains SP
54. Tuttle Educational SF
55. Mt Jefferson SP
56. New River SP
57. W Kerr Scott Reservoir
58. Rendezvous Mountain SF
59. Doughton Park
60. Stone Mountain SP
61. Cumberland Knob Rec Area

Introduction

North Carolina's mountain region begins abruptly at the western edge of the Piedmont plateau, where the eastern slope of the Blue Ridge Mountains rises as much as 2,000 feet. The mountain region is small—it covers less than one-tenth of the state's total area—but is notable for its dramatic landforms and ecological diversity. The Appalachian Mountains lie on a northeast–southwest axis between Maine and Georgia, an orientation which is maintained in North Carolina. They're one of the oldest mountain ranges on earth, having eroded over several hundred million years to their present state. The major mountain chains in North Carolina—the Smokies, Blue Ridge, Nantahala and Black—include some of the Appalachians' most formidable terrain and loftiest peaks. The mountains reach their highest elevation of 6,684 feet on Mt. Mitchell. Forty-two other peaks in the state top 6,000 feet.

The mountain summits and slopes are blanketed with forests, with a diversity of plant and animal species that is almost unmatched at this latitude. More tree species are found in Great Smoky Mountains National Park alone than in all of Europe. The flora and fauna that inhabit the North Carolina mountains are typically encountered only across distances as great as 1,000 miles. Species characteristic of the boreal, or northern, forest; the Southern Appalachian hardwood forest; and the mixed deciduous forest are all found in the mountain province.

The boreal forest is found on the state's highest peaks and mountain ridges. With species adapted for harsh, cold weather, this is the forest community that covers parts of New England and most of Canada. Spruces, firs and other conifers are the predominant tree species. Although the forest's difficult climate limits the number of plant species, wildflowers, shrubs, mosses and lichens are not uncommon. Mammal species that inhabit the forest include the black bear and bobcat. The climate of the boreal forest is the harshest encountered in North Carolina. Temperatures at the highest elevations rarely exceed 80°, even during the hottest summer days. In winter, they often drop well below freezing. Snow is common, with annual averages between 50 and 100 inches at most locations. Sudden storms that seem to arise out of thin air are also common, and of concern to backcountry travellers.

Moving down the mountain slope, the next forest community encountered is the Southern Appalachian hardwood forest. Actually, it's not one type of forest, but rather a collection of forest types that has come to be treated as a unique classification because of its incredible botanical diversity. The predominant tree species vary according to several factors—altitude, available light, and available moisture. At higher elevations the spruces and firs characteristic of the boreal forest are still encountered. Lower down, but at altitudes high enough to have been inaccessible to loggers, virgin tracts of yellow poplar, eastern hemlock, sugar maple, American beech and northern red oak are found in moist, dark coves. On the slopes with greater exposure oaks and pines dominate. Understories of both areas are dominated by rhododendron trees, which grow in dense, impenetrable thickets known as hells. As in the boreal forest, large mammals are rare. Black bear, white-tailed deer and bobcat are the primary species. The red wolf has been reintroduced recently into Great Smoky Mountains National Park. Non-native wild boars, which deprive bears and squirrels of important food sources, have been a destructive force for more than 50 years.

The lowest elevations in the mountains have been logged. The forests on these lower slopes are passing through the various stages of succession: first pines take root and reach maturity; then oaks begin to grow and crowd out the pines, which cannot tolerate the shade that the oaks create; finally other hardwood species, notably beeches, maples and yellow poplars, begin to compete with the oaks, until the forest attains a climax state as a mixed deciduous forest. The understory of the forest at the lower altitudes is generally more open than higher up the mountains, particularly if it's been logged within the last 50 years. Rhododendron, mountain laurel and dogwood are the dominant species. Animal species are the same as in the Southern Appalachian forest.

Although it comprises a relatively small area, the mountain region provides the large majority of opportunities in North Carolina for backcountry travel, particularly extended backpacking trips. A greater percentage of the land is publicly owned than elsewhere in the piedmont or coastal regions. Major holdings are the Nantahala National Forest, the Pisgah National Forest, Great Smoky Mountains National Park and the Blue Ridge Parkway. Visitors come from all over the eastern half of the country to see and spend time in the magnificent forests of these ancient uplands.

The mountains offer opportunities for outdoor recreation year-round. Summer is pleasant, lacking the heat and humidity of the Piedmont and coast. Spring and fall are crisp, with cool days and often chilly nights. Winters are cold and bring snow to the higher elevations.

Tusquitee Ranger District

Nantahala National Forest

Tucked in the remote, sparsely populated southwest corner of the state, the Tusquitee Ranger District covers 158,579 acres in Cherokee and Clay Counties. Boundaries are formed by Georgia (S), Tennessee (W), the Cheoah Ranger District (N) and the Wayah Ranger District (E). Much of the district is characterized by scenic high valleys and rolling mountains that are less rugged and imposing than elsewhere on the Nantahala National Forest. The exception is the eastern edge of the district, where the mountain terrain is rocky and steep. A portion of the Southern Nantahala Wilderness occupies the extreme southeast corner of the Tusquitee Ranger District. Almost all opportunities to explore the backcountry are found among the mountain ridges and peaks in this portion of the district. Recreation in other parts of the District centers on Hiwassee Lake, Apalachia Lake and Chatuge Lake, all of which were created by the construction of Tennessee Valley Authority dams on the Hiwassee River. Recreation facilities on the district include 2 developed car campgrounds and 3 primitive campgrounds which are also accessible by car.

Murphy is in the center of the district. Andrews (NE) and Hayesville (SE) are the only other towns of any size.

contact: District Ranger, US Forest Service, 201 Woodland Drive, Murphy, NC 28906; 704/837-5152.

getting there: US-19 and US-64 provide the primary accesses to the district. To get to the RS go to the jct of US-19 and US-64 in Murphy. From there, take US-19 SW 0.3 mi to a traffic light at Hiwassee St. Turn L and go 0.3 mi to the RS entrance, L.

topography: In the center of the district, the high, broad valleys of the Valley and Hiwassee Rivers give way gradually to rolling, rounded mountains. Mountains in the district are the Unicoi (NW), Snowbird (N), and the Valley River, Tusquitee and Nantahala (E). Highest elevations in the district are on Tusquitee Bald Mtn (5,249 ft) and Standing Indian Mtn (5,499 ft), located on the border with the Wayah RD. **maps:** see individual listings below.

starting out: The district RS is open M–F 8 am–4:30 pm. You can buy topo maps and a small selection of guidebooks here. Other info about the district is also available. Crowds are minimal throughout the district, making it a good alternative to the more crowded Wayah RD or Cheoah RD on busy summer weekends.

activities: Hiking, Camping, Canoeing/Kayaking, Fishing.

hiking: Although hiking opportunities are somewhat limited, the Tusquitee RD includes a number of long trails that can be connected for long trips. Trail access is at the Fires Creek Area, Southern Nantahala Wilderness and Chunky Gal Mountain Area. The Appalachian Trail follows the district's SE boundary for approx 12 mi. Shorter trails are located at Hiwassee Lake and Chatuge Lake.

camping: Car campgrounds are located at Hiwassee Lake and Chatuge Lake. More primitive car camping is available at 2 areas in the Fires Creek Area and at a small campground near the N end of the Chunky Gal Mountain Area. Opportunities for backcountry camping are abundant at the district's eastern edge.

canoeing/kayaking: Paddling opportunities on the district are found on 3 lakes—Hiwassee Lake, Apalachia Lake and Chatuge Lake.

fishing: Fires Creek and Big Tuni Creek both offer opportunities for trout fishing. The 3 major lakes are popular with anglers casting for largemouth and smallmouth bass and walleye.

Hiwassee Lake Area

At more than 6,000 acres, Hiwassee is the second largest of a string of 3 Tennessee Valley Authority lakes along the Hiwassee River, and the largest that lies entirely within North Carolina. Due to a narrow channel, the lake has an elongated, dragon-like shape and a 180-mile shoreline. Its primary tributaries are the Hiwassee River, Valley River and Nottely River. Hiwassee Lake empties into Apalachia Lake at its western end; Murphy, the largest town (population 5,000) in the area and the Cherokee County seat, is at the eastern end. The lake is scenic, with emerald green water surrounded by mountainous National Forest land blanketed with a pine/hardwood forest. Most area recreation is centered around the lake, with only limited opportunities for exploring the backcountry. 2 rec areas—Hanging Dog and Cherokee Lake—provide facilities for camping, picnicking, and hiking. Apalachia Lake has no developed rec areas on its shores and therefore receives less use than Hiwassee. It's a good option on busy summer weekends. Murphy (E) and Hiwassee Village (W) are the closest towns.

getting there: To get to Hanging Dog Rec Area, from downtown Murphy take Peachtree Rd (SR-1326), which becomes the Joe Brown Highway, 4.4 mi W to the rec area entrance, L. • To reach Cherokee Lake Rec Area, from the jct of US-64 and US-19 in Murphy, take US-64 W 8 mi to NC-294. Turn R and go 2.8 mi to FR-313 and a FS sign, R. The road dead ends after 0.5 mi at the rec area parking lot.

topography: Elevation on Hiwassee Lake is approximately 1,500 ft. The immediately surrounding countryside consists of rolling foothills with gradual elevations gains. The Unicoi (NW) and Snowbird Mtns (NE) ascend to greater heights in the distance. **maps:** USGS-FS Murphy, Persimmon Creek, Unaka.

starting out: Facilities are at Cherokee Lake (water, flush toilets) and Hanging Dog Rec Areas (pit toilets, water, pay phone). Cherokee Lake is a day-use area only. It has 20 picnic tables on a gentle grassy slope shaded by pines and dogwoods overlooking the placid lake. There's also a shelter with tables and grills. Hanging Dog has 2 picnic areas—1 overlooks the lake and has a few tables and a shelter. The other is loop D of the campground, which is used for picnicking when the sites aren't being used by campers.

activities: Canoeing/Kayaking, Fishing, Camping, Hiking.

canoeing/kayaking: Paddlers have a choice of 3 lakes—Hiwassee, Apalachia and Cherokee. Hiwassee Lake, the largest of the 3, is the major recreational lake in the SW corner of the state. Bass boats and water skiers are a presence, but the sparse population of the region and the lake's serpentine shape help keep traffic light and spread out. Scenery is similar to the other man-made lakes in NC: 5 or 6 feet of red clay at the waterline, and above it a relatively young mixed pine/hardwood forest. The FS owns almost all of the land surrounding the lake, so development isn't really a factor. Access to Hiwassee is at Hanging Dog, where there's a boat ramp. Another ramp is located on SR-1326 (the Joe Brown Highway) between Hanging Dog and Murphy, 3.5 mi W of Murphy.

Immediately W of Hiwassee is Apalachia Lake, which occupies a long, narrow channel between the larger lake and the Tennessee state line. Although considerably smaller than Hiwassee, Apalachia also receives much less boat traffic, making it a good bet for paddling. Most of the shoreline is owned by the NF. Access points are below Hiwassee Dam and at Apalachia Dam.

Cherokee Lake is a small impoundment connected to the S end of Hiwassee Lake. Little more than a mile long, it's best suited to a short paddle or a fishing trip. The lake is uncrowded; go on a weekday and you'll likely have it to yourself. Access is at the picnic area, where a portage of about 50 yds is necessary.

fishing: Fishing in Lake Hiwassee is for largemouth and small-mouth bass and walleye. Although there's some space along the banks at Hanging Dog with room to cast, most anglers fish from a boat. Fishing at Apalachia Lake is from a boat only, as there are no developed rec areas along its shores. Cherokee Lake, on the other hand, has a long handicapped accessible pier at the picnic area, as well as 2 smaller piers along the hiking trail. There's a large grassy bank—ideal for casting from—as well. One of the advantages to fishing Cherokee Lake from a canoe is the absence of power boats. Species in Apalachia and Cherokee are the same as in Hiwassee. Trout populations are supported by the Valley River and Persimmon Creek. Both are Hatchery Supported.

camping: The car campground at Hanging Dog is the only developed campground in the area. 66 sites are laid out in 4 loops in a large wooded area on the lakeshore. The mid-sized sites each include a table, grill, lantern post and tent pad. Privacy is not great, but is helped by the forest cover, which is fairly dense. Some sites are at lakeside, with room to launch a canoe or kayak. Modern restrooms (no showers) are centrally located. The fee is $4/night. The campground is open May 1–Oct 15.

Backcountry camping is permitted on NF lands around Hiwassee Lake and Apalachia Lake.

hiking: There are 3 hiking trails on the shores of Hiwassee Lake—1 at Cherokee Lake Picnic Area and 2 at Hanging Dog. The *Cherokee Lake Trail* (#83) is a short (0.3 mi), easy trail that follows the forested lakeshore from the picnic area to Persimmon Dam, providing access to 2 small fishing piers along the way. The trailhead is signed and the trail, well worn by fishermen, is easy to follow. The 2 trails at Hanging Dog Rec Area meander through approx 4 mi of the hardwood/pine forest that covers the mountain slopes that rise from the lake. Both trails follow narrow dirt footpaths and are easy to moderate to hike. The 2.1-mi *Hanging Dog Interpretive Trail*, aka the *Ramsey Bluff Trail* (#81) follows a ridgeline above the lake between camping loops B & D. There are 10 interpretive stations along the route, with guides available at the trailheads. The 1.5-mi *Mingus Trail* begins at a small parking area across from camping loop B. All trailheads are signed and both trails are blazed with blue bars.

Fires Creek Area

Located at the eastern edge of the district in Clay County, the Fires Creek Area is a 14,000-acre wildlife management area that has been set aside as a sanctuary for black bears. High mountain rims surrounding Fires Creek define the geography of the area. With only one access along a gravel forest road, the backcountry remains relatively isolated and offers an excellent opportunity for an extended backpacking trip. Except for a small, scenic picnic area and a couple of primitive campgrounds, the area is undeveloped. Although formerly logged, the mountainsides and river corridors are now heavily forested with hardwoods, pines, and a lush understory of rhododendron and laurel. There are outstanding views of the Fires Creek watershed and the Nantahala Mountains from a series of balds along the eastern rim, accessible only by hiking trail.

Hayesville (S) is the closest town.

getting there: From the jct of US-64 and NC-69 in Hayesville, take US-64 4.8 mi W to a svc station and SR-1302 (9.4 mi E of the jct of US-64 and US-129 in Murphy). Turn R and go 0.9 mi to a bridge crossing and bear R onto SR-1300. Go 3 mi and turn left at a FS sign onto unmarked gravel SR-1344, which becomes FR-340. Go 1.9 mi to the Leatherwood Falls Picnic Area and trailheads, L. FR-340 continues approx 10 mi along Fires Creek, with numerous pullouts.

topography: The region is defined by Fires Creek, flowing E to W, and a series of steep, rugged ridges that rise N (Valley River Mtns) and S (Tusquitee Mtns), and, above the creek's headwaters, E. Highest elevations are along these E mtns; Signal Bald, Tusquitee Bald, and Potrock Bald all top 5,200 ft. Fires Creek descends to 2,000 ft. **maps:** USGS-FS Hayesville, Andrews, Topton.

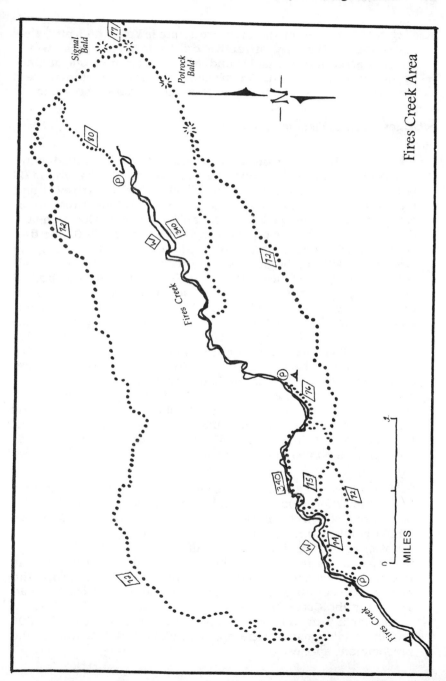

Fires Creek Area

starting out: Facilities in the area are limited. You'll find pit toilets and water in the very attractive creekside picnic area, which includes about a dozen tables and grills isolated from one another by heavy forest growth. An arched footbridge provides access across Fires Creek. The picnic area is handicapped accessible.

activities: Hiking, Fishing, Camping.

hiking: 6 trails cover more than 35 mi of the ridges, balds, and creeks of the Fires Creek watershed. At 25 mi, the *Rim Trail* (#72) is the signature trail in the area. It follows old forest roads and narrow footpaths along a series of ridges above Fires Creek in an elongated loop, with the 2 signed trailheads about 200 yds apart. One is in the picnic area, the other 0.1 mi E on FR-340. The trail is irregularly blazed, but not difficult to follow. Hiking is strenuous, with an elevation gain of more than 3,000 ft, though there are easy stretches. Water is infrequent along the trail. 3 other trails (#75, #76, #80) provide access to the *Rim Trail* from points along FR-340 and Fires Creek, making shorter loops possible. Trailheads are signed along FR-340. These trails make short (1.25-1.5 mi), steep ascents on narrow, rocky footpaths. Another trail connection is with the 22-mi *Chunky Gal Trail* (#77); its N terminus is between Signal and Tusquitee Balds and it runs SE to a jct with the *AT* and the Southern Nantahala Wilderness. 2 more trails begin in the picnic area. One is a very short, easy walk through the picnic area along the creek. The other, *Cover Trail* (#74), is a moderate trail that follows Fires Creek for almost 5 mi, providing good fishing access. The first mi of this trail is paved. Some trails are open to horses as well as hikers.

fishing: Fires Creek is a medium to large sized trout stream that flows E to W for about 12 mi between its headwaters and the FS boundary just S of the picnic area. For most of its course it follows a mild gradient through lush coves of rhododendron and a mixed forest of conifers and hardwoods. Although gravel FR-340 follows it almost to its headwaters, the road is little-travelled and the region fairly remote. Fishing pressure is not heavy, with the highest concentration at the picnic area. Access is from the road and along the *Cover Trail* (#74). Fires Creek is Wild Trout water, except for a 1-mi Hatchery Supported stretch between SR-1300 and the wildlife management area boundary. Rainbow trout is the predominant species.

camping: There are no developed campgrounds in the Fires Creek area. A primitive car accessible campground, known as Huskins Branch Hunt Camp, (but labeled Fires Creek on the USGS-FS topo), is located at the SW edge of the area, 0.8 mi S of the picnic area on FR-340. The only facilities at this site are pit toilets. A better bet for primitive car camping is along FR-340, where there are numerous pullouts with small campsites. Another possibility is the Bristol Horse Camp, a former primitive horse camping area located on FR-340 that has been converted to a primitive car campground with pit toilets and water.

Backcountry camping is allowed throughout the Fires Creek area (except at signed wildlife clearings), with the *Rim Trail* providing the best opportunities.

Chatuge Lake

Chatuge Lake is the easternmost of a string of Tennessee Valley Authority lakes on the Hiwassee River. It is located in Clay County on the North Carolina/Georgia state line, with about half of the 7,050-acre lake lying in Georgia. Most of the 133-mile shoreline is privately owned and much of it is developed; only the peninsula that contains Jackrabbit Mountain Rec Area is on National Forest lands. Nevertheless, the lake still provides a pleasant and attractive setting for a day or weekend spent canoeing, kayaking or fishing. Waterskiing, sailing and powerboating are all popular on the lake, but the numbers aren't so large as to spoil the lake's scenic alpine charm. The rec area has a developed campground, picnic area, small swimming beach, boat ramp and a pair of short hiking trails that wind through the Southern Appalachian forest which covers the area's rolling mountain terrain.

Hayesville (NW) is the closest town.

getting there: From the jct of US-64 and NC-69 S of Hayesville, take US-64 E 4.7 to NC-175. Turn R and go 0.9 mi to a fork in the road. Bear R, continuing on NC-175, and go 2.5 mi to Jackrabbit Rd (SR-1155). Turn R and go 1 mi to the rec area entrance.

topography: Lake elevation is 1,927 ft. The immediately surrounding countryside rises moderately to an elevation of 2,250 ft on Jackrabbit Mtn. **maps:** USGS-FS Hayesville, Shooting Creek, Hiwassee, Macedonia.

starting out: Restrooms, water fountains and a pay phone can all be found at the rec area. There's a day-use fee of $2 to use the swimming beach or picnic area (no charge for use of the boat ramp and hiking trails). The picnic area has individual tables and grills, as well as a shelter. It's located on one of the lake's many coves, and is shaded by a grove of pines and scattered hardwoods.

activities: Camping, Canoeing/Kayaking, Fishing, Hiking.

camping: The car campground has 103 sites arranged in 3 large loops on and near the lakeshore. Each site has a picnic table, grill, lantern post and tent pad. Some are located in isolated pockets along the lake and offer nice views and lots of privacy; others are spread out in relatively open clearings without much privacy. Modern restrooms with hot showers are centrally located. The fee is $8/night. The campground is open May 1–Oct 15. There are no opportunities for backcountry camping in the immediate area, though the Fires Creek Area (N) and Chunky Gal Mtn Area (E) are only a short drive away.

canoeing/kayaking: Although Chatuge Lake seems to have several drawbacks as a paddling destination—small size, popularity with waterskiers, a developed shoreline, and a dam—it is actually rather appealing. In truth, it doesn't get that much traffic, its numerous coves make it easy to slip out of the main channel, and much of the development along its shores is tasteful and unobtrusive. Its small size makes it well-suited for a short day or half-day trip, and a 4 mi paddle will put you in Georgia. Access is from the boat ramp in the rec area.

fishing: Chatuge Lake is known primarily for its smallmouth bass fishing. Other game species taken include largemouth and bodie bass, crappie and bluegill. Anglers have the option of fishing from a boat or from shore. To facilitate bank fishing, a number of fish locators—underwater cover of small trees and plants designed to create an optimum fish habitat—are maintained along the shoreline. These can be reached from the main trail loop that circles Jackrabbit Mtn. There's plenty of room at these spots to allow for casting even a flyrod. A mapboard near the boat ramp and trailhead shows the trails and location of the fishing spots.

hiking: The *Jackrabbit Mtn Scenic Trail* (#384) has 2 loop options that circle the mountain and part of the lakeshore for a total distance of about 3 mi. The signed trailhead is located near the boat ramp. The trails, blazed with blue and orange, follow well-worn footpaths through a hardwood and pine forest. Placards which describe the habitat of a Southern Appalachian forest are posted along the trail. Trails are improved with footbridges and benches and are easy to hike.

Chunky Gal Mountain Area

Chunky Gal Mountain is a 10-mile long mountain ridge that takes its name from an Indian legend: a plump Indian girl fell in love with a boy who came from a rival neighboring tribe. To discourage the young girl's affections, her parents banished the young man to the wilderness. Instead of surrendering her love, she followed him into the mountains, which have honored her in name ever since. The Chunky Gal Mountain area is remote, and generally unvisited except by foot travelers hiking the *Chunky Gal Trail* or the *Appalachian Trail*, which connects at the former trail's southern terminus. The region is located between the Fires Creek Wildlife Management Area (NW) and the Southern Nantahala Wilderness (SE). Access to both is possible via the *Chunky Gal Trail*. US-64 passes through the area at Glade Gap, with trail access and views east and west.

Hayesville (W) and Franklin (E) are the closest towns.

getting there: The easiest vehicle access is via US-64. From the jct of US-64 and NC-69 S of Hayesville, take US-64 E 15.6 mi to Glade Gap, where the *Chunky Gal Trail* crosses the hwy. (The trail access can be difficult to locate; it's next to a jct with a FR, L). To reach the S trailhead, continue 3 mi to the jct with FR-71. Turn R and go 0.8 mi to a jct and continue L on FR-71, which becomes a rough, gravel road. At 2.5 mi reach a small parking area at Park Gap and trailheads to *Park Creek Trail* and *Park Ridge Trail*. Continue 2.6 mi to Deep Gap and access to the *AT* and the *Kimsey Creek* trailhead. To reach the N trailhead, see the Fires Creek Area or directions to the Bob Allison primitive campground, below.

topography: Elevations along the rugged mountain ridges that the *Chunky Gal Trail* follows reach 5,200 ft at the trail's N terminus near Signal Bald. The low point along the trail is 3,000 ft, where

Big Tuni Creek flows through the Bob Allison campground. **maps:**
USGS-FS Topton, Shooting Creek, Rainbow Springs.

starting out: The only developed facilities in the area are at the Bob
Allison primitive campground, where there are water spigots and a
pit toilet. It's located on Big Tuni Creek 3 mi E of the *Chunky Gal
Trail's* N terminus. The portion of the trail S of US-64 is also
shown on the USFS map Southern Nantahala Wilderness and
Standing Indian Basin.

activities: Hiking, Camping, Fishing.

hiking: 22-mi *Chunky Gal Trail* (#77) is the single trail that defines
this area. It is somewhat unusual for a long trail, in that both of its
endpoints are jcts with other trails, and can only be reached on
foot. The N trailhead is at the E end of the 25-mi *Rim Trail* (#72),
between Signal Bald and Tusquitee Bald. Its S end is a jct with the
AT (#1), 3 mi SW of the Deep Gap trailhead and parking area. This
trailhead is on the border of the Southern Nantahala Wilderness
and the Standing Indian Basin Area. With all these long trails
connected, backcountry expeditions of days or weeks are
possible. Shorter hikes are possible by using the vehicle access
points on US-64 or at the Bob Allison campground. The *Chunky
Gal Trail* follows a series of high mountain ridges, with good views
at various points along the route. Water is scarce along much of
the trail, as it follows elevations that are above the headwaters of
local creeks. The trail is blazed with white bars, and trail accesses
are signed. It is infrequently used.

camping: The Bob Allison primitive campground is located along
the *Chunky Gal Trail* approx 3 mi from its N terminus. The
camping area is a grassy clearing beside Big Tuni Creek. It has 6
picnic tables and a number of fire rings, though individual sites
are not really defined. Water spigots and a pit toilet are the only
facilities. Campers have done a poor job of keeping the area
attractive. A better option is backcountry camping, permitted along
the entire length of the trail. To reach Bob Allison, from US-64
turn N onto Cold Branch Rd (SR-1330) near the turn for Chatuge
Lake and Jackrabbit Mtn Rec Area and go 4.2 mi to the end of the
road. Turn R onto SR-1307 (L it is 7.2 mi to Hayesville). Go 1.6 mi
and turn L onto gravel SR-1311, which becomes FR-440. Go 4.3
mi to the camping area, R.

fishing: For most of its route, the *Chunky Gal Trail* is well above the headwaters of area creeks. An exception is Big Tuni Creek, which the trail crosses at the Bob Allison campground and then follows for a couple of miles to near its headwaters below Signal Bald. Big Tuni is a small to medium sized creek that follows a boulder strewn course N to S for about 7 mi before emptying into Tusquitee Creek. A pine and hardwood forest with an understory of rhododendron provides good cover on both banks. It is Hatchery Supported. Access is via the hiking trail and along FR-440.

Southern Nantahala Wilderness

The Southern Nantahala Wilderness covers 24,500 acres of steep, rugged mountainous terrain in North Carolina and Georgia. 10,900 acres are in NC, divided between the Tusquitee and Wayah Ranger Districts. Although the boundary between the two districts is not much more than a line on a map, it delimits a significant difference: the portion of the wilderness that lies within the Wayah District is laced with a pattern of regularly used trails that connect it to both the *AT* and the popular Standing Indian area. By contrast, the Tusquitee portion has no maintained hiking trails and is remote and isolated. Almost all visitors to this part of the wilderness experience it from the *AT*, which skirts its boundary for 15 miles. FR-56 does enter the area from Georgia, but follows a narrow strip of land not technically within the wilderness. In short, this region provides ample opportunity for exploring the backcountry at its most primitive and isolated. Standing Indian Mountain provides the best views of the surrounding area.

Hayesville (W) and Franklin (E) are the closest towns.

getting there: Access from NC is at Deep Gap. To get there, turn S onto FR-71 18.6 mi E of the US-64/NC-69 jct in Hayesville. Go 0.8 mi to a jct and continue L on FR-71, which becomes a rough, rugged gravel road. At 2.5 mi reach trailheads to *Park Creek Trail* and *Park Ridge Trail* at Park Gap with a small parking area. Continue 2.6 mi to Deep Gap and the *AT* and *Kimsey Creek* trailheads.

topography: The Tallulah River runs N to S through the heart of the area, splitting it in half and draining the deep coves and precipitous mountainsides that rise E and W and culminate along the Blue Ridge. Rocky escarpments and heath balds are scenic highlights along the ridge. Standing Indian Mtn (5,499 ft) is the highest point; the lowest is on the Tallulah River at the NC/GA state line (2,253 ft). **maps:** USGS-FS Rainbow Springs, Hightower Bald (GA); USFS Southern Nantahala Wilderness and Standing Indian Basin.

starting out: There are no facilities in this remote, seldom travelled area. The USGS-FS topos are recommended over the USFS area map due to their larger scale. Be sure to bring both map and compass, as trails in the wilderness are primitive.

Campfires are prohibited in the wilderness.

activities: Hiking, Camping.

hiking: There are 2 distinctly different hiking options in this part of the wilderness. The *AT* (#1) begins following the wilderness boundary about 1 mi after entering NC from GA. It continues N 6 mi to Deep Gap, where it turns SE and enters into the heart of the designated wilderness. Here it follows the Tusquitee/Wayah line 9 mi to the Carter Gap shelter, where it turns N again and leaves the Tusquitee RD. The *AT* is regularly used (though not heavily here), blazed with white bars, easy to follow, and has signed trailheads. The 2 FS trails that enter the wilderness, on the other hand, are not maintained and are rarely used. The *Deep Gap Branch Trail* (#377) and the *Beech Creek Trail* (#378) follow primitive, unmaintained footpaths that are not blazed or signed. They cover about 8 mi between them, generally following the 2 creeks for which they're named. NC access is from the Deep Gap trailhead. All trails in the wilderness are strenuous.

camping: There are no developed camping facilities in the area. 3 shelters—Muskrat Creek, Standing Indian, and Carter Gap—are located along the *AT*. There are a couple of good roadside campsites at the Deep Gap trailhead. Backcountry camping is permitted throughout the wilderness (no fires); Standing Indian Mtn, with spectacular views and a nearby spring for water, is the most popular spot.

Cheoah Ranger District
Nantahala National Forest

The Cheoah Ranger District occupies 120,000 acres in a remote part of the state in Graham and Swain counties. Boundaries are formed by the Cherokee National Forest in Tennessee (W), Great Smoky Mountains National Park (N), Wayah Ranger District (E) and Tusquitee Ranger District (S). This isolated part of the state was settled late and sparsely by Europeans; populations remain sparse, and today only one major highway runs through the district. The district includes some of the largest, emptiest tracts of land in the mountains. Major backcountry areas are located in the district's western half in the Unicoi and Snowbird Mountains, an area that contains the unforgettable 3,800-acre Joyce Kilmer Memorial Forest and 17,000-acre Kilmer-Slickrock Wilderness. Other recreational activities are on Fontana and Santeetlah Lakes, which both enjoy beautiful mountain settings. The Nantahala River, with the popular and scenic Nantahala Gorge, is on the district's eastern boundary.

Robbinsville is near the center of the district, and is the only town of substantial size. Fontana Village is a vacation resort near Fontana Dam.

contact: District Ranger, US Forest Service, Route 1, Box 16-A, Robbinsville, NC 28771; 704/479-6431.

getting there: Primary highway access to the district is on US-129 from the SE and NW, and on NC-28 from the E. To get to the RS, from the jct of Main St and US-129 in downtown Robbinsville, take US-129 N 1 mi to a FS sign and SR-1116. Turn L and go 1.1 mi to the RS, L.

topography: The district is dominated by several impressive mountain chains—the Unicoi, Snowbird and Cheoah. The most dramatic of these are the Unicoi, with peaks more than a mile high. The mountains are heavily wooded, with all the tree species of the Southern Appalachian forest represented. **maps:** see below under individual listings.

starting out: The RS sells a complete selection of topo maps for the district, as well as a small number of guidebooks. Modern restrooms and a water fountain are on the premises. Hours are M–F 8 am–4:30 pm, and on weekends & holidays during the summer. 2 trail loops begin behind the RS. *Camp Santeetlah Trail* follows a paved path and features an observation deck overlooking the site of a former CCC camp that operated from 1934-41. *Cheoah Trail* is a 2.3-mi forest management trail blazed with white arrows. Trailheads to both are clearly signed.

activities: Hiking, Camping, Fishing, Canoeing/Kayaking, Mountain Biking.

hiking: The Cheoah RD offers some of the best hiking opportunities in the mountain region. The Kilmer-Slickrock Wilderness and Snowbird Area both feature extensive trail networks that provide access to large, roadless backcountry areas. In all there are more than 200 mi of hiking trails on the district, including a 30-mi segment of the *Appalachian Trail.*

camping: There's a wealth of camping options on the district. Developed car campgrounds are located at each of the 5 areas described below, except for the Snowbird Area. These campgrounds are all small, and lack the harried atmosphere of some of the larger campgrounds on the busier districts. Primitive roadside camping is available on the forest roads in the vicinity of the Kilmer-Slickrock Wilderness and the Snowbird Area. These 2 areas also provide the best opportunities for backcountry camping. The S shore of Fontana Lake can be used for camping by canoeists and kayakers.

fishing: The district is popular with both lake fishermen and fly-fishermen who pursue trout in the cool mountain creeks. The 2 major lakes described below have populations of largemouth and smallmouth bass, with several other species of game fish also present. The number of miles of trout water is not as high as on some of the other districts, but the quality is exceptional. The Kilmer-Slickrock Wilderness and Snowbird Area both offer the chance to combine fishing and backpacking deep in the backcountry.

canoeing/kayaking: Primary paddling opportunities are on flat water. Lake Santeetlah offers an intimate setting, while Fontana Lake provides an opportunity for extended trips.

mountain biking: The 38 mi of multi-use trails at Tsali Rec Area are on every short list of best and most popular biking trails in the state. Period. Other opportunities for mountain biking are on the many dirt and gravel forest roads that cross the district and receive only a modicum of auto traffic.

Snowbird Area

Snowbird is a large backcountry area defined by the watershed of Snowbird Creek, which drains a portion of the Unicoi and Snowbird Mountains. Located at the western edge of the state and bordering the Cherokee National Forest in Tennessee for a short distance, Snowbird is a region of steep, rugged mountains, lush coves blanketed in dense, impenetrable rhododendron slicks, and a beautiful mountain creek that features a series of waterfalls. Although the region was barely settled until this century, timber interests were quick to exploit the natural wealth of the forest, laying railroad tracks along Snowbird Creek and logging most of the watershed. Operations did not cease until the early 1940s, when the Forest Service acquired the land. The main appeal of the area to visitors today is the extensive network of hiking trails (closed to all other uses) and the chance to spend an extended amount of time in a remote, little-travelled backcountry area.

Robbinsville (NE) is the closest town.

getting there: From the district RS outside of Robbinsville, turn L onto SR-1116 and go 2.3 mi to SR-1127. Turn R and go 2.1 mi (at 0.8 mi pass the Snowbird Picnic Area), and Bear L at a fork in the road onto SR-1115. Go 2.2 mi to where SR-1115 turns sharply L. Make the turn and continue 1 mi to a pair of bridges. Immediately after the 2nd, turn R onto SR-1120 and go 6 mi (at 2.1 mi the road enters the NF and becomes gravel FR-75) to the end of the road and trailheads at Junction, the site of a former logging camp.

topography: The terrain throughout the area is rugged and mountainous, with the highest elevations atop the Unicoi Mtns near the headwaters of Snowbird Creek. A forest of hardwoods and pines is in the process of regenerating itself after extensive logging. Elevations are between 5,429 ft on Hooper Bald at the NW corner of the area, and 2,200 ft on Snowbird Creek. **maps:** USFS Snowbird Area; USGS-FS Santeetlah Creek, Big Junction.

starting out: The backcountry area beyond Junction is completely undeveloped. A pit toilet is located at the trailhead and parking area. Water sources are abundant, but be sure to treat all water before drinking. The USFS Snowbird Area map ($3) shows all hiking trails on a large scale topo. It's available at the RS or camping supply stores.

activities: Hiking, Fishing, Camping.

hiking: Snowbird is an area of long trails: the 7 hiking trails cover a total distance of more than 37 mi. Trails ascend the ridges of the Unicoi and Snowbird Mtns and follow beside Snowbird and Sassafras Creeks. Loops of up to 20 mi are possible, and all trails can be connected with one another. The *Big Snowbird Trail* (#64) follows a wide RR bed left over from logging days; other trails follow rugged single tracks. Although some blazes are present and trail improvements such as footbridges are found, in general the trails are kept in a primitive state. Be sure to bring a map and compass, and plan on rock hopping or wading all stream crossings. Trails are generally moderate to hike, with some easy and some difficult stretches. All trails are accessible from the parking area at the end of FR-75, where the trailheads are clearly signed.

fishing: Snowbird Creek is a beautiful, boulder-strewn trout stream that flows W to E for a distance of more than 14 mi between its headwaters at the TN state line and the FS boundary. In terms of fishing, the creek is divided into two distinct parts. Below Junction to the FS boundary, the creek is followed by FR-75. This stretch is Hatchery Supported and sees quite a lot of fishing pressure. Access from the road is easy and there are numerous pulloffs. Above Junction, however, the road ends and the only way to get upstream is by wading or hiking *Big Snowbird Trail,* which follows the creek all the way to its headwaters 10 mi upstream. Access from the trail is difficult in many places, due to the dense growth of rhododendron. This section of the creek is designated Wild Trout, and receives considerably less fishing pressure than the downstream section. Throughout its long midsection, Snowbird is a medium to large creek with excellent cover and a moderate gradient. Brown, brook and rainbow trout are all caught in the creek.

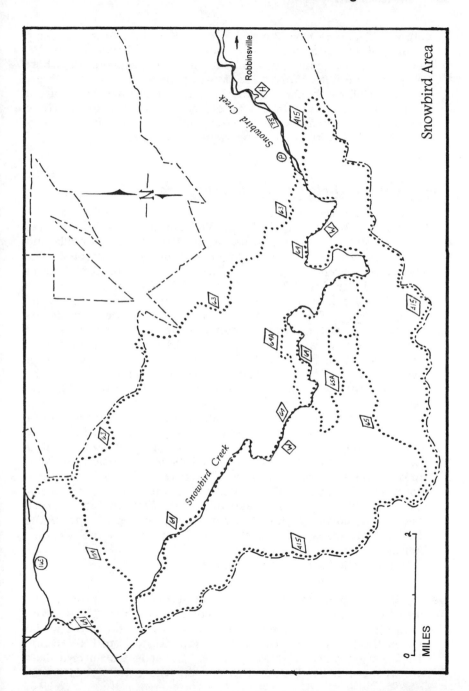

Snowbird Area

camping: Campers have 2 options in the Snowbird Area: car camp at one of the numerous sites along FR-75 between the FS boundary and Junction, or backpack into the backcountry, where camping is permitted anywhere. Most of the sites along the forest road are well established; many have a picnic table. There are a couple of sites at Junction, where there's also a pit toilet. There are no designated sites in the backcountry, though backpackers won't have difficulty spotting previously used areas.

Joyce Kilmer-Slickrock Wilderness Area

Located at the western edge of the state just south of the Smoky Mountains, the Kilmer-Slickrock Wilderness is a wild, roadless region of steep, rocky ridges, cascading streams, heath balds and one of the few remaining virgin forests on the east coast. The wilderness covers more than 17,000 acres, with 3,800 acres designated the Joyce Kilmer Memorial Forest, in honor of the World War I soldier (killed in action in France) and author of the poem "Trees." The special appeal of the wilderness is its remoteness and the awesome beauty of the virgin forest preserved in the Kilmer Forest. As a result of the bankruptcy of the timber company that once owned this tract of land, the forest was never logged. If you've never seen an old-growth forest up close, the difference with a second-growth forest can be startling. Massive hardwoods and hemlocks, a cool, damp floor that receives little direct sunlight, and an overwhelming abundance of mosses, ferns, and other floor-level vegetation create a primeval world painted almost entirely in shades of green. A large variety of fauna inhabits the wilderness as well, including black bear, wild boars and wild turkey. The wilderness occupies the eastern slope of the Unicoi Mountains, which form the border with Tennessee. The northwest corner of Kilmer-Slickrock actually is in TN; the Citico Creek Wilderness, covering 15,891 acres on the western slope of the Unicoi Mountains, is entirely in TN and forms the western boundary with Kilmer-Slickrock.

Robbinsville (SE) is the closest town.

getting there: Directions are to 3 different access points to the wilderness. To reach the Joyce Kilmer Memorial Forest, from the RS, turn L onto SR-1116. Go 2.4 mi to SR-1127. Turn R and go 9.1 mi (at 8.8 mi the Rattler Ford Group Campground is L) to FR-416 and the forest entrance, L (Ahead on SR-1127 it is 4.5 mi to a dead end with scenic overlook and trailhead). R is gravel FR-416, with

Horse Cove Campground at 0.3 mi, R & L. • To get to the Wolf Laurel trailhead on the S perimeter of the wilderness, from the RS, turn L onto SR-1116 and go 2.4 mi to SR-1127. Turn R and go 6.9 mi. Turn L onto an unmarked road and then immediately R, onto gravel FR-81. Go 6.8 mi and turn R at a FS sign onto FR-81F. At 4.4 mi reach the Wolf Laurel Hunter Camp, L, and at 4.9 mi reach the parking area, trailhead and signboard. • To reach the Big Fat Gap trailhead and the N part of the wilderness, take US-129 5.6 mi N of the jct with Old US-129. Turn L at a bridge over the Cheoah River onto single track, gravel FR-62. (Or, from the bridge across Lake Cheoah at the county line, take US-129 S 1.9 and turn R onto FR-62.) Keep R around a hairpin curve at 0.3 mi. At 7.2 mi reach the trailhead and large parking area.

topography: The steep ridges and rugged mountain slopes of the wilderness are drained by 2 major arteries: N–S flowing Slickrock Creek, and W–E flowing Little Santeetlah Creek. Elevations are between 5,341 ft on Stratton Bald and 1,086 ft at the mouth of Slickrock Creek. **maps:** USFS Joyce Kilmer-Slickrock and Citico Creek Wilderness; USGS-FS Tapoco, Santeetlah Creek, Whiteoak Flats.

starting out: Facilities are limited to the perimeter of the wilderness. Water and restrooms are at the entrance to Kilmer Memorial Forest, where there's also a small, scenic picnic area with tables and grills beside Little Santeetlah Creek. This area is always the most crowded in the wilderness; nevertheless, a hike through the giants of this awe-inspiring forest should not be passed up (avoid it during high winds and storms, however, as falling trees and branches can be deadly). Best views of the wilderness are from the Hangover, where rock outcrops provide 360° unobstructed vistas.

activities: Hiking, Camping, Fishing.

hiking: A network of more than 60 mi of hiking trails criss-crosses the NC portion of the wilderness and surrounding area. The trails have been intelligently laid out to allow access to all of the various topographic regions encountered in the wilderness: heath balds; rocky ridgelines and outcrops; cool, moist coves; boulder-strewn creeks and waterfalls; and virgin forest. Within the wilderness, the trail network has also been designed so that all trails can be connected, accommodating extended trips into the backcountry.

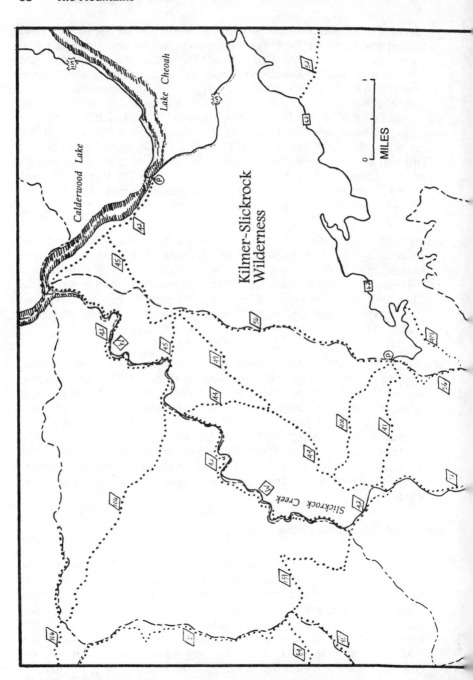

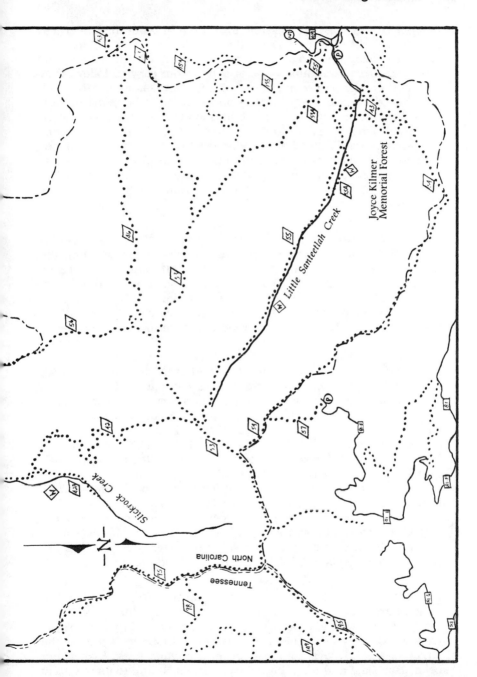

Further connections are possible into the portion of the wilderness that lies within TN and the adjacent Citico Creek Wilderness. Trails are maintained in a primitive state; although the majority are well worn from continuous use and therefore easy to follow, they are neither blazed nor improved. Stream crossings are by rock hopping or wading. The treadway on many trails is rocky, muddy, or both. (An exception to these conditions is the 2-mi *Joyce Kilmer Memorial Trail* [#43]. A National Recreation Trail, it has been thoughtfully constructed along wide level paths that are improved with footbridges, steps, handrails and benches.) All trailheads at the wilderness boundary are signed, as are most trail jcts within the wilderness. All trails can be reached from the 3 access points listed above.

camping: Backcountry camping is one of the most popular activities in the wilderness. Sites are numerous, both along the major creeks and in mountain clearings. Although there are no developed camping facilities within Kilmer-Slickrock, a number of options are available just outside its boundaries. The Horse Cove car campground has 17 sites in a lush cove near the mouth of Horsecove Branch (opposite the road entrance to the Kilmer picnic area). The sites are small and crowded together, with minimal privacy. Nevertheless, they fill up early on summer weekends. Each site has a picnic table and grill, and there are restrooms with flush toilets. The fee is $5/night. The campground is open all year. Another option for car camping is along the forest roads S and E of the wilderness. FR-81, a gravel road that follows the beautiful Santeetlah Creek for about 7 mi, has numerous designated sites starting 3 mi W of SR-1127. FR-62 between US-129 and Big Fat Gap has a couple of areas with primitive sites near the Bear Creek Hunter Camp.

For large groups, there's the Rattler Ford Group Campground, located near the entrance to Kilmer Forest. 4 sites are located in an open area beside Santeetlah Creek. Facilities include modern restrooms with hot showers. Each site can accommodate 50 people, with fire rings, picnic tables and water. Reservations are required. The fee is $25/night. Open Apr 6–Oct 31.

fishing: Within the wilderness, Slickrock Creek and Little Santeetlah Creek are the 2 primary fishing destinations. The 2 creeks are similar, and between them drain most of the wilderness on the NC side. Slickrock Creek, which flows S to N and is the larger of the 2, crosses almost the entire wilderness. Rising just below Bob Bald and the S boundary, it flows N 8 mi to its mouth at

Calderwood Lake. Little Santeetlah Creek begins not far E of Slickrock's headwaters and flows E 4 mi to Santeetlah Creek. Slickrock is a beautiful, medium to large creek with several water-falls, numerous cascades and a boulder strewn bed. Santeetlah Creek is slightly smaller with similar characteristics. Flowing beneath the massive old-growth trees in Kilmer Forest and over moss covered logs and boulders, its beauty is exceptional. Hiking trails provide access to the entire length of both creeks; Slickrock is the remoter of the 2. The Kilmer Forest access road and picnic area are both beside Little Santeetlah Creek along its last half-mile, a stretch that is often crowded. Both creeks are Wild Trout waters.

Outside the wilderness and 1,000 ft below the rim that forms its S boundary, Santeetlah Creek flows 10 mi W to E between Johns Branch and Santeetlah Lake. This is the largest creek in the area, as well as the most heavily fished; gravel FR-81 runs beside it for most of its length, providing easy access. (This is also a popular roadside camping area.) Nevertheless, Santeetlah is an attractive stream with good cover and excellent pools. It is Hatchery Supported.

Lake Santeetlah

3,000-acre Lake Santeetlah may be the most attractive lake in western North Carolina. Flanked by the Cheoah Mountains (E), the Snowbird Mountains (S), the Unicois (W), and the Smokies (N), the lake is situated amidst some impressive alpine scenery. Only a small portion of its shoreline is developed; the rest is owned by the National Forest. Like all other mountain lakes in NC, it is man-made, formed when Santeetlah Dam was built on the Cheoah River at what is now the lake's northern end. Santeetlah Creek also feeds into the lake. Santeetlah Lake is a popular spot with fishermen, canoeists and kayakers. Given its proximity to the Kilmer-Slickrock Wilderness and Great Smoky Mountains National Park, it can provide a nice water-based diversion from backpacking trips.

Robbinsville (SE) is the closest town.

getting there: There are 3 boat ramps on the lake. In addition to a ramp at Cheoah Point Rec Area, there are boat ramps at Massey Branch (across SR-1116 from the district RS) and at Avey Branch (1.6 mi E on FR-416 from the jct with SR-1127 and the entrance to Kilmer Memorial Forest). To get to the Cheoah Point Rec Area from

Robbinsville, take US-129 N 5.1 mi to SR-1145. Turn L and go 1.4 mi to the campground entrance, L. The boat ramp is 0.2 mi further ahead.

topography: The lake occupies a narrow floodplain with numerous coves along the Cheoah River. Elevation is 1,940 ft. Beyond the shoreline the terrain is mountainous, with impressive ranges in all 4 directions; the Smokies (N) and the Unicoi (W) have the highest peaks and steepest slopes. **maps:** USGS-FS Robbinsville, Santeetlah Creek, Tapoco.

starting out: Facilities near the lake are at the Cheoah Point boat ramp/campground and picnic area (restrooms, water); and at the RS across from the Massey Branch boat ramp (restrooms, water, info).

activities: Canoeing/Kayaking, Fishing, Camping.

canoeing/kayaking: In a region that draws canoeists and kayakers for its whitewater, Santeetlah is one of the most popular *lakes* with paddlers. A beautiful mountain setting, numerous intimate channels and coves, and relative lack of power boats all contribute to its appeal. Although too small for any extended paddling expeditions, an overnight trip is possible, with camping at Cheoah Point Campground or at undesignated backcountry sites along the lakeshore. See above for directions to the 3 boat ramps.

fishing: Lake Santeetlah supports both warm- and cold-water species of fish. It is best known for its largemouth and smallmouth bass, but also supports populations of walleye, rainbow and brown trout, and bluegill. Fishing is done primarily from boats.

camping: Located on the eastern shore of the lake, Cheoah Point Campground is a developed campground that is usually full for the weekend by early Friday evening during the peak season. Fishermen seem to make up most of the traffic, with boat trailers often crowding the campground loop road. Most of the 26 sites are small and pretty close together; a few are isolated and offer more seclusion. Each site has a picnic table and grill. There are pit toilets and water at the campground, but no showers. Sites cost $5/night. The campground is open Apr 14–Oct 31.

Backcountry camping is allowed along the lake's perimeter.

Some sites are located at roadside along FR-416; a better bet is to paddle out onto the lake and find your own along the shoreline.

Fontana Lake Area

Located in the shadow of the Smoky Mountains, Fontana Lake covers 11,685 acres along the course of the Little Tennessee River. The largest lake in western North Carolina, it was created with the construction of Fontana Dam in 1945. The dam and lake are part of the extensive Tennessee Valley Authority system. The north shore of the lake is entirely within Great Smoky Mountains National Park; the southern shore is on the Cheoah Ranger District, with several developed rec areas, described below. Fontana Lake occupies a long, narrow floodplain in the mountains between the dam at its western end and the Little Tennessee and Tuckaseigee to the east. With the Smokies forming the northern shoreline and the Cheoah Mountains to the south, the lake offers some of the most attractive scenery in the southeast. For this reason it is popular with recreational boaters of all types, though the lake's remote location helps keep the number of visitors relatively low.

Fontana Village (W) and Bryson City (E) are the closest towns.

getting there: There are numerous access points along the lake's S shore. To reach Fontana Dam and a private boat launch and marina, take NC-28 1 mi E of Fontana Village. Turn L (the dam is 1 mi ahead straight) onto the Fontana Dam Rd and go 0.1 mi to the first R. Take the turn and go 0.2 mi to the parking area and marina. • To reach the Cable Cove Rec Area, take NC-28 4.7 mi E of Fontana Village to a FS sign and SR-1287 (FR-520). Turn L and go 1 mi to the campground, R, or continue ahead to the boat ramp at 1.7 mi. • Tsali Rec Area—listed separately below—also has lake access.

topography: The elevation on the lake is around 1,700 ft, with fluctuations in water level of up to 130 ft. The lake is surrounded by rugged, mountainous terrain covered by an extensive Southern Appalachian hardwood forest. Elevations in the Smokies top 6,000 ft. **maps:** USGS-FS Noland Creek, Tuckaseigee, Fontana Dam.

starting out: Facilities are at Cable Cove Rec Area and Fontana Dam, where there's a visitors center with several useful amenities.

Among these are restrooms with hot showers (popular with *AT* hikers), a pay phone, picnic area with tables and grills, and several scenic overlooks. Additional services are available in nearby Fontana Village, a vacation resort made up of the numerous cabins that were built to house the 5,000 men who worked on the dam in the 1940s.

activities: Canoeing/Kayaking, Fishing, Hiking, Camping.

canoeing/kayaking: Fontana Lake has 240 mi of shoreline, much of it along isolated coves and in small branches away from the lake's main channel. The lake is one of the few in NC where an extended paddling/camping expedition is possible. There are a number of backcountry campsites along the N shore in Great Smoky Mountains NP (backcountry registration rules apply) and primitive camping is permitted anywhere on Nantahala NF lands, which make up the S shore. Powerboats and sailboats are present on the lake, but not in such numbers that they significantly detract from the lake's appeal. Boat ramps are located near Fontana Dam, at Cable Cove Rec Area and at Tsali Rec Area (see separate listing below).

fishing: Fontana Lake is known for its bass (smallmouth, large-mouth and white) and walleye fishing, and in 1994 a state record 41-lb muskellunge was caught from the lake. Other species of game fish found in the lake include channel and flathead catfish, bluegill and crappie. Trout are also present, though more so in the creeks which roll out of the Smokies and feed the lake. Fishing on the lake is done primarily from a boat.

hiking: Hiking in the Fontana Lake area is along either the *Appalachian Trail* (#1) or the trails of Great Smoky Mountains National Park. (On the NF side of the lake, there are trails at Tsali Rec Area, covered separately below.) The *AT* actually crosses Fontana Dam before entering the NP, where it continues for 69 mi. In the other direction, the trail enters the general vicinity of Fontana Lake on the Nantahala River at Wesser (beside the Nantahala Outdoor Center). From there, it's a 30-mi hike across the Cheoah and Yellow Creek Mountains to the dam. An *AT* shelter is located near the dam on its S side. Hikers have dubbed it the "Fontana Hilton" because of the luxury of hot showers available at the dam visitors center. The trail is blazed with white bars and is easy to follow. Hiking along this segment is moderate to strenuous.

Within GSMNP, the *Lakeshore Trail* follows the lake's N shoreline for 20 mi. It is accessible at several points by boat. The trail connects with several other trails, which connect in turn to the national park's entire network of more than 800 mi of trails (see the GSMNP section for more information).

camping: Campers planning to spend a night or more on the lakeshore have several options. For car camping, there's a 26-site developed campground at Cable Cove Rec Area. Popular with boaters, each of the sites is long enough to accommodate a trailer. The sites are large, but are bunched together on either side of the dirt campground road. Privacy is minimal, as the area has been cleared of most trees and vegetation. Each site has a picnic table, grill and lantern post. There are water spigots and pit toilets. Sites cost $5/night. The campground makes a good basecamp for exploring the lake, but doesn't have much appeal of its own. The campground is open Apr 14–Oct 31.

If you're backcountry camping, you have your choice of the S shore, located on NF lands, or the N shore, located entirely within GSMNP. Primitive, low-impact camping is permitted anywhere on NF lands (except where posted otherwise). If you're camping in the NP, you'll have to stay at one of the designated backcountry sites. There are 7 sites along the lakeshore. 3 sites—#s 87, 78, & 72—are only accessible by boat; 4 other sites—#s 90, 86, 81, & 77—are mainly hike-in sites, but can also be reached by boat. A backcountry camping permit is always required. See the GSMNP chapter for more details.

Tsali Rec Area

The Tsali Rec Area is situated on a peninsula situated between Fontana Lake and the Little Tennessee River. The rec area is at the eastern edge of Cheoah Ranger District and the eastern end of the lake; the Nantahala River Little Tennessee River and Tuckaseigee River all drain into the lake near the rec area. Aside from the natural beauty of the setting, Tsali has become renowned among mountain bikers of the southeast as one of the premier destinations in the region. On weekends the parking lot fills with vehicles sporting bike racks and license plates from Tennessee, South Carolina, Georgia and Virginia. The rec area is also well-situated to serve as a base for paddling excursions or fishing trips on Lake Fontana. Tsali takes its name from the Cherokee Indian who was one of the thousand who escaped the Trail of Tears to

Oklahoma by hiding out in the Smokies. Word was conveyed to Tsali that if he surrendered to the US Army and faced the death penalty (a soldier had been killed during his escape), the other Cherokees who had fled to the mountains would be granted immunity and allowed to stay. He agreed, and was granted his request that the firing squad to execute him be made up of Cherokees.

Bryson City (E) is the nearest city.

getting there: From the jct of NC-28 and US-19 SW of Bryson City, take NC-28 W 3.5 mi to a FS sign and SR-1286 (the jct with NC-143 is 8.3 mi W). Turn R onto the gravel road (it becomes FR-2550) and go 1.5 mi to the campground and rec area parking lot.

topography: Fontana Lake's elevation is 1,708 ft (water level fluctuates by as much as 130 ft). Elevations along the trails rise about 300 ft on mild to moderate slopes. Forest cover is predominantly hardwoods, with pines interspersed. **maps:** USGS-FS Noland Creek.

starting out: Water, restrooms and a pay phone are all located in the campground. There's also water, restrooms and a bike washing stand in the main parking lot. The trails at Tsali are open to bikers and horses on a rotating schedule. A current schedule is always posted on the signboard at the parking lot or you can get one from the district ranger station. The RS will also send you a trail map.

activities: Camping, Mountain Biking, Canoeing/Kayaking, Fishing, Hiking.

camping: Tsali has a 41-site car campground laid out in 2 large loops. The area has been mostly cleared of trees, though enough remain to provide a decent amount of shade. Sites are average in size and pretty close to one another; privacy is minimal. Each of the sites has a picnic table, grill and tent pad. There's one shower/restroom facility, as well as a flush toilet. The fee is $10/night. The campground is popular with mountain bikers, so sites fill up pretty regularly on warm weather weekends. The campground is open Apr 14 to Oct 31.

mountain biking/hiking: There are 38 mi of multi-use trails at Tsali. The easy to moderate trails follow the ridges and shoreline of

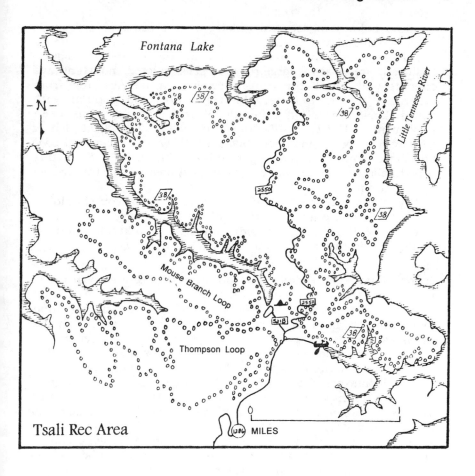

Fontana Lake

Little Tennessee River

38

38

2550

38

38

2550

Mouse Branch Loop

5A18

Thompson Loop

38

Tsali Rec Area

1286

MILES

Fontana Lake along several quiet coves. Treadways are single track and abandoned forest roads. Trails are blazed, though heavy use has made them easy-to-follow in any case. The signed trailheads are all at the large rec area parking lot. Although always open to foot travel, the trails receive their heaviest use from mountain bikers. Because the trails are also popular with equestrians, a rotating schedule of trail use days has been implemented. The 1995 schedule is as follows: *Tsali Trail* (right & left loops) is open to mountain bikes Su, M, W & F; *Thompson Loop* and *Mouse Branch Loop* are open to bikes Tu, Th & Sa. Since this schedule is subject to change, it's a good idea to call the district RS for current status.

If you're planning on hiking the trails at Tsali, you should be aware that the use from mountain bikers is as heavy as anywhere in the state. Horse use is considerably lighter, so keeping to trails on days when they're closed to bikes is a good idea.

canoeing/kayaking: Paddlers can put in at the rec area boat ramp. From there, you can explore the numerous small coves and branches that surround Tsali or head out for a longer expedition along the 240 mi of shoreline on the 11,685-acre lake. With the Smokies rising majestically on the N shore, the scenery on Fontana rivals that of any other lake in the state. Despite this beauty, the lake never seems to be crowded, though powerboats and sailboats are a presence. Tsali is near the eastern edge of Lake Fontana, where the Nantahala, Little Tennessee and Tuckaseigee all empty into it. The north shore of Fontana Lake and Great Smoky Mountains NP is only about a 2 hr paddle away. 9 mi in the other direction is the bottom of Nantahala Gorge, probably the most popular whitewater run in the state. Tsali can be used as an easy-access base camp for either of these options.

fishing: Fontana is regarded as a good fishing lake for a number of species: largemouth, smallmouth and white bass, muskellunge (a state record 41-pounder was caught in 1994) and walleye. Other game species found in the lake are channel and flathead catfish, and sunfish. Fish attractors have been constructed, and are indicated by yellow markers. Anglers typically fish from boats.

Wayah Ranger District

Nantahala National Forest

The Wayah Ranger District encompasses 134,000 acres of the Nantahala Mountains in Macon, Swain, and Jackson counties. Major rivers on the district are the Little Tennessee, Tuckaseigee, and Nantahala. Boundaries are formed by the Tusquitee Ranger District (SW), Cheoah Ranger District (NW), Great Smoky Mountains National Park and Cherokee Indian Reservation (N), Highland Ranger District (E), and Georgia (S). The district takes its name from the Cherokee word for wolf. Primary opportunities for backcountry travel are concentrated in the southern and western portions of the district. The Standing Indian Basin and Wayah Bald Area offer the best environments for extended backpacking trips. A portion of the Southern Nantahala Wilderness is at the southern edge of the district, and continues into Georgia.

Franklin, located near the district's center, is the largest city. Bryson City (N) and Sylva (NW) are the only other towns of any size.

contact: District Ranger, US Forest Service, 90 Sloan Rd, Franklin, NC 28734-9064; 704/524-6441.

getting there: Primary access to the Wayah RD is on US-64 from the E or W, and on US-441/23 from the N or S. To get to the ranger station, take US-64 1 mi W of its jct with US-441/23 to Sloan Rd (SR-1153). Turn R and go 0.2 mi to the RS entrance, R.

topography: The Nantahala is the major mountain range on the district. Although not the highest mountains in the state, they are rugged and often steep, particularly along the eastern slope. Standing Indian Mtn (5,499 ft), Albert Mtn (5,250 ft), Wine Spring Bald (5,440 ft) and Wayah Bald (5,342 ft) are the highest peaks in the district. **maps:** see below under individual listings.

starting out: Major backcountry areas are W and SW of Franklin. Before heading out, stop by the district RS; they sell topo maps, *Bartram Trail* maps, brochures, and can answer questions about local conditions. There are also a water fountain and restrooms here. Hours are M–F 8 am–4:30 pm. Wayah Bald and Standing Indian Basin are both popular destinations, though there is plenty of opportunity in both areas to escape into the relatively untravelled backcountry.

activities: Hiking, Camping, Fishing, Canoeing/Kayaking.

hiking: The large complex of hiking trails on the district is located in the Standing Indian Area. Shorter trail networks can be found at Nantahala Lake and Wayah Bald. 2 long trails—the *Appalachian Trail* and the *Bartram Trail*—pass through the district. The *AT* winds through the Nantahala Mtns for 51 mi between Deep Gap and US-19 at Wesser. The *Bartram Trail* is on the district for 35 mi.

camping: Campers options on the district are somewhat limited. A single large developed car campground is located at Standing Indian Area. Backcountry camping is a better bet, with good sites on the long trails near Wayah Bald and in the extensive backcountry at Standing Indian Area.

fishing: The Nantahala River offers the trout angler long stretches of water with varying characteristics. A large system of smaller creeks drains the Standing Indian Area; other trout creeks are located in the valleys below Wayah Bald. Nantahala Lake supports populations of bass and several other game species.

canoeing/kayaking: The Nantahala River Gorge is the most popular whitewater run in the state. Flat water is found on Nantahala Lake.

Nantahala Lake Area

With an elevation of 3,013 feet, Nantahala Lake sits at the highest altitude of any lake in North Carolina. Like the other lakes in the region, it's man-made, created when a dam was built across the Nantahala River. Situated between the Tusquitee Mountains to the west and the Nantahala Mountains to the east, the lake is cradled in one of the most attractive areas on the Nantahala National Forest. Although there is plenty of opportunity for backcountry exploration in the region surrounding the lake, the lake itself is not really a hub of any major recreational activity. Fishing is good, but the lake is small and not particularly attractive.

Andrews (W) and Franklin (E) are the closest towns.

getting there: From the jct of US-64 and US-441/23 W of Franklin, take US-64 W 3.7 mi to Old Murphy Rd. Turn R and go 0.2 mi to Wayah Rd (SR-1310). Turn L and go 14.2 mi to a boat ramp, L. To get to Appletree Group Campground, continue on SR-1310 2.3 mi (at 1.2 mi reach a signed trailhead to the *Bartram Trail*) to Junaluska Rd (SR-1400). Turn L and go 2.4 mi to the campground entrance, R.

topography: Lake elevation is 3,013 ft. London Bald and Piercy Bald—both over 4,500 ft—are the highest elevations in the area. The lakeshore is forested with hardwoods and conifers. Higher elevations are further E on Wayah Bald and W on Tusquitee Bald. **maps:** USGS-FS Topton.

starting out: Although the lake is the geographic center of this region, there's no real center of activity. The lands around the lake are a patchwork of private and public holdings. Facilities at Appletree, which are the only ones in the area, are for the use of campers only. You're not likely to run into crowds at any of the areas described below.

activities: Hiking, Canoeing/Kayaking, Fishing, Camping.

hiking: The 68-mi *Bartram Trail* (#67) passes through the area, providing the best opportunity for long hikes. The trail skirts the lakeshore for a short distance before continuing downstream on the banks of the Nantahala River. From the lake, Wayah Bald is 7.5 mi E, with exceptional views from an historic observation tower. The trail is blazed with yellow bars and is easy to follow (the section N of Nantahala Lake is more obscure and overgrown, but can still be followed). The trailhead on SR-1310 is signed and has parking. The other hiking opportunities in the area are on a network of trails that begin in the Appletree Group Campground and pass to the W of it through a dense hardwood/pine forest. The longest of these is the 9-mi *London Bald Trail* (#19C). It connects to 5 other trails, which cover a combined distance of more than 11 mi. Loops of varying distance are possible, as is a connection with the *Bartram Trail*. These trails receive fairly regular use from campers at Appletree, but are otherwise lightly travelled. Trails are blazed and generally easy to follow; hiking is easy to moderate. Trailheads are inside the campground (if the gate is locked, park outside and hike 0.3 mi to the trailhead, L) and on SR-1400 3.5 mi W of the campground. The trailhead to *Junaluska Trail* (#19) and *London Bald Trail*, located here, is difficult to find. The trail marker and trail are set back from the road amidst dense vegetation across from Little Choga Rd about 20 yds E of the county line sign.

canoeing/kayaking: Despite its high altitude and mountain setting, Nantahala Lake is disappointing as a paddling environment. The lake is small and lacks coves or secluded branches. Also, it's a rather unattractive lake, with a shore that is packed dirt for about 5 feet above the waterline. Powerboats are also a presence, though the lake is rarely crowded.

fishing: Nantahala Lake supports populations of largemouth and smallmouth bass and walleyes. Fishing is from a boat. Below the dam, the Nantahala River is a medium to large stream that supports trout. Access is from FR-308, SR-1310 or the *Bartram Trail*. In general, the further you go downstream from the dam the more attractive the river and the better the fishing. The gradient varies from almost flat (between the dam and Appletree) to steep (near the gorge). Fishing pressure on this section of the river is moderate The river is Hatchery Supported below the lake. Another local trout stream is Jarrett Creek, which feeds the lake from the E. It's a small to medium creek that is followed by SR-1310. Access is from the road. Jarrett Creek is Wild Trout water. Fishing pressure is light.

camping: The only developed campground in the area is the Appletree Group Camp. It features 4 sites in a large, attractively landscaped clearing beside the Nantahala River. Each site has picnic tables, grills and water. There are modern restrooms and showers with hot water. There's also a large sports field and a picnic shelter. Capacity is 25–50, depending on the site. Reservations are required and the fee is $30–60. The campground is open Apr 1–Oct 31.

Backcountry camping is allowed anywhere along the hiking trails, except where posted. Best opportunities are along the *Bartram Trail*.

Nantahala River Gorge

The Nantahala River Gorge is a 9-mile stretch of the river between Beechertown and Wesser that is without doubt the most popular whitewater run in the state. Although the gorge and river possess great natural beauty, for most visitors paddling seems to push all other concerns into the background. Canoeists and kayakers travel from all over the southeast and beyond to run the river, and a shantytown of rafting companies has sprung up along US-19, which runs close beside it. Although the gorge is not the place to go if you're looking for isolated, pristine wilderness, it does offer a thrilling whitewater run in a beautiful natural setting.

The closest city is Bryson City (N), though there are numerous services along the river at the bottom of the gorge.

getting there: The bottom of the gorge is 8 mi S of Bryson City. There are 3 river access points in the gorge. The Nantahala River Launch Site is located at the jct of US-19 and SR-1310, 8 mi S of Wesser. The entrance is on SR-1310. • 2.8 mi downriver (N) on US-19 is the Ferebee Memorial Rec Area, L. • The takeout point is 8 mi N on US-19, just after the Nantahala Outdoor Center and the jct with Silvermine Rd (SR-1103).

topography: Nearly vertical walls rise more than 1,000 ft E and W of the river. While in the gorge, the river drops a total of 265 ft. **maps:** USGS-FS Hewitt, Wesser.

starting out: The river can only be run when the Nantahala Power and Light Company is operating; fortunately it operates most days from at least 9 am–5 pm. Call 704/321-4504 for a recorded message giving current operating times. Facilities in the gorge include modern restrooms and water at the NF Launch Site and pit toilets and a small picnic area at Ferebee. The Nantahala Outdoor Center compound—with outdoor store, restaurants, hotels, guides and clinics—straddles the river in Wesser. It's generally regarded as the best whitewater paddling school in the nation.

Lifejackets are required while on the river and alcohol is prohibited. Camping is not allowed between US-19 and the river or on the islands in the river between the NF Launch Site and the take-out at Wesser.

activities: Kayaking/Canoeing, Fishing, Hiking.

kayaking/canoeing: The river features an almost continuous run of class II-III rapids across a width of 60-100 ft. Nantahala Falls, just before the takeout, is class III-IV; Wesser Falls, just downstream of the take-out, is class V and unrunnable. Put in at the FS Launch

Site or at Ferebee. The takeout is just downriver from the NOC. US-19 runs beside the river with numerous pullouts and overlooks, allowing for advance scouting; spectators are not uncommon at these spots. Although not a technically difficult river to run, the Nantahala does require a certain level of skill. Beginners should seek instruction before attempting the river.

fishing: Under different circumstances, the Nantahala might be regarded as one of the premier trout fishing runs in the state. But with US-19 providing easy access and diminishing the beauty of the gorge, and the almost continuous parade of canoes, kayaks and rafts, it's something of an oddity instead. Nevertheless, it offers one of the few opportunities in NC to fish big trout water. If the crowds bother you, come at night; it's the only trout stream in the mountains open to night fishing. Keep in mind that the stretch of river above the boat put-in is almost always much less crowded, though you'll probably see more fishermen. The river is shallow enough in most places to permit wading and the gradient is mild to moderate. Access is from US-19. It's Hatchery Supported.

hiking: The primary hiking opportunity in the area is the *Appalachian Trail* (#1), which crosses the Nantahala River and US-19 in Wesser at the Nantahala Outdoor Center. From there, you can hike S to Wayah Bald (18 mi; elevation gain: 3,600 ft) or N to Fontana Dam and the Great Smoky Mountains National Park (29 mi). The high point along this segment is Cheoah Bald, at just over 5,000 ft. Hiking along both segments is moderate to strenuous. The *AT* is blazed with a white bar and is easy to follow. The trailhead is signed, with parking nearby.

Standing Indian Basin

The Standing Indian Basin is a large backcountry area southwest of Franklin near the state border with Georgia. The Nantahala River rises in the area, and flows north through its center. The Nantahala Mountains and Standing Indian Mountain rise to elevations of more than a mile on either side of the river. A large network of hiking trails and some excellent trout streams are the major recreational attractions in the area. The 24,515-acre Southern Nantahala Wilderness is adjacent to the south and west, furthering the opportunity for extended backcountry expeditions. The *Appalachian Trail* passes through both the wilderness and Standing Indian Basin, and provides a trail connection to the

Chunky Gal Mountain Area and Wayah Bald. Flora in the area is that typical of the Southern Appalachian forest, with bogs found at lower elevations along the Nantahala river. Rock outcrops at Standing Indian and Pickens Nose provide scenic vistas, as does the fire tower (capacity: 2) on Albert Mountain. The hiking trail to Pickens Nose, which passes through a narrow corridor of rhododendron and mountain laurel, is particularly beautiful. Also adjacent to the area is the Coweeta Hydrologic Laboratory, an outdoor lab dedicated to studying the effects of man on forest ecosystems.

Franklin (NE) is the closest city.

getting there: The main access to the area is on FR-67, which follows the upper stretch of the Nantahala River, with most trailheads in the area located along its route. From the jct of US-64 and US-441/23 W of Franklin, take US-64 W 12 mi to a FS sign and Old US-64. Turn L and go 1.9 mi to FR-67. Turn R and go 1.8 mi to the Standing Indian Campground, R. Or continue ahead to the Backcountry Information Center at 2.1 mi. The road continues S (pavement ends here) for another 9 mi, with numerous pullouts and trailheads along the route.

topography: The topography of the region is defined by the steep mountain ridges that rise E and W of the Nantahala River, which drains the basin. Elevations along the E edge reach 5,250 ft on Albert Mtn in the Nantahala range. On the W edge, Standing Indian Mtn reaches the highest point on the basin rim at 5,499 ft. Elevation along the Nantahala River drops as low as 3,300 ft.
maps: USFS Southern Nantahala Wilderness and Standing Indian Basin; USGS-FS Rainbow Springs, Prentiss.

starting out: Although the Standing Indian Basin is popular and has a paved access, it is still possible to escape into the remote backcountry, though at peak times that means avoiding the most popular trails. Facilities in the area are limited. There are restrooms, water and a pay phone at the campground. There's also an adjacent picnic area with an A-frame shelter and a few tables and grills. A $2/vehicle fee is charged for parking in the day-use area. The Backcountry Information Center consists of a 3-panel information board with a map of the area and regulations. A copy of the area map published by the USFS is worth having; it shows trails and permitted usages and has a large enough scale to be useable as a topo.

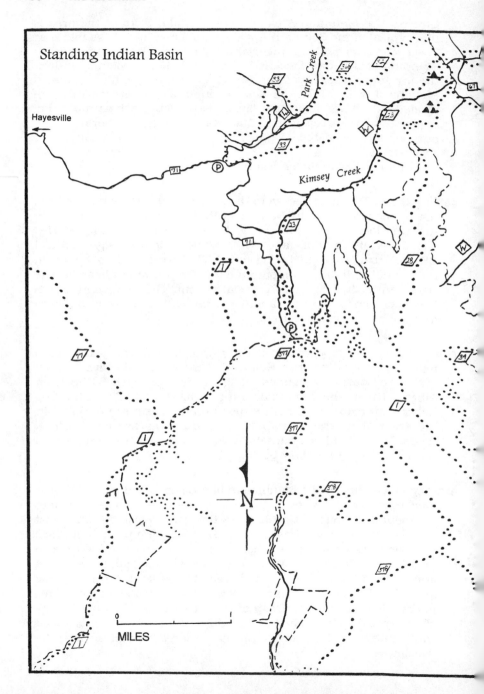

Standing Indian Basin

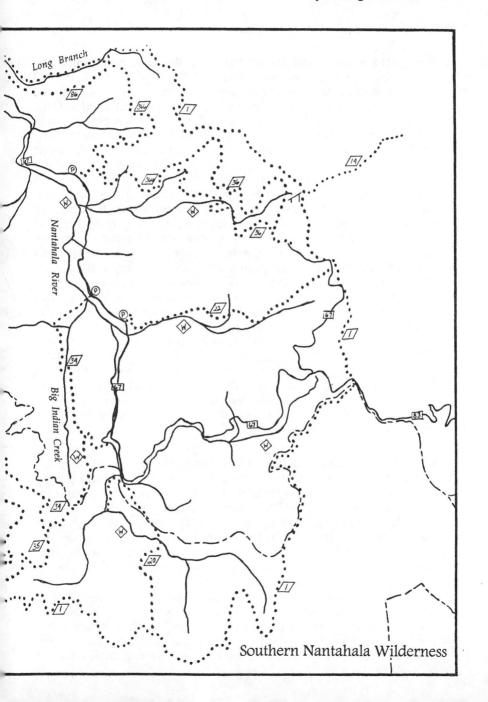

Long Branch

Nantahala River

Big Indian Creek

Southern Nantahala Wilderness

activities: Hiking, Camping, Fishing.

hiking: There are almost 70 mi of trails in the area, including a 20-mi section of the *Appalachian Trail* (#1). The trails have been laid out in a manner that makes numerous connections and extended backcountry trips possible. Most of the trails begin along the Nantahala River and then either follow feeder creeks through dimly lit, moist coves, or rise along rocky ridges to precipitous overlooks. A few short trails lead to interesting natural features or scenic waterfalls. Some trails are open to horse travel. Trailheads are all clearly signed, and are concentrated along FR-67, which has numerous pullouts. Several trails begin at or near the Backcountry Information Center. Most of the trails in the area are blazed with blue bars. They're generally easy to locate and follow. Hiking on most trails is moderate, with short sections that are either easy or strenuous. Use is average to heavy, which has resulted in fairly well-worn paths. Treadways are typically narrow dirt single tracks, though rocky sections are not uncommon, particularly beside creeks and at higher elevations. Trail improvements include numerous footbridges across creeks, as well as log steps or stairs where soil erosion is a problem.

The *AT* enters the area near Standing Indian Mtn and follows a high, winding path along the Blue Ridge and Nantahala Mountains, with precipitous drops and spectacular vistas until leaving the area at Wallace Gap. Access to the trail is at Deep Gap (see Southern Nantahala Wilderness for directions) and at several points along FR-67. The trail is blazed with the familiar white bar and is easy to follow, with moderate to strenuous hiking.

camping: The Standing Indian car campground has 84 sites arranged in 5 loops. 3 of the loops are connected in a large grassy meadow mostly cleared of trees that offers little privacy, though the sites are large. The other 2 loops are in heavily wooded areas, with considerable privacy and more of a wilderness setting. All sites include a picnic table, grill, lantern post and tent pad. There are centrally located modern restrooms and hot water showers. Sites cost $8/night. The campground is popular, and fills on weekends and late summer weekdays. It's open Mar 31–Dec 15.

Adjacent to the main campground is the Kimsey Creek Group Camp. This area features 3 group sites in a large grassy clearing with the creek running through its center. Each site has a few picnic tables, a large fire pit, water spigot, pit toilet and lantern post. The fee is $20/night and reservations are required. It's open

Apr 1–Oct 31.

The Hurricane Creek Primitive Camping Area is another car camping option. It consists of 2 small open fields beside FR-67, one for the use of horse campers, one for backpackers and car campers. The only improvement is a pit toilet. There is no water supply and the odor of horse manure can be strong. To get there, take FR-67 2.1 mi S from the Backcountry Information Center.

Backcountry camping is permitted throughout the Standing Indian Basin. In addition, 4 shelters are located along the section of the *AT* that passes through the area—2 of them are inside the Southern Nantahala Wilderness.

fishing: There are some excellent opportunities for backcountry trout fishing on area creeks. The Nantahala River rises near the S end of the Standing Indian Basin, where the Hemp Patch Branch, Yellow Patch Branch and Mooney Branch all come together. From there the river flows N 7 mi to the edge of NF lands. This section of the river is medium to large, with a mild to moderate gradient and excellent cover. Access to the river is from FR-67. Its size and easy access make it the most popular fishing river in the area, though if you get away from the campground, an empty stretch is not hard to find. The river supports native populations of brown and rainbow trout. Several of the creeks which feed the Nantahala also offer good trout fishing. Among these, Kimsey Creek, Big Indian Creek, and Park Creek are largest and easiest to fish. These are all remote, small to medium creeks with stunning natural beauty. Fly casting can be difficult on some parts of these creeks due to heavy cover. Access is by hiking trail. All waters are Wild Trout.

Wayah Bald Area

Located west of Franklin, the Wayah Bald Area is dominated by several high rounded balds and the steep slopes of the Nantahala Mountains. The area is of historical importance, and a couple of structures remain from the early days of the Forest Service. Wilson Lick, built in 1913, served as the first ranger station on the Nantahala National Forest. Its grounds are open to visitors as an historical site, though the building itself is closed. Wayah Bald and 12,000 acres of surrounding land were purchased in 1912 under the Weeks Law. Atop the bald is a stone observation tower built by the Civilian Conservation Corps in 1937. The views from the tower are extraordinary, extending all the way to the Smoky

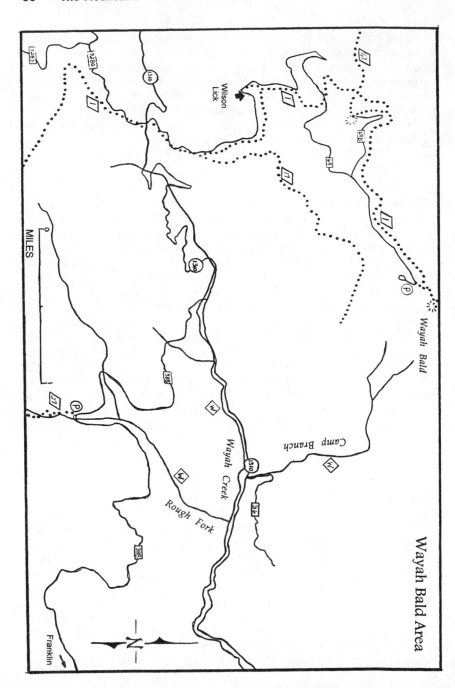

Wayah Bald Area

Mountains and Georgia. The primary opportunity to explore the backcountry is along either the *Appalachian Trail* or *Bartram Trail*, both of which cross Wayah Bald. The bald takes its name from the Cherokee word for wolf.

Franklin (SW) is the closest town.

getting there: From the jct of US-64 and US-441/23 W of Franklin, take US-64W 3.0 mi to Old Murphy Rd. Turn R and go 0.2 mi to Wayah Rd (SR-1310). Turn L and at 3.2 mi reach the Arrowwood Glade Picnic Area, R. At 6.4 mi reach FR-388, L, a single-track gravel road. (2.1 mi up the road is the signed trailhead to the *A. Rufus Morgan Trail* [#27] and a small parking area.) At 7.2 mi reach Wayah Gap and FR-69, R, and the entrance to Wayah Crest Picnic Area, L. Turn R onto FR-69, a rugged, single-track gravel road. Go 4.4 mi (at 1 mi reach the *Shot Pouch Trail* [#17], R) to a cul de sac and large parking area for Wayah Bald.

topography: Wayah Bald (5,342 ft) is the centerpiece and defining natural feature of this region. It's located atop the Nantahala Mountains, which fall away steeply to the east of the bald. The bald, which actually has only a very small treeless area around the observation tower, is surrounded by a corona of oaks twisted and stunted by harsh weather. Low elevations are along Wayah Creek to the S, between 2,300-3,000 ft. **maps:** USGS-FS Wayah Bald.

starting out: This is a dispersed area with facilities at several locations. There's a pleasant picnic area at Arrowwood Glade with modern restrooms, water, a single shelter and about a dozen tables and grills. Alcohol is not allowed and the area closes 10 pm–7 am. Wayah Crest is another picnic area, with 3 tables and grills, a pit toilet (no water source) and access to the *AT*. There's also a small picnic area on Wayah Bald beneath a canopy of wind-bent oaks. Pit toilets are located along the short paved trail to the observation tower. Wayah Bald is a popular tourist stop and is frequently crowded. The views are extraordinary, however. Nearby Wine Spring Bald, though slightly higher than Wayah Bald, is covered in a small forest of communications antennae.

activities: Hiking, Fishing, Camping.

hiking: 2 long trails—the *Appalachian Trail* (#1) and the *Bartram Trail* (#67)—cross Wayah Bald, with several shorter trails also located in the area. The *Bartram Trail* enters the area from the E on a steep ascent up Trimont Ridge. The ascent is at the end of an 11.5-mi section of the trail which begins at the Wallace Branch Trailhead and ends at a jct with the *AT* 100 yds N of Wayah Bald. From there, the trail continues W to Nantahala Lake, 7.5 mi down the W slope of the mountain. The well-designed and -constructed trail is clearly marked with yellow bar blazes and signed trailheads. Creek crossings are improved with footbridges. To reach the Wallace Branch trailhead, from the district RS turn R onto Sloan Rd (SR-1153) and go 100 yds. Turn L onto Old Murphy Rd (SR-1442) and then immediately R onto Pressley Rd (SR-1315) and go 1.7 mi to the end of the road and trailhead. The *AT*, which enters the area from the S at US-64 near the entrance to the Standing Indian Basin Area, runs perpendicular to the *Bartram Trail*, crossing it near Wayah Bald. From US-64 to Wayah Bald is 13 mi; the trail continues N 18 mi to the Nantahala River and US-19 at the Nantahala Outdoor Center in Wesser. The *AT* is blazed with a white bar and is clearly signed. Hiking on both trails is moderate to strenuous; the approaches to Wayah Bald are the most difficult segments. The 2 trails are most heavily used on and near Wayah Bald, where they become one along a paved path that provides access to the observation tower from the parking lot.

fishing: Although the area is not regarded as a prime trout fishing destination, there are some nice small creeks that do support trout. Wayah Creek is the largest of these, but runs mostly through private property posted against trespassing. The segment that is on NF land is between Arrowwood Glade and Wayah Crest. It is accessible from SR-1310. Camp Branch and Rough Fork are two small, steep creeks that empty into Wayah Creek. Both offer about a mile of fishable stream in very tight conditions. Reach Camp Branch on FR-316, off of SR-1310. To get to Rough Fork, follow directions above to the *A. Rufus Morgan Trail*. A relict forest road follows the creek downstream. All waters are Wild Trout.

camping: There are no developed campgrounds in the area. 3 shelters—Siler Bald, Cold Spring and Rufus Morgan—are located along the segment of the *AT* described above. Backcountry camping is permitted throughout the area, except where posted otherwise. There are good sites along both long trails.

Great Smoky Mountains National Park

Great Smoky Mountains National Park is a vast mountain preserve to which superlatives seem to cling: it's the largest wilderness preserve in the Southern Appalachians; its 10 million annual visitors are the most of any national park (almost three times as many as second-place Yosemite); there are more different tree species in the park (150) than on the entire continent of Europe. The park covers more than half a million acres of mountainous terrain blanketed with deciduous and spruce-fir forests on the both sides North Carolina/Tennessee border. 275,895 acres are located in North Carolina, occupying primarily the crest ridge and eastern slope of the magnificent Smoky Mountains. The mountains take their name from the white, smoke-like haze that often fills their valleys and lower slopes, leaving the higher elevations and peaks exposed above a sea of clouds. Plant communities that coexist within the park are more typically found over the 1,000-mile distance between Canada and Georgia. Although extensive logging took place in the last century, significant tracts of virgin forest remain. The park's great botanical diversity is one of the primary reasons it has been designated an International Biosphere Reserve. Mammals thrive there as well: there are approximately 500 black bears in the park, the largest population in the state, and the previously eradicated red wolf has recently been reintroduced. The park offers the backpacker, naturalist and outdoor photographer one of the most exciting and memorable environments on the East Coast.

Bryson City (S), Cherokee (S) and Gatlinburg, TN (N) are the closest towns.

contact: Superintendent, Great Smoky Mountains National Park, Gatlinburg, TN 37738; 615/436-1230.

getting there: Access to the NC side of the park is via US-129 and NC-28 at its W end, US-441 (which becomes Newfound Gap Rd inside the park) in the center, and the BRP and I-40 in the E portion.

topography: With the exception of the Black Mtns to the E, the Smoky Mtns are the highest, steepest and most rugged uplands on the east coast. The Smokies lie on a NE-SW axis, with the crest line forming the NC/TN border. Drainages generally flow S and N, except in the E portion of the Park. Elevations in the park are between 6,643 ft on Clingmans Dome and 1,500 ft on Big Creek where it leaves the park. **maps:** NP Great Smoky Mountains Trail Map; Trails Illustrated and Earthwalk Press both publish 1:62,500 scale waterproof maps that cover the entire park. See individual listings below for USGS topo sheets.

starting out: Ranger stations are located at Twentymile, Deep Creek, Smokemont, Cataloochee and Big Creek. A Backcountry Registration Station is located at each. Park trail maps are available for a 50¢ donation. Pets are not permitted in the backcountry. They're allowed in the campgrounds and picnic areas, but must be kept on a leash.

activities: Hiking, Camping, Fishing, Canoeing/Kayaking, Mountain Biking.

hiking: With more than 850 mi of trails, the park is one of the premier hiking destinations in the East. Among those trails is the nation's most famous, the *Appalachian Trail* (#1), which travels through the Park for 69 mi, where it reaches its highest point and passes through some of the most unforgettable and spectacular scenery along its entire route. Trails in the park have been laid out to ensure that a hiker can spend an almost unlimited amount of time in the backcountry without ever having to backtrack or drive to a different trail network; almost all trails can be connected in one way or another. Trails are not blazed, though frequent use makes most easy to follow. Trailheads and trail jcts are almost always signed, with distances to other trails and landmarks given (usually correctly). The large majority of trails in the park are open to horses. Despite the vast numbers of people who visit the park annually, only a small fraction (less than 70,000) spend a night in the backcountry. The result is that while trails near parking areas and campgrounds are often crowded, backcountry trails are likely to be empty.

camping: Campers in the park have the choice of car camping at developed campgrounds or camping in the backcountry at designated sites or shelters. There are 5 developed campgrounds on the NC side of the park—Deep Creek, Smokemont, Balsam Mtn, Cataloochee and Big Creek. Campgrounds are generally open from May 15–Oct 31, with some fluctuation due to weather. Smokemont has some sites available year-round. Smokemont is also the only campground at which reservations are accepted. Although the car campgrounds offer convenience, they've suffered from budget cuts and are by no means high on a list of park attractions.

Backcountry camping is permitted at 55 sites on the NC side, spread throughout the S half of the park. In addition to these sites, there are 14 shelters, most of them located along the AT. Sites are typically unimproved except for fire rings, though some have picnic tables or food storage containers. Permits are required for all backcountry camping. These permits are free, and can be picked up at self-registration stations at any of the ranger stations. To camp at one of the shelters or at a rationed backcountry site, you must obtain reservations by calling the Backcountry Reservation Office. The phone number is 615/436-1231 and it's open daily 8am–6pm. Reservations can be made up to a month in advance; these sites (particularly the shelters) fill early. Sites close occasionally due to overuse or animal problems. Backcountry camping outside of the designated sites is prohibited. You can stay 3 nights at a campsite, 1 night at a shelter. Groups larger than 8 are not allowed. Consult the *Great Smoky Mountains Trail Map & Guide*, available at all ranger stations, for additional information.

fishing: With more than 300 fishable streams, the park provides the most extensive native trout habitat in the state. All three species of mountain trout are present, with smallmouth bass found at lower elevations. The park is a protected brook trout refuge, with efforts underway to sustain and expand the range of the only truly native species of trout in the southern Appalachians. The possession of brook trout within the park is prohibited. If you hook one, you must release it unharmed immediately. The park has its own fishing regulations that are separate and distinct from NC regulations. Rules are as follows: A NC or TN fishing license is necessary (trout stamp not required); daily creel limit is 5 fish total; minimum length is 7" for rainbow and brown trout and smallmouth bass; only artificial lures and flies on a single hook can be used; season is all year; some waters are protected brook trout habitat and are closed to all fishing. Up-to-date regulations are available in the park pamphlet *Fishing Regulations*.

canoeing/kayaking: Flat-water paddling is available on 11,685-acre Fontana Lake, which forms the park's S boundary for 29 mi. The lake is ideal for combined paddling/fishing trips and touring, with several backcountry campsites located along the N shore. Put-ins are located on the lake's S shore.

mountain biking: Although mountain bikes are prohibited on all hiking and bridle trails within the park, they are allowed on park roads. On the NC side, the road best suited to backcountry bike travel is the steep, unpaved Heintooga Round Bottom Rd, located in the Balsam Mtn area. Another possibility is the unpaved park road that runs between the Big Creek and Cataloochee areas.

Twentymile Area

The Twentymile area is located in the remote southwest corner of the park. Boundaries are formed by Lake Cheoah on the Little Tennessee River to the south, by the state line with Tennessee to the west and north, and by Twentymile Ridge and the *Appalachian Trail* to the east. The Joyce Kilmer-Slickrock Wilderness in the Nantahala National Forest, with additional opportunities for backcountry travel, is nearby to the southwest. The area takes its name from its location—20 mi downstream from where the Tuckaseigee River empties into the Little Tennessee River (now Fontana Lake).

Fontana Village (S) is the closest town.

getting there: From the Texaco Station near the entrance to Fontana Village, take NC-28 W 6.1 mi to the entrance, R (no trailers permitted). The trailhead and small parking area 0.2 mi ahead.

topography: Although elevations in this corner of the Park are lower than in many other locations, the terrain is still quite rugged. Deep, narrow valleys shelter cool, moist coves where hardwoods, rhododendron, mosses and ferns flourish. The ridges feature several grassy balds. At 4,949 ft, Gregory Bald is the highest point in the area. Lowest elevation is on Lake Cheoah at 1,276 ft. **maps:** USGS Fontana Dam, Cades Cove, Tapoco, Calderwood.

starting out: Park trail maps are available at the Backcountry Registration Station. It's located beside the RS, which has no facilities. This is one of the less frequently visited areas of the park. It's a good place to escape the crowds that clog the central part of the park on peak days. The parking area is small, with room for only about 15-20 cars.

activities: Hiking, Fishing, Camping.

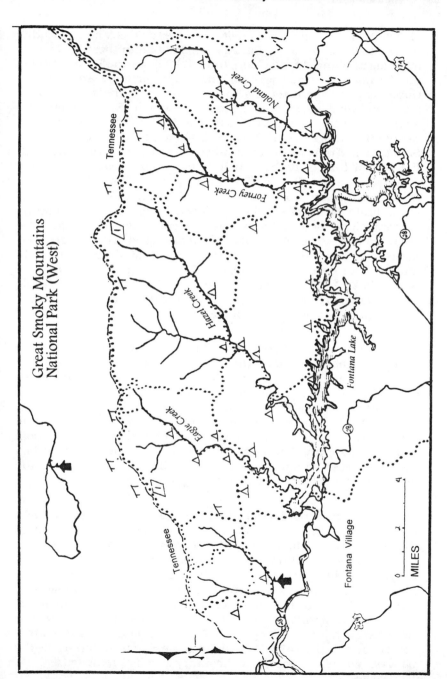

Great Smoky Mountains
National Park (West)

hiking: 21 mi of hiking trails follow the area's creeks and ascend to the crest line of the Great Smokies. In addition to these trails, a 7-mi segment of the *Appalachian Trail* (#1) follows the E boundary of the Twentymile area. Loops of 7 mi, 15 mi or more are possible. Numerous trail connections to other parts of the park can be made, allowing for trips of almost any length. Scenic highlights along the trails are deep, lush coves along the creeks and panoramic views from Gregory Bald and the fire tower on Shuckstack. Trails in the area range from easy to strenuous, with the easiest hiking in the S half of the region along Twentymile Creek and Dalton Branch. Trails are easy to follow on treadways that are either dirt roads or single-track footpaths. Signs at trail jcts indicate distances to other trails and landmarks. Trail improvements include footbridges over the several creeks that drain the area, though some crossings are unimproved. Horses are permitted on all area trails except for the first 4 mi of the AT and a 3-mi connector trail between *Twentymile Trail* and *Wolf Ridge Trail*. Access to all trails is from the signed trailhead at the Twentymile parking area, except for the *AT*, which is reached from the Fontana Lake Area access point on Fontana Dam Rd (see below).

fishing: Twentymile Creek and Moore Springs Branch are the primary streams that drain the area. Both creeks form high on the steep S slope of the Great Smokies' main ridgeline and flow S for about 5 mi to their confluence 0.7 mi N of the RS. The 2 creeks share similar characteristics: both are medium sized and follow a very rocky bed over a moderate to steep gradient. Cover is exceptional, as is the natural beauty of both creeks. Access to both is along hiking trails, though much of Moore Springs Branch has no trail access and must be waded upstream. See above under the main park heading for park fishing regulations.

camping: There's no developed campground in the area. 4 backcountry sites—#s 93, 95, 92, 13—are widely spaced throughout the area. Hiking distance to reach the sites from the RS is between 2 and 7.5 mi. The Birch Spring Gap shelter is located on the *AT* 5.2 mi N of the trailhead on NC-28. The shelter and site #13 are rationed. A free permit is required to camp at any of the sites. It can be filled out at the backcountry registration station near the trailhead and parking area. Rationed sites and shelters must be reserved in advance. Stop by a RS, the Fontana Dam visitors center, or call 615/436-1231 daily 8 am–6 pm. Camping in the park outside of designated backcountry sites is prohibited.

Fontana Lake Area

The Fontana Lake area stretches east-west along most of the lake's north shore and includes the watersheds of Eagle Creek and Hazel Creek. Perhaps the most isolated and infrequently visited part of the park, the north shore area was spared from greater crowds when the proposed North Shore Road was abandoned after only a small segment had been built. Intended to connect Bryson City and the Fontana Dam, construction was halted when environmentalists and local citizens raised objections to the road's potential impact on the park. The north shore was populated until the construction of Fontana Dam in the 1940s. Numerous small cemeteries remain in the area and are tended by family members of the buried.

Fontana Village (S) and Bryson City (E) are the closest towns.

getting there: From the Texaco station in Fontana Village, turn E on NC-28. Go 1.8 mi to Fontana Dam Rd and continue straight (rather than following NC-28 to the R). Go 0.8 mi to the dam and overlook. At 2.3 mi reach the end of the road and trailheads. Another access is that described below for the Forney Creek Area. From there, it's about a 4-mi hike to the E endpoint of the *Lakeshore Trail*.

topography: Eagle Creek and Hazel Creek are 2 of the major drainages on the S slope of the Great Smokies' main crest. They form not far below steep, rugged mountain ridges that top out at over 5,500 ft and empty into Fontana Lake (1,708 ft), the lowest elevation in the area. Highest peaks are Thunderhead Mtn (5,527 ft) and Silers Bald (5,607 ft). **maps:** USGS Tuskeegee, Thunderhead Mtn, Fontana Dam, Cades Cove, Noland Creek, Silers Bald.

starting out: This is a very large area with only a single vehicle access, located in its extreme SW corner. As many people arrive to the area by boat or on foot as by car. The area has no RS or developed facilities. The Fontana Dam visitors center located on Fontana Dam Rd can provide backcountry camping permits and park information. Because the backcountry area is vast and access is limited, the number of hikers along the trails is generally small.

activities: Hiking, Fishing, Camping, Canoeing/Kayaking.

hiking: This is an area of long trails, with most of the mileage along the two creeks and Fontana Lake. In all, there are 55 mi of trails, plus another 26.7 mi on the *Appalachian Trail* (#1), which follows the ridge crest along the area's W and N perimeter between Fontana Lake and Silers Bald. The region's 3 longest trails are the 20.5-mi *Lakeshore Trail*, which roughly parallels the lake's N shore; *Eagle Creek Trail*, which follows the creek for 14 mi to its headwaters and continues to a jct with the *AT*; and 14.5-mi *Hazel Creek Trail*, which follow the entire length of the creek before joining *Welch Ridge Trail* near the *AT*. Trail connections are numerous in the area, allowing for loops that would take anywhere from 1 to 4 or 5 days to hike. The shortest possible loop from the parking area is 13 mi. Scenic highlights along the trails include Lake Fontana, the deep coves through which the creeks flow, and the balds and openings along the *AT* near Thunderhead Mtn and Silers Bald, which permit outstanding views. Hiking on the trails is moderate to strenuous. Trails are not blazed (the *AT*, blazed with white bars, is an exception), but are easy to follow. Trailheads and trail jcts are signed, with distances to other trails and landmarks listed (usually correctly). Improvements include footbridges at many of the creek crossings. Horses are permitted on many of the trails, particularly those that follow old roads. The only auto-accessible trailhead is located at the end of Fontana Dam Rd on the N side of the dam; *Eagle Creek Trail*, *Hazel Creek Trail* and points along the *Lakeshore Trail* can be reached by boat.

fishing: Eagle Creek and Hazel Creek are 2 of the most highly regarded trout streams in the park. The creeks share similar characteristics in that both head up near the crest of the Smokies and flow SW to Fontana Lake. At 14 mi, Hazel Creek is the longer; Eagle Creek covers 8 mi. Both creeks are medium in size and follow a moderate to steep gradient over boulder and rock strewn courses with exceptional pooling. Access to both is by hiking trail. The difficult access keeps fishing pressure light, though you'll probably bump up against at least a couple of other fly fishermen. In addition to these creeks, there are many more miles of fishable trout waters on the smaller creeks that drain into Eagle Creek and Hazel Creek. These creeks are mostly small in size with limited trail access, though there are a couple of exceptions. 4 stretches of water at higher elevations are protected brook trout habitat and are closed to all fishing: Gunna Creek above the trail crossing at 3,080 ft; Defeat Branch above its confluence with Bone Valley Creek; Walkers Creek above the falls at 3,400 ft; and the headwaters of Hazel Creek above the cascades. These closed waters are all relatively short stretches and do not significantly impact area fishing. See above under main park heading for fishing regulations.

Another option for anglers is Fontana Lake, which supports populations of largemouth, smallmouth and white bass, muskies and walleye. Fishing is from a boat, with plenty of small coves perfect for maneuvering a canoe or kayak into. State fishing regulations apply on the lake.

camping: There are no developed campgrounds in the area. Backcountry campsites, however, are abundant, including 4 designed for boat access from Lake Fontana. In all, there are 19 sites, with 6 shelters spread out along the *AT*. Backcountry sites are located in 1 of 3 general areas: on the N shore of Fontana Lake (#s 90, 87, 86, 81, 77, 78, 76, 75, 98, 72), on Eagle Creek and its tributaries (#s 91, 89, 88, 96, 97) and on Hazel Creek (#s 85, 84, 83, 82). Of these, only #83 is a rationed site. Campers must fill out a (free) permit to stay overnight in the backcountry. Permits are available at the Fontana Dam visitors center or at any RS. The *AT* shelters and the rationed site must be reserved through the Backcountry Reservation Office. See above under main Park heading for information regarding reservations and other backcountry camping regulations. Camping outside of the designated sites is prohibited.

canoeing/kayaking: The N shore of 29-mi long Fontana Lake is fully contained within the park, presenting an excellent opportunity for extended canoe or kayak touring. Although the lake is popular with all kinds of watercraft, traffic is light enough for a relatively undisturbed paddling trip. The scenery from the lake is some of the best in the state. There are numerous landing sites along the N shore at backcountry campsites and trail access points. Boat launches are located on the S shore, at NF rec areas as well as at private marinas. On the Cheoah RD, there are put-ins at Tsali Rec Area and at Cable Cove Rec Area. There's also a private launch near the Fontana Dam. The Cable Cove launch provides the shortest route to backcountry site #s 90, 87, 86, 81, 77, & 78; the shortest route to site #72 is from Tsali. Paddling distance from put-in to campsite is between 2 and 6 mi.

Forney Ridge Area

The watersheds of Forney Creek and Noland Creek define the Forney Ridge Area. Natural boundaries are formed by Welch Ridge to the west, Noland Divide to the east, the eastern end of Fontana Lake to the south, and the crest of the Smokies—including Clingman's Dome—to the north. The uncompleted segment of the North Shore Rd, nicknamed "The Road to Nowhere," is in this part of the park. The road passes through a tunnel near Noland Creek where it ends abruptly. Originally intended to connect Bryson City and the Fontana Dam, construction was halted due to the pressures of environmentalists and local citizens concerned about the environmental impact of the road. Hiking through the tunnel without a flashlight is one of the eerier experiences you can have in the park.

Bryson City (SE) is the closest town.

getting there: From the RR depot in downtown Bryson City, take Fontana Rd—known locally as "The Road to Nowhere"—N 8.6 mi (at 2.8 mi reach the NP entrance; at 7.8 mi is a parking area and trailhead, L) to a parking area and trailheads, R, just before the tunnel and end of the road. An alternative access is from the Clingmans Dome parking area, with access to the *AT, Forney Creek Trail* and *Forney Ridge Trail.*

topography: The terrain in the N portion of this area is as rugged and steep as anywhere in the Appalachian Mtns. In the NE corner, Clingmans Dome (6,643 ft) sits atop the Smoky Mtns. Forney Ridge runs S from Clingmans Dome, with elevations from 6,500-4,500 ft. Forney Creek and Noland Creek straddle the ridge and drain the area. Fontana Lake—the lowest point in the area—has an elevation of 1,708 ft. From the lake to Clingmans Dome—a trail distance of only 12 mi—the elevation gain is 4,935 ft. **maps:** USGS Noland Creek, Silers Bald, Clingmans Dome, Bryson City.

starting out: With easy access from Bryson City, this area receives more visitors than the more remote regions to the W—but not many more. Even during peak foliage season in October, trails in the backcountry can be nearly deserted. The parking lot at Clingmans Dome is always crowded, as is the first mile of each trail that begins there; beyond that, the crowds vanish. There are restrooms and water along the short paved trail that leads to the summit and overlook.

activities: Hiking, Fishing, Camping.

hiking: This area includes some of the most challenging and rewarding trails in the park. The primary trails follow Forney Creek, Forney Ridge and Noland Creek, with connecting trails running between them. Many different trail combinations can be made to form loops, with distances that range from 3 to 40 mi. Connections to other areas of the Park are also possible. There are more than 65 mi of trails in the area, including 4.6 mi of the *Appalachian Trail* (#1) between Clingmans Dome and Silers Bald. This is one of the most scenic stretches of the trail, featuring large grassy openings allowing spectacular views that encompass the entire W half of the park. As in the rest of the park, trailheads and most trail jcts are signed, but trails are not blazed. Improvements include footbridges across creeks, particularly at lower elevations. Trails follow a combination of old homesteader roads and narrow footpaths. Aside from the views from the *AT*, scenic highlights include the creeks and Andrews Bald on *Forney Ridge Trail.*

fishing: Forney Creek and Noland Creek drain most of the watershed on either side of Forney Ridge and are the 2 primary trout habitats in the area. Both creeks flow S from near the crest of the Smokies and empty into Fontana Lake. If followed upstream to their headwaters, the creeks cover about 11 mi each, though the names of both change as they are fed by smaller creeks near Clingmans Dome. Both are medium sized creeks that flow over very rocky beds down an average to steep gradient, with slow, shallow stretches near Fontana Lake. Access to both is via hiking trails, which follow almost their entire distance. Many of the feeder creeks support trout and provide an opportunity to fish more intimate waters. 3 stretches of water in the area are protected brook trout habitat and are closed to all fishing. These are Huggins Creek (a tributary of Forney Creek) above the cascade at 3,700 ft and Noland Creek and Salola Branch upstream from their confluence. See above under the main park heading for fishing regulations.

camping: There are no developed campgrounds in the area. Backcountry camping is permitted at any of 14 sites and at 1 *AT* shelter. Most backcountry sites are located on either Forney Creek (#s 74, 73, 71, 70, 69, 68) or Noland Creek (#s 66, 65, 64, 63, 62, 61). Of these, only 2 (#s 71 & 61) are rationed. Hiking distance from the Fontana Rd trailhead to the sites is between 1 and 10 mi. The Double Spring Gap Shelter is located on the *AT* 2 mi W of Clingmans Dome. Free permits are required for camping at all backcountry sites; they're available at the Deep Creek campground and at all ranger stations. Camping outside of the sites is prohibited. Reservations are necessary to use the rationed sites and the shelter. See above under the main park heading for information about making reservations and other backcountry camping regulations.

Deep Creek Area

The watersheds of Deep Creek and Indian Creek define this part of the park. Noland Divide and Thomas Divide provide natural boundaries to the west and east, respectively. The backcountry area ascends north all the way to the Smokies' summit ridge. In addition to the magnificent woodlands and dramatic mountainous terrain that are the park's primary attractions, there are 3 scenic waterfalls on Indian Creek not far from the Deep Creek campground. Innertubing on Deep Creek is a popular activity, with several private concessions that supply the innertubes just outside the park boundary.

Bryson City (S) is the closest town.

getting there: From the RR depot in downtown Bryson City, take Depot St (SR-1336) 0.2 mi to Ramseur St. Turn L and go 50 yds to Deep Creek Rd (SR-1337). Turn R and go 2.3 mi to the NP entrance. Continue straight 0.2 mi to the campground entrance, R, or 0.6 mi to the trailheads and parking area. The entire route is signed.

topography: This area is defined by Deep Creek, which flows S off the crest of the Smoky Mtns, and 2 steep, rugged ridges—Noland Divide and Thomas Ridge—that parallel the river to the E and W. Elevations on these ridges reach 5,000 ft. Highest point is Mt Collins (6,188 ft) at the area's N edge; low point, on Deep Creek, is 1,800 ft. **maps:** USGS Bryson City, Clingmans Dome, Smokemont.

starting out: Facilities are at the Deep Creek campground and picnic area, where there are restrooms, water and a pay phone. The picnic area includes about 25 tables and grills spread out over a very large meadow. There's also an open-air shelter. With Bryson City only 3 mi away and the popular car campground, the S edge of this area can get a little crowded.

activities: Hiking, Camping, Fishing.

hiking: Primary opportunities for hiking in the area are along Deep Creek, Noland Divide and Thomas Ridge. 75 mi of hiking trails are concentrated in the Deep Creek basin, with ridge trails E and W. A 7.9-mi segment of the *Appalachian Trail* (#1) provides another hiking possibility. This part of the trail is closely paralleled by the Clingmans Dome Rd between Clingmans Dome and Newfound Gap, though the road is out of sight for most of the distance. Access to most area trails is at the Deep Creek trailhead, from which loops of 3 to 40 mi can be made, with longer hikes made possible by connections with trails in other regions of the park. Other access points to area trails are on the Newfound Gap Rd and on Clingmans Dome Rd. Trailheads are signed, as are most trail jcts, with mileages to other trails or natural landmarks given. Although there are no trail blazes, the trails are generally easy to follow, particularly at the lower elevations, where most trails follow old dirt roads. Trails are improved with numerous footbridges at the lower elevations, though creek crossings at higher altitudes are by rock hopping. Hiking is generally easy near the Deep Creek campground, with difficulty increasing as you move N. Ridge trails have significant elevation gains. Best views of the Deep Creek Basin are from pulloffs along Newfound Gap Rd near the gap. Horses are permitted on the trails in the S half of the area.

camping: Deep Creek campground has 100 sites arranged in 2 general areas. One is a loop with 58 tent/RV sites; the other is a long grassy clearing beside the creek with 42 tent only sites. All sites include a picnic table, grill and tent pad. Privacy is minimal throughout the campground. Modern restrooms (no showers) are located throughout the campground. The fee is $8/night. The campground is open from May 15–Oct 31.

There are 9 backcountry campsites (#s 60, 59, 58, 57, 56, 55, 54, 53, 52) in the Deep Creek area. 8 of these are located along Deep Creek, at distances between 3 and 9 mi from the parking area and trailheads near the campground. These sites can also be reached by hiking S on *Deep Creek Trail* from its N terminus on Newfound Gap Rd. A free permit, required for all backcountry sites, can be filled out at the Deep Creek campground. Site #s 57 & 55 are rationed. Reservations are required to camp at these sites. See above under the main park heading for additional backcountry camping rules.

fishing: Deep Creek is the major drainage in the area and one of the most popular trout streams in the park. The creek features a wide range of conditions, from a small, steep headwater section, to a rocky, medium-sized mid-section with excellent pooling and some fast water, to a large, shallow, low-gradient tailwater section near the campground. This lower part of the creek in particular can get crowded. Access to almost the entire 13 mi of the creek in the NP is by hiking trail. Left Fork, which joins the creek at backcountry campsite #55, is one of the larger creeks that drain into Deep Creek. Still, it's relatively small, and can only be fished by wading upstream. Indian Creek is the other primary feeder of Deep Creek, emptying into it about a mile above the campground. It is small to medium in size and follows a moderate gradient. Access is from the *Indian Creek Trail*, which follows it for more than 4 mi. Sahlee Creek, which empties into Deep Creek up near its headwaters, is protected brook trout habitat and is closed to all fishing. See above under the main park heading for fishing regulations.

Smokemont Area

The Smokemont Area is situated in the busy central section of the Park. The Newfound Gap Rd (US-441 outside the park) passes through the area, carrying thousands of vehicles daily between Cherokee, NC and Gatlinburg, TN. Most of the cars seem to stop at the parking lot at Clingmans Dome. The Highway follows close beside the Oconaluftee River, the area's major drainage. Bradley Fork drains the watershed between Richland Mountain and Hughes Ridge, the area's eastern boundary. A visitors center is located near the southern entrance to the area, and the Cherokee Indian Reservation is adjacent to the south. Also here is the western terminus of the Blue Ridge Parkway, which continues northeast to Shenandoah National Park in Virginia, a distance of 469 mi.

Cherokee (S) is the closest town.

getting there: The heavily trafficked Newfound Gap Rd passes through the center of this area. From the park boundary with the Cherokee Indian Reservation, driving N it's 0.6 mi to the W terminus of the BRP, 1.4 mi to the Visitors Center, 4.5 mi to the campground and 16.9 mi to Newfound Gap. From there it's 6.9 mi L on the Clingmans Dome Rd to the very large parking area and paved access to the observation tower.

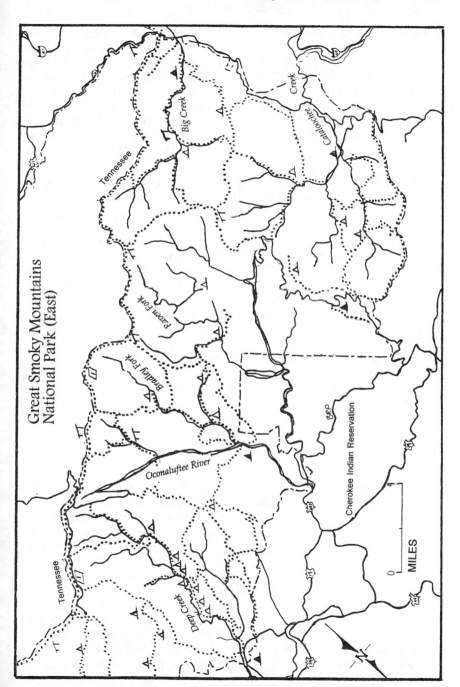

Great Smoky Mountains
National Park (East)

topography: The Oconaluftee River and Bradley Fork drain the area between Thomas Ridge (W) and Hughes Ridge (E). Richland Mtn is located between the 2 creeks. All 5 of these geographic features are oriented roughly N–S, with the lofty summit ridge of the Smokies forming the N perimeter. Elevations in the area are between 4,500 and 5,500 ft on the ridges and 2,000 ft on the Oconaluftee where it leaves the Park. High point in the area is Mt Kephart (6,217 ft), one of the summits on the crest ridge. **maps:** USGS Smokemont, Mt Guyot, Clingmans Dome, Mt Le Conte.

starting out: The park receives 10 million visitors each year; most of them can be found driving up and down the Newfound Gap Rd, which runs between Cherokee, NC and Gatlinburg, TN. The town of Cherokee is a tourist mecca of Indian kitsch that has to be experienced to be believed. Even on weekdays, the Smokemont Area keeps pretty busy. In short, if you're looking for wilderness solitude, this is the part of the park to avoid. In terms of crowd density, the contrast between the Smokemont area and other parts of the park can be shocking.

Facilities in the area are at the visitors center, which includes restrooms, a pay phone, exhibits on local history, an info desk, guided tours and a small bookstore and gift shop. Additional facilities are at the Collins Creek picnic grounds, located 1.9 mi N of Smokemont campground. Several dozen picnic tables and grills are spread out across a large wooded area. Restrooms and water are in the area. Restrooms and water can also be found at the Clingmans Dome parking lot.

activities: Hiking, Camping, Fishing.

hiking: There are 58 mi of trails in the area, including a 10.4-mi segment of the *Appalachian Trail* that follows the highest ridgeline in the Smokies along the area's N perimeter. The network of trails begins at the Smokemont campground on the Oconaluftee River and fans out in 3 directions between the natural barriers formed by Thomas Ridge (W), Hughes Ridge (E) and the summit line of the Smokies between Newfound Gap and Pecks Corner. A couple of other trailheads are located on Newfound Gap Rd. Loop hikes of various distances (minimum is 5.1 mi) can be made by connecting 2 or more trails. There are 3 trail connections with the *AT*, as well as several connections to trails E and W of the area. The primary trail corridors are along Bradley Fork and Hughes Ridge, with a pair of connector trails running between the 2. All but 2 trails in the area are open to horses. Trailheads and trail jcts are signed and trails are easy to follow. Creek crossings at lower elevations are improved with footbridges; at upper elevations, rock hopping or wading may be necessary.

camping: With 140 sites, Smokemont is the largest developed campground on the NC side of the Park. Sites are closely spaced in a long, narrow clearing near the confluence of Bradley Fork and the Oconaluftee River. The area is semi-wooded, but the small sites afford little privacy. This is a campground that will appeal to those who need to car camp or who don't mind a little crowding. Each site has a picnic table and a grill. Modern restrooms are located at regular intervals around the campground. The fee is $11/night with reservations, $8 without. The campground is open year-round, with 35 sites available during the off-season Nov 1–May 14. Reservations are accepted May 15–Oct 31. For information, call 800/365-2267.

There are also 2 group sites at Smokemont. Capacity at these sites is 15 and 20. The fee is $18 and $23/night, respectively. Groups sites are available May 15–Oct 31, with reservations accepted at the above number.

There are 3 backcountry sites and 2 shelters in the Smokemont Area. Sites #48 and 50 are located on Chasteen Creek, which empties into Bradley Fork 1.2 mi above Smokemont campground. #49 is on the upper stretch of Bradley Fork. #50 is the only site that's rationed. Hiking distances from Smokemont are between 1.2 and 4 mi. In addition to the backcountry sites, there are 2 shelters in the area. One of these, Icewater Spring shelter, is located on the *AT*, 3 mi E of Newfound Gap. The other, Kephart Shelter, is on the *Kephart Prong Trail*. Permits are necessary for all backcountry camping, with reservations required for rationed sites and shelters. Permits can be filled out at Smokemont. See above under the main park heading for information about making reservations and additional backcountry camping regulations.

fishing: The Oconaluftee River and Bradley Fork are the primary trout waters in the area. The Oconaluftee is a medium to large creek that flows SE between Newfound Gap and the visitors center before turning S and leaving the park. The river's gradient is mild at the lower elevations, but increases to moderate and then steep as you move upstream. Pooling and cover are both excellent. The river's only drawback is that the very busy Newfound Gap Rd runs close beside it for its entire length. This makes access easy, but increases fishing pressure and diminishes the natural setting.

Bradley Fork heads up near the crest of the Smokies and flows S to the Smokemont campground where it empties into the Oconaluftee. Like that river, its gradient varies with elevation from mild to steep. Bradley Fork is slightly smaller than the Oconaluftee. Access is via the Bradley Fork Trail, which follows it upstream from the campground for 5 mi. In addition to these 2 creeks, both have several feeder creeks that offer trout fishing on a smaller scale. Conditions on these creeks can be very tight, particularly for fly-fishermen. 2 stretches of water are protected brook trout habitat and are closed to all fishing: Taywa Creek; Gulf Prong and Chasm Prong above their confluence near the headwaters of Bradley Creek. See above under the main heading for park fishing regulations.

Balsam Mountain Area

In contrast to the often crowded Smokemont Area adjacent to the west, the Balsam Mountain Area is a remote mountain habitat favored more by black bears than by tourists. Vehicle access is from the Blue Ridge Parkway, where Heintooga Ridge Road ends at a picnic area and campground perched atop a mountain (elevation 5,310 feet). A rugged dirt and gravel road descends to the valleys in the shadow of Balsam Mountain. The backcountry area extends north deep into the heart of the park. Natural boundaries are formed by Hughes Ridge (W), Tricorner Knob and the summit ridge of the Smokies (N), and Balsam Mountain. The Cherokee Indian Reservation is adjacent to the southwest.

Maggie (SE) is the closest town.

getting there: From the BRP, turn N at mp 458.2 onto Heintooga Ridge Rd (closed in winter) and go 8.3 mi to the campground entrance, L. Continue straight 0.4 mi to the picnic area.

topography: Balsam Mtn, with a summit of 6,122 ft on Balsam Corner, forms the E perimeter of this area. At the N edge, Mt Chapman (6,300 ft) and Mt Sequoyah (6,000 ft) dominate the crest of the Smokies. Hughes Ridge forms the W boundary. The elevation at the Balsam Heintooga Overlook near the picnic area is 5,335 ft. Elevations on Straight Fork, the area's major drainage, drop to 3,100 ft. **maps:** USGS Smokemont, Mt Guyot, Bunches Bald, Luftee Knob.

starting out: The Heintooga Overlook and picnic area are at the S edge of this large backcountry area. Heintooga Round Bottom Rd—a narrow gravel single-track closed to trucks, trailers and buses—descends the mountain to Straight Fork, which it follows to the Cherokee Indian Reservation, a distance of 14 mi. Access to most area hiking trails is along this road. The road is gated after dark and closed in winter. Facilities are at the scenic picnic area and include restrooms and water, in addition to several dozen picnic tables and grills spread out over a wide area.

activities: Hiking, Camping, Fishing, Mountain Biking.

hiking: There are 45.8 mi of hiking trails in the area, including a 5.2-mi segment of the *Appalachian Trail* (#1). The trails are laid out in such a manner that they can be connected to form a spectacular 29-mi loop around the mountain ridges and summits that form the area's perimeter. Shorter loops of 6 mi or more are also possible. Access to these loops, and to all but 3 trails, is on the Heintooga Round Bottom Rd near Round Bottom. Trailheads are clearly signed and trails are easy to follow, though they are not blazed. All area trails follow mountainous terrain; hiking is moderate to strenuous. The trailhead to 2.6-mi *Flat Creek Trail* is in the picnic area. Trailheads to 4.5-mi Polls Gap Trail and 6.5-mi Rough Fork Trail are on Heintooga Ridge Rd, 2.7 mi back down the road from the picnic area (6.1 mi N of the BRP). There's a small parking area left. These trails are used much less heavily than the trails in the middle of the park. All trails in the Balsam Mtn area are open to horses.

camping: The Balsam Mtn car campground has 45 sites situated in a heavily wooded area. The sites are small and close together, but the dense foliage improves privacy. 6 of the sites are tent only. Each site includes a picnic table and grill. There are 2 comfort stations with flush toilets, but no showers. The fee is $8/night. firewood is sold for $2/bundle. The campground seems not to get very busy, and an atmosphere of mountain isolation pervades. Black bears are abundant in the area. The campground is open from late May–Oct. There's a 7 day limit.

Backcountry camping is available at 3 backcountry campsites (#s 47, 44, 42) and 3 shelters. Hiking distance to the campsites is between 0.2 and 4.2 mi. Site #47 is rationed. 2 of the shelters—Pecks Corner and Tricorner Knob—are located on the *AT*. Hiking distance from Heintooga Bottom Round Rd is 10 and 11 mi, respectively. Laurel Gap Shelter is on Balsam High Top at an elevation of 5,500 ft. A 4.5-mi uphill hike is necessary to reach the shelter. Permits are required for all backcountry camping. You must have reservations to camp at a rationed site or at any of the shelters. See above under the main park heading for information.

fishing: Raven Fork and Straight Fork are the primary drainages of the basin that lies between Balsam Mtn and Hughes Ridge. Straight Fork is a medium sized creek that flows S off of Balsam Mtn for about 10 mi before leaving the Park and entering Cherokee tribal lands.The gradient is low to moderate over most of this stretch. Access is along Heintooga Round Bottom Rd at the lower stretch SW of Round Bottom; access above that is only by wading. Raven Fork is a small to medium sized creek with an average gradient that runs roughly parallel to Straight Fork on its W side. Access to this creek is via the *Enloe Creek Trail*, which crosses it at backcountry site #47, 1.8 mi from the trailhead. No road or trail follows Raven Creek. Several stretches of water in the area are protected brook trout habitat and are closed to fishing. These are Bunches Creek; Stillwell Creek; Enloe Creek; the 3 forks of Raven Fork above their confluence; and Straight Fork and Balsam Corner Cree above their confluence.

mountain biking: The Heintooga Round Bottom Rd is a narrow, winding, unimproved single-track gravel and dirt road that runs 14-mi one-way from the picnic area to Round Bottom, where it becomes a 2 way road that continues for another 14 mi to the Cherokee Reservation and through to the town of Cherokee. The road is closed to trucks, buses and trailers, and receives little use except for hiking trail access. It's well suited to mountain bike travel, though with a descent of 2,300 ft, bikers will have to decide whether to continue on to Cherokee (and either ride the BRP back up to Balsam Mtn or arrange a vehicle shuttle) or pedal back up to the picnic area. The ride is easy or strenuous, depending on the direction of travel. The road is closed in winter and gated after dark. All other trails in the area are closed to bikes.

Cataloochee Area

Unlike most of the park on the North Carolina side, the Cataloochee Area includes an extensive valley with broad areas cleared of forest. Signs of settlement are still abundant, with numerous historic buildings such as the Palmer Chapel and Beech Grove Schoolhouse from the turn of the century still extant and open to the public. These buildings are scattered discreetly across the valley, and add a quaint touch to the mountain environment. The backcountry extends west from the park boundary, encompassing the watersheds of Cataloochee Creek, Caldwell Fork and Palmer Creek. Access to the area is limited to a single dirt and gravel road, limiting the number of visitors. While the terrain is less spectacular than the mountain heights to the west, this is one of the most delightful corners of the park. Wildlife is commonly seen grazing at the edge of woodland and meadow.

Dellwood (S) is the closest town.

getting there: From I-40 take exit 20 onto US-276. Go 0.1 mi and turn R onto Cove Creek Rd (SR-1331). Go 7.5 mi (at 3.6 mi the pavement ends. At 5.8 mi reach the entrance to the NP) to a jct with a paved road, L (Big Creek is straight ahead 16 mi N). Take the turn and go 3.1 mi to the campground entrance, L. Continue 0.5 mi to the RS and Backcountry Registration Station, R. At 1.7 mi reach a trailhead. The road ends after another 0.9 mi at a trailhead and parking area.

topography: The Cataloochee Valley is a broad area of open fields and gently rolling mountains—a stark contrast to the severe terrain of much of the rest of the park. The valley is hemmed in by Balsam Mtn (W), Mt Sterling Ridge (N) and the Cataloochee Divide (S). Elevations are between 2,500 ft on Cataloochee Creek and 6,155 ft on Big Cataloochee Mtn. **maps:** USGS Dellwood, Cove Creek Gap, Bunches Bald, Luftee Knob.

starting out: Apart from those at the campground, there are no facilities in the area. A Backcountry Permit Station is located in front of the RS.

activities: Hiking, Camping, Fishing, Mountain Biking.

hiking: 37 mi of hiking trails follow the major creeks in the scenic Cataloochee Valley and ascend to the surrounding ridges. Trails throughout most of the area are easy to hike, with trails on the perimeter moderate to strenuous. This is a popular horseback riding area, and horses are allowed on all trails but one. Most trailheads are located along the park road W of the campground. Numerous loop options are possible (6 mi is the shortest), as the trails connect to one another and to trails to the W and N. Trailheads and trail jcts are signed. Trails are not blazed, but are not difficult to follow. Treadways include both single-tracks and old roads that remain from when the area was settled. Trail use is light.

camping: The car campground has 27 sites, arranged in a single large loop. The area is shaded by a canopy of hardwoods, but privacy at the sites is fairly minimal. Each site includes a picnic table and grill. A comfort station has flush toilets, but no showers. Sites cost $6/night. The campground is open mid-May–Oct. Despite a relatively isolated location, the campground stays pretty busy throughout the season.

Backcountry campers have 3 sites (#s 39, 41, 40) to choose from. The sites are situated beside 3 different creeks. Hiking distance from the nearest trailhead is between 1.5 and 5 mi. Permits (free) are required to camp in the backcountry. They can be filled out at the Backcountry Permit Station beside the RS. See above under the main park heading for additional information.

fishing: Cataloochee Creek is the area's major drainage. It forms at the confluence of Palmer Creek and Rough Fork 2 mi W of the campground and flows E about 8 mi before leaving the park. It's medium to large in size and follows a mild gradient. Access is from the road. It's a popular creek that gets a fair amount of fishing pressure. 2 other creeks in the area—Caldwell Fork and Palmer Creek—offer more remote fishing: These creeks are both medium in size and follow rocky beds over a mild to average gradient. Caldwell Creek is about 5 mi long, Palmer Creek is about 4. Cover and pooling on both are exceptional. 2 stretches of water in the area are protected brook trout habitat and are closed to fishing—Lost Bottom Creek and Correll Branch. See above under the main park heading for fishing regulations.

Big Creek Area

The Big Creek Area is located at the remote eastern edge of the park. It is bounded by Tennessee (N), Tricorner Knob (W) and the Cataloochee Area (S). The backcountry area is relatively small and is defined by the watershed of Big Creek, which runs through the heart of the area. Although I-40 passes by just outside the park, there are no towns in the vicinity, and the number of visitors to the area is relatively small. A scenic picnic area and small

campground are both located near the area's entrance.
Newport, TN (N) is the closest town.

getting there: From I-40 take exit 451 in TN. Go 0.2 mi on an unmarked road. Turn L across a bridge and follow the Pigeon River for 1.2 mi on a poorly paved road to the CP&L plant where the road reenters NC. Continue ahead on SR-1332 0.9 mi to a jct with the NP road S to Cataloochee (16 mi). Continue straight and at 0.3 mi reach the RS, R. Another 0.7 mi ahead is the picnic area parking lot.

topography: This area is defined by the Big Creek watershed. The mountainous terrain on the area's ridges is as rugged and steep as anywhere in the park. Elevations top out at 6,621 ft on Mt Guyot, with several other summits above 6,000 ft. Elevation on Big Creek drops as low as 1,500 ft. **maps:** USGS Cove Creek Gap, Luftee Knob, Waterville, Hartford.

starting out: Facilities in the area are at the picnic ground, which has modern restrooms and water fountains. The picnic area includes a dozen tables and grills on a scenic bluff overlooking Big Creek. There's also a pay phone and pit toilet at the RS. Food and a small selection of trail supplies are available at Mountain Mama's Country Store, located near the NP entrance on SR-1332. The store caters to hikers, and carries the only supplies in the vicinity. Hours are 8 am–8 pm.

activities: Hiking, Fishing, Camping.

hiking: 42 mi of hiking trails fan out S and W from the trailheads near the picnic area. In addition to these, a 15.7-mi segment of the *Appalachian Trail* (#1) follows the ridgeline that forms the area's N and W perimeters, beginning in Davenport Gap and culminating on Mt Guyot. There are 2 general categories of trail: easy trails that follow the major drainages of the area, and strenuous ridge trails that ascend to the highest points on the area's borders. Loops of various length (16 mi is the minimum) and difficulty can be formed by joining 2 or more trails. Connections with other parts of the park can also be made. Trails follow a combination of single-track dirt paths and old logging roads. Most trails, including the segment of the *AT*, are open to horse travel.

fishing: Big Creek forms in the shadow of looming Mt Guyot and flows E about 13 mi before crossing the NP boundary. By the time it reaches the campground, it's a large creek with water flowing over rock formations and around boulders in cascades and small falls. The gradient is moderate over most of its course. Access is via *Big Creek Trail*, which follows it for 9 mi. 3 of the creek's tributaries are protected brook trout habitat and are closed to fishing: Big Creek and Yellow Creek upstream from their confluence; Gunter Fork above the trail crossing; and McGinty Creek.

camping: The car campground at Big Creek has 12 tent-only sites. Cars are parked in a central lot and campers walk 20-100 ft to the campsites, which are in a lightly wooded area. Privacy is average, though with so few sites crowding is not a problem. Each site includes a picnic table and grill. There's a centrally located restroom facility, but no showers. The fee is $6/night. The campground often fills during the summer. It's open May 15–Oct 31.

For backcountry camping, there are 3 backcountry sites (#s 36, 37, 38) and 1 shelter, located on the *AT*. Hiking distance to the sites is between 5 and 6 mi. The shelter is located at the western edge of the Big Creek area on Tricorner Knob. On the *AT*, it's a 15.7-mi hike from the access point at Davenport Gap; from the campground/picnic area, the shortest route is 16-mi. Reservations are required for the shelter and backcountry sites, all 3 of which are rationed. See above under the main park heading for camping rules and regulations.

Highlands Ranger District
Nantahala National Forest

The Highlands Ranger District occupies approximately 113,000 acres in Transylvania, Macon and Jackson Counties. District boundaries are formed by Georgia and South Carolina (S), the Pisgah Ranger District of the Pisgah National Forest (E), and the Wayah Ranger District of the Nantahala National Forest (W). The Blue Ridge Parkway forms much of the northern boundary. In 1981 the district's size was increased substantially with the purchase of the 39,000-acre Roy Taylor Forest. The forest is located in the northeast corner of the district, between the Blue Ridge Parkway and the Tuckaseigee River. It includes Rich Mountain, the Tuckaseigee Gorge and Panthertown Valley. Most of the other National Forest holdings are in the southwest corner of the district, surrounding the vacation community of Highlands. This area features numerous scenic attractions, including Whiteside Mountain, numerous waterfalls including Whitewater Falls, at 411 feet the highest falls east of the Rockies, and the Cullasaja River Gorge. 2 Wild and Scenic Rivers—the Chattooga and the Horsepasture—flow through the district. The Ellicott Rock Wilderness, with 3,900 acres in North Carolina, is on the border with South Carolina and Georgia.

Highlands and Cashiers are the largest towns in the district. They are located in the southern part of the district.

getting there: Major access to the district is on US-64 from the E and W, and on US-23 and the BRP from the N. To reach the district RS, from US-64, turn N onto Flat Mountain Rd (SR-1544) 2.4 mi E of downtown Highlands. Go 2 mi to the RS, L. There's also an information center located in downtown Highlands on US-64 50 yds E of the jct with NC-106.

contact: District Ranger, US Forest Service, 2010 Flat Mountain Rd, Highlands, NC 28741; 704/526-3765.

topography: With dozens of waterfalls, the cliffs of Whiteside Mtn, Tuckaseigee Gorge and Cullasaja Gorge, Highlands contains some of the most interesting and spectacular geology in the southern Appalachians. The mountains, however, are generally less rugged and towering than elsewhere in the state. Highest elevations are in the Roy Taylor Forest on Rich Mtn (5,583 ft). **maps:** see individual sections below.

starting out: Maps, brochures, guide books and other information are available at the visitor information center in downtown Highlands. Hours are M–Sa 10 am–4:30 pm, Su 1–4:30pm. Many of the areas described below feature one of the area's many stunning natural attractions. For this reason they are popular stops among the many tourists who come to the Highlands area to vacation.

activities: Hiking, Camping, Fishing, Mountain Biking.

hiking: The Highlands RD is an area of many short trails designed to provide access to the regions many scenic natural attractions and 2 long trails—the *Bartram Trail* and *Foothills Trail*. Most of the latter is located in SC, with about 25 mi in NC close to the state line. The *Bartram Trail* follows the path of the famed naturalist for 68 mi, about 11 of which are on the Highlands RD.

camping: Camping facilities on the district include a small developed car campground, several primitive campgrounds that are accessible by auto on forest roads, and backcountry camping. Opportunities for this last option are best in the Ellicott Rock Wilderness and the Blue Valley Area.

fishing: Anglers have their choice of some of the largest trout water in the state on the Cullasaja River, Whitewater River and Chattooga River. Fishermen not wanting to venture into the backcountry or grapple with heavy water and slippery rocks can fish the small, stocked lake at Cliffside Lake Rec Area.

mountain biking: Several areas on the district have forest roads (both open and gated) that are well suited to mountain bike travel. The most extensive network is in the Blue Valley Area. Panthertown Valley also has a number of trails.

Cullasaja River Gorge Area

The Cullasaja (pronounced cul-a-SAY-ja) River heads up north of Whiteside Mountain and flows southwest through Highlands, where it is dammed and forms man-made Lake Sequoyah. Below the dam, the river enters a steep, narrow gorge where it drops 1,400 ft. The gorge features 3 scenic waterfalls that are among the numerous popular tourist attractions in the Highlands area. Bridal Veil Falls, Dry Falls and Cullasaja Falls can all be reached with little effort from US-64, which follows the river from Highlands to Franklin. Although the gorge is prized for its natural beauty, there's little opportunity to explore it in a backcountry setting. Hiking trails in the area are located at Van Hook Glade and Cliffside Rec Area, adjacent camping and day-use areas, out of sight of the river and gorge. Probably the best way to get a sense of the river and its environs is to get in it, with rod and reel.

Highlands (E) is the closest town.

getting there: US-64 parallels the river between Highlands and Franklin. To reach points described below, from the jct of US-64 and NC-106 in downtown Highlands, take US-64 W. The gorge begins after 2 mi. There are numerous pullouts along the highway for scenic views and river access. At 3.2 mi is the Dry Falls parking area, L. At 4.2 mi reach the entrance to Van Hook Glade Campground, R. The entrance to Cliffside Rec Area is at 4.3 mi, R.

topography: The character of the Cullasaja River takes many forms as it descends through the gorge: whitewater, cascades, falls, and even stretches of flat water occur. On either side, the gorge's walls rise up to 1,000 ft above the river. Elevations on the river drop from 3,600 ft on Lake Sequoyah to 2,200 ft below Cullasaja Falls. **maps:** USGS-FS Scaly Mountain, Highlands.

starting out: The best way to see the gorge is from US-64. There are a number of pullouts along the route, with access to the river and the 3 scenic falls. Facilities are at the campground and at Cliffside Rec Area, a very attractively designed day-use picnic area. Unless you're a camper at Van Hook Glade, there's a $2/vehicle fee to enter Cliffside. The rec area features a small trout-stocked lake, a large picnic area with shelters, tables and grills, pit toilets, and a modern shower/restroom facility (cold water only) housed in an historic CCC building. The area is open sunup to sundown, with water on May 1–Oct 31.

activities: Hiking, Camping, Fishing.

hiking: Area trails are not actually in the gorge, nor do they follow the river. They're concentrated in the mountains above Pinecliff Rec Area. A network of short trails covers a distance of about 5 mi, including a loop around Cliffside Lake and a mountain trail that offers scenic vistas from a hewn-timber gazebo. The trails receive fairly heavy use from campers at Van Hook Glade and picnickers at Cliffside. Signed trailheads are located at both areas. Trails follow well-worn single-track paths with improvements that include steps and footbridges. The trails are not blazed, but are easy to follow.

camping: Campers in the area stay at Van Hook Glade Campground, which has 20 sites in a very scenic wooded glade across the highway from the river. Sites are well spaced and large, with excellent privacy. Each site has a picnic table, grill, lantern post and tent pad. Firewood is available for $3/bundle. There are flush toilets, but no showers. The fee is $8/night. The campground is open Apr 15–Oct 31.

fishing: The Cullasaja River is the primary fishing location in the area. It's a large river with a varying character. Anglers will find cascades and falls, massive rock formations, deep pools and stretches of flat water. Parts of the river simply can't be fished due to the ruggedness of the gorge; you'll have to work around these. Access is along US-64, which spoils some of the beauty of the gorge, but makes getting on the river relatively easy. The river is Hatchery Supported.

The other option is 8-acre Cliffside Lake, a popular spot with local bait fishermen. It's located inside the rec area, and is stocked with trout throughout the spring and summer. Fishing is from the bank, which is open around the lake's perimeter. There's also a small pier.

Glen Falls Scenic Area

Like many of the other backcountry areas on the Highlands Ranger District, the Glen Falls Scenic Area provides trail access to one of the region's natural attractions. Glen Falls is a series of 3 falls on the upper reaches of the East Fork of Overflow Creek. The falls are more accurately described as cascades, as the water twists, tumbles and slides through the flumes and rock formations that form the upper bed of the river. Opportunity for backcountry travel is limited here, as the area is small and bordered by private property to the north and west. A morning or afternoon is sufficient time to hike the 2 trails. The hiking trail that follows the creek can be used as a connector to the Blue Valley, 2 miles south.

Highlands (N) is the closes town.

getting there: From the jct of US-64 and NC-106 in downtown Highlands, take NC-106 S 1.9 mi to gravel SR-1618. Turn L and then immediately R at the FS sign. Go 1 mi to where the road ends at the parking area and trailheads.

topography: There are 2 prominent topographical features to the Glens Falls area: the series of cascading falls and Chinquapin Mtn, which reaches an elevation of 4,200 ft. The steep mountain

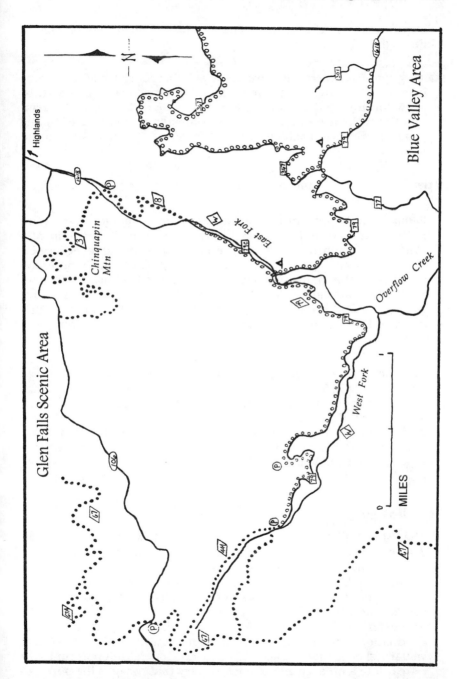

slopes are blanketed with a pine/hardwood forest. **maps:** USGS-FS Highlands.

starting out: The Glen Falls area is a popular tourist stop and day-hike area. The area is too small, and the hiking trails too short, to allow for any kind of extended trip. The *Glen Falls Trail* is steep and the rocks around the falls are slippery; a good pair of hiking boots is essential. Facilities are in Highlands, 2 miles back up the road.

activities: Hiking, Camping.

hiking: 2 trails begin at the parking area—the popular, 1.5-mi *Glen Falls Trail* (#8) and the less-travelled, 1.6-mi *Chinquapin Mtn Trail* (#3). Trailheads to both are at the parking area described above; both are signed. The trails are not blazed, but continuous use keeps the path well worn and easy to follow. Hiking is moderate to strenuous. The *Chinquapin Mtn Trail* ends on the mtn, with views of the Blue Valley. *Glen Falls Trail* follows the E Fork down to FR-79C and the Blue Valley, where there's camping and fishing.

camping: There are no developed camping facilities in the area. The *Glen Falls Trail* is generally too steep to allow for camping, though at the S end of the trail is FR-79C with good backcountry sites along E Fork and the E Fork primitive campground at the end of the road (see Blue Valley Area below for details). Camping along the *Chinquapin Mountain Trail* is also a good bet, with scenic views of the Blue Valley.

Blue Valley Area

The Blue Valley is located near the southwest corner of the district, where it presses up against the Georgia state line. It's an area of small creeks that flow through lush coves, a series of scenic waterfalls, and mild mountain ridges covered with a dense forest of hardwoods, hemlocks and pines. The valley was formerly settled, though now human populations are sparse and limited to its eastern side. The Blue Valley is unlike many of the other destinations on the Highlands Ranger District in that it lacks a visually spectacular attraction. Instead, it offers an opportunity to retreat into a quiet corner of backcountry that escapes the notice of the many tourists who visit the region.

Highlands (N) is the closest town.

getting there: From downtown Highlands take NC-28 S. Go 5.9 mi to a NF sign and Blue Valley Rd (SR-1618). Turn R and go 2.1 mi (at 0.5 mi the pavement ends and the road becomes FR-79) to the Blue Valley primitive campground. At 3.7 mi reach the East Fork primitive campground. Beyond this point the road is narrow and rugged. At 6.8 mi reach the end of the road and trailheads.

topography: The Blue Valley is defined by Overflow Creek and the mountains that surround it. Elevations along the creek are between 3,300 ft at its headwaters and 2,400 ft where it forks. The mountain ridges to the N and W are mostly mild, though there are some steep areas. The area is heavily forested with a dense understory of shrubs and rhododendron. Blue Ridge, which marks the W perimeter of the area, is also on the perimeter of the Tennessee Valley. Creeks in the Blue Valley flow E to the Atlantic, rather than W. **maps:** USGS-FS Highlands, Scaly Mtn.

activities: Hiking, Camping, Mountain Biking, Fishing.

starting out: The Blue Valley is the most extensive backcountry area on the district and offers the best opportunity for an extended backpacking trip. Although numerous forest roads cross the valley, particularly at its E end, the area has a remote and isolated feel. There are no facilities, except for the 2 primitive campgrounds described below.

hiking: The Blue Valley features 3 short hiking trails that cover a total distance of 4 mi and the *Bartram Trail* (#67), which passes along the W edge of the valley for 3.7 mi between the Hale Ridge Rd trailhead (GA) and the Osage Mtn Overlook. The 68-mi trail begins not far S of here at Beegum Gap, GA. It continues NW to Porterfield Gap on the Cheoah RD. It's blazed with yellow bars and is easy to follow. Hiking along the Blue Ridge, the W limit of Blue Valley, is easy to moderate. 2 other trails in the area, the *West Fork Trail* (#444) and *Hurrah Ridge Trail* (#4), provide short connections to the *Bartram Trail* from the end of FR-79. One trailhead is signed, the other is not. These trails are not blazed, but are not difficult to follow. Both trails are steep and strenuous to hike. To reach the Hale Ridge Rd access to the *Bartram Trail*, take NC-106 out of Highlands 7.5 mi (at 5.9 mi pass the Osage Mtn Overlook and another trail access, L) to Hale Ridge Rd (SR-

1625). Turn L and go 2.1 mi (at 1.9 mi cross into GA) to Bald Mtn Rd (FR-7). Turn L and go 1.1 mi to the signed trailhead, R. Trailheads to the *Bartram Trail* are clearly signed. The only other hiking trail in the area is the *Glen Falls Trail* (#8), which has its S terminus on gated FR-79C beside the East Fork primitive campground. From the start of the forest road, it's 1.5 mi to the scenic falls, 2 mi to the N trailhead and parking area described above under Glen Falls Scenic Area.

camping: Camping in the Blue Valley is at 1 of 2 primitive campgrounds, at any of several sites along FR-79 or in the backcountry. The 2 primitive campgrounds are similar. There are no facilities at either, with only a couple of picnic tables to distinguish the areas. Neither campground has water, though both are located near creeks (water should be treated). These campgrounds are best suited to groups, as both are in small clearings without designated sites.

Another option for primitive car camping is along FR-79 W of the East Fork campground. There are several pullouts with previously used sites in small clearings.

Backcountry camping is allowed anywhere on NF land, except where posted. There are good sites along E Fork and the *Bartram Trail*.

mountain biking: Although there are no single tracks in the Blue Valley, there are more than 15 mi of forest road—both open to autos and gated—available for backcountry riding. The 2 major arteries are FR-79 and FR-367. Both are moderate rides on dirt and gravel roads that see very little vehicle traffic. In fact, you're unlikely to see even a single car or truck. FR-79C is a gated road that runs along E Fork for about half a mi before joining the *Glen Falls Trail* (foot travel only). With campsites along FR-79, this is a good area for an overnight bike/camp/hike trip.

fishing: The E Fork and W Fork of Overflow Creek are both small to medium creeks (E Fork is slightly larger) that support populations of native trout. Both creeks have outstanding natural cover, which can make casting a problem. E Fork is the more open of the 2, particularly at the E Fork campground and along FR-79C. Each creek offers at most a mile or 2 of fishable water, with access along FR-79 and FR-79C. Both creeks are Wild Trout waters.

Whiteside Mountain Area

Whiteside Mountain is one of the several outstanding natural attractions in the area. Rising dramatically from the valley floor, the mountain features the highest cliffs on the east coast. The granite cliffs along the mountain's southern face are between 450 and 750 feet high. The alternating light and dark bands of rock are visible from miles around, but are best seen from the mountain summit. The light rock is feldspar and quartz, the dark is granite. Vegetation on the mountain is dominated by an oak forest and an abundance of wildflowers, shrubs, and lichens. Peregrine falcons nest on the mountain, and can be seen in spring and summer rising on thermals; they were reintroduced to the area in 1985. The mountain is a protected Peregrine Falcon habitat.

Cashiers (E) and Highlands (W) are the closest towns.

getting there: From the jct of US-64 and NC-28 in downtown Highlands, go E on US-64 5.5 mi to Whiteside Mountain Rd (SR-1600). Turn R and go 1 mi to the parking area, L.

topography: Elevation at the top of Whiteside Mtn is 4,930 ft. From there the S and E faces of the mountain drop away in sheer cliff faces of up to 750 ft. The base of the mountain is at only 2,800 ft. **map:** USGS-FS Highlands.

starting out: Views from the top of the mountain are spectacular and unlike those anywhere else in the state. For this reason, Whiteside Mountain is one of the most heavily touristed attractions in the Highlands/Cashiers area. You won't get away into remote, unspoiled backcountry here, but the views and geology are worth a visit anyway. Camping is not allowed on the mountain or along the hiking trail.

activities: Hiking.

hiking: The single hiking trail in the area is the *Whiteside Mountain Trail* (#70), a National Recreation Trail. The 2-mi loop ascends a narrow footpath through a hardwood forest to the exposed clifftops (guardrails have been erected to help prevent fatal missteps) along the S face of the mountain. Views S are of the Chattooga River Gorge and Georgia. At the E edge of the mtn are views E and N. The trail continues down the backside of the mountain on an old road. The heavily trafficked trail is easy to follow and often crowded (most people hike up and back the road segment). Hiking is moderate.

Chattooga Wild and Scenic River

The Chattooga River begins inconspicuously in the mountains near Cashiers. As it flows south, however, it widens rapidly, and for the next 50 miles it's one of the most spectacular waterways in the southeast. For its first 10 miles the river is in North Carolina; after that, it forms a 40-mile segment of the border between South Carolina and Georgia. The river has features that are no longer common in the southeast: unspoiled natural beauty, a lack of development along its banks and, most importantly, no dams. For these reasons it was designated a Wild and Scenic River in 1974. The river is a popular whitewater destination among kayakers and canoeists, though paddling is not allowed on the North Carolina section. The river has perhaps gained most fame as the setting of the movie *Deliverance*.

Highlands (NW) and Cashiers (NE) are the closest towns.

getting there: From the jct of US-64 and NC-28 in downtown Highlands, take Main St, which becomes Horse Cove Rd (SR-1603) S out of town. Proceed 4.7 mi to gravel Bull Pen Rd (FR-1178). Turn R and go 1.3 mi to Ammons Branch Primitive Campground. At 1.9 mi is a small parking area and trailhead to *Ellicott's Rock Trail*, R. At 3 mi reach a short, unsigned drive L that leads to a parking area. At 3.3 mi reach the "iron bridge" across the river. Most people park their cars here, though this has caused erosion problems. The previous parking lot is preferred.

topography: The Chattooga River flows through a rugged gorge with cliff faces of 400-500 ft in many places. The river banks are heavily forested with conifers, hardwoods and an understory of rhododendron. Elevations on the river are between 2,800 ft where the Wild & Scenic designation begins and 2,413 ft at the iron bridge. **maps:** USFS Chattooga Wild and Scenic River; USGS-FS Cashiers, Highlands.

starting out: Access to the Chattooga River is on a bumpy gravel forest road in the most remote part of the district. Although this keeps crowds to a minimum, the area is still relatively popular among the adventurous. The iron bridge and the stretch of river just above it are the busiest places. There are no facilities in the vicinity.

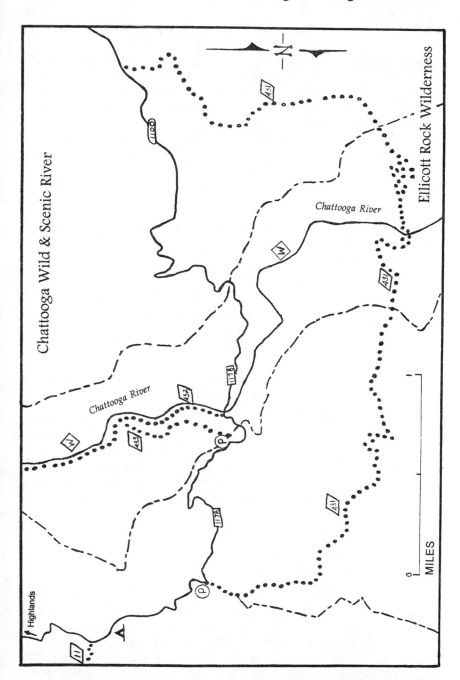

activities: Hiking, Fishing, Camping.

hiking: Although there are plans to construct a trail alongside the NC segment of the river for its entire length, presently hiking options are limited in the area. 2 hiking trails cover a total distance of 3 mi on the W bank of the river. The *Chattooga River Trail* (#432) follows the river N from the iron bridge 1.5 mi before coming to a dead end. The *Chattooga River Loop Trail* (#433) connects and forms a loop to the parking lot above the iron bridge. Both trails are popular and heavily used by day-hikers. Most hikers start out at the iron bridge trailhead, which is signed. Trails are easy to follow, but not blazed.

fishing: By east coast standards, the Chattooga is large trout water. The river heads up 10 mi N of the iron bridge, and by the time it reaches the bridge it is moving a lot of water. Rather than the usual problems of overhanging branches and thick rhododendron slicks, anglers have to contend with heavy water and rapids. Access is at the iron bridge on Bull Pen Rd. From there, a hiking trail follows the river upstream for about 1.5 mi. The river can be fished to the NF boundary, about 6 mi N. It narrows considerably as you head upstream. The river is Wild Trout waters.

camping: Backcountry camping is allowed anywhere along the river (except on private property, which includes a small segment of the river S of SR-1107 near the N end of the Wild & Scenic designation). Campers are requested to make camp at least 50 ft from the river. If you don't want to backpack into the backcountry, you can stay at Ammons Branch, a primitive camping area located on Bull Pen Rd. This is a very primitive campground, with only a couple of picnic tables and an ancient pit toilet. There is no water supply. Individual sites are not marked, but there's enough room for at least 4 or 5 groups.

Ellicott Rock Wilderness

The Ellicott Rock Wilderness is spread out over 3 states: North Carolina, South Carolina and Georgia. Approximately half of the wilderness—3,900 acres—is located in NC. The Wild and Scenic Chattooga River flows through the heart of the area, dividing it into 2 roughly equal halves. The wilderness takes its name from the mid-river rock that supposedly marks the tri-state border. The actual border is marked by Commissioner's Rock, located about

10 ft downstream from Ellicott Rock. It's inscribed LAT 35 AD 1813 NC SC.

Highlands (NW) and Cashiers (N) are the closest towns.

getting there: Bull Pen Rd (FR-1187) forms the N boundary of the wilderness and provides the only access. To get there from the jct of US-64 and NC-28 in downtown Highlands, take Main St, which shortly becomes Horse Cove Rd (SR-1603) out of town. Proceed 4.7 mi to gravel Bull Pen Rd (FR-1178). Turn R and go 1.9 mi to the N terminus of the *Ellicott Rock Trail*, R. To reach the N trailhead to *Bad Creek Trail*, continue ahead another 4.3 mi. The trailhead and a small parking area are R.

topography: The Chattooga River is the dominant natural feature of the wilderness. The terrain on either side rises steeply in places, though in general the mountain ridges are relatively mild. The area is heavily forested, and the river corridor is lined with tangles of rhododendron trees. Elevations are between 3,660 ft on Ellicott Mtn and 2,270 at Ellicott Rock in the Chattooga River. **maps:** USGS-FS Highlands, Cashiers.

starting out: There are no facilities in the vicinity. The busiest part of the wilderness is the steel bridge on Bull Pen Rd. There's no trail access to the wilderness there, but the Chattooga River is popular as a swimming hole and sunbathing area. Canoeing and Kayaking are not allowed on the river in NC.

activities: Hiking, Fishing, Camping.

hiking: In terms of hiking trails, the NC section of the wilderness is symmetrical: 2 trails of equal length begin on Bull Pen Rd on opposite sides of the river and descend about 3.5 mi to Ellicott Rock and the river itself. Together, *Ellicott's Rock Trail* (#431) and *Bad Creek Trail* (#431) cover a distance of 7 mi, following old road beds and then, as they near the river, single track footpaths. Both trailheads are signed and the trails are easy to follow, though blazes are irregular. Hiking is moderate. Because both trails are one-way paths to the river, loops are not possible, except by using 4 mi of Bull Pen Rd as a connector. For longer hikes, a connection can be made with the *Chattooga River Trail*, which runs S beside the river in SC/GA for about 30 mi before ending at US-76.

fishing: The Chattooga River is a popular trout stream, and fishing is encouraged as a part of river management. The river is large by NC standards, and features boulder gardens, rock formations, and lots of rapids, which attract canoeists and kayakers from around the southeast. The NC section of the river, however, is not open to paddling, so anglers will only have the water to contend with. Access is either at the iron bridge on Bull Pen Rd, or by hiking the 3.5 mi to Ellicott Rock and fishing upstream from there. The iron bridge is about 2 mi N from the rock. The Chattooga is Wild Trout water.

camping: Primitive backcountry camping is allowed throughout the wilderness, except within 50 ft of the river.

Whitewater Falls Scenic Area

Upper Falls on the Whitewater River is a gorgeous double cascade of water that plummets over an exposed rock face into a deep gorge. The 411-foot drop makes it the highest waterfall east of the Rockies, a fact that no doubt accounts for much of its popularity as a tourist stop. The area above the falls has been developed to accommodate all visitors, including the physically challenged: a paved path leads from the parking lot to the scenic overlook. Beyond the heavily touristed area, however, there is ample opportunity to escape into the backcountry. The river below the falls is one of the more picturesque stretches of water in the state, with rock formations and massive boulder piles that force the water into cascading drops and deep pools. The falls are located at the southern end of the district, about a mile north of the South Carolina state line.

Cashiers (N) is the closest town.

getting there: From the jct of US-64 and NC-107 in Cashiers, take NC-107 S for 9 mi (after 8 mi it becomes FR-101 at the state line) to paved FR-106. Turn L and go 2.3 mi to paved FR-107. Turn L and go 1 mi to the state line and the start of NC-281. Proceed another 0.2 mi to the entrance and parking lot, R.

topography: The Whitewater River plunges 411 ft at the falls into a steep gorge with walls that rise more than 500 ft on either side. The top of the falls are at almost 2,600 ft; a mi downstream the river has dropped to 1,950 ft. **maps:** USGS-FS Cashiers.

starting out: Anticipate crowds, regardless of when you visit. The short path to the overlook is paved and heavily trafficked. Even the steep trail down to the river gets pretty busy in summer. The backcountry doesn't really begin until you cross the footbridge at the bottom of the gorge and begin hiking on the *Foothills Trail*. There are restrooms and an info board at the parking lot. Camping is not allowed between the parking lot and the overlooks or on the *Foothills Trail* E of NC-281 in NC.

activities: Hiking, Fishing, Camping.

hiking: There are 2 options here: the short paved trail that leads to a scenic overlook with postcard perfect views of Upper Falls, or the 80-mi *Foothills Trail* (#436). The *Whitewater Falls Trail* (#7) is about 200 yds on a level, paved walkway that ends at the first overlook. The *Foothills Trail*, most of which is in SC, crosses the trail here. From the overlook, the trail runs E and W, including a steep, 0.5-mi descent on switchbacks to the Whitewater River and a steel bridge across it. The trail is maintained cooperatively by the Nantahala NF, Sumter NF and Duke Power Co and runs between 2 SC state parks—Oconee and Table Rock. Approx 25 mi are located in NC, where the trail roughly parallels the state line. Hiking on the white-blazed trail is moderate to strenuous. Designated primitive campsites are located along the trail, including 5 in NC. One possible 2- or 3-day hike is from the Whitewater Falls area to the Horsepasture National Scenic River, a distance of 11 mi one-way. For additional information about the trail contact the Foothills Trail Conference, PO Box 3041, Greenville, SC 29602.

fishing: In addition to its natural beauty, the Whitewater River is a fishable trout river. Conditions here are different than on most other trout streams in the state. The Whitewater is a large, fast river, with ample room to cast. Although the gradient is steep, massive boulders and rock formations create large areas of natural pooling. Access is via the *Foothills Trail*, which follows the river between the Upper Falls and the SC state line. The river is Wild Trout water. If you're hiking the Foothills Trail E, bring a rod to fish the Horsepasture River, a remote river that has been designated Wild & Scenic. It's Hatchery Supported.

camping: Although there are no developed camping facilities in the area, backcountry camping is allowed on NF land (not at the

Whitewater Falls parking area) and there are designated primitive sites along the *Foothills Trail*. Camping is not permitted on the trail E of NC-281 in NC.

Pisgah Ranger District

Pisgah National Forest

Located southwest of Asheville in Buncombe, Haywood, Henderson and Transylvania Counties, the Pisgah Ranger District covers approximately 157,000 acres of mountain woodlands. It is the most popular forest district in the state for outdoor recreation, with 4 developed car campgrounds, 5 group campgrounds, more than 340 miles of hiking and mountain biking trails, and dozens of miles of top quality trout streams. The Blue Ridge Parkway passes through the district for more than 40 miles, adding to the opportunities for backcountry travel and providing numerous vantage points from which the mountain and valleys of the district can be viewed. Mount Pisgah, for which the district and National Forest are named, overlooks the district from just beyond its boundaries on the Blue Ridge Parkway. The district is the location of many scenic attractions that draw tourists from around the state, including Looking Glass Falls, Sliding Rock, Graveyard Fields and Looking Glass Rock. The Pisgah Ranger District has an historical significance as well: it was here that professional forestry began in the United States. In the latter part of the 19th century, George Vanderbilt owned more than 125,000 acres of land in the area. He hired 2 men—Gifford Pinchot (who became the first Chief of the Forest Service) and the German forester Carl Schenck—to manage the land for forest conservation. The Cradle of Forestry in America—a 6,500-acre National Historic Site—commemorates the vision and achievements of these men.

Asheville (NE), Hendersonville (E), Brevard (SE) and Waynesville (NW) are the closest cities.

contact: District Ranger, US Forest Service, 1001 Pisgah Highway, Pisgah Forest, NC 28768; 704/877-3265/3550.

getting there: Primary access to the district is on the BRP, which abuts NF land for almost 40 mi. US-64/NC-280 parallels the district on the SE boundary and provides the other major access. The district Ranger Station is located on US-276 2 mi N of Brevard.

topography: Topographically, the district divides into 2 distinct regions, with the BRP forming the dividing line. The terrain N of the Blue Ridge is typically rugged and steep, and includes the district's highest peaks. At 6,214 ft, Black Balsam Knob is the highest of these. S of the Blue Ridge, the terrain is considerably milder, with peaks generally under 4,500 ft. One unusual feature of this area is the Pink Beds, a complex of upland bogs that cover approx 1,000 acres. Elevations on the district drop as low as 2,000 ft. **maps:** USFS Pisgah District Trail Map; see below under individual listings for USGS topo maps.

starting out: The Pisgah RD receives more visitors than any other forest district in NC. The busiest spots are along the BRP and US-276, which can both become clogged with traffic during the peak season. Many of the backcountry areas also become crowded during peak season, particularly the Shining Rock Wilderness and Black Balsam Knob Area. Areas least likely to be crowded are the N Fork Mills River Area and the S Fork Mills River Area. If you're planning on spending any time in the area, a copy of the USFS Pisgah District Trail Map, which covers most of the district, provides an excellent overview. Its scale is too small to use as a topo for backcountry pathfinding, but it shows all area trails, allowed uses, and rec areas. (NOTE: Trail numbers shown on the map are not the same as the USFS trail numbers.) Additional information can be picked up at the RS, the Forest Discovery Center at the Cradle of Forestry in America, The Forest Place in downtown Brevard, or at one of the developed campgrounds. All 3 have a small selection of maps and guide books for sale. RS hours are M–F 8 am to 4:30 pm; summer hours are daily from 9 am to 5 pm. Restrooms, water, a pay phone and a message board are all located outside.

activities: Hiking, Mountain Biking, Fishing, Camping.

hiking: With more miles of hiking trail than any other national forest district, the Pisgah RD has a trail to satisfy every hiking taste. Each of the areas described below has a substantial back-country area that's laced with an extensive trail network. The trails are laid out in a manner that fosters trail connections, and dozens of possibilities for extended backpacking trips exist. The district includes 2 long trails—the *Art Loeb Trail* and the *Mountains-to-Sea Trail*, which, when completed, will be the state's longest trail.

mountain biking: There are more miles of trails open to mountain bikers on the Pisgah RD than on all the other national forest districts combined. Bikers will find extensive networks that include single tracks as well as gated and open forest roads. The greatest concentration of trails is at the Davidson River Area, S Fork Mills River Area, N Fork Mills River Area and Lake Powhatan Area. Trails in the different areas can be connected, making this one of the only regions in the state where long trips that combine biking with camping are a possibility. Bikers should note that some trails in the district are only open to bike traffic seasonally.

fishing: Fishing on the Pisgah RD is for rainbow, brown and brook trout in cool mountain creeks, and the district is home to some of the most popular stretches of water in North Carolina. The major areas of activity are the Davidson River Area and the 2 branches of the Mills River.

camping: Campers on the district have several options. There's a very large developed car campground at the Davidson River Area; smaller car campgrounds are located at Lake Powhatan, N Fork Mills River and at the N edge of the Middle Prong Wilderness. Primitive roadside car camping is available at a small number of sites at the W end of the S Fork Mills River Area. With 2 designated wildernesses and several other extensive backcountry areas, opportunities for backcountry camping abound. Shining Rock, Middle Prong, Davidson River, S Fork Mills River and N Fork Mills River all provide excellent possibilities. The Shining Rock Wilderness and Davidson River Area are often crowded.

Middle Prong Wilderness

The 7,900-acre Middle Prong Wilderness is a pristine, roadless region of steep, rocky ridges, damp hardwood coves and gurgling mountain streams. Located in the Great Balsam Mountains, it was created in 1984 by the North Carolina Wilderness Act. Prior to that, much of the area had been logged. The forest that is present today is mostly second growth, with the spruces and firs typical of a northern forest at the highest elevations and the hemlocks and hardwoods of the Southern Appalachian forest in the coves, hollows and along the lower slopes. The wilderness is bounded mainly by other publicly held land—The Blue Ridge Parkway to the south and west, Shining Rock Wilderness and the Black Balsam Knob Area to the east, and additional Forest Service land to the north. The West Fork of the Pigeon River forms most of the eastern boundary. The wilderness is an excellent destination for backpacking or trout fishing in very primitive conditions.

Waynesville (NW) and Canton (NE) are the closest towns.

getting there: The BRP forms the wilderness' S and W boundary and provides trail access. Trailheads are located at Buckeye Gap (mp 425.5) and Haywood Gap (mp 426.7). Trailheads are also located at Sunburst Campground. To get there, exit the BRP at mp 423.3 onto NC-215. Take the road N 8.6 mi to the campground and campground entrance, L.

topography: Rugged mountain slopes covered with spruce-fir and Southern Appalachian hardwood forests dominate the terrain W of the W Fork of the Pigeon River. The highest point is 6,140 ft on the E slope of Richland Balsam (the peak is just outside the wilderness). Fork Ridge runs N-S and bisects the area, with elevations that top out at 5,900 ft. Elevations on the Pigeon River drop to 3,100 ft. **maps:** USFS Shining Rock and Middle Prong Wilderness; USGS-FS Sam Knob.

starting out: The Middle Prong Wilderness receives fewer visitors than the larger and better known Shining Rock Wilderness adjacent to the E. Concentrations of people tend to be at Sunburst, which is a popular day-use area and small campground. Facilities there include restrooms, water and a small picnic area. The best map of the area is the USFS Wilderness map. Unless you're already familiar with the Middle Prong Wilderness, a topo map and compass are essential equipment.

Group size is limited to 10. Campfires are not allowed in the wilderness.

activities: Hiking, Camping, Fishing.

hiking: 3 trails form 2 major N–S routes between Sunburst Campground and the BRP. Together the trails cover 14 mi of rugged mountainous terrain. Near the BRP they join the *Mountains-to-Sea Trail* (#440), which passes through the wilderness between Haywood Gap and NC-215. Several loops of varying distance can be formed, and connections with the trails of the Black Balsam Knob area and Shining Rock Wilderness are also possible. This affords the opportunity for an extended backpacking trip. Although the trails are fairly heavily used, they

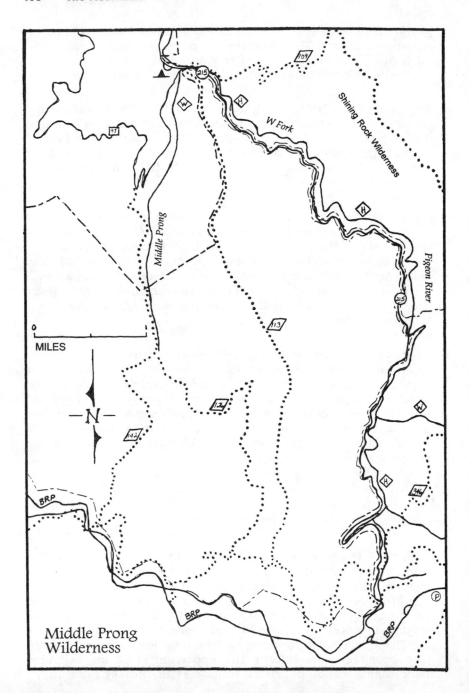

Middle Prong
Wilderness

are maintained in a primitive condition. Trailheads—located along the BRP and at Sunburst—are generally signed and easy to locate. The trailhead at Sunburst is an exception; it's difficult to find. Trails are not blazed or improved.

camping: Camping is either at the small car campground at Sunburst Campground just N of the wilderness boundary or in the backcountry. There are 14 sites at Sunburst in a small, scenic clearing between a heavily forested embankment on one side and the Pigeon River on the other. NC-215 is also adjacent. Traffic is light, but the highway's presence detracts from the setting. Each of the sites has a picnic table and grill. Privacy is minimal. There are restrooms with flush toilets. The fee is $4/night. The campground is open Mar 1–Nov 1.

fishing: There are 9 mi of fishable trout streams in the area. The W Fork of the Pigeon River is a medium to large stream that flows N along the E boundary of the wilderness from near the crest of the Blue Ridge. The river has a steep gradient and some magnificent rock formations and boulder fields. Fishing is best near the Sunburst Rec Area, where the river levels out somewhat. Access is from NC-215. There's no hiking trail along the river, and it's difficult or impossible to reach in many places. The river is Hatchery Supported. Inside the wilderness, Middle Prong is a medium to large creek that flows N for 5 mi through the heart of the wilderness before emptying into W Fork just above Sunburst. Access to the river is on gated FR-97 and *Haywood Gap Trail*. It is Wild Trout water.

Shining Rock Wilderness

The Shining Rock Wilderness covers 18,500 acres of roadless, pristine backcountry in the Great Balsam Mountains. The wilderness features high, rugged mountain slopes that top out at over 6,000 feet, with numerous peaks above 5,800 feet. These peaks and upper slopes are covered with the vegetation of the spruce-fir forest more typical of northern latitudes. Lower elevations are blanketed with the tree and plant species found throughout the great Southern Appalachian forest. The forest is second growth, as the region was heavily logged up to the first half of this century. Shining Rock is the oldest designated wilderness in North Carolina and was one of the original tracts of land included in the federal system of wilderness areas created by the

1964 Wilderness Act. Middle Prong Wilderness is adjacent to the west, and the beautiful Black Balsam Knob area abuts to the south, increasing the opportunity for extended backcountry hiking trips.

Waynesville (NW), Brevard (SE) and Asheville (NE) are the closest cities.

getting there: From the BRP, turn N onto US-276 at mp 411.8. Go 2.8 and turn L at the large NF sign to reach the Big East Fork parking area and trailheads. A smaller parking area is located 0.1 mi back up US-276. There's also trail access from the Black Balsam Knob parking lot and Sunburst Rec Area.

topography: The Shining Rock Wilderness includes some of the most rugged terrain on the district. Grassy Cove Top (6,040 ft) and Cold Mtn (6,030 ft), both part of the Great Balsam Mountain chain, are the highest peaks. Shining Rock (5,940 ft) is at the geographic center of the wilderness. Major drainages are the E and W Forks of the Pigeon River and N Prong Shining Creek. The lowest elevations are on W Fork Pigeon River, which drops to 3,100 ft.
maps: USFS Shining Rock Wilderness and Middle Prong Wilderness; USGS-FS Shining Rock, Sam Knob, Cruso

starting out: The Shining Rock Wilderness is the most popular backcountry destination on the Pisgah Ranger District. As a result, it has suffered from overuse in recent years. Although there are remote areas on its 18,500 acres for those willing to make the effort, hikers and backpackers seeking solitude and a wilderness experience are likely to be disappointed. Most crowded trails are those than run N and W to Shining Rock. A topo map and compass should be considered essential equipment for travelling in the wilderness. The USFS wilderness map has a large enough scale to be usable as a topo map. There are no facilities in the wilderness. Sunburst Campground and picnic area, on the W perimeter, has toilets and water.

Campfires are not permitted in the wilderness. Group size is limited to 10.

activities: Hiking, Camping, Fishing.

hiking: Most visitors to Shining Rock come to hike the trails—for a day, a weekend or a week. 8 trails create a network of more than 35 mi, with most trails concentrated in the wilderness' E and S

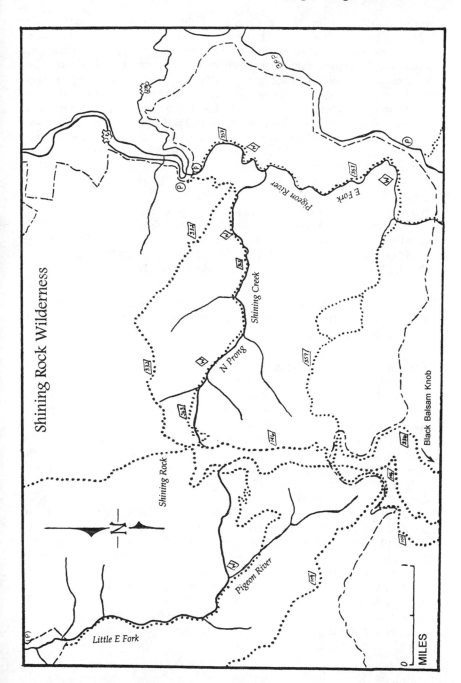

Shining Rock Wilderness

Pisgah River

Shining Creek

E Fork

N Prong

Shining Rock

Black Balsam Knob

Pigeon River

Little E Fork

MILES

halves. The trails are maintained in a primitive condition; trailheads are signed, but there are no blazes and creek crossings are by rock hopping or wading. They typically follow single tracks, though creekside trails often follow the old railroad beds of the timber companies that formerly logged the region. Hiking on the trails is moderate to strenuous, with elevations above 5,000 ft along many of the trails. Easier trails follow the creeks. Horses are permitted on 2 trails: the *Ivestor Gap Trail* (#101) and *Little East Fork Trail* (#107). Connections with trails in the Middle Prong Wilderness and the Black Balsam Knob Area are possible, increasing the opportunity for extended backpacking trips. The last 8 mi of the *Art Loeb Trail* (#146) are in the wilderness. This trail can be followed S 30 mi to the Davidson River Rec Area. Access to most trails is at Big East Fork trailhead or from the parking area on FR-816 near Black Balsam Knob. From there, it is a little more than a 2-mi hike to reach the wilderness. Trailheads to less travelled parts of the wilderness are at Sunburst and Daniel Boone Camp at the end of Little E Fork Rd.

camping: The closest developed campgrounds are at Mt Pisgah (BRP) and Sunburst. Backcountry camping is permitted throughout the wilderness.

fishing: The 3 major creeks that flow out of the wilderness offer good native trout fishing. The creeks—E Fork Pigeon River, N Prong Shining Creek, and Little E Fork Pigeon River—are all similar in character. They are medium to large with a mild to average gradient and very rocky beds, with massive boulders creating ideal pooling. Cover is provided by hemlocks, hardwoods and understory shrubs. Each has 3 to 4 miles of fishable water in the wilderness. All 3 creeks are accessible by hiking trails which follow them from near their headwaters to the wilderness boundary. All 3 are Wild Trout waters.

Another option is the West Fork Pigeon River, which heads up S of the wilderness below the Blue Ridge and flows N on the W side of Fork Mountain, where it marks the wilderness' W boundary. Below its headwaters, the river quickly becomes a medium to large stream that follows a steep gradient through some stunning rock formations and boulder gardens. NC-215 winds alongside the river between the BRP and Sunburst. The highway provides the only access, as no trail follows the river. The easiest access for fishing is across from Sunburst Rec Area. The river is Hatchery Supported.

Black Balsam Knob Area

At 6,214 feet, Black Balsam Knob is the highest peak in the district. Like much of the surrounding terrain, the mountain is treeless, with low shrubs, grasses and wildflowers the dominant vegetation. Two fires in the first quarter of the century scorched the earth and left the area barren. The result of those fires today is one of the more unusual mountain environments in the southern Appalachians. Instead of the typically dense spruce-fir and hardwood forests found at these elevations, the mountain slopes and alpine meadows are open, with views that extend for miles, revealing the contours of the land. East of the knob is Graveyard Fields, so named for the raised mounds of earth that once caused the area to resemble a cemetery. The force of the fires that devastated the area was so great that the mounds were obliterated. Today, Graveyard Fields is a beautiful valley covered with rhododendron and laurel and featuring a series of scenic waterfalls on Yellowstone Prong. The area is bounded by the Shining Rock Wilderness (N), Middle Prong Wilderness (W), and the Blue Ridge Parkway (S). Across the highway is another scenic highlight of the region—the Devil's Courthouse. Spectacular views from the overlook encompass Pilot Mtn, Rabun Bald in Georgia, Whiteside Mountain and Rich Mountain.

Waynesville (NW) and Brevard (SE) are the closest towns.

getting there: Vehicle access to this area is from the BRP. To reach the Black Balsam Knob Area parking lot and trailheads turn N onto FR-816 at BRP mp 420.3. At 0.7 mi reach the trailhead parking area for the *Art Loeb Trail*. At 1.3 mi the road ends at a large parking area and trailheads. • The Devil's Courthouse parking area is at BRP mp 422.4. • Graveyard Fields is at BRP mp 418.8. The area can also be reached by hiking in from the Shining Rock Wilderness.

topography: Area geography is dominated by rounded balds and alpine meadows with vegetation that includes grasses, shrubs, rhododendron, mountain laurel and abundant wildflowers. In some areas the understory is extremely dense. The entire area is at a high altitude, with most of the area more than a mile high. Lowest elevation is about 4,200 ft. **maps:** USFS Shining Rock Wilderness and Middle Prong Wilderness; USGS-FS Sam Knob, Shining Rock.

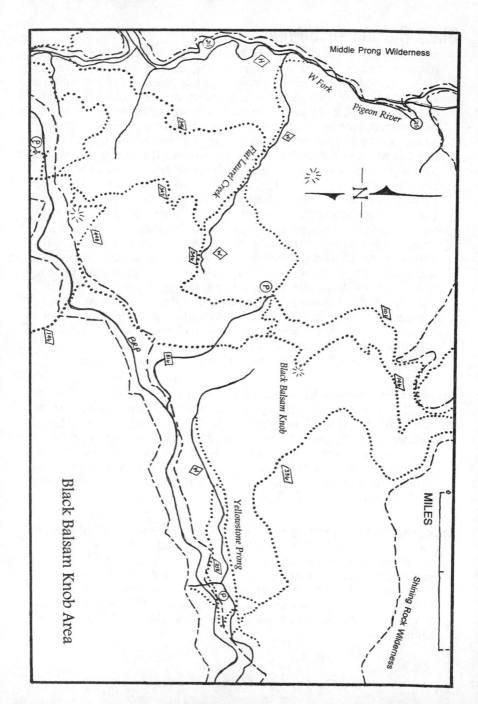

Black Balsam Knob Area

starting out: This is a popular area with easy access from the BRP. The attraction here is the uniqueness and beauty of the alpine setting, not the chance to find solitude in a wilderness setting (except in winter, perhaps). The least crowded area is W and S of the parking lot at the end of FR-816. The only facilities in the area are pit toilets, located at the parking area.

activities: Hiking, Camping, Fishing, Mountain Biking.

hiking: The trails on and around Black Balsam Knob offer an unusual but welcome circumstance in the southeast: the chance to hike on mountains and through valleys not blanketed with forest and allowing unobscured vistas. A network of 7 trails covers 18 mi, extending into all sectors of this area. Among these are segments of 2 long trails, the *Art Loeb Trail* (#146) and the yet-to-be-completed *Mountains-to-Sea Trail* (#440). The trails can be connected in a variety of combinations, making loops of varying distance possible. All trailheads are clearly signed. Most trails are blazed and all except a few primitive, unmaintained trails are easy-to-follow. The trails at Graveyard Fields are improved with steps, footbridges and benches. Trail use is generally heavy, with both day-hiking and backpacking popular. The trail at Devil's Courthouse is partially paved. Several trails are open to horses, pack animals (llama tour operators use the area) and mountain bikes.

camping: The nearest developed campgrounds are at the Mt Pisgah Rec Area on the BRP and at Sunburst Campground (see Middle Prong Wilderness). Backcountry camping is permitted anywhere on NF land except within 1,000 ft of roads. Camping is not allowed on BRP land.

fishing: Although not a primary fishing destination, there are a couple of creeks in the area that support trout. The best and most accessible of these is Flat Laurel Creek, a small creek with about 2 mi of fishable water between its headwaters and where it empties into W Fork Pigeon River. Access is along *Flat Laurel Creek Trail* (#346) and a very primitive secondary trail. You have to make an effort to fish this creek, and the rewards aren't great, though there are some very nice cascades and pools along its lower stretch. The creek is Wild Trout water.

mountain biking: 3 trails—The *Ivestor Gap Trail* (#101), the *Graveyard Ridge Trail* (#336), and *Flat Laurel Creek Trail* (#346)—are open to bikes. The trails cover a total distance of 9.2 mi. Riding is easy to moderate. Although the grade is generally mild, the trails are very rough and rocky in places. Access is at the parking lot at the end of FR-816. Trails are easy to follow. Trail use is heavy. Other trails that connect to these 3 are not open to bikes.

Davidson River Area

The Davidson River Area is a popular area with campers, fishermen and day visitors who come to see the local scenic attractions. The area is defined by 2 highways and a river—the Blue Ridge Parkway, which forms the northern boundary; US-276, a part of the Forest Heritage National Scenic Byway and the major access to the area, and the Davidson River, which flows out of the Blue Ridge through the heart of the region. Most visitors pass through on US-276, with short stops at the 2 main scenic attractions: Looking Glass Falls and Sliding Rock. Beyond the highway, however, are the true attractions of the area: 80 miles of trails open to hikers, bikers and horses; spectacular vistas from 3 mountains with striking geologic formations; and some of the best trout water in the state.

Brevard (SE) is the closest town

getting there: From the jct of NC-280 and US-276 in Brevard, turn NW onto US-276 and go 1.2 mi to the entrance to Davidson River Campground, L.

topography: The topography of this area is defined by the Davidson River and the numerous small creeks and branches that feed it. The river rises near the crest of the Blue Ridge and flows E toward Brevard and the French Broad River. The terrain on either side of the river is varied, with rolling mountain slopes interrupted by the exposed rock formations and sheer cliffs on Looking Glass Rock (3,969 ft), John Rock and Cedar Rock Mtn (4,055 ft). Highest elevations and most rugged mountain terrain are on the S slope of the Blue Ridge, at the NW end of this area. **maps:** USFS Pisgah District Trail Map; USGS-FS Pisgah Forest, Shining Rock, Sam Knob.

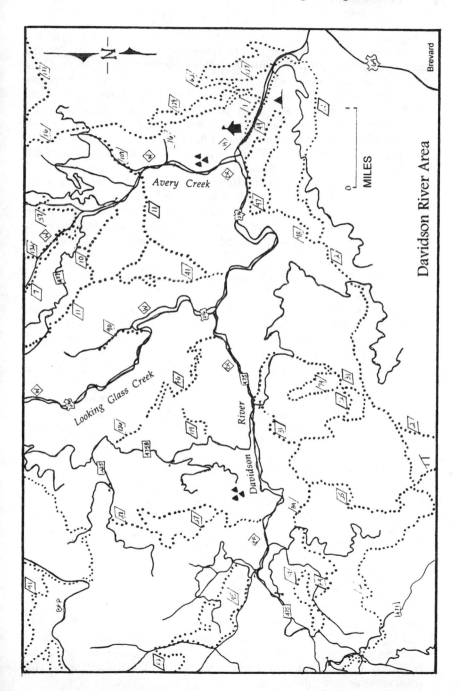

Davidson River Area

starting out: The RS and visitor center is located 0.25 mi N of the Davidson River Campground. Facilities include water, a pay phone and restrooms outside. The Davidson River Area is one of the busiest areas on a very busy district. The most popular destinations in the backcountry are Looking Glass Rock, John Rock and the Davidson River, which seems to attract more fly fishermen than any other body of water in the state. The fish hatchery located beside it is also a popular tourist stop. Additional facilities are at Sycamore Flats, a large picnic ground located on the N bank of the Davidson River 0.8 mi S of the campground. Dozens of picnic tables are scattered across a large grassy meadow shaded by hardwoods. Flush toilets and water are centrally located. The picnic area is open from 7 am to 9 pm. Alcohol is not permitted. In addition, there are many individual roadside picnic sites with tables and grills located along US-276.

activities: Hiking, Camping, Fishing, Mountain Biking.

hiking: A network of 20 trails covering more than 70 mi provides access to all the various features of the area: hardwood and hemlock forests, cool mountain creeks, rugged peaks with rock outcrops and unobstructed vistas, and steep mountain ridges. The layout of the trails makes possible loops of many lengths and connections with trails in the S Fork Mills River Area, The Black Balsam Knob Area, and the Shining Rock and Middle Prong Wildernesses make backcountry expeditions of several days or more feasible. The longest trail in the area is the 30-mi *Art Loeb Trail* (#146), a National Recreation Trail that travels from the Davidson River Rec Area entrance to the NW corner of Shining Rock Wilderness. Most trails in the district are blazed and follow treadways that have become clearly defined from heavy use. Hiking is generally moderate to strenuous, with some easy sections on level terrain along the area's creeks. Trailheads are clearly signed, with permitted uses and difficulty rating marked on each post. Hikers should beware that a large percentage of trails are open to mountain bikes. Most trails are accessible from the entrance to the campground, at the ranger station, and along FR-475, particularly behind the fish hatchery.

camping: Campers in the area have their choice of a developed campground, 3 group camps or backcountry camping. Reservations are accepted at Davidson River Campground and are required at each of the group camps. Call 800/280-2267 for reservations and information.

With 161 sites, the Davidson River Campground is the largest on the district. The campground is laid out in a series of consecutive loops, which makes it seem less massive than it actually is. Some of the loops are in open meadows, others are lightly forested. Each site has a table, grill and lantern post. A restroom/shower facility (hot water) is located at the center of each loop. Privacy varies with each loop, though it's better than might be expected at such a large campground. The fee is $11/night. Some sites can be reserved in advance. The campground is open all year.

White Pines Group Camp is located in a large clearing beside Avery Creek. There are 2 sites, each with a capacity of 25. Sites include picnic tables, tent pads and pit toilets. The fee is $25/night. Reservations are required. To get to the campground go 0.6 mi N of the RS to FR-477, a wide gravel road that follows Avery Creek. Turn R and go 0.25 to the parking lot, R. The group camp is open year-round.

The 2 other group camps—Cove Creek and Kuykendall—are located not far from each other and share a vehicle access. (Access to Cove Creek is normally from FR-475; however a storm in the fall of 1994 washed the road out.) To reach the campgrounds, from US-64 in Brevard go 3.4 mi SW and turn R onto Kathy's Creek Rd. Turn L immediately onto Selica Rd (SR-1338). After 0.2 mi the pavement ends and the road becomes FR-471. At 1.4 mi come to the gated entrance to Kuykendall Group Camp, R. There's a single large grassy clearing that can accommodate 100 people. Facilities include pit toilets and water pumps. The fee is $50/night. Reservations are required. Kuykendall is open year-round. To reach Cove Creek Group Camp, continue on FR-471 6.6 mi to the jct with FR-475 and the *Art Loeb Trail*. Turn R and proceed 2.9 mi to the gated campground entrance, L. There are 2 sites, each with a capacity of 100 people. Pit toilets and water are at the sites. The fee is $50/night for each site. Reservations are required. Cove Creek is open year-round.

Backcountry camping is permitted throughout the Davidson River Area, except where posted. There are 2 shelters—Butter Gap and Deep Gap—along the *Art Loeb Trail*. As this is such a popular area for backpacking, there are numerous pre-established sites along most trails.

fishing: The Davidson River is arguably the premier destination on the district—perhaps in the state—among fly fishermen in pursuit of trout. On spring and summer weekends, the river near the fish hatchery is always the busiest stretch of water on the district. The Davidson is a medium-sized river with a mild to average gradient and some deep pools. Access is from FR-475 and US-276, which together parallel the river for most of its length. The forest road has numerous pullouts. 2 different regulations apply to fishing on the Davidson. From its headwaters downstream 20 mi to Avery Creek, the river is Catch & Release/Artificial Flies Only; below Avery Creek, normal Hatchery Supported regulations are in effect. This lower stretch of the river gets busy too, with campers and spin casters mixing with the fly fishermen. 2 other creeks in the area offer fishable stretches of trout water. Avery Creek and Looking Glass Creek are both medium-sized streams that cover about 5 mi before emptying into the Davidson not far above the campground. Looking Glass Creek is followed for its entire course by heavily travelled US-276, the district's primary highway. There are numerous pullouts and river access is easy, though the highway detracts considerably from the setting. Avery Creek is a little more remote, though access is still from a road that parallels the creek—gravel FR-477. Both creeks are Wild Trout waters.

mountain biking: All but a few trails in the Davidson River Area are open to mountain bike traffic. The longest and most significant trail closed to bikes is the *Art Loeb Trail*. Aside from that, there are still approx 38 mi of trails—mostly single track—that riders can choose from. Riding is typically moderate to strenuous. Trailheads are clearly signed with permitted uses indicated on each marker. Several trails in the area are only open to bikes between Oct 15-Apr 15. See above under hiking for additional trail information.

Pink Beds Area

The Pink Beds are an extensive system of upland bogs that are unusual in the Southern Appalachians. The area is located in an elevated valley little more than 1,000 feet below the crest of the Blue Ridge, yet more closely resembles habitats found on the coastal plain. Despite the ruggedness of the surrounding mountain terrain, the Pink Beds are virtually flat, with expanses of dark, moist earth interlaced with meandering creeks. Rhododendron and laurel flourish in the damp habitat, and the area may take its name from their showy display of blooming flowers every June and July. Adjacent to the Pink Beds is the Cradle of Forestry in America National Historic Site. A Forest Discovery Center, numerous buildings with historical significance, and a pair of interpretive trails describe and recreate the early days of professional forestry in America.

Brevard (SE) is the closest town.

getting there: From the BRP, turn S onto US-276 at mp 411.8. At 3.3 mi reach FR-1206, L, a rough, gravel road. (To reach roadside camping sites and access to the S Fork Mills River Area, take the road 3.3 mi to FR-476.) At 3.7 mi reach the parking lot for the Pink Beds Picnic Area and trailheads, L. 0.2 mi further S on the L is the entrance to the Cradle of Forestry in America.

topography: The Pink Beds Area is characterized by a broad expanse of nearly flat terrain in the shadow of the rugged slopes of the Blue Ridge. Hemlocks, pines and a dense understory of rhododendron and laurel comprise most of the forest cover. Elevations are between 3,200 and 3,300 ft. **maps:** USGS-FS Shining Rock, Pisgah Forest, Cruso, Dunsmore Mtn.

starting out: Facilities are at the Pink Beds Picnic Area (water, flush toilets) and at the Cradle of Forestry in America (restrooms, water, pay phone, vending machines). The picnic area has a dozen tables and grills and several small shelters in a large clearing. It's open 7 am–9 pm. The Cradle of Forestry in America—with hiking trails, historic buildings and a Forest Discovery Center that features exhibits on forest ecology and management—is located immediately S of the Pink Beds Picnic Area. The CFA is open 10 am–6 pm daily from May 1 to Nov 1. An entrance fee is charged.

activities: Hiking, Camping, Fishing, Mountain Biking.

hiking: Trails in the area begin at the Pink Beds Picnic Area and at the CFA. The 5-mi *Pink Beds Loop Trail* (#106) is an easy trail that provides the best opportunity to explore the unusual environment of the Pink Beds. The easy-to-follow trail is blazed with orange bars and begins at a signed trailhead in the picnic area parking lot. The trail is improved with numerous footbridges across the area's many small drainages. It's bisected by a segment of the *Mountains-to-Sea Trail* (#440) and a mile-long spur trail connects with the 12-mi *S Mills River Trail* (#121), allowing for extended backpacking trips. These 2 trails are moderate to strenuous, and are generally unimproved. Hikers should be aware that the N half of the *Pink Beds Loop Trail* is open to bikes Oct 15 to Apr 15. Another long trail that is in the area (trailhead is on US-276, 2.4 mi S of the BRP) is the 6-mi *Buck Spring Trail* (#21), which follows a ridgeline along the steep S slope of the Blue Ridge to the Pisgah Inn and nearby Mt. Pisgah. Hiking is moderate along the trail.

Other trails in the area are 2 that are located in the Cradle of

Forestry in America. The easy, 1-mi *Forest Festival Trail* includes stops at interpretive posts that describe timber practices and some of the predominant plant communities found in the area. The *Biltmore Campus Trail* offers a chance to see the buildings that housed the first school of forestry in the US. The trail is an easy, 1-mi walk. Both trails are paved, and both begin behind the Forest Discovery Center. The primary purpose of these trails is educational and both receive very heavy use. Trail maps and guides are available inside.

camping: There are no developed campgrounds in the area. Car campers can pull over at any of 5 designated primitive sites along FR-476. Backcountry camping is permitted throughout the area. The trail that follows the S Fork Mills River is one popular area with numerous sites. A shelter is located on *Black Mountain Trail* a quarter-mi W of Buckhorn Gap.

fishing: Although the Pink Beds area forms a large basin of water-logged earth and is criss-crossed by numerous creeks and drainages, its shallow, slow-moving waters are poor trout habitat. To find fishable water, you have to go beyond the bogs. The headwaters of the S Fork Mills River, one of the premier native trout streams in the state, are located within the Pink Beds area. The medium-sized river flows S and E 20 mi over a mild to average gradient. Access is via the *South Mills River Trail* (#121), which parallels the river for 12 mi on an old RR bed. The river is Wild Trout water.

mountain biking: Most trails in the area are open to bikes for at least part of the year. The easiest trail is the 2.5-mi N half of the *Pink Beds Loop Trail* (the S half is closed to bikes). Bikers can use the trail Oct 15–Apr 15. Longer rides are possible on the 12-mi *S Mills River Trail* or the 10-mi *Black Mountain Trail*, which skirts the S edge of the Pink Beds. These offer more challenging rides than the *Pink Beds Loop*, with some rugged terrain and stream crossings. Both trails are open to bikes year-round. Treadways are generally single-track, though the *S Mills River Trail* follows a wide RR grade alongside the river. These trails can all be connected to each other for extended bike/camp trips.

South Fork Mills River Area

The South Fork of the Mills River begins as one of the many small, meandering creeks that interlace the boggy environment of the Pink Beds. As it flows southeast, it gains in size and momentum, becoming the major drainage of the watershed between Laurel Mountain to the north and Black Mountain to the southwest. The surrounding area—bounded by FR-1206 and Black Mountain—is more remote and less visited than many of the other areas on the Pisgah Ranger District. The terrain is mountainous, but with slopes and ridges that are less rugged and imposing than in many other locations on the district. Forest cover, which includes the major species of the Southern Appalachian forest, is heavy. The South Fork Mills River area is well-suited to backpacking trips, with outstanding opportunities for trout fishing along the way.

Brevard (SW) and Hendersonville (E) are the closest cities. The community of Mills River (NE) is also close.

getting there: From the jct of US-276, US-64, and NC-280 in Brevard, take NC-280 5 mi N to Turkey Pen Rd (FR-297) on the Henderson/Transylvania county line. Turn L onto the narrow, winding gravel road and go 1.3 to a dead end at the large parking area and trailheads. (The parking lot is often full on summer weekends.) If you're coming from the N or E, Turkey Pen Rd is 6.3 mi SW of the jct of NC-191 and NC-280 in the community of Mills River. • An alternate access to the area is to go through the Pink Beds Area. From US-276 (3.3 mi S of BRP mp 411.8; 0.6 mi N of the Cradle of Forestry in America) turn E onto gravel FR-1206. Go 3.3 mi to FR-475. Turn R and go 1.2 mi to the end of the road and trailhead.

topography: From its headwaters in the Pink Beds to Turkey Pen Gap, the S Fork Mills River drops from 3,200 to 2,400 ft. The area's mountainous terrain is relatively mild, with elevations rarely rising more than 1,000 ft above the riverbed. **maps:** USGS-FS Pisgah Forest, Dunsmore Mtn.

starting out: Aside from the Shining Rock Wilderness and Middle Prong Wilderness, the S Fork Mills River Area is one of the most remote and isolated regions on the district. Local roads end at the area's perimeter; access is by foot, horse, or mountain bike only. There are no facilities in the area. A 2-panel info board at the Turkey Pen Rd parking area shows a trail map and gives short descriptions of the area's trails.

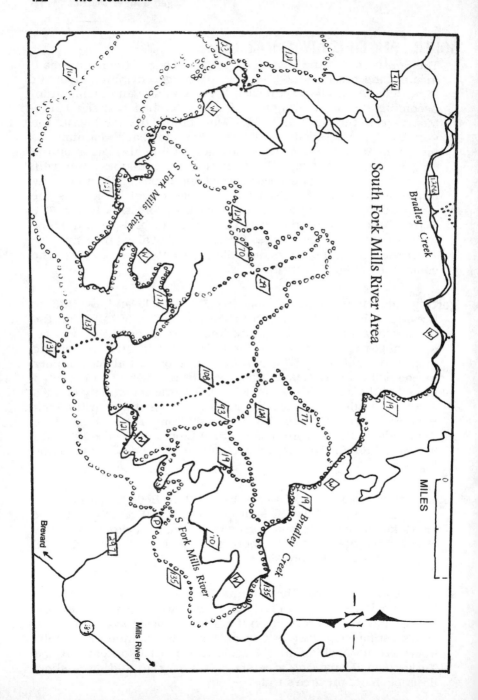

South Fork Mills River Area

activities: Hiking, Fishing, Mountain Biking, Camping.

hiking: The backcountry around S Fork Mills River is an area of long trails and longer loops. The *S Mills River Trail* (#121) is longest, following the river for more than 12 mi. 9 other trails make connections along its route, which follows an old RR grade. There are 12 trails in the area, with a combined length of more than 30 mi. Although several trailheads provide access to the area, the trailheads at the end of Turkey Pen Rd lead to the greatest concentration of trails. Trailheads are clearly signed and trails are blazed, though many trail junctions are not signed. Improvements along the trails are rare. An exception is the S Mills River Trail, which features a series of footbridges between Turkey Pen Gap and Cantrell Creek. Hiking is generally moderate, though there are some river crossings on Bradley Creek and on the upper portion of S Fork Mills River which can be difficult when the water is high. Most trails are open to use by mountain bikers, though the traffic is not nearly so heavy as in other parts of the district.

mountain biking: Most trails in the area are open to mountain bikes year-round. Trailheads are signed, with current usage allowances clearly marked. Trail treadways vary from narrow, rocky single-tracks to wide, sandy RR grades. Many of the river crossings on the major creeks are unimproved. Riding is moderate on most trails, with some easier stretches along the creeks. Short rides, long loops and extended backcountry bike/camp expeditions are all possible in this large area.

fishing: S Fork Mills River is the signature trout stream in the area, supporting populations of native browns and rainbows. Unlike the 2 other rivers on the district with similar characteristics—the Davidson and N Fork Mills—The S Fork Mills River is Wild Trout water. Consequently it receives much less fishing pressure, particularly from those intent on catching dinner. The river is medium to large, with a mild to average gradient and outstanding cover and pooling. Access is via hiking trail only, with trailheads at Turkey Pen Gap and near the Pink Beds. The river is 20 mi long, with 15 mi on NF land. 1 other area creek worth mention is Bradley Creek. It's a medium-sized creek that rises near the crest of the Blue Ridge and flows S 6 mi to a confluence with S Fork Mills River. A hiking trail follows it upstream from near Turkey Pen Gap to FR-1206, which runs beside it for several miles. It too is Wild Trout water.

camping: There are no developed camping facilities in the area. With the numerous long trails and the possibility of so many loop connections, this area is ideal for backcountry camping. You can make camp anywhere in the backcountry. The most popular sites are along the river.

North Fork Mills River Area

Located in a bowl-shaped basin between the Blue Ridge and the National Forest boundary near the start of the broad valley through which the North Fork of the Mills River flows, this area features a small car campground and a network of multi-use trails that are particularly popular with mountain bikers and equestrians. The eponymous river is also a favorite trout stream that is stocked regularly during the spring. Although access to the area is on a paved road, there is a substantial backcountry area that is more difficult to reach, requiring hiking or biking. The area is covered with a second-growth hardwood forest, with lush coves of rhododendron and laurel along the numerous creeks that drain the area.

Mills River (E) is the closest town.

getting there: From the BRP at Bent Creek Gap (mp 400.2), turn S onto unsigned FR-5000, a rugged gravel road. At 3.6 mi come to a jct with FR-142, R (on FR-142 it's 0.5 mi to the end of the road and several trailheads). Continue on FR-5000 2 mi to the end of the road at a jct with FR-1206 (paved) and the campground. • Alternately, from the community of Mills River at the jct of NC-280 and NC-191, take NC-280 N 0.9 mi to N Mills River Rd (SR-1345). Turn L and go 4.9 mi to the campground and the start of FR-1206.

topography: Area geography is defined by the broad, fertile valley of the Mills River to the E, and the mountains of the Blue Ridge to the N and W. Between is the N Fork Mills River watershed. Elevations along the Blue Ridge are between 5,721 ft (Mt Pisgah) and 3,270 ft (Bent Creek Gap). The campground is at 2,400 ft. **map:** USGS-FS Dunsmore Mtn.

starting out: The trails in the backcountry are particularly popular with equestrians and mountain bikers. The trailhead at the end of FR-142 can get pretty crowded on summer weekends. The campground/picnic area is also a busy area, with the adjacent N Fork Mills River a popular trout fishing area. The picnic area is located in a large clearing shaded by sweetgum, dogwoods, and other hardwoods. Facilities here include dozens of picnic tables and grills, a sports field, water, modern restrooms and a pay phone. The area is open year-round, with water off Nov through Mar.

activities: Hiking, Fishing, Camping, Mountain Biking.

hiking: More than 25 mi of multi-use trails fan out N and W of the N Mills River campground. In addition to the official hiking trails, there are dozens of miles of gated forest roads open to non-vehicular travel. Although popular with mountain bikers and horseback riders, these trails also offer an excellent opportunity for hikers and backpackers to venture into the backcountry. Trails cover a variety of geography, from the rugged summit ridge of Laurel Mtn to the remote headwaters of Big Creek near the BRP. Trails originate in 3 locations: the end of FR-142 (where the greatest number of trails and gated forest roads begin), along FR-5000 and along FR-1206. Most trails can be connected to form loops of varying length. Trailheads are generally signed, though a good topo map will help you negotiate the network of forest roads, which often aren't signed. Most trails are blazed, though inconsistently in places. There are no improvements along these trails; creek crossings are by rock hopping or wading. Hiking is moderate to difficult, with easy stretches along the forest roads and on trails that follow creeks. Trails on the S slope of Laurel Mtn, with access points along FR-1206, are as lightly used as any trails on the district.

camping: The 32-site N Mills River Campground is a popular car campground arranged in 2 loops beside the river. Sites are closely spaced in a wooded area that offers some degree of privacy, though not much. Each site has a picnic table, grill and lantern post. There are flush and pit toilets, as well as water spigots. The fee is $5/night. The campground is open year-round, with no water between Nov 1 and Apr 1 (no fee either). The campground is often full on weekends after Memorial Day. Another car camping possibility is at designated primitive roadside sites along FR-5000 and FR-142. There are 12 sites in all, without improvements. Car camping is not allowed along the roads except at these sites.

Backcountry camping is permitted throughout the area, except where posted. The most popular areas are along the N Fork Mills River and Big Creek, accessible by hiking trail and gated forest road.

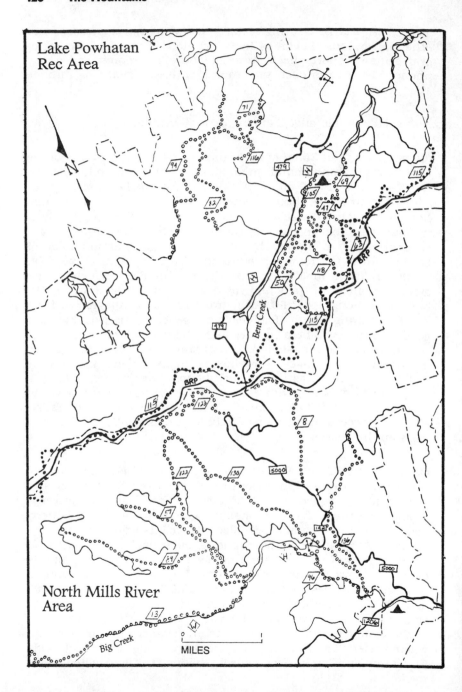

Lake Powhatan
Rec Area

North Mills River
Area

Bent Creek

Big Creek

MILES

mountain biking: Between single-tracks and gated forest roads, there are more than 50 mi of trails open to mountain bikers in the area. The trails cover a wide variety of terrain, with trails that range from easy to strenuous. Although this is a popular locale among NC riders, it gets less use than the trails across the BRP at Lake Powhatan. Short loops, long loops, and even longer backtracks are all possible on the high density network of trails and gated roads. The large majority of trails begin at the end of FR-142, where there are 2 gated forest roads and several single track trails. Riding covers the complete range of difficulty levels, from easy to strenuous.

fishing: The primary fishing destination is the N Fork Mills River, a medium to large stream that flows SE 2 mi from the Hendersonville Reservoir to the campground. This stretch of water follows a mild gradient over a boulder strewn course. The upper segment of the river, accessible by trail, is a very nice stretch of water. The section near the campground is the most heavily fished, with easy access from FR-1206. The river is Hatchery Supported with Delayed Harvest regulations in effect.

2 other creeks with good trout habitat flow through the area—Big Creek and Fletcher Creek. Both are small to medium sized creeks located above the reservoir in the remote backcountry. These creeks cover a distance of about 7 mi between them as they flow S and E out of the Blue Ridge and drain into the reservoir. Because a 2 mi hike or bike ride is necessary to reach these creeks, they receive little fishing pressure. Both creeks are Wild Trout waters.

Lake Powhatan Recreation Area

As the area on the district closest to Asheville, Lake Powhatan inevitably receives a lot of visitors. In fact, the area is something of a mecca among local mountain bikers, who come to ride the miles of single track and forest road trails. At the center of the area is the Lake Powhatan campground and day-use area. In addition to a full service campground, there's a lake with swimming beach and picnic area, as well as a network of hiking/biking trails. Outside the campground gate, the Bent Creek Research and Demonstration Forest covers 6,300 acres that were established in 1925 as the first research area dedicated to studying the regeneration of the Southern Appalachian forests. Also nearby is the North Carolina Arboretum, a component of the University of North Carolina. The

424-acre preserve features gardens and trails. A $3/vehicle entrance fee is charged. The Arboretum is open M–F 8:30 am to 4 pm. Call 704/665-2492 for additional information. The Lake Powhatan area appeals primarily to car campers, mountain bikers and day-users who come to swim or fish in the lake. The backcountry area is rather limited and is likely to disappoint backpackers looking for an escape into pristine wilderness.

Asheville (NE) is the closest city.

getting there: From the BRP, exit at mp 393.7 on the W side of the French Broad River. Follow the exit ramp 0.3 mi to NC-191. Turn L and go 0.3 mi to a FS sign at Bent Creek Ranch Rd (SR-3480). Turn L and go 0.3 mi to a fork in the road. Turn L onto Wesley Branch Rd (SR-3484) and go 2.3 mi to the rec area entrance. Or, if you're coming from Asheville, from the jct of I-26 and NC-191, take NC-191 1.9 mi to Bent Creek Ranch Rd (SR-3480). Turn R and follow directions above.

topography: Elevations along most of Bent Creek are between 2,000 and 2,300 ft. The creek flows through a wide corridor where the mountains have been smoothed into rounded hills and flattened ridges. More rugged terrain is found on the area's perimeters, particularly to the N, along Stradley Mtn, and in the SE corner. Bent Creek Gap, where FR-479 and the BRP intersect, is at 3,270 ft. **maps:** USGS-FS Dunsmore Mtn, Skyland.

starting out: The Lake Powhatan Rec Area—with campground, picnic area, lake, beach and trails—is at the center of this area. It's open officially from May 15 to Oct 31, though dates vary depending on the weather. Unless you're camping, there's a $3/vehicle fee to park in the Rec Area. If you want to use the picnic area, lake or swimming beach, you'll have to pay it. Out of season, or if you won't be using the Rec Area facilities, park in the large designated area outside the main gate across from the start of FR-479. In addition to water and toilets, facilities include vending machines, an ice machine and a pay phone located near the entrance.

activities: Hiking, Mountain Biking, Fishing, Camping.

hiking: About half of the hiking trails in this area are within the Powhatan Rec Area; the other half are outside the main gate, mostly N of Bent Creek. There are about 20 mi of trails in all. That's not counting the 16-mi *Shut-in Trail* (#115), a part of the

Mountains-to-Sea Trail (#440) that runs between the French Broad River and the Pisgah Inn on the BRP. It skirts the S edge of the rec area with several spur trails providing connections. Access is at the jct of the BRP and NC-191, where there's a small parking area 400 ft from the signed trailhead. Lake Powhatan trails cover the whole range of difficulty levels, with most trails easy to moderate to hike. Trails are signed and blazed, and improved with footbridges across creeks. Most trails are short, through longer loops combining 2 or more are possible. The trails within the rec area grounds are closely grouped, with trailheads at the lake and along the gravel road (FR-806) that leads to it. Hikers should be aware that almost all hiking trails within the rec area are open to mountain bikes Oct 15–Apr 15. Permitted trail use is clearly indicated on trailhead markers.

Trails outside the rec area can be reached via the gated forest roads along FR-479. Trailheads to 2 trails are 1 mi E of the rec area entrance on Wesley Branch Rd (SR-3484) behind a 2-panel info board. Some of these trails are not clearly signed or blazed, though heavy use keeps them relatively easy to locate and follow.

mountain biking: The Lake Powhatan area is a magnet for local mountain bikers. Almost all trails within the rec area proper are open to mountain bikes between Oct 15 and Apr 15. (A notable exception is the 16-mi *Shut-In Trail.*) These trails are single track, well-worn from use, and generally easy to moderate to bike. Trails are blazed and trailheads are signed (see above for locations) with permitted uses clearly indicated. More popular with area bikers, however, are the trails outside the gates. These combine gated logging roads and single-tracks to create a network that covers more than 20 mi. Better yet, they're open year-round and foot traffic is minimal. The terrain along these trails is generally more rugged than within the rec area proper. The main trailhead and gathering spot is the parking area outside the rec area gate across from FR-479. A large trail map and info board gives a synopsis of each trail. Access to trails in the N half of the area begin at gated forest roads along FR-479. A good several-day bike/camping trip could include a tour of Powhatan trails, a climb up FR-479 to Bent Creek Gap on the BRP and back down the other side on FR-5000 to hook up with the numerous trails in the N Mills River Area.

camping: The central attraction at the Powhatan Rec Area is the 98-site car campground. The campground is laid out in 4 large loops set amidst gently rolling forested hills. The sites are moderately sized and fairly close together. Each site has a tent pad, picnic table, grill and lantern post. There's a shower/restroom facility (hot water) in the center of each loop. Sites cost $10/night. Firewood is available for $3/bundle. Reservations are accepted for some campsites. Call 800/280-2267 at least 10 days in advance. There's a $7.50 surcharge for this service.

Outside the rec area, there are 6 roadside primitive campsites along FR-479. Sites are indicated by brown signs with a tent icon, and are undeveloped except for fire rings left from one group to the next. Camping elsewhere along this road is prohibited.

Backcountry camping is permitted outside the rec area. The most popular sites are along Bent Creek.

fishing: Lake Powhatan and Bent Creek are the primary fishing opportunities in the area. Bent Creek is a small to medium sized stream that covers about 5 mi between its headwaters near the BRP and its confluence with the French Broad River, just outside the Pisgah RD boundary. Lake Powhatan is a small, man-made lake inside the Rec Area. Both lake and creek are stocked with brown and rainbow trout. There's a handicapped accessible fishing pier on the lake beside the dam that is often crowded, as well as other places along the shore to cast from. Multi-use trails follow the creek for 2 mi below the dam. Above it, Bent Creek Gap Rd (FR-479) runs alongside it almost to its headwaters. This area is also heavily used by roadside campers. Cover along this portion of the creek is poor to average. If you just want quick, easy stream access, give it a try; if you're looking for backcountry solitude, look elsewhere.

Mount Pisgah Recreation Area

Blue Ridge Parkway

The land on and around Mt Pisgah was once a part of George Vanderbilt's vast forest holdings. It was here that he built the Buck Spring Hunting Lodge, connected to his famous Biltmore Estate by a 20-mi trail. Today the National Park Service runs an inn near the site, with outstanding views of Mt Pisgah and the Blue Ridge. Early visitors to the area named Mt Pisgah for the mountain from which Moses saw the promised land. A short hiking trail leads from the rec area to the summit, where there is an observation platform that permits 360° views of the surrounding countryside. The area is best suited for day-hikes, with opportunities for longer trips into the backcountry on the trails that enter the Pisgah National Forest, adjacent to the south and east.

Asheville (NE) is the closest city.

contact: Superintendent, Blue Ridge Parkway, 400 BB & T Building, 1 Park Square, Asheville, NC 704/298-0398.

getting there: The rec area is located on the BRP between mp 407 and mp 409, 20 mi SW of Asheville. US-276 is the closest highway access.

topography: At an elevation of 5,721 ft, Mt Pisgah is the dominant geographical feature in the area. The mtn looms over the narrow summit ridge of the Blue Ridge, which drops off sharply, particularly to the SE. Area terrain is very rocky and rugged. **maps:** USGS Cruso, Dunsmore Mtn.

starting out: The Pisgah Rec Area is one of the more developed areas on the BRP, with an inn, gas station, large campground, hiking trails and picnic areas. A map of the area that includes hiking trails is available at the campground. A small selection of camping supplies is available at the gas station store. Pay phones are also there, as well as at the inn. A large picnic area with modern restrooms and water fountain is located 0.1 mi S of the trailhead parking lot. It includes several dozen tables and grills scattered around the perimeter of a large meadow bordered by rhodo- dendron, oaks and maples.

activities: Camping, Hiking.

camping: Directly across from the Pisgah Inn is a 140-site car campground. Sites are arranged in 3 handsomely landscaped loops, with half of the sites in the tents-only loop C. Although the sites are fairly small and close together, the dense forest understory adds considerably to privacy. Each site has a picnic table, grill and lantern post. Comfort stations (no showers) and hand water pumps are centrally located. Sites cost $9/night. Sites are generally available, except on the busiest summer weekends, when the campground fills early. The campground is open from May 1–Oct 31. The campground phone number is 704/235-9109.

Backcountry camping is permitted anywhere on NF lands,

except where posted. Camping is not allowed on BRP land, which includes all of Mt Pisgah and the summit trail leading to it.

hiking: There's a fairly large network of trails in the area, with 2 short trails leading to scenic overlooks on Mt Pisgah and Fryingpan Mtn, and longer trails forming connections with the trails of the Pisgah RD to the S and E. The strenuous, 1.6-mi trail to the summit of Mt. Pisgah is the area's most popular trail. The longest trail in the area is the 16-mi *Shut-In Trail* (#345). This National Recreation Trail, which is also a part of the *Mountains-to-Sea Trail* (#440), was built by George Vanderbilt in the 1890s to connect his estate and hunting lodge. The trail runs NE along the BRP to a terminus near the French Broad River. It's blazed with white bars. Other long trails that begin in the area are the 7.4-mi *Laurel Mtn Trail* (#121), 5-mi *Big Creek Trail* (#102) and 6.5-mi *Buck Spring Trail* (#104). These trails all run one-way to various parts of the Pisgah RD and are not really suitable for forming loops. All trailheads are signed, and are concentrated at the Pisgah Inn parking lot and at another parking lot at BRP mp 407.5. Hiking in the area is mostly moderate to strenuous. Area trails are shown on the USFS Pisgah District Trail Map.

French Broad Ranger District
Pisgah National Forest

The French Broad Ranger District occupies 80,335 acres in remote Madison and Haywood Counties. Most of this land is spread out in a long, narrow corridor on the southeastern slopes of the Bald Mountains along the border with Tennessee. Boundaries are formed by Great Smoky Mountains National Park (SW) and Tennessee (NW), with the Toecane Ranger District adjacent on a narrow strip of land to the northeast. The Pigeon River and French Broad River both flow through the district. Primary recreational activities are along a 78-mile segment of the *Appalachian Trail*, on the French Broad River, and in the remote backcountry along the Bald Mountains, where there's an extensive network of hiking trails and numerous native and stocked trout streams. There are 2 recreation areas—Rocky Bluff and Murray Branch—with facilities for picnicking at both and for camping at Rocky Bluff.

Hot Springs is the only town on the district and is located near its center.

contact: District Ranger, US Forest Service, PO Box 128, Hot Springs, NC 28743; 704/622-3202.

getting there: Primary highway access to the district is on I-40, which runs past the Harmon Den Area, and on US-25/70, which goes through Hot Springs at the center of the district. The district RS is located on US-25/70 in the town of Hot Springs.

topography: Elevations on the French Broad River, which flows through the center of the district at its lowest point, are approx 1,300 ft. Highest elevations are on the summits of the Bald Mountains, which follow the NC/TN line. Camp Creek Bald (4,844 ft), Bluff Mtn (4,686 ft) and Max Patch Bald (4,629 ft) are the highest of these. **maps:** see below under individual listings.

starting out: Hot Springs is at the center of the district, which is in a very sparsely populated part of the state. There are a few cafes in town, and a couple of food stores, but not much else. Whatever you need, bring, as you're not likely to find it once you're here. The Nantahala Outdoor Center operates a small outdoor store near the French Broad River put-in under the bridge. The district RS sells topo maps and a small selection of guide books. They can also provide you with up-to-date info on local conditions, trail closings, etc. The RS is open weekdays from 8 am to 4:30 pm.

activities: Hiking, Camping, Canoeing/Kayaking, Mountain Biking, Fishing.

hiking: Hiking trails on the French Broad RD are dispersed over a wide area. All 4 backcountry areas described below have trail networks, though total mileage at each of the areas is relatively small. Hikers wanting to take longer trips can access the *Appalachian Trail* at any of several points. The trail passes through the district for 78 mi between Sam's Gap (NE) and Davenport Gap (SW).

camping: There's a single developed car campground on the district at Rocky Bluff Rec Area. Primitive roadside camping is available in the Harmon Den Area, and at a few sites in the Camp Creek Bald Area. Backpackers can camp on the *AT*, or along one of the district's other trails. Best locations are in the Harmon Den Area and Camp Creek Bald Area.

canoeing/kayaking: Paddling opportunities are primarily on the French Broad River, which is the largest river in the state's mountain region. The Pigeon River is another large river that flows through the district. The stretch that runs from the power plant on the state border into Tennessee is a popular whitewater run.

mountain biking: The district features a couple of trails that are open to bikes. These are located in the French Broad River Area. In addition to these designated trails, the forest roads of the Camp Creek Bald Area, rarely travelled by autos, provide another good option.

fishing: Both the Harmon Den Area and Camp Creek Bald Area are home to some remote mountain creeks that support rainbow, brown and brook trout. The creeks are relatively small, but the setting is beautiful, particularly near Camp Creek Bald. The French Broad offers fishing for bass and muskie, as well as several other game species.

Harmon Den Area

The Harmon Den area is located at the western edge of the district. The Great Smoky Mountains National Park forms the western boundary, with Tennessee to the north. Although I-40 runs right through the middle of the area, a lack of nearby cities and no paved access to the backcountry make this one of the most remote and little-used areas on the Pisgah National Forest. As a result, wildlife flourishes here: the area is a protected ruffed grouse habitat; white-tailed deer, rabbits, rodents, and, at night, bats, are also all readily seen. The scenic highlight of the area, and one of the natural treasures of the state, is the bald on Max Patch Mountain. Views of the Smokies, Snowbird Mountain and Black Mountains are superb, and the mountain seems to explode in an abundance of wildflowers in spring and summer.

Hot Springs (NE), Waynesville (S) and Canton (SE) are the closest towns.

getting there: From I-40, take exit 7 (Harmon Den). Turn N onto gravel Cold Springs Rd (FR-148). Go 3.7 mi (with pullouts at 0.5 & 3.3 mi) to a jct. Keep L and go 3.1 mi to Roberts Gap (with parking and trailhead) and the jct with Max Patch Rd (SR-1182). To the L it's 1 mi (with parking & trailheads at 0.6 and 0.7 mi) to parking

for Max Patch Bald, R. • From Hot Springs, take NC-209 S 12.9 mi
to Caldwell Corner Rd (SR-1165). Turn R and go 2.9 mi to Meadow
Fork Rd (SR-1175). Turn L and go 3.5 mi to gravel Max Patch Rd
(SR-1182). Turn R and go 4.8 mi to Roberts Gap.

topography: Elevations in the area are between 4,629 ft on Max Patch
Mtn and 1,400 ft where the Pigeon River leaves NC. Generally, the
higher elevations and more rugged terrain are along the N and E
edges of Harmon Den. The Pigeon River, a major waterway, flows
through the W half of the area. The area was heavily logged in the
1930s; today it's covered with hardwood and pine forests, except
for Max Patch Mtn and the surrounding area, where grasses and
wildflowers flourish on treeless balds. **maps:** USFS Harmon Den
Trail Map; USGS-FS Lemon Gap, Fines Creek, Cove Creek Gap,
Waterville.

starting out: The Harmon Den area is undeveloped and remote,
without facilities or water supply. If you'll be in the area for more
than a day, be sure to bring a water filter. The best map of the area
is the new USFS Harmon Den Trail Map. You can buy one at the
RS in Hot Springs for $3.

activities: Hiking, Fishing, Camping.

hiking: The primary hiking trail in the area is the *Appalachian
Trail* (#1). It follows the NC/TN border for about 21 mi between
Lemon Gap, at the area's NE edge, and Davenport Gap, located
near the area's W boundary and inside GSMNP. In addition to the
AT, there are another 17 mi of trails, most open to horses as well
as hikers. Trailheads are signed, easy to locate, and have small
parking areas. Most are clustered around Roberts Gap, on FR-148
and SR-1182. There are 5 trails in this vicinity, all open to horses.
They follow old disused forest roads and narrow footpaths along
creeks and ridge lines. Hiking is moderate to strenuous. Blazes
are irregular (except on the *AT*, blazed with white bars), though the
trails are generally easy to follow. The scenic highlight of the area
is Max Patch Bald; it can be reached by hiking 0.8 mi on the *AT* or
a 0.3-mi spur trail that leads from SR-1182. 2 other trails in the
area, *Rube Rock Trail* (#314) and *Groundhog Creek Trail* (#315),
are located further W and can only be reached via the *AT*. Both
trails descend to a terminus at I-40, though access from the
interstate is no longer possible.

fishing: There are 3 creeks in the Harmon Den area that support trout—Cold Springs Creek, Hurricane Creek, and Roaring Fork. All are similar in character, in that they're small, 5–6 mi long, and descend on an average gradient. Also, none gets much fishing pressure. Cold Springs Creek and Hurricane Creek flow E to W and empty into the Pigeon River. FR-148 runs alongside Cold Springs Creek, providing easy access. Hurricane Creek can be reached via FR-233 (4WD only), which begins at the jct of SR-1175 and SR-1182. Roaring Fork starts out near Max Patch Mtn, and flows E to Meadow Fork. This upper portion of the creek can only be reached via the *AT*, in one of the most scenic parts of the Harmon Den Area. All 3 creeks are Hatchery Supported.

camping: There are no developed camping facilities in the Harmon Den area. There are 2 shelters along the *AT*, at Lemon Gap and Deep Gap. Backcountry camping is allowed along all trails, and, if you must, along FR-148, where there are a few frequently used sites beside pullouts. A night spent on Max Patch Bald is a memorable experience; on a weeknight you might even have the mtn to yourself. Thus far, the no-trace ethic has prevailed on the mtn, where signs of previous campers are almost nonexistent. Water is available at a small creek along the *AT* about 50 yds E of the SR-1182 access. It should be treated.

Rocky Bluff Recreation Area

The Rocky Bluff Recreation Area is located on a bluff high above Spring Creek, near the northern end of a gorge that the river has carved from the surrounding mountains. Access to the gorge is limited; it's best viewed from one of several pullouts along NC-209. West of the gorge are the Bald Mountains, with form a natural barrier along the border with Tennessee. Opportunities for backcountry travel in the area are mostly along the *Appalachian Trail*, which ascends from the French Broad River in Hot Springs to the crest of the mountains along the state line. Within the rec area, there are a pair of trails, a developed campground and Spring Creek, which is a stocked trout stream.

Hot Springs (NE) is the closest town.

getting there: From downtown Hot Springs, take NC-209 S 3.2 mi to the Rec Area entrance, L. To reach the trailhead to the *Shut-In Trail* and access to the *AT*, continue S on NC-209 3.3 mi to SR-

1173 at a small sign for the community of Bluff. Turn R and go 1.6 mi (at 0.7 mi the pavement ends) to a dead end at the trailhead and parking area.

topography: The geography of the area is dominated by the Spring Creek Gorge, with rocky bluffs that rise 500 ft from the river. Bluff Mtn (4,686 ft), located SW of the rec area, is the highest peak in the area. Area terrain outside the gorge is not particularly rugged. **maps:** USGS-FS Spring Creek,Lemon Gap.

starting out: Facilities are at the rec area, with water and toilets at the small picnic area. The picnic area includes 13 tables and grills in a small area shaded by hardwoods and hemlocks. The best views of the gorge are from NC-209, which has several pullouts.

activities: Camping, Hiking, Fishing.

camping: Rocky Bluff Rec Area includes a 30-site car campground. The campground is very attractively landscaped and is one of the nicest on the NF. A mixture of sites is laid out in 2 loops: some are in an open area shaded by a canopy of hardwoods and pines, while others are more secluded, perched on the steep, forested hillsides above Spring Creek. Privacy varies with the sites. Each site has a picnic table, grill, lantern post and tent pad. The restrooms have flush toilets, but no showers. The fee is $5/night. The campground is open May 1–Oct 31.

As this is primarily a day-use area, opportunities for backcountry camping are few. The *AT* offers the best possibilities. There are 2 shelters along the 13-mi stretch between Hot Springs and Lemon Gap–at Deer Park Mtn and Walnut Mtn.

hiking: There are 2 options for hiking in the area: short day-hike loop trails that are located in the rec area, or the *Appalachian Trail* (#1), which passes nearby along a winding, 14-mi path between Hot Springs and Lemon Gap. The moderate, 1.2-mi *Spring Creek Trail* (#312) descends from the campground to Spring Creek, with several overlooks along the route. The 2.6-mi *Van Cliff Loop Trail* (#313) is more strenuous, involving some steep climbs. It crosses NC-209 twice. Both trails are blazed with yellow bars and improved with steps and benches, though the treadways are rocky in places. Trailheads are clearly signed. Another trail, the 2-mi, moderate *Shut-In Trail* (#296), is located about 4 mi from the rec area (see above for directions) The unblazed trail follows an old forest road along Shut-In Creek to its terminus at SR-1183. The little-used trail is easy to follow, but rocky and muddy in places. Access to the *AT* is at the same trailhead. This section of the *AT* offers some exceptional views as it climbs from the French Broad River to a series of mountain summits along the NC/TN border. Hiking on the segment is moderate to strenuous. The trail is blazed with white bars and is easy to follow. The access point described above is 6.6 mi SW of Hot Springs, 7.4 mi NE of Lemon Gap.

fishing: Spring Creek is a large trout stream with an average gradient and excellent cover as it flows through a steep gorge and past the rec area. The streambed is strewn with rocks and boulders, creating good pooling. Access is along the *Spring Creek Trail*. From the Rec Area, the creek can be followed upstream about 10 mi, though trails only follow it for a short distance. The 13-mi segment of the river on NF land is Hatchery Supported. Shut-In Creek is a smaller, more remote creek that can be reached by hiking the *Shut-In Trail*, or by driving on Upper Shut-In Rd (SR-1183). If you hike in, you'll walk 2 mi along East Fork (too small to fish) before reaching the creek. Access to SR-1183 is on US-25/70, about 4 mi W of Hot Springs.

French Broad River Area

The French Broad is the largest river in the mountainous region of North Carolina. Where it flows through Hot Springs and the French Broad Ranger District, it's 200-300 feet across. On the east bank of the river across from Hot Springs is a high, rocky bluff known as Lover's Leap. The chalky cliffs provide excellent views back out over the river and town. Their name comes from a Cherokee legend about a girl who jumped to her death after her lover was killed by a jealous rival. Backcountry activities in this area include paddling the river, which has some heavy whitewater interspersed with long flat stretches, and hiking or biking on a number of trails, among them the *Appalachian Trail*, that are dispersed over a wide area.

Hot Springs is located on the river's W bank, across the bridge from the rec area and trailheads.

getting there: From downtown Hot Springs, take US-25/70 E 0.3 mi across the bridge. Turn L onto River Rd (SR-1304). Go 0.3 mi to a jct. To the L it's 0.4 mi on Silvermine Rd to the Silvermine trailhead and parking area. To the R it's 4.1 mi (pavement ends at 3.1 mi) on River Rd (SR-1304) to the Murray Branch Rec Area, L.

topography: Elevations on the river are around 1,300 ft at Hot Springs. On the E bank, chalky cliffs rise precipitously from the river to heights of 2,400 ft. The S slope of the Bald Mtns, located to the N of the river on the NC/TN state line, features some rugged terrain and elevations up to 3,670 ft on Rich Mtn. **maps:** USGS-FS Hot Springs.

starting out: Facilities in the area are at Murray Branch Rec Area, a picnic area with tables, grills, flush toilets, water fountains and a pleasant bank from which to watch the French Broad River flow past. A stand of pines provides shade. At the other end of the road (under the bridge) are a couple of river running outfitters.

activities: Canoeing/Kayaking, Hiking, Mountain Biking, Fishing Camping.

canoeing/kayaking: Between the bridge on SR-1151 in Barnard and the bridge on US-25/70 in TN, the French Broad River flows N and W for 20 mi. This stretch of water features several different characteristics, with class III–V whitewater on the segment between Barnard and Murray Branch Rec Area and much flatter water below the rec area, with only occasional class II–III water. The upper section is for advanced paddlers only, while the lower section is more suitable to novice or intermediate skill levels. Whatever segment you paddle, keep in mind that the French Broad is a very large river that moves a lot of water. The US-25/70 bridge in Hot Springs and the Murray Branch Rec Area can both be used as put-in/take-out points. The river is runnable year-round, except during period of very high or very low water.

hiking: There are more than 24 mi of trails in the area, including almost 9 mi of the *Appalachian Trail* (#1) between Hurricane Gap near Rich Mtn and the French Broad River. The *AT* begins under the US-25/70 bridge at the base of Lover's Leap Rock. From there it ascends the white bluff to scenic overlooks of the river and the town of Hot Springs, before continuing to Rich Mtn. A short spur trail leads to an observation tower with outstanding views. The section ends at Hurricane Gap, where there is an access point. To get there, take US-25/70 4 mi E of Hot Springs to FR-476 (it's 0.5 mi past the overpass). Turn L and go 4.6 mi on the rugged gravel road to Hurricane Gap and the *AT*. Hiking on this section of trail is moderate to strenuous. Trailheads are signed and the trail is blazed with white bars.

Other trails in the area are located across from the Murray Branch Rec Area, where 2 trails form a 4-mi loop on the ridges overlooking the French Broad River. These trails follow rocky, single-track footpaths through terrain that is moderate to strenuous to hike. The trailhead is signed.

In addition to the *AT*, 2 other trails begin at the Silvermine trailhead and cover a distance of almost 5 mi. These trails allow for loops of varying distance, with the *AT* used as a part of each loop. Both trails are blazed and the trailheads are clearly signed beside a large trailmap at the parking area. Hiking is moderate to strenuous. 2 more trails are described below under mountain biking.

mountain biking: In addition to the trails described above, 2 area trails are open to both hikers and bikers. The 3.5-mi *Laurel River Trail* (#310) follows a major tributary of the French Broad River through an area of great natural beauty and botanical diversity. The one-way trail is an easy hike or ride that ends at the confluence of the Laurel and French Broad Rivers. To get to the trailhead, take US-25/70 approx 5.5 mi from Hot Springs to a jct with NC-208. Keep R on US-25/70 but pull over immediately to the R at a large parking area near some dumpsters. The trailhead is at the end of the parking lot. It's not signed, but it's not difficult to locate either. The trail crosses a private residence near its start that is posted against trespassing. Stick to the trail there.

The other trail is the 3.5-mi *Mill Ridge Trail* (#280). Most of this trail follows an old logging road around a scenic loop with mountain views and abundant wildlife (wild turkeys seem to favor the area). Forest cover is patchy along the trail, with numerous openings that are the result of clear-cutting. The trail is not blazed, but is easy to follow. Hiking or biking is easy to moderate. To get there, take US-25/70 about 3 mi E of Hot Springs to a concrete overpass. Turn L just beyond the bridge at an *AT* sign. Go 0.2 mi and turn L again. Cross the bridge and go 0.7 mi on a gravel road to a sign. The small parking area is 50 yds, L.

fishing: The French Broad offers fishing for largemouth and small-mouth bass, channel and flathead catfish, and muskellunge. Fishing is typically done from a boat, though many parts of the river provide a real challenge to the boater who tries to fish and pilot a boat. Fishing solo from a canoe or kayak is not really possible, as the current is too swift. If there are 2 of you, one could fish while the other paddles. The stretch of river below Murray Branch is best suited for this. Bank fishing is another possibility. The best conditions are at the Murray Branch Rec Area, where there's a large grassy bank with plenty of room for casting. The final option is wading, though if you choose this method, be aware that the French Broad is a large river with some heavy water. Most of the river is too deep and the water too fast for this.

camping: There are no developed camping facilities in the area. Backcountry camping is permitted throughout the area, except at Murray Branch Rec Area and where posted. The best opportunities are along the *AT*.

Camp Creek Bald Area

The Camp Creek Bald area is located at the northern extent of the French Broad Ranger District in Madison County. Like many other parts of the district, the region occupies the eastern slope of the Bald Mountains, the chain that forms a natural barrier between North Carolina and Tennessee. The *Appalachian Trail* follows the summit line of these mountains along the western edge of the area, and provides the easiest foot access to the backcountry. Apart from hikers on the *AT*, this part of the district receives few visitors.

Hot Springs (SW) is the closest town.

getting there: Directions are to 3 main access points to the area, listed S to N. To reach the S terminus of the *Pounding Mill Trail*, take US-25/70 E out of Hot Springs and go approx 5.5 mi to a jct with NC-208. Turn L and go 3.5 mi to a jct with NC-212. Keep L on NC-208 and go 3.5 mi to the trailhead, R (2 mi further W is the area's S access to the *AT*). The trailhead is obscure and difficult to locate. It's at the end of a L curve in the road. • To get to the trailheads to *Hickey Fork Trail* and *White Oak Trail*, follow the directions above to the jct on NC-208 and NC-212. Take NC-212 N 7 mi to SR-1310. Turn L onto the gravel road (it becomes FR-465 after 0.5 mi) and go 1.2 mi to a small parking area, R. The trailhead to *Hickey Fork Trail* is 100 yds ahead. To reach the trailhead to *White Oak Trail*, continue on FR-465 1.3 mi to a fork in the road. Bear L and go 0.6 mi to the end of the road and trailhead, L. • To reach *Fork Ridge Trail* (*Big Creek Trail* on the USGS topo) take NC-212 N 11 mi from its jct with NC-208 to the

Carmen Church of God and SR-1312 (4 mi further N is the area's N access to the *AT*). Turn L and go 1.3 mi to a low concrete bridge and the start of FR-111. Continue 1 mi to a primitive camping area and trailhead, L.

topography: Camp Creek Bald is on the TN border at the W perimeter of this area. At 4,844 ft, it's the highest peak on the district. The rugged eastern slope of the Bald Mtns are drained by numerous small to medium sized creeks, among them Big Creek and Hickey Fork. Elevations drop as low as 2,000 ft. Forest cover is mixed pine and hardwoods, with lush riparian coves dominated by rhododendron. **maps:** USGS-FS Greystone, White Rock, Hot Springs, Davy Crockett Lake, Flag Pond.

starting out: Although state roads are never far away, this area can seem as wild and remote as any in the mountains. Trailheads are frequently unsigned or impossible to locate, most trails are primitive and rarely used, and you could spend days in the backcountry without seeing another soul. Make sure you have a map and compass with you when you go. Views from Camp Creek Bald are exceptional. There are no facilities in the area.

activities: Hiking, Fishing, Camping.

hiking: A loose network of more than 36 mi of hiking trails, including a 20-mi segment of the *Appalachian Trail* (#1), provides access to the backcountry. The *AT* generally follows a route along the ridgecrest of the Bald Mountains on the NC/TN border, reaching its highest point on Camp Creek Bald. This portion of the trail is defined by NC-212 at the N end and NC-208 at the S end. The trail is blazed with white bars and access points (both are on the state line) are signed. Hiking along the trail is moderate to strenuous. Most other trails in the area provide connections to various points on the *AT*. Several of the trails can be connected to each other, allowing for loops of varying distance. These trails are considerably more primitive; locating and following them can be a challenge. Blazes are irregular, and most trailheads are unsigned. Trails are generally unimproved. An exception is the *Hickey Fork Trail* (#292), which begins by crossing a new wooden footbridge and follows a path that is clearly blazed with orange bars. Trails follow a combination of single-track paths and old logging roads. Trail use throughout the area on trails other than the *AT* is light.

fishing: Several creeks in the area support good populations of native trout. The E and W Forks of Hickey Fork are both small to medium creeks that follow a mild to average gradient through lush coves that offer excellent cover and a challenge to fly-casters. There's about 6 mi of fishable water between the 2 creeks. Access to E Prong is on FR-465; access to W Prong is along the *Hickey Fork Trail*. Both creeks are Wild Trout waters. Big Creek features similar fishing conditions on a 3-mi stretch of water from the headwaters to the NF boundary. Access is from FR-111, a narrow single-track gravel road. This portion of the creek is Hatchery Supported.

camping: There are no developed campgrounds in the region. Backcountry camping is permitted throughout the area. There's one primitive roadside camping area on FR-111 at the trailhead to *Fork Ridge Trail*. There are 3 *AT* shelters in the area—Little Laurel, Jerry Cabin and Flint Mountain.

Holmes Educational State Forest

Holmes Educational State Forest is a 235-acre preserve dedicated to education and forest management. It's located southwest of Hendersonville in the foothills of the Blue Ridge Mountains. Facilities in the forest are intended primarily as educational tools: there's a Forestry Center, several outdoor exhibits, an amphitheatre, and regularly scheduled primary school trips. Backcountry travellers will enjoy walking along the quiet trails over semi-mountainous terrain covered in a mixed hardwood/pine forest. The preserve was originally developed in the 1930s by the Civilian Conservation Corps as a nursery; it was designated a state forest in 1972. The forest is open from mid-March to the Friday before Thanksgiving.

Hendersonville (NE) is the closest town.

contact: Forest Superintendent, Holmes Educational State Forest, Route 4, Box 308, Hendersonville, NC 28739; 704/692-0100,

getting there: From the jct of US-25 & US-64 in Hendersonville, go 0.5 mi S on US-25 to Kanuga St (SR-1127). Turn R and go 9.7 mi to the state forest entrance, L.

topography: A small escarpment that rises approx 500 ft is aligned on an E–W axis. The mountain slope is fairly steep, though the forest has some level areas too. Elevations are between 2,160 and 2,680 ft. **maps:** USGS Standingstone Mtn.

starting out: A map of the forest and additional information can be picked up at the ranger station. Facilities are available near the main parking area, and include restrooms and water. There's a pleasant picnic area there with tables and grills. Forest hours are Tu–F 9 am–5 pm, Sa and Su 11 am–8 pm. If the forest is closed, you can park outside the gate (don't block it) and still hike the trails.

activities: Hiking, Camping.

hiking: 5 trails cover a total distance of 5 mi. Trails are intended as much to assist in forest education as they are to provide a means of exploring the backcountry. Highlights include the *Talking Tree Trail*, which features a number of stations where trees describe themselves and their uses to a recorded music accompaniment; and the *Forest Demonstration Trail*, where management and logging techniques are stressed. The well-constructed trails are blazed with hiker icons and are easy to follow. Hiking is easy to moderate. Access to all trails is from the main parking area. Improvements include handrails, steps, interpretive stations and a viewing platform.

camping: There are 6 primitive backcountry sites in the SF. Each site includes a fire ring, but no other improvements. The sites are very well spaced in a heavily wooded area, allowing for a maximum of privacy. Several pit toilets are located in the area. There's no water supply in the immediate vicinity.

There's also a group camping area with 4 sites. Facilities here include cold-water showers and a water supply. Both camping areas can be reached by hiking about 1 mi from the main parking area or from a separate entrance on the Old CCC Rd. There is no fee for camping in the forest.

Craggy Gardens Recreation Area

Blue Ridge Parkway

The Craggy Gardens are so named because of the extensive growth of Catawba rhododendron that covers a series of rocky balds. The flowers of the rhododendron bloom throughout the month of June, covering the mountains in a profusion of pink and purple. The peak period occurs around the middle of the month, with slight variations due to seasonal weather patterns. The rhododendron trees share the balds with several other vegetation types, among them wildflowers, grasses, laurel, blueberry and azalea. Rock outcrops are frequent on the balds, affording unobstructed vistas. Lower elevations are blanketed by a mixed pine/hardwood forest. The Craggy Gardens is a designated state Natural Heritage Area. The area is a popular stop with tourists and motorists travelling the Blue Ridge Parkway. Although the gardens remain busy throughout the summer season, the highest density of visitors occurs in June.

Asheville (SW) is the closest city.

contact: Superintendent, Blue Ridge Parkway, 400 BB & T Building, 1 Pack Square, Asheville, NC 28801; 704/298-0398.

getting there: Craggy Gardens Rec Area is located on the BRP 15 mi NE of Asheville. The visitor center is at mp 364.6. Entrance to the picnic ground is at mp 367.5. Craggy Pinnacle Parking lot is at mp 364.1.

topography: The heath balds that characterize the area are covered in rhododendron, laurel, flame azalea and blueberry. Although the balds are generally rounded, much of the terrain is rocky and rugged. Peaks are Craggy Knob (5,526 ft), Craggy Pinnacle (5,892 ft) and Craggy Dome (6,085 ft). **maps:** USGS Craggy Pinnacle, Montreat.

starting out: Facilities at the visitors center include restrooms, water and a one-room museum. The museum has some small exhibits on the flora of the area, particularly azalea, laurel and rhododendron. It also has a good selection of nature and guide books. It's open daily 9 am–5 pm, May 1–Oct 31 (dates may vary slightly depending on seasonal weather). Facilities are also located at the very large picnic area. Several dozen tables and grills are spread out in several tiers in a beautifully landscaped meadow. Restrooms and water are in the area.

activities: Hiking, Camping.

hiking: Craggy Gardens features several short trails that lead through the rhododendron slicks on the mountain balds to summits where vantage points offer outstanding views. The *Craggy Gardens Trail* and *Craggy Pinnacle Trail* are both less than a mi long and ascend on moderate to strenuous grades to Craggy Knob and Craggy Pinnacle, respectively. These very popular trails are easy to locate and follow. Trailheads are clearly signed at 2 large parking areas. Improvements include steps, benches and a timber shelter on Craggy Knob built by the CCC in 1935. In addition to these 2 trails, connections can be made to a couple of longer trails, most notably the yet-to-be-completed *Mountains-to-Sea Trail* (#440). A 30-mi segment of the trail passes through the Craggy Gardens on a route between Glassmine Falls Overlook and the French Broad River. Vehicle access to the *MST* is at the Greybeard Mtn Overlook (mp 363.5). The trailhead is signed and the trail is blazed. Hiking is moderate to strenuous. Other trails in the area are the 3-mi Snowball Trail (#170) and the 4-mi Douglas Falls Trail (#162). Both trails can be reached from the *MST*.

camping: There are no developed camping facilities in the area. Backcountry camping is permitted on NF land on the *MST* and on the other 2 NF trails. Camping is not allowed on BRP land.

Toecane Ranger District
Pisgah National Forest

The 76,000 acres of the Toecane Ranger District are widely dispersed in 2 main areas. The northern section of the district is made up of a long, narrow string of land holdings that hug the Tennessee border. Scenic highlights on this section of the district include the Roan Gardens and the Nolichucky River Gorge. 2 other large parcels of land are located northeast of Asheville. The dominant natural feature of this region is the Black Mountains, a small, J-shaped chain that includes Mt. Mitchell, the highest peak east of the Rockies. On these lofty peaks can be seen the southernmost occurrence of the northern forest that blankets much of New England and Canada. Also apparent is the sad fate of the Fraser fir, the species that has been dying out due to insect infestation and pollution. The dead, gray husks of these trees cover the highest elevations of the Black Mountains. Although the Toecane Ranger District doesn't offer a lot of any particular backcountry activity, it does offer some of the best of each available in the state, with memorable opportunities for backpacking, river-running and fishing. The district is named for the Toe and the Cane Rivers.

Burnsville and Spruce Pine are located between the district's 2 main land holdings. Black Mountain and Asheville are close to the southern tracts.

contact: District Ranger, US Forest Service, P.O. Box 128, Burnsville, NC 28714; 704/682-6146.

getting there: Primary highway access to the S portion of the district is on the BRP, which forms the SE boundary. Access to the N portion is via US-19W, NC-197 and NC-261. The district RS is in Burnsville on US-19 Bypass. Hours are M–F, 8 am to 4:30 pm.

topography: In the S part of the district, the Black Mountains dominate the geography, with 5 peaks that rise above 6,500 ft, including Mt Mitchell, the highest point in the Appalachians. In the district's N section, a couple of mountain chains—the Iron Mtns and the Bald Mtns—form a natural border with TN. Peaks in these ranges are generally between 5,000 and 6,000 ft. The Nolichucky is the largest river on the district. It passes through a gorge with 1,000-ft cliffs near the TN border. **maps:** see below under individual listings.

starting out: Because of its small size and dispersed lands, the Toecane RD offers fewer opportunities for extended backcountry travel that do most of the other mountain forest districts. What it lacks in size, however, it makes up for in scenic grandeur. With the Black Mtns in the S half, and the heather and grassy balds along the *AT* in the N half, the district contains 2 of the state's natural treasures. The Roan Gardens draw the largest concentration of visitors to the district, particularly during June when the gardens are in full bloom. Maps, brochures and other information can be picked up at the district RS in Burnsville.

activities: Hiking, Fishing, Camping, Canoeing/Kayaking.

hiking: The largest network of hiking trails is in the Black Mountains Area. These trails wind up the mountains' E slope, connecting to the trails in Mt Mitchell SP. The Roan Mtn Area provides the other major opportunity for hiking on the district. The *Appalachian Trail* passes over the mountain as it follows a route that hugs the state line. The trail is on the district for approx 37 mi.

fishing: The Nolichucky is a good smallmouth bass river, with muskies also present. The South Toe River drains the E slope of the Black Mountains. The river and the tributaries that flow down off the steep mountain ridges offer excellent fishing for rainbow, brown and brook trout. The Elk Falls Area also has trout fishing, though on a more limited basis.

camping: There are 2 developed car campgrounds in the Black Mountains area—Black Mountains and Carolina Hemlocks. This is also the best area for backcountry camping. The *AT* provides additional opportunities, with shelters and trailside sites.

canoeing/kayaking: Whitewater paddling is available of the Noli-chucky River, one of the premier runs in the state.

Nolichucky River

With the possible exception of the Linville Gorge, the Nolichucky is the most spectacular and inaccessible gorge in the state. The cliffs on either side of the river rise so steeply and suddenly from the river's banks, that the highway that runs side-by-side with the railroad along the river east of the gorge is forced away from the river and up over a mountain into Tennessee before it can rejoin the river's course. The railroad is the Clinchfield CSX, and it runs along the south bank of the river all the way through the gorge. Depending on your point of view, this either adds a dash of historical romance or detracts from the gorge's natural beauty.

Burnsville (SE) and Chestoa, TN (E) are the closest towns.

getting there: In the small community of Poplar, from NC-197 turn W onto FR-5580 at a small boat launch sign. The parking area and boat launch are 0.2 mi ahead, just across the RR tracks. The take-out is at the bridge in Chestoa, TN. To get there take NC-197 E to the state line where it becomes TN-395. Continue to US-19W/23. Turn S and go through Erwin and cross the river. The turn for the bridge in Chestoa is 1.3 mi ahead.

topography: The river runs in a steep, narrow gorge between the Unaka Mtns to the north and the Bald Mtns to the south. As the mountains near the river, they drop precipitously—as much as 2,000 ft in some places. Elevations on the river are between 2,000 and 1,600 ft. **maps:** USGS-FS Huntdale, Chestoa.

starting out: The Nolichucky is one of the most popular rivers in the state for rafting and kayaking. The parking lot at the put-in can get to be a very busy place on weekends. Facilities there are limited to a pit toilet and an information board.

activities: Kayaking/Canoeing, Fishing.

kayaking/canoeing: The 10-mi run through the gorge is one of the most beautiful and challenging stretches of whitewater in NC. The rapids are almost continuous Class III-V across a large river that is generally more than 100 ft across in most places. The river should not be attempted by inexperienced paddlers. Once you enter the gorge, there's no way out except to run the river to the take-out. For a description of individual rapids, see Benner & Benner: *Carolina Whitewater*.

fishing: The Nolichucky offers good fishing for smallmouth bass and muskellunge. The only way to fish the river is by wading, and access is very limited in the gorge. The easiest place to get in the river is at the boat put-in in Poplar. Anglers have 2 other challenges to deal with: heavy water that can be difficult to wade; and raft, canoe and kayak traffic. Of these, the first is probably the more serious, as the boat traffic is relatively light, particularly compared to that encountered in the Nantahala Gorge.

Roan Mountain Area

"The Roan," as this area is locally known, is the highest point in the Roan Massif, a small mountain chain on the North Caro-lina–Tennessee state line. Most of the mountain summits in this area are balds, treeless peaks covered in grasses or rhododendron trees. Not a state that occurs naturally below the tree line, the baldness of the region is the result of earlier timber harvesting. When extensive slicks of rhododendron took root on the logged peaks, efforts were made to maintain the condition and preserve the resulting natural beauty. Those efforts continue today, and the Roan Gardens are regularly thinned to prevent the encroachment of the spruce-fir forest that covers the lower mountain slopes. Goats, who eat unwanted plant species, are being used as part of this ongoing project. The Roan encompasses 600 acres of rhododendron garden and 850 acres of boreal forest.

Bakersville (S) is the closest town.

getting there: From the jct of NC-226 and NC-261 in Bakersville, take NC-261 N 12.8 mi to Carver's Gap on the NC/TN state line. The 1.9-mi road to Roan Gardens (closed in winter) and a parking area for the *AT* and Round Bald are L.

topography: Area geography is dominated by the distinctive balds on Roan Mtn—Roan High Knob (6,286 ft) and Round Bald (5,826). Roan High Knob is a heath bald, with rhododendron and laurel covering the rounded summit. Round Bald is almost completely devoid of trees and shrubs; grasses and wildflowers are the dominant vegetation. A spruce-fir forest covers the mountain slopes. Carver's Gap (5,512 ft) is located between the 2 balds.
maps: USGS-FS Carvers Gap.

starting out: Although this area can get crowded any time during the warm months, peak season is usually the last 2 weeks of June, when the rhododendron are in full bloom. Facilities at the Roan Gardens include an information center, restrooms, water, and several picnic areas with tables. From Nov to May, the access road is gated and the Roan Gardens and Roan High Knob are only accessible by foot or cross-country skis; the water is turned off during this period.

activities: Hiking, Camping.

hiking: The primary hiking trail in the area is the *Appalachian Trail* (#1), which passes over both balds as it follows the NC/TN border. Easiest access to the trail is at the parking lot in Carvers Gap. From there, the trail ascends 0.4 mi E to Round Bald and 1.4 mi W to Roan High Knob. The trail access is signed and the trail is blazed with white bars. Hiking is moderate. Improvements include RR tie steps on the slopes of both balds to help impede soil erosion. Views from the trail are exceptional. In addition to the *AT*, there are several shorter trails on the summit of Roan High Knob. 1.2-mi *Cloudland Trail* (#171) is signed and begins in one of the summit parking lots. The trail is wide, level and easy to follow. It features several scenic overlooks, including one at its terminus at Roan High Bluff. The 1.5-mi *Roan Mountain Gardens Trail* (#290) is a National Recreation Trail that loops through the gardens on Roan Mountain. It features 16 interpretive panels and a viewing platform. The treadway is paved.

camping: There are no developed camping facilities in the area. Backcountry camping is permitted throughout the area on NF lands, except within the Roan Gardens. There are many good sites along the *AT*. There are also 3 shelters on the AT within 5 mi of Carvers Gap. The shelter on top of Roan High Knob is the highest altitude shelter on the entire trail. Roan Highlands Shelter is 3 mi E of Carvers Gap; the Overmountain Shelter is 1.7 mi E from there. Because of the delicate natural environment on the balds, it's essential to practice no-trace camping in the area.

Elk Falls Area

The Elk Falls area is located on a small tract of remote national forest land not far from the border with Tennessee. The broad valley through which the Elk River runs has been mostly cleared for small-scale agriculture. A handful of homesteads line the river and the setting seems to recall an earlier time. The scenic 50-ft falls are located at the end of this valley, where the river channel narrows and forest resumes. This is a pleasant area for picnicking or trout fishing, with little opportunity for backcountry travel.

Elk Park (S) is the closest town.

getting there: From NC-19E in Elk Park, turn onto SR-1303 (across the road from the Belco service station) and go 0.3 mi to Elk River Rd (SR-1305). Turn L and go 3.9 mi (pavement ends after 2.3 mi) to a small parking area and the picnic grounds.

topography: The picnic area is at the end of an open valley, which ends at the Elk Falls. Beyond the falls, the land is undeveloped and the valley is considerably narrower. Elevation at the picnic area is 2,800 ft. **maps:** USGS-FS Elk Park.

starting out: The picnic area features half a dozen tables and grills, most of which are on a grassy bank of the river. There are no toilets or water supply. Crowds are usually minimal. You won't need a topo map for this small area.

activities: Hiking, Fishing.

hiking: The *Big Falls Trail* (#172) is the only hiking trail in the area. The easy quarter-mi trail leads from the picnic area through a forest to the falls. The treadway is wide and level and improvements include steps and a bench. The trailhead is signed.

fishing: The Elk River is a large Hatchery Supported trout stream. Much of the area surrounding the NF tract is private property posted against trespassing. This leaves only about 2 mi of fishable water. Nevertheless, it's a nice area for a day-trip. At the picnic area, the river is open and follows a mild gradient with little pooling. Below the falls, the river flows over and around large rock formation and boulders, and cover is quite good.

Black Mountains Area

The steep, rugged terrain on the eastern slope of the Black Mountains encompasses most of this area. The South Toe River forms the E extent of those mountain ridges, which rise to the highest peaks east of the Mississippi. The mountain slopes are heavily forested, with the vegetation of the boreal forest at the highest elevations and lush coves below covered with a dense carpet of hardwoods, rhododendron and laurel. At the start of this century, the forests were logged, though some stands of virgin trees do remain. Although access to this area is relatively easy, the remote nature of the mountains makes them an ideal sanctuary for all kinds of wildlife. They are also ideal for backcountry backpacking trips. Area boundaries are formed by the crest of the Black Mountains and Mt Mitchell State Park to the west and the Blue Ridge Parkway to the east.

Black Mountain (SW) and Burnsville (NW) are the closest towns.

getting there: Access to the Black Mtn Campground and nearby trails and creeks is on unpaved FR-472 (S Toe River Rd). From the BRP, exit W at mp 351.9 onto unsigned, gravel FR-472. Trailheads and river access are along the first 5 mi. At 4.8 mi, come to the campground entrance, L. • Another access from the BRP (mp 344) is to take NC-80 W 2.2 mi to FR-472. Turn L and go 1.5 mi to a sharp curve, R (FR-2074 continues straight to the BRP). The campground is 0.6 mi ahead, R. Trail access to the area is also possible from either the BRP or Mt Mitchell State Park.

topography: The S Toe River flows through a basin E of the Black Mtns, the highest mtn chain E of the Mississippi. Elevations along the river are between 4,000 and 2,900 ft. Elevation on Mt. Mitchell, the highest of the Black Mountains, is 6,684 ft. 5 other peaks are above 6,500 ft. The terrain between the S Toe River and the Black Mtns is rugged and steep. Forest cover is spruce-fir at higher altitudes and Southern Appalachian hardwoods in the coves and on lower slopes. **maps:** USFS South Toe River Trail Map; USGS-FS Mount Mitchell, Celo, Old Fort, Montreat.

starting out: The S Toe River area can get pretty crowded during the summer season. FR-472 is a popular primitive car camping spot, and the S Toe is becoming increasingly popular among fly fishermen. The only facilities in the area are at the campground, but are for the use of campers only. There's a pay phone near the entrance. Neal's Creek Information Center, located 0.7 mi E of Black Mtn Campground, sells USFS trail maps, USGS topos and books of local interest. If it's closed, check at the campground for info. A picnic area with half a dozen tables and grills is located in a riverside meadow 1.2 mi N of Black Mtn Campground on FR-472. The USFS S Toe River Trail Map is a good guide to the area, but is too small-scale to be very useful for orienteering. If you're going into the backcountry, you'll want the USGS topo sheets instead.

activities: Hiking, Fishing, Camping.

hiking: More than 30 mi of hiking and bridle trails ascend the ridges on either side of the S Toe River. These trails provide access to some of the most rugged terrain on the east coast, culminating on the towering peaks of the Black Mtns. Most of the trails in the area can be connected to form loops of varying length. Connections can also be made to the trails in Mt Mitchell SP,

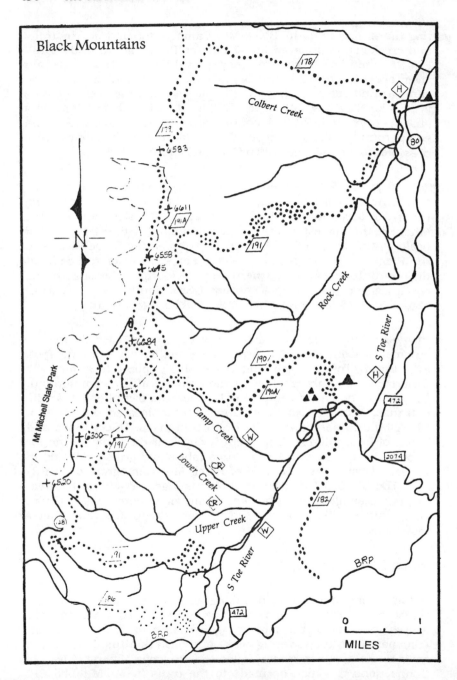

Black Mountains

increasing the opportunity for extended backpacking trips. With the exception of the area's longest trail—18-mi *Buncombe Horse Range Trail* (#191)—all trails are open to hikers only. Trailheads are located at pulloffs along FR-472 between the BRP and the Black Mtn campground. Trailheads are all clearly signed, with markers that indicate trail name and number, permitted use, and difficulty. Most trails are blazed. Hiking is generally moderate to strenuous, with significant elevation gain on all but one trail. Trail use is moderate. A short trail leads from Black Mtn Campground to scenic Setrock falls.

fishing: The headwaters of the S Toe River are located just N of the BRP. From there, the river quickly gains size as it flows NE for roughly 5 mi before leaving NF land. For most of this stretch, the S Toe is a medium to large stream, with numerous smaller creeks feeding it from the steep watershed of the Black Mountains. It is an outstanding stretch of trout water, with all 3 species present. The gradient is average to mild, with the river flattening out and losing depth as it moves downstream. Access is from FR-472, which has numerous pullouts. 2 designations apply on this part of the river: from the headwaters to the concrete bridge 1.4 mi above the campground, the river is Wild Trout water; below there to the NF boundary (about 3 mi) Catch & Release/Artificial Flies Only rules are in effect.

Many of the feeder creeks that drain into the S Toe from the N and S offer fishable stretches of water. These creeks are typically small, with heavy cover and an average to steep gradient. Access is from abandoned logging roads or by wading and rock-hopping the creeks from FR-472. In all, these creeks offer more than a dozen mi of trout water. 2 of these creeks—Upper Creek and Lower Creek—are Catch & Release/Artificial Lures Only. All other creeks are Wild Trout waters.

camping: Black Mtn Campground is a busy, 45-site car camp-ground laid out in 2 large loops. The campground is geared toward car and RV campers; spaces are in an area largely cleared of trees, with minimal privacy. Each site has a grill, picnic table and lantern post. 3 comfort stations provide toilets and sinks, but no showers or hot water. The fee is $8/night. There's a pay phone near the self-pay station. The campground is open from mid-Apr to Oct 31.

Briar Bottom Group Campground is adjacent. Each of its 6 sites includes picnic shelters with fireplaces and grills, costs $25/night, and has a capacity of 50 people. It too is open from mid-Apr to Oct 31.

Backcountry camping is permitted throughout the area on NF land. There are established sites along most trails.

Carolina Hemlocks Recreation Area

Carolina Hemlocks is a campground and day-use recreation area located on the east bank of the South Toe River. The river, which flows south to north, marks the bottom of the eastern slope of the Black Mountains, a compact chain of towering peaks that are the highest east of the Rockies. The mountains are blanketed with 2 distinct forest communities: the spruce-fir dominated boreal, or northern, forest and the hardwoods more typical of this latitude that comprise the dominant species of the Southern Appalachian forest. Wildlife abounds on these rugged mountain slopes, and the area offers one of the few opportunities in the state to take an extended backpacking trip through an environment more typical of New England and Canada than the South.

Burnsville (NW) and Spruce Pine (NE) are the closest towns.

getting there: From the BRP, exit at mp 344.2 onto NC-80 W. Take NC-80 5.3 mi to the rec area entrance, L.

topography: The rec area is on the S Toe River at an elevation of 2,800 ft. The area is at the bottom of the eastern slope of the Black Mtns, the highest chain in the Appalachians. The terrain on the mountain slopes is rugged and steep. Elevations along the crest of the Black Mtns are above 6,600 ft. **maps:** USFS South Toe River Trail Map; USGS-FS Celo, Mt Mitchell.

starting out: Carolina Hemlocks is a popular campground and day-use area. Facilities there include a large picnic area in a wooded area with a dense understory of rhododendron. In addition to a couple dozen tables and grills, there's a picnic shelter beside the river. Reservations are necessary, and a fee is charged. The rec area also includes a sandy area on the bank of the river where there's a natural swimming hole. Unless you're camping, a $2/vehicle entrance fee is charged at the rec area. The rec area is open Apr 14–Oct 31.

activities: Camping, Hiking, Fishing.

hiking: 2 trails begin near the rec area. 3.7-mi *Colberts Ridge Trail* (#178) follows a steep ridgeline ascent to the summit of the Black Mountains at Deep Gap, an elevation gain of 3,000 ft. There the trail connects to the spectacular, 12-mi *Black Mtn Crest Trail* (#179). The other trail in the area—18-mi *Buncombe Horse Range Trail* (#191)—begins not far away and climbs to a lofty ridgeline which it follows before descending again to FR-472 between the Black Mtn campground and the BRP. This trail provides connections to all the trails in the Black Mtn Area and Mt Mitchell SP. Hiking on both trails is strenuous. The trailheads are clearly signed with markers that indicate trail name and number, permitted uses and difficulty. To reach them, go 0.3 mi N of the rec area on NC-80 to Colbert Creek Rd (SR-1158). Turn L and go 0.3 mi to a small parking area, R and the trailhead to #178. Continue ahead 0.4 mi to a fork. Bear R and go 0.2 mi to the trailhead of #191. In addition to these official trails, there are numerous other unofficial trails and abandoned logging roads in the area.

camping: Carolina Hemlocks is used primarily for its 31-site car campground. Each of the sites, which are arranged in 2 small loops—one on either side of NC-80—includes a picnic table, grill and lantern post. Privacy is average at the sites. The fee is $8/night. 3 sites are for tents only. The campground is handsomely landscaped in a wooded area above the east bank of the S Toe River. There are 2 comfort stations with flush toilets and sinks. The campground is open Apr 14–Oct 31.

Backcountry camping is permitted on NF lands outside the rec area. Backpackers will have little difficulty in locating sites.

fishing: The S Toe River flows through the rec area. It's a large stream there, with a mild gradient and some deep pools created by the many rock formations that form its bed. With the campground right beside the river, this stretch of the river gets a lot of fishing pressure. The river is Hatchery Supported downstream from Clear Creek, which is about a mile above the rec area.

Mount Mitchell State Park

Mount Mitchell is a long, narrow Park that covers 1,677 acres of the summit ridge of the Black Mountains, a short, J-shaped chain that includes Mt Mitchell, the highest peak east of the Rockies. The climate on the mountains is more typical of New England or Canada than of the South, and has resulted in an ecosystem also more typical of northern latitudes. Recorded temperature extremes on the mountains are –34° F and 81° F, with an annual avg of 44°. The mountains receive an average annual snowfall of 104 inches. The spruce-fir forest, well-adapted to these conditions, covers the mountains, though the overwhelming majority of the fraser firs are dead or dying, victims of the non-native balsam woolly aphid (and possibly the effects of acid rain).

Mount Mitchell is named for Elisha Mitchell (1793-1857), a professor of mathematics at the University of North Carolina who first saw the Black Mountains in 1827 and 1828. In 1835 he climbed and measured 3 of the peaks, determining that they were the highest in the state. A dispute with Senator Thomas Clingman led him to reclimb and remeasure the mountains in 1857. It was during this trip that he slipped over the edge of a waterfall and fell to his death. A museum (open Apr to Oct) near the summit features exhibits on Dr. Mitchell, other explorers and local inhabitants, as well as area geology and ecology.

The park is located off the Blue Ridge Parkway northeast of Asheville. It's open year-round.

contact: Superintendent, Mount Mitchell State Park, Route 5, Box 700, Burnsville, NC 28714; 704/675-4611.

getting there: From the BRP, turn N onto NC-128 at mp 355.4. The park gate is 2.4 mi ahead.

topography: The Black Mtns are the highest mtns in the Appalachians and therefore the highest in the East. The topography here is as steep and rugged as anywhere else in the state. Mt Mitchell (6,684 ft) is the highest peak E of the Rockies. 5 other peaks top 6,500 ft. Forest cover is that typical of a spruce-fir forest. **maps:** USGS Mt Mitchell, Montreat.

starting out: Park maps and brochures are available at the park office, located in a stone and log building just inside the main gate. A large signboard there includes a park map and advice to hikers and backpackers. A summit concession stand (open daily Jun to Aug and on weekends only in Sep and Oct) sells refreshments, souvenirs and a small selection of maps and books. The park also has a restaurant (open May to Oct) in a large rustic lodge with views out over the Black mountains. Restrooms are at all 3 locations. A pay phone is at the restaurant. A picnic area behind the trailhead to *Deep Gap Trail* includes 2 rustic shelters and a dozen or more picnic tables scattered in a heavily wooded area of red spruce and fraser fir.

The park is open year-round, though the BRP closes during severe winter weather. The park office is open May 1 to Oct 31. Vehicles left overnight in the park must be registered with the park office.

Pets must be kept on a leash. Alcohol is not allowed.

activities: Hiking, Camping.

hiking: There are more than 10 mi of hiking trails within park boundaries. Trails range from an easy 0.75-mi nature trail loop with available interpretive guide to a moderate 6-mi trail that passes over or near the 5 summits above 6,500 ft. A 4-mi loop between the park office and the Mt Mitchell summit is another option. A short trail up a series of stone steps leads from the summit parking area to the summit observation tower, with spectacular 360° views. All park trails are clearly signed and blazed. Trailheads are concentrated at the summit parking area and the park office. Treadways are generally narrow and rugged, befitting the mountainous terrain. The summit and nature trails are exceptions. In addition to the park trails, 3 trails continue beyond park borders and connect with the large network of trails in the S Toe River Area of the Pisgah NF. Among these, the strenuous 5.5-mi *Mt Mitchell Trail* (#190) leads to the Black Mtn Campground. Most park trails draw crowds on summer weekends; the summit trail receives the heaviest use.

camping: There's a 9-site tents-only primitive campground accessible by a short hike from a parking lot off the main park road. The sites are well-spaced in a beautiful mountainside spruce-fir forest. There's a centrally located modern restroom facility and each site includes a tent pad, picnic table and grill. The fee is $9/night. The sites fill up fast during peak season.

Another camping option is to hike out of the park and camp in the backcountry on NF lands. The Commissary Ridge and Deep Gap shelters (shown on the park map) are no longer available for camping, though tent camping in the areas is permitted. Backcountry tent camping is permitted on all NF lands, unless otherwise posted.

Crabtree Meadows Recreation Area

Blue Ridge Parkway

Crabtree Meadows is a small rec area with a large developed campground, restaurant and hiking trail that leads to a scenic falls on Crabtree Creek. Although the backcountry area is not particularly extensive, it's a quiet, peaceful area of rhododendron and hardwoods, which makes a nice stopover from driving on the Blue Ridge Parkway. The rec area is rarely crowded, and the campground can serve as a useful base camp for hiking in the Pisgah National Forest.

Spruce Pine (NE) and Marion (E) are the closest towns.

contact: Superintendent, Blue Ridge Parkway, 400 BB & T Building, 1 Pack Square, Asheville, NC 28801; 704/298-0398.

getting there: The entrance to Crabtree Meadows is located on the BRP at mp 338.9. NC-80 provides the closest highway access.

topography: Although the Blue Ridge drops off steeply across the parkway to the E, the terrain around Crabtree Meadows is relatively mild. Elevations are between 3,200 ft at the falls and 3,920 ft. **maps:** USGS Celo.

starting out: Facilities at Crabtree Meadows include a camp store, gas station and restaurant/gift shop. Hours at the camp store and gas station are 10 am–8 pm; the restaurant is open 10 am–6 pm. Restrooms and a pay phone are located at the restaurant. Crabtree Meadows is one of the quieter, less-visited stops on the BRP. The rec area is open May 1–Oct 31.

activities: Camping, Hiking.

camping: The car campground at Crabtree Meadows has 95 sites arranged in 3 large loops. 22 sites are for RVs only. Sites are fairly close together in large grassy clearings. Privacy is minimal, but the campground is rarely full; on quiet weekdays it can seem like you have the place to yourself. Each site has a picnic table, grill and tent pad. Comfort stations (no showers), water fountains and hand water pumps are centrally located. Sites cost $9/night.

Firewood is for sale at the gas station. The campground is open
May 1–Oct 31.

hiking: *Crabtree Falls Trail* is a strenuous 2.5-mi loop that begins
near the entrance to the campground. The trail descends 1 mi on a
wide, graded footpath to a scenic waterfall. The trailhead is signed
and the trail is easy to follow, though it's not blazed. Improvements
include benches, log steps and footbridges. A trail map is
available at the campground.

Lake James State Park

Lake James is a 6,510 acre man-made lake that sits in the shadow
of the Blue Ridge Mountains and Linville Gorge. The lake is fed by
the Linville River and the Catawba River, as well as several smaller
drainages. The scenic lake, which has a shoreline of 150 miles, is
used primarily by boaters and fishermen. The state park is located
on a small, 585-acre parcel of land on the lake's south shore.
Created in 1987, Lake James is the newest of North Carolina's
state parks. The setting is scenic, with the mountain peaks of the
Blue Ridge and Linville Gorge visible to the west and north. Most
visitors to the park come to use its extensive picnic grounds.
There's also a semi-primitive campground and a couple of boat
ramps within the park. The park is open year-round.
    Nebo (S) and Marion (SW) are the nearest towns.

contact: Superintendent, Lake James State Park, PO Box 340, Nebo,
NC 28761; 704/652-5047.

getting there: From Marion, go E on I-70 approx 5 mi to the jct with
NC-126 in the community of Nebo. Turn L onto NC-126 and go
2.9 mi to the park entrance, L.

topography: Although it lies in the shadow of the Blue Ridge
Mountains to the W and N, Lake James is actually part of the
Catawba River Valley. Rolling hillside typical of the western
piedmont rises from the lake shore. **maps:** USGS Marion East,
Glen Alpine, Ashford, Oak Hill.

starting out: You can pick up a map and brochure as well as additional information in the park office, located in a new, modern building that also houses restrooms, a water fountain and a pay phone. The park is designed to serve the lake; there's little opportunity to explore the backcountry here. Extensive picnic grounds border the lake near the park office with numerous sites containing tables and grills. Towering pines provide ample shade. There's also a large, open air shelter which is free, unless reserved in advance.

Alcohol is prohibited in the park. Pets must be kept on a leash.

activities: Canoeing/Kayaking, Fishing, Camping, Hiking.

canoeing/kayaking: Although Lake James sees its share of powerboats, it isn't nearly as crowded as the larger piedmont recreational lakes to the east. The elongated shape of the lake and its many small coves help make the lake seem often less crowded than it really is. Although the lakeshore is partially developed (particularly near the park), most of the scenery is unspoiled forest, with mountain silhouettes in the distance. The lake is served by almost a dozen boat ramps; 2 are on state park property. To reach the Hidden Cove boat ramp, leave the park and turn L onto NC-126 and drive 0.6 mi to a boat access sign. Turn L and go 0.3 to the boat ramp and parking lot. The Canal Bridge access (open 24 hrs) is also located on NC-126, 2 mi NE of the park.

fishing: Due to its location on the perimeter of the mountains and piedmont, Lake James supports both cool- and warm-water species of fish. Largemouth, smallmouth and white bass, walleye, muskellunge, white bass, crappie, catfish, redbreast and bluegill are all regularly fished for. Boat fishing is the most popular method, though there is a small pier near the park office and a number of places along the shore from which it's possible to cast.

camping: Lake James has one of the most attractive campgrounds in the state. 20 well-spaced sites—reached by a short hike—are spread out on one side of a wooded peninsula on the lake's S shore. 2 sites are handicapped accessible. Most sites have excellent views of the lake—some are perched right over the water with nothing but lake, trees and sky in sight. Each site has a picnic table, grill and lantern post. Water spigots are found throughout the campground. A shower/restroom facility is located near the campground parking lot. Sites cost $9/night. Firewood can be purchased for $2.50/bundle. The campground is closed Dec 1—Mar 15.

hiking: Hiking opportunities in the park are limited to 2 short, easy trails. Total distance covered is just over a mile. The well-defined, easy-to-follow trails pass through the young pine-hardwood forest that covers much of the land around the lake. Both trails end at a scenic lakeside overlook with wooden decks and benches.

Linville Falls Recreation Area
Blue Ridge Parkway

The Linville Falls Rec Area is situated between the Blue Ridge Parkway (N) and the spectacular Linville Gorge Wilderness (S). The primary attractions at the rec area are a large developed campground and a network of short hiking trails that provide a number of access points to the river and scenic falls. The river and rec area are named for William Linville, who along with his son was killed by Indians here in 1766.
Linville Falls (W) is the closest town.

contact: Superintendent, Blue Ridge Parkway, 400 BB & T Building, 1 Pack Square, Asheville, NC 28801; 704/298-0398.

getting there: The entrance to the rec area is located on the BRP at mp 316.3. NC-181 (E) and US-221 (W) are the closest highway accesses to the BRP.

topography: The Falls, which drop 100 ft over a massive rock formation, are located near the start of the Linville Gorge. Terrain in the rec area is mountainous, but not particularly rugged. Elevations are between 3,600 and 3,000 ft. Forest cover is hardwoods with an understory of rhododendron. maps: USFS Linville Gorge Wilderness, USGS Linville Falls.

starting out: A large signboard with a trailmap is located on the wall of the visitors center. There are restrooms here (open seasonally), a water fountain and pay phone. There's also a pay phone at the campground entrance. Across from the campground is a large picnic area beside the Linville River. In addition to picnic tables and grills, there are restrooms and water fountains. Swimming in the river is not permitted on NPS land. The rec area is frequently crowded.

activities: Hiking, Camping, Fishing.

hiking: 6 short trails covering a total distance of 3 miles fan out from the visitors center. The trails follow both banks of the river, leading to several vantage points that provide views of the falls. Trails are well worn and easy to follow. In general, they're designed for casual strolls rather than arduous hikes. Although there are some strenuous sections of trail, hiking on most trails is easy to moderate. Trailheads and junctions are signed, with distances posted. Improvements include benches, steps, handrails, shelters and observation platforms. Access to all trails is at the large rec area parking lot.

camping: The 70-site car campground occupies a very large meadow near the river. The sites are arranged in 2 loops. They're fairly closely spaced, with minimal privacy due to the lack of forest cover. Each site has a picnic table, grill and lantern post. 3 comfort stations (no showers) are centrally located. Sites cost $9/night. The campground is open May 1–Oct 31.

Backcountry camping is not permitted on BRP land. It's allowed in the adjacent Linville Gorge Wilderness (see below under separate heading for details).

fishing: A short stretch of the Linville River passes through the rec area on BRP land. The river is large and shallow above the falls and follows a mild gradient. It's Hatchery Supported.

Grandfather Ranger District

Pisgah National Forest

Located on the eastern slopes of the Blue Ridge Mountains, the Grandfather Ranger District covers 187,000 acres in McDowell, Burke, Avery, Watauga and Caldwell Counties. The district is bounded by the crest of the Blue Ridge and the Blue Ridge

Parkway on the west, and the eastern edge of the Appalachian Mountains to the east. There's one designated wilderness area on the district, the 10,975-acre Linville Gorge Wilderness. Another large backcountry area is the Wilson Creek watershed, located in the shadow of Grandfather Mountain, which at 5,837 feet is the highest mountain in the Blue Ridge range. The views from the mountain, which encompass much of the district, are exceptional. The most popular activities on the district are backpacking and trout fishing. The highest concentration of backcountry visitors is found in the Linville Gorge Wilderness and the Wilson Creek Area.

Towns close to the district are, from N to S, Blowing Rock (N), Linville (NW), Lenoir (NE), Spruce Pine (W), Marion (S), Old Fort (S) and Black Mountain (SW).

contact: District Ranger, US Forest Service, Route 1, Box 110-A, Nebo, NC 28761-9707; 704/652-2144.

getting there: Primary access to the district is via the BRP, which runs its entire length. Other highways that enter the region are I-40 and US-70 from the S, US-321 from the N and E, and US-221 from the W. The district RS is located at exit 90 (Nebo-Lake James) on I-40.

topography: The Linville Gorge features the district's most spectacular geography. The river that carved it from granite and quartzite over millions of years flows S through the center of the district. The Blue Ridge, with elevations over 4,500 ft, runs NE-SW, forming a large segment of the district's N and W boundary. The mountains in the center of the district are at lower altitudes than those further W, with elevations generally under 4,000 ft. The E slope of the ridge is also the E edge of the Appalachians. **maps:** see below under separate headings.

starting out: Maps, brochures, permits for camping in the Linville Gorge Wilderness and other information are available at the district RS. Hours are M–F, 8 am to 4:30 pm. The Linville Gorge Information Cabin provides the same information and services. It's open daily 9 am–5 pm, between Apr and Oct.

activities: Hiking, Camping, Fishing, Mountain Biking, Canoeing/ Kayaking.

hiking: The Grandfather RD includes 2 major backcountry areas with extensive networks of hiking trails—the Linville Gorge Wilderness and the Wilson Creek Area. Between them, the 2 areas have more than 140 mi of trails, most of which are only open to hikers. The Curtis Creek Area offers a smaller number of trails.

camping: The district lacks a large developed car campground. There are small primitive, car accessible campgrounds in the Wilson Creek Area and Curtis Creek Area. Primitive roadside camping is also available in these areas. Wilderness camping is the best option on the district, with major backcountry areas in the Linville Gorge Wilderness and at Wilson Creek Area and Curtis Creek Area.

fishing: The Linville River offers fishing for trout and smallmouth bass on a large scale. The Wilson Creek Area may have the largest concentration of high-quality trout streams in the state outside of Great Smoky Mountains National Park. In all, there are more than 100 mi of fishable creeks there. Curtis Creek is another good trout stream; several tributaries are also in the area. A couple of creeks near the Old Fort Picnic Area round out the district's opportunities for trout fishing.

mountain biking: Mountain biking opportunities on the district are limited. 2 trails in the Wilson Creek Area are open to bikes. The area also has an extensive network of forest roads that don't get too much auto traffic.

kayaking/canoeing: Wilson Creek Gorge offers advanced paddlers a short, challenging whitewater run on a beautiful stretch of river.

Old Fort Picnic Area

Old Fort is a relatively secluded picnic area located in a large, shaded clearing between Swannanoa Creek and a mountain ridge. There's a picnic shelter there, as well as about 20 tables and grills in the very scenic, pleasant setting. Andrew's Geyser is a local landmark located just up the road. To reach it, take Mill Creek Rd (SR-1407) 2.1 mi to a parking area, L. The unremarkable geyser shoots a 50 ft stream of water out of a rock that's in the center of a large fountain-like cement structure. Several picnic tables are scattered across a large meadow. The geyser was used to mark the start of the Blue Ridge for the trains that looped around it before beginning their ascent up the mountain. The Old Fort area is a pleasant place to spend a quiet afternoon, but doesn't offer much opportunity for backcountry travel.

The closest town is Old Fort (E).

getting there: From I-40, get off at exit 73 (Old Fort). Take Catawba Ave 0.4 mi into Old Fort and the jct with US-70. Turn L and go 0.3 to Old US-70 (SR-1400) and a NF sign. Turn R and go 2.5 mi to a small parking area at the picnic area, L.

topography: The picnic area is located in an open grove near the confluence of Swannanoa Creek and Mill Creek at an altitude of 1,600 ft. Heavily forested Youngs Ridge rises steeply to the S, with an elevation gain of more than 1,000 ft. **maps:** USGS-FS Old Fort, Black Mtn.

starting out: This is a small area best suited to day-trips. Facilities at the picnic area include water and pit toilets. The picnic area can be used year-round, but the gate is closed and the water is turned off Nov 1–Mar 31.

Camping is not allowed in the picnic area.

activities: Hiking, Fishing.

hiking: 2 hiking trails, covering a total distance of approx 4.5 mi, begin in the picnic area. The 4-mi *Kitsuma Peak Trail* (FS #205) is a moderate trail that ascends Youngs Ridge from the picnic area and ends at an overlook on I-40. The trailhead is signed, and the trail is easy to follow, but not blazed. It's a good trail for a day-hike, but there are no connecting trails, so longer loops are not a possibility. Also beginning in the picnic area, at the far end, is an easy, half-mi, unsigned, unblazed loop trail that follows Swannanoa Creek through rhododendron slicks before returning to the picnic ground on the slope of the ridge.

fishing: Both Swannanoa Creek, which runs parallel to the picnic area, and Mill Creek support populations of trout. Swannanoa is a small, shallow creek with a mild gradient and good cover. Casting is very tight on the creek, and it's really only fishable for a short stretch near the picnic area. Swannanoa Creek is Wild Trout water. Nearby, Mill Creek flows into the area from the NW. It's a shallow, medium creek with a mild gradient and rather poor cover between the picnic area and Andrew's Geyser. Mill Creek Rd runs beside it, providing easy access. Above Andrew's Geyser, the gradient increases, and cover improves. Access here is more limited as well, as the road becomes gravel and then ends. A 6-mi stretch of the river is fishable, though only the upper stretch has much appeal as a backcountry setting. Mill Creek is Hatchery Supported. A third creek in the area is Jarrett Creek, which parallels Mill Creek to the E and is similar in character. The major difference is that there is no vehicle access to Jarrett Creek, though a trail runs beside it. The creek crosses Old US-70 and joins Mill Creek 1 mi W of Old Fort. It is Wild Trout water.

Curtis Creek Area

The Curtis Creek Area is located in McDowell County between the Blue Ridge Parkway to the north and US-70 and I-40 to the south. It's a large backcountry area that is largely inaccessible except by bushwhacking. Curtis Creek flows north to south through the heart of the area; FR-482, a bumpy, steep gravel road, provides the only access. The center of the area is a small primitive campground. A sign near the entrance to the campground describes the historical significance of the region: On August 29, 1912, by authority of the Weeks Act, it became the first tract of National Forest land purchased in North Carolina.

Old Fort (S) is the closest town.

getting there: From I-40, take exit 73 (Old Fort) and turn onto Catawba Ave. Go 0.4 mi into Old Fort and the jct with US-70. Turn R and go 1.9 mi to a FS sign and Curtis Creek Rd (SR-1227). Turn L and go 5.1 mi (pavement ends after 2.6 mi; at 3.7 mi the road becomes FR-482) to the Curtis Creek Campground. The road continues N 5.7 mi to a jct with the BRP at mp 347.5.

topography: Elevations on Curtis Creek are between 4,000 ft at its headwaters on the S slope of the Blue Ridge and 1,800 ft at the campground. Although located in the foothills of the Appalachians, the terrain is fairly rugged and steep on either side of the creek. **maps:** USGS-FS Old Fort.

starting out: Curtis Creek is one of the more scenic and pleasant car campgrounds on the district. Facilities there are the only ones in the area, and include water and pit toilets. The campground is open all year, though FR-482 closes during bad weather. This area is one of the remoter, less-travelled backcountry areas on the Grandfather RD.

activities: Hiking, Camping, Fishing.

hiking: 3 trails in the area cover a total distance of 13 mi. The trails ascend the ridges on either side of Curtis Creek, ultimately climbing through hardwood forest to several of the area's peaks. All trails are one-way, without the possibility of forming loops or connections. Hiking is moderate to strenuous, but is made more challenging by the frequent obscurity of the treadways. The trails are not blazed and are seldom travelled. There are no improvements; the few creek crossings are by rock hopping. A good topo map and compass and the skills to use them are essential for travelling the backcountry in this area. The trailhead to the 2-mi *Hickory Branch Trail* (#213) is signed and located at the rear of the campground. 3.1-mi *Snooks Noose Trail* (#211) begins about 100 yds S of the campground across from a small parking area and an open field. The trailhead is unsigned and the trail can be difficult to locate. The trailhead to 8-mi *Mackey Mountain Trail* (#216) is at the jct of FR-482 and gated FR-1188, 3.8 mi N of the campground. The trail is not signed or blazed, but is easy to find and follow.

camping: The Curtis Creek Campground has 7 sites nestled in a small, scenic clearing between the creek and a mountain ridge. The sites are well-spaced, but in an unsheltered meadow, which diminishes privacy. Each site has a picnic table, lantern post and grill. There are pit toilets at the campground. The campground is open all year. No fee is charged.

A second option for car campers is to park at one of the many pull-offs along FR-482 and make camp along the creek. This is a popular option, and there are numerous established sites.

Backcountry camping is allowed throughout the area on NF lands. This is an infrequently used area with few established sites.

fishing: There are 2 nice trout streams in the area. Curtis Creek flows S for about 10 mi from its headwaters to US-70 and the entrance to the area. On its lower 5 mi Curtis Creek is a medium-size stream that flows through a broad flood plain with numerous openings in the cover and easy access from SR-1227. This portion of the creek is Hatchery Supported. Above the confluence with Newberry Creek and the end of SR-1227, the creek is smaller, more remote, and more challenging to the fly caster, as the cover becomes very dense. The gradient also becomes steeper as the creek flows down off the Blue Ridge, but access is still easy on gravel FR-482. This section of the river is Wild Trout Water. Newberry Creek is similar to this stretch of Curtis Creek, with excellent cover, a moderate gradient, and about 4 mi of fishable water. Access is on an old jeep trail that begins at the end of FR-482A. The lower stretch of this creek flows through private property posted against trespassers. Newberry Creek is Catch & Release/Artificial Lures Only.

Linville Gorge Wilderness

The Linville River heads up high on Grandfather Mountain, where it begins a long descent that carries it through one of the most spectacular gorges on the east coast before emptying into Lake James. The Linville Gorge Wilderness is a 10,975-acre preserve that encompasses 12 miles of the river and the soaring cliffs on either side that rise 2,000 feet from its waters. There is no terrain more dramatic in appearance or more challenging to hike in the state. Its exceptional natural beauty and recreation potential were first officially recognized in 1951, when the US Forest Service designated it a wilderness. In 1964, it joined Shining Rock as one of the original components of the National Wilderness System. Much of the terrain of the Linville Gorge is steep and inhospitable, covered in a dense forest of hardwoods and pines. At higher elevations, massive granite and quartzite rock formations and exposed cliffsides preclude even the hardiest vegetation from gaining a foothold. Although presently named for an explorer killed by Indians in 1766, the name given the river by the Cherokees is more apt: *Eeseeoh*, they called it, "river of many cliffs."

Linville (N) and Spruce Pine (W) are the closest towns.

getting there: There are 2 main ingresses to Linville Gorge, one on each rim. The W rim is reached via the Kistler Memorial Highway. To get there take US-221 from its jct with the BRP at mp 317.5. Go S on US-221 0.7 mi to NC-183. Turn L and go 0.7 mi to a NF sign and the start of the Kistler Highway, a rugged dirt and gravel state road that follows the gorge for its entire length. Trailhead parking areas are located along the road. To reach Wiseman's View, go 4 mi and bear L onto FR-458. The parking area is 0.3 mi ahead. • Access to the E side of the gorge is at and near the Table Rock Picnic Area. To get there take NC-181 S from its jct with NC-183. Go 3 mi and turn R onto Gingercake Rd (SR-1264) at the FS sign. Go 0.3 mi and bear L onto Table Rock Rd (SR-1261). After 0.9 mi the pavement ends. The road becomes FR-210, with pulloffs at trailheads. At 5.3 mi bear R at the NF sign onto FR-210B. Follow the steep, winding, single lane road (it's paved after 1.5 mi) for 2.8 mi to the Table Rock parking area. (NOTE: this road is closed Jan–Mar.)

topography: The gorge offers some of the most spectacular geological formations east of the Rockies and the Grand Canyon. Sheer cliffs rise 500-1,500 ft from the Linville River at the bottom of the gorge. Highest elevation (4,120 ft) is atop Gingercake Mtn on the E rim. Elevations on the river are between 1,300 and 3,000 ft. **maps:** USFS Linville Gorge Wilderness; USGS-FS Linville Falls, Ashford.

starting out: The Linville Gorge is probably the most heavily visited backcountry area in NC. To cope with the number of people, a free permit system has been put in place for those wanting to spend a night or more in the wilderness (see below under camping for details). The highest concentrations of hikers are at the Table Rock Picnic Area and at the Linville Falls Rec Area, just N of the wilderness (trails connect the 2 areas). Facilities are at Table Rock (pit toilet, no water) and at an information cabin located on the Kistler Memorial Highway, 0.5 mi S of its jct with NC-183, where there are pit toilets. Information and backcountry camping permits are available at the cabin daily Apr–Oct, 9 am–5 pm. The USFS Linville Gorge Wilderness map is an excellent topo map and guide to the area. Be sure to bring a compass too.

activities: Hiking, Camping, Fishing.

hiking: 39 mi of hiking trails follow the gorge's E rim, the river's W bank, and numerous steep, rugged descents between the 2 rims and the river. The several trails that make connections between the W rim and the river are as rugged and challenging as any in the state. Because of the shape of the gorge and the limited amount of land level enough to accommodate trail building, most trails travel in a straight line. There are only a few loop options, located on the W side of the gorge. The longest loops include

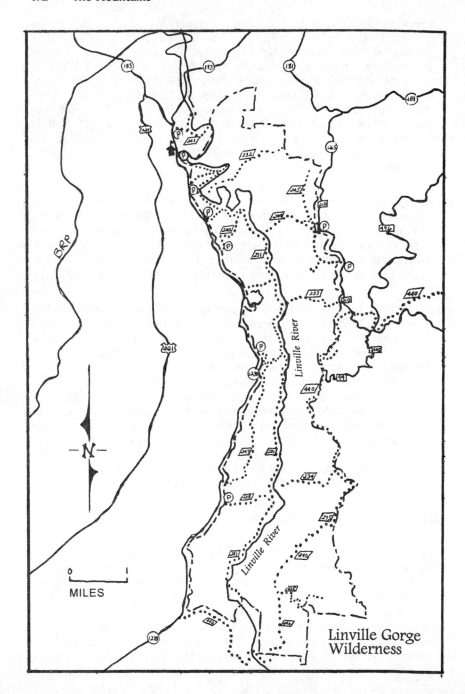

Linville Gorge
Wilderness

segments of the Kistler Highway. The 2 longest trails, 8-mi *Shortoff Mountain Trail* (#235) (part of the *MST* [#440]) and 9-mi *Linville Gorge Trail* (#231) run N–S along the E rim and the river, respectively. Trailheads are generally signed, but trails are not blazed. The *MST*, blazed with white bars, is an exception. In general, heavy use keeps the trails relatively easy to follow, though some primitive trails are an exception. As in any wilderness setting, a compass and large scale topo map are essential equipment. Trails are not improved and all river crossings are by rock hopping or wading.

camping: Backcountry camping is one of the most popular activities in the wilderness. Because of the large number of people wanting to spend a night or more in the backcountry and the fragility of the environment, a permit system has been established for peak periods. A permit is required for anyone intending to camp in the wilderness on weekends and holidays between May 1 and Oct 31. There's a 2-night limit during this period. Permits can be obtained in advance from the district RS in Marion. Walk-in permits are available at the information cabin on Kistler Highway.

The closest car campground is at the Linville Falls Rec Area on the BRP.

fishing: The Linville River is one of a handful of rivers and creeks in NC that qualifies as big trout water—at least by east coast standards. The river also supports a population of smallmouth bass. It's an exceptionally scenic river, with cascades, whitewater and deep pools sculpted by impressive rock formations and building-sized boulders. The gradient throughout the gorge is moderate to steep, with wading and fishing from mid-river rocks the typical method. Access to the river is on the *Linville Gorge Trail*, which follows the W bank for the length of the gorge. The trail has numerous connectors to the W rim, though these are extremely steep and rugged. Access from the E rim is more limited, though there are a couple of primitive trails that descend on narrow, steep footpaths to the river. The river is Hatchery Supported.

Wilson Creek Area

The Wilson Creek area is a large region in the northeast corner of the district. Its boundaries are formed by the Linville Gorge Wilderness (W) and the National Forest boundary on the other 3 sides. The town of Edgemont—once a thriving timber community but now nearly deserted—is in the center of the area. An atmosphere of desertion pervades the area, and the network of rugged, gravel forest roads that wind along steep ridgelines and provide access to the more remote portions of the area leave one with a sense of having travelled back in time. These mountains are also home to the mysterious Brown Mountain lights, flickering, dancing lights that can sometimes be seen at night. Although local legends explaining them have been around for more than a century, their exact cause is not known. Today, the area sees a large number of visitors; the extensive network of hiking trails, a dozen high-quality trout streams, prime hunting habitat, and excellent opportunities for wilderness camping are the primary draws. In addition, the lower stretches of Wilson Creek, where the water widens and tumbles over and around massive boulders and ledges, offers challenging whitewater to kayakers and canoeists.

Linville (NW), Blowing Rock (N), and Lenoir (E) are the closest towns.

getting there: To get to Edgemont and the nearby Mortimer Rec Area,, take Adako Rd (SR-1337) from Collettsville 3.3 mi SW to a FS sign at Playmore Beach Rd (SR-1328). Turn R and drive 11.6 mi (the road becomes gravel after 1.4 mi) beside Wilson Creek to the end of the road and the jct with NC-90. Turn L and reach the rec area R at 0.1 mi. • If you're arriving from the N or W, there are a number of access points on NC-181, the BRP, and US-221. 2 that provide quick access to a number of trailheads are SR-1511 and FR-464.

topography: The Wilson Creek watershed is a large bowl-shaped basin SE of the major ridgeline of the Blue Ridge. Elevations in the area are between 1,100 and 3,700 ft. Major ridges run NW-SE. A number of these ridges end abruptly at exposed rock outcrops and cliffs, offering excellent views. **maps:** USFS Wilson Creek Area Trail Map; USGS-FS Chestnut Mtn, Grandfather Mtn.

starting out: Mortimer Rec Area and the nearby community of Edgemont are good places to start out from, as they're convenient to the largest concentration of hiking trails and trout streams. A large scale map of the area is essential to navigate the forest roads that traverse the area, as most are not found on even detailed highway maps. If you don't bring one with you, pick up a copy of the Wilson Creek Area Trail Map, produced by the FS, at the general store in Edgemont. The map includes trail information, rules and regulations, and advice on backcountry travel.

In addition to those at the campgrounds and in Edgemont, facilities are located at 2 picnic areas: Barkhouse and Mulberry. Barkhouse is located on NC-181 6.7 mi S of the BRP. It includes tables, grills, a hand water pump and pit toilets in an attractive clearing shaded by oaks and pines with an understory of rhododendron. It's open year-round. Mulberry has picnic tables and grills, but no restrooms or water. It's located near Boone Fork Campground on SR-1368 and is also open year-round.

activities: Hiking, Fishing, Camping, Kayaking/Canoeing, Mountain Biking.

hiking: A network of more than 75 miles of hiking trails extends into all reaches of the Wilson Creek Area, with the greatest concentration of trails located in the area between Edgemont and the Mortimer Rec Area (E) and the BRP (W). There's a wide variety of trail types, including short easy paths that lead to outstanding views from clifftop overlooks, creekside trails that follow the area's principal drainages as they snake through mountains and ridges and plunge down spectacular waterfalls, and ridgetop trails with numerous spurs dropping down into the river valleys. Trails range in length from 0.5 mi to almost 15 mi, with much longer loops possible. They have been laid out in a manner that makes possible backcountry expeditions of several days or more. Most trails are moderate in difficulty, with strenuous segments along the steeper ridges and easy stretches along some of the creeks. Treadways are rocky single tracks. Trails are generally blazed, and frequent use keeps most well-defined, though locating spurs and some of the more remote trails can be difficult. Trails are unimproved, so all stream crossings must be done by rock hopping or wading, depending on the water level. Trailheads are signed and easy to locate. Although you'll find them scattered throughout the region, a large concentration is along FR-464 between Edgemont and the BRP.

fishing: With more than 100 mi of trout streams, the Wilson Creek Area is one of the premier fishing destinations on the Pisgah National Forest. Most of the area's acreage is contained within the Pisgah Game Lands, which means that all streams are designated as Public Mountain Trout Waters. Because of heavy fishing pressure, many of the creeks have special regulations. Wilson

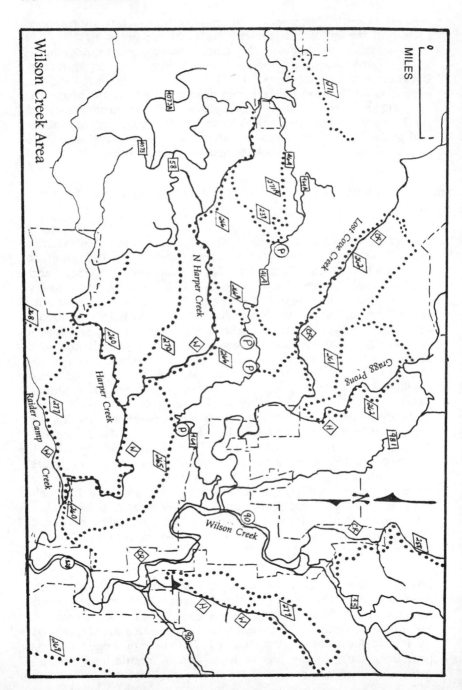

Wilson Creek Area

Creek, which flows S out of the Blue Ridge through the heart of the area, is the major artery. It's a medium to large stream for most of its length, and becomes one of the more spectacular short stretches of whitewater in the state when it enters Wilson Creek Gorge. The portion located on game lands (21 mi) is Catch & Release/Artificial Lures Only. The 6-mi segment between Phillips Branch (near the start of the gorge) and the Brown Mtn Beach Dam (6 mi) is Hatchery Supported.

Wilson Creek is fed by a number of creeks that flow down off of the W slope of the Blue Ridge. Among these are (N to S) Gragg Prong, Lost Cove Creek, N Harper Creek, Harper Creek and Raider Camp Creek. Upper Creek and Steels Creek are located S of these and flow S, rather than E. The creeks are all roughly similar in character, with mild to average gradients across a medium to large sized streambed, good pooling due to frequent rock formations and numerous boulders, and excellent cover. Hiking trails run beside all of these creeks, providing easy access (though most creeks have long stretches that can only be reached by wading or bushwhacking). All are Wild Trout waters with the following exceptions: the 16 mi of Lost Cove Creek on game lands are Catch & Release/Artificial Flies Only; Gragg Prong, Webb Creek, Thorpe Creek from the falls to the NC-90 bridge (1 mi), and Boone Fork Pond, near the Boone Fork campground, are all Hatchery Supported.

camping: The 22-site car campground at Mortimer Rec Area is the only developed campground in the Wilson Creek Area. It's centrally located, and is convenient to all rec opportunities in the vicinity. The campground is situated in a long, narrow forest clearing. Sites are closely spaced, with minimal privacy. Each site has a picnic table, grill and lantern post. Several pit toilets and water spigots are located in the campground. The fee is $4/night. The campground fills quickly on weekends during peak season. There's also an adjacent picnic area, which is much nicer than the campground itself. The campground is open year-round; with water off Nov–Mar; there's no fee during this period.

Another option for car campers is the Boone Fork Rec Area. Located about 5 mi E of Mortimer, it's not part of the Wilson Creek Area, but is close enough to make it a good second choice if Mortimer is full. 17 small, closely space sites are arranged in a loop. Each has a picnic table, grill and lantern post. Pit toilets are centrally located, as are hand water pumps. No fee is charged. The campground is closed Jan–Mar. To get there from Lenoir, take NC-90 5.3 mi from its jct with N Main St to Mulberry Creek Rd (SR-

1368). Make a R and go 4.6 mi to a FS sign. Turn R onto gravel FR-2055. The campground is 2 mi ahead.

Backcountry camping is permitted throughout the Wilson Creek Area. It's very popular, and there are numerous well-established campsites located along most of the trails. Using these instead of making a new campsite minimizes impact. No trace camping is the rule. Water is readily available in most areas, as many trails follow creeks. All drinking water should be treated.

kayaking/canoeing: Wilson Creek Gorge is a beautiful 2.5-mi stretch of river with water that forms cascades, pools, and mini falls as it tumbles and twists through impressive rock formations and boulder gardens that feature some massive rocks. For expert paddlers, this is one of the premier short runs in the state. The whitewater is class IV-V, depending on water levels, with ledges posing the primary challenge. Wilson Creek is large at this point in its course, with a width of 60-100 ft. The gorge is located between the FS boundary and Deer Horn Park. You shouldn't have much trouble finding the put-in or take-out, as this is a very popular area that draws a crowd on pleasant summer weekends. In addition to river-runners, sunbathers, innertubers and fishermen all use this stretch of the river. Access is at numerous pullouts along SR-1328, which runs beside the creek. The gorge should not be attempted except by those with considerable whitewater experience.

mountain biking: Only 2 trails in the area are currently open to mountain bikers. The moderate, 15-mi *Wilson Ridge Trail* (#269) is, however, the area's longest trail. The S trailhead is on Playmore Beach Rd (SR-1328), 3 mi N of its jct with Adako Rd (SR-1337). The trail's N terminus is on FR-45, about 2.5 mi N of its jct with NC-90. Another access is mid-trail where it crosses NC-90 a little more than 2 mi E of the Mortimer Rec Area. Elevations on the Wilson Ridge Trail are between 1,400 ft, near the S terminus, and 2,800 ft on Joe White Mtn. Water is scarce on this trail, so be sure to bring enough with you. The other trail open to bikes is the moderate 2.4-mi *Woodruff Branch Trail* (#256). This trail begins just up the road on FR-45 from the N end of the *Wilson Ridge Trail*. Its other trailhead is on NC-1362.

Grandfather Mountain

Grandfather Mountain is a 3,000-acre privately-owned nature preserve that encompasses the highest mountain in the Blue Ridge Mountains. It's been designated a North Carolina Natural Heritage Area and a United Nations International Biosphere Reserve. The preserve is managed to accommodate both short auto visits that take in the major scenic attractions, as well as longer hiking trips into the backcountry. The mountain ridge, which rises more than 3,000 feet from the valleys below, includes some of the most rugged and spectacular terrain in the state. Upper elevations are blanketed by the spruce-fir forest more typical of New England and Canada than of the South. Sadly, the Fraser firs on the mountain are suffering the same degradation that is afflicting them in the Black Mountains and Smoky Mountains, though at a slower rate. A small insect called the balsam woolly aphid is the culprit. One of the uncommon features of the mountain is the many rocky crags and outcrops at the highest elevations. Views from these heights are extraordinary. The mile-high swinging bridge is a well-known, frequently photographed landmark. Grandfather Mountain is open year-round.

Linville (SW) is the closest town.

contact: Grandfather Mountain, PO Box 129, Linville, NC 28646; 800/468-7325 or 704/733-4337.

getting there: From the jct of NC-221 and NC-105 in Linville, turn N on NC-221 at the large Grandfather Mtn sign. Go 2.2 mi up the winding road to the entrance gate, L. Or, from the BRP (mp 305.3), take NC-221 1 mi S to the entrance gate, R.

topography: The terrain on and around Grandfather Mtn is among the most rugged in the state. The mountain, which is actually a ridge with four peaks, rises abruptly from a valley that is more than 3,000 ft below. Calloway Peak, at 5,964 ft the highest point on the mountain, is also the highest peak in the Blue Ridge Mountains. **maps:** Grandfather Mtn Trail Map; USGS Grandfather Mountain.

starting out: Grandfather Mountain opens at 8 am and closes at 5 pm in winter, at 6 pm in spring and fall, and at 7 pm in summer. Unless you're camping overnight, you must return to your car at least one hour before closing. The mountain operates on a fee and permit system. Admission at the main gate, from which you can drive to the top of the mountain, is $9/adult, $5/child (4-12 yrs). If you're entering the mountain on foot, via one of the hiking trails, the backcountry permit fee is $4.50/day for adults and $2.50 for children. Permits can be purchased at the Grandfather Mtn Entrance, Connect 4 Sports (Linville), Grandfather Mtn Country Store, Footsloggers (Boone), Mast Store Annex (Valle Crucis), High Mountain Expeditions (Blowing Rock), Taylor Country Store (Foscoe) and Edge of the World Outfitters (Banner Elk). Season hiking passes, good for 1 year, are sold for $20. Be sure to get a copy of the large scale topo map that's free with the permits; it shows trails, campsites, water sources, overlooks and other features of the mountain. Facilities at Grandfather Mountain include a visitors center with gift shop and snack bar, a museum with exhibits on area flora and fauna, and a small zoo. Restrooms are at the entrance gate, in the museum and in the visitors center. There's a pay phone at the main gate.

Possession of alcohol, firearms, or knife blades exceeding 6 inches is prohibited. Dogs must be kept under their owner's control. Fishing is not permitted in the mountain's streams. Hiking off-trail and rock climbing are not allowed.

activities: Hiking, Camping.

hiking: 8 trails cover almost 12 mi of mtn terrain. The 3 longest trails form a rough Y shape, coming together near Calloway Peak. 2 of these trails, *Grandfather Trail* and *Daniel Boone Scout Trail*, have been designated National Recreation Trails. Trail lengths on the mtn range between 0.3 mi and 2.7 mi. Loops aren't really possible; if you want to begin and end at the same point, you'll have to backtrack. There are 3 main trailheads, which provide access to all of the trails: at the visitor center, on NC-105 in Foscoe, and from the *Tanawha Trail* (park at the Boone Fork Parking Area, BRP mp 299.9). Trailheads, like the trails themselves, are all clearly marked and signed. Blazes are colored bars. Getting lost on the mountain is unlikely. Most of the trails are moderate to strenuous to hike; an exception is *Grandfather Trail*, which is one of the most challenging—and rewarding—hiking trails in the state. Inexperienced hikers should not attempt this trail. At the other extreme, the *Black Rock Trail* is an easy, 1.3-mi nature trail with 35 interpretive stations and several overlooks from rock outcrops. Hikers not camping on the mtn must return to their vehicles at least one hour before closing time.

camping: There are 13 designated backcountry campsites and 1 shelter on Grandfather Mtn. Camping at other locations on the mtn is not allowed. Water is available from springs or creeks near a number of the sites, but others, particularly those on the mtn ridge, have no water source nearby. Campfires are not permitted at most of the mountaintop sites. Technically, there's no fee to camp—you pay for each calendar day you are on the mtn. A single night would therefore cost $9/adult (2 days @ $4.50/day).

Tanawha Trail
Blue Ridge Parkway

The *Tanawha Trail* takes its name from the Cherokee word for fabulous hawk. The name is apt, considering some of the spectacular views afforded from the trail, which seem to be from a bird's eye. Completed in 1993, the trail closely follows the Blue Ridge Parkway for a distance of 13.5 miles between Beacon Heights and the Julian Price Memorial Park. Among the scenic highlights along the trail are dense thickets of rhododendron and mountain laurel, a mountainside strewn with massive boulders, fields of heather and wildflowers, and hardwood mountain forests. The trail also passes below the impressive architectural achievement of the Linn Cove Viaduct, which seems to hang in thin air from the side of Grandfather Mountain.

Blowing Rock (E) is the closest town.

contact: Superintendent, Blue Ridge Parkway, 400 BB & T Building, 1 Pack Square, Asheville, NC 28801; 704/298-0398.

getting there: The trail runs alongside the BRP between mileposts 305.5 (1.5 mi S of Linn Cove Viaduct) and 297.1 (Julian Price Memorial Park campground). There are more than half a dozen parking areas with access to the trail between these points. The Beacon Heights parking area is 0.1 mi S of the jct of the BRP and US-221.

topography: The trail follows the E side of Grandfather Mtn at elevations between 4,200 and 4,600 ft. Although it passes over some steep, mountainous terrain, elevation gains along the trail are relatively slight. **maps:** USGS Grandfather Mtn, Valle Crucis, Boone.

starting out: A trail map and information sheet can be picked up at the Linn Cove Visitor Center or the Julian Price Memorial Park. There are restroom facilities, pay phone and water at both. The Linn Cove Visitor Center has an exhibit on the construction of the viaduct and additional BRP information, as well as a small book and gift shop.

Camping is not permitted along the trail. Pets must be kept on a leash.

activities: Hiking.

hiking: The 13.5-mi trail is easy to strenuous, with the most difficult segment winding through a field of massive boulders above the Linn Cove Viaduct. The tail is signed with a distinctive feather logo at all access points. Boardwalks and wooden stairs are among the trail improvements. Water is available from a number of springs and creeks along the trail. The trail intersects several trails that are part of Grandfather Mountain, Inc; a permit is required to hike them. The trail connects to the *Mountains-to-Sea Trail* (#440) at the Beacon Heights area.

Julian Price Memorial Park
Blue Ridge Parkway

Julian Price acquired the lands of the park that bears his name in the 1930s and 1940s for the purpose of developing a recreation area for the employees of the insurance company he owned. His untimely death in 1946 forestalled those plans, but the donation of the property by his heirs to the National Park Service allowed for the creation of a park open to the general public. The 4,200-acre Price Park has a little something to offer everyone. The park's central feature is a 134-site campground. Across the street is Price Lake, with canoes for rent and plenty of open space along the banks from which to cast for trout. Nearby are the trailheads to 10 mi of hiking trails that circle two lakes and follow a pair of creeks into the backcountry. Among these is the N terminus of the exceptional 13.5-mi *Tanawha Trail*, located at the campground. Picnickers will find an abundance of tables and grills spread out over several scenic acres along Boone Fork just up the road. All of these facilities are at roadside, which makes Price Park one of the most popular destinations on the BRP. The park is open year-round, though facilities close from Nov to May.

Blowing Rock (E) and Boone (NE) are the closest towns.

contact: Superintendent, Blue Ridge Parkway, 400 BB & T Building, 1 Pack Square, Asheville, NC 28801; 704/298-0398.

getting there: The park is located between mp 295.1 and 298 on the BRP W of Blowing Rock. US-221 is the closest highway access.

topography: Elevations at Price Park are between 3,400 ft on Price Lake and 3,920 ft on Green Knob. The generally mild terrain is covered by a dense hardwood forest that has been cleared in the rec areas. **maps:** USGS Boone, Valle Crucis.

starting out: Maps, brochures, and other information are available at the campground office. A pay phone is there also. Restrooms and water fountains can be found in the campground and at the large picnic area 1 mi up the road.

Pets must be kept on a leash.

activities: Camping, Hiking, Canoeing, Fishing.

camping: There's a 198-site RV/tent campground that sprawls across both sides of the BRP near Price Lake. Most of the sites are relatively close together, though rhododendron plantings add a measure of privacy. Each site includes a tent pad, picnic table and grill. The fee is $9/night. Firewood can be bought for $3/bundle. 6 restroom facilities (no showers) are spread throughout the area, as are numerous water spigots. Some sites are reserved for RVs only. The campground is open from May through Oct.

hiking: 3 trails totalling almost 10 mi are located in Price Park. *Price Lake Trail* is an easy, 2.3-mi loop that weaves through a pine forest as it circles the small scenic lake. The trailhead is located at the lake parking lot on the BRP. *Boone Fork Trail* is a moderate 5-mi trail that follows 2 mountain streams—Boone Fork and Bee Tree Creek. The trail forms a loop that passes through the campground near its trailhead in the picnic ground. The moderate, 2.3-mi *Green Knob Trail* begins in the parking area at Sims pond and follows Sims Creek before ascending up Green Knob to an elevation of 3,920 ft.

canoeing: Canoes can be rented for use on 47-acre Price Park. The rental shack and boat launch are located near the parking lot at Boone Fork Overlook. The rental rate is $4/hr. The rental shack is open 8:30 am–6 pm daily. Private boats are not allowed on the lake.

fishing: Trout fishermen have their choice of 2 small lakes or a creek. Price Lake can be fished from its banks or from a canoe (but not from the dam). The lake is hatchery supported. Boone Fork, which empties into the lake, is a small creek with good cover. It's accessible via the *Boone Fork Trail* for about 2 mi. Regulations are Catch & Release/Artificial Flies Only. Sims Pond supports a small population of native trout. It's beside the BRP, with an adjacent parking lot. Fishing pressure is moderate on the lakes, lighter on Boone Fork.

Moses H. Cone Memorial Park

Blue Ridge Parkway

Shortly before the turn of this century, Moses Cone, reputed "Denim King" of the textile industry, began acquiring land just north of Blowing Rock. Having relocated to the area from New York in order to be nearer the resources his trade required, Cone turned the same energies that had made him an entrepreneurial success to the task of creating a mountain estate. He built the 20-room Flat Top Manor, constructed three lakes and stocked them with fish, imported and protected deer, and laid out a 25-mi network of carriage trails as a gift to his wife. Cone died in 1908, and in 1950 his wife deeded the estate to the National Park Service, so that it might be used as a "pleasuring ground" for the public. Today, the Cone estate is administered as a part of the Blue Ridge Parkway, but it still evokes a bygone era of grandeur and aristocracy, and of wilderness tamed by the hand of man. It is ideal for equestrians and for hikers wanting to spend an hour or a day exploring mountain ecology minus the rigors normally associated with backcountry travel.

The park covers 3,517 acres on either side of the BRP. It's open all year, with facilities open from May to Oct. The manor houses the excellent Southern Highlands Handicraft Guild, where the work of local artisans is displayed and sold.

Blowing Rock (S) is the closest town; Boone is about 10 mi N.

contact: Superintendent, Blue Ridge Parkway, 400 BB & T Building, 1 Pack Square, Asheville, NC 28801; 704/298-0398.

getting there: The park is located on the BRP between mp 292 and mp 295. From Blowing Rock, the BRP can be reached by taking either US-221 or US-321 N for about 1 mi. From Boone, take US-221/321 S approx 8 mi.

topography: The undulating terrain of the estate features both open meadow and hardwood forest. The plant species that cover the grounds reflect the Cones' naturalist interests: plantings of rhododendron, laurel, apple, sugar maple and cherry trees can all be seen. Highest elevations are at the N end of the park on Rich Mtn and Flat Top Mtn (4,558 ft). Low point is on Bass Lake (3,560) **maps:** USGS Boone.

starting out: An information center is located in the manor house, which is also home to the Southern Highlands Handicraft Guild. Trail maps and parkway brochures are available there also. The book shop has a comprehensive selection of nature and travel guidebooks. Restrooms and a water fountain are also on the premises. The manor is open from 9 am to 5:30 pm, May 1 to Oct 31. The large porch out front provides excellent views down the mountain to Bass Lake and the S half of the park. Horseback riding is one of the park's most popular activities. Horses can be rented by the hour or day at stables located on US-221 between the BRP and Blowing Rock. In winter, the carriage trails make ideal tracks for cross-country skiing.

Bicycles are not allowed on any of the park's trails. Pets must be kept on a leash.

activities: Hiking, Fishing.

hiking: The park has a network of more than 25 mi of wide, well-graded carriage roads that are open to hikers and equestrians alike. There's a 0.5-mi self-guided nature trail for hikers only that begins near the manor house. Because the park is so popular with equestrians, hikers should be prepared to share the trails with horses. The network of roads are laid out in a manner that accommodates either short strolls or more rigorous day-long hikes. The manor house is a centrally located starting point, providing access to all trails, which fan out N and S on both sides of the

BRP. Other trailheads are located on the vehicular roads that run through the park. Most of the carriage roads are easy to hike, with several that ascend to the park's highest elevations providing a moderate challenge. Their surface is mostly cinders and crushed gravel, but you can expect mud and puddles after frequent spring and summer rains. The carriage roads are not blazed, though most are signed at trailheads and junctions. Stream crossings are by bridge, and benches have been placed along the more popular routes.

fishing: Although the park is not a primary fishing destination in the NC mountains, 2 of the lakes that Moses Cone built do support fish, mainly trout and bass. 16-acre Trout Lake is designated as Wild Trout water. It can be reached by a pleasant 1 mi hike from Cone Manor across hillside meadows and down coves so dense that the trail becomes a corridor through an otherwise impenetrable curtain of rhododendron thickets. Vehicle access is also possible by taking Flannery Fork Rd 0.5 mi N from its jct with the BRP at mp 294.7. The NE corner of the lake provides clear banks from which to cast, while a foot trail winds through the deep forest that surrounds the rest of the lake. Boats are not allowed on the lake. This is also true of 22-acre Bass Lake, which is located in the S half of the park and can be seen beyond the famous Cone apple orchards from the front porch of the manor house. From there, the hike downhill follows two winding carriage roads for approx 2.5 mi. A parking lot near a large park sign on US-221 about 0.5 mi N of downtown Blowing Rock is the closest vehicle access (about 0.2 mi) to the lake. A carriage road circles the lake, and its banks have been cleared of forest, making casting possible from just about anywhere.

South Mountains State Park

South Mountains State Park covers 7,334 acres of rugged mountainous terrain in Burke County. The area is part of a transition zone between the Appalachian Mountains and the Piedmont Plateau. Although technically located on the Piedmont, the South Mountains are eastern outliers of the Blue Ridge Mountains. Despite peaks that fall short of 3,000 feet, they include some of the most rugged terrain in the region. Their steep slopes and boulder-strewn stream beds have been carved by the drainages of the Catawba River watershed. Prior to European settlement, the mountains served as a natural buffer between the frequently warring Cherokees, who occupied lands to the west, and the Catawbas, who lived on the Piedmont to the east. Although virtually all areas of the park are now blanketed with dense forest, the area was once heavily logged—sections of second- and third-growth forest are still in early stages of succession, with species of pine predominant. The park was also at one time a Civilian Conservation Corps camp; many of the roads which are now used exclusively by hikers, bikers, and equestrians were built by corps volunteers. Opened as a state park in 1975, South Mountains has been left largely undeveloped, offering an extensive backcountry more typical of the national forests and parks than of other state parks. The park is well-suited to short day-hikes and longer multi-day backpacking trips. It's open year-round.

Morganton (N) is the closest city.

contact: Superintendent, South Mountains State Park, Route 1, Box 206-C, Connelly Springs, NC 28612; 704/433-4772.

getting there: From I-85, get off at exit 105. Take NC-18 S 10.9 mi to Sugar Loaf Rd (SR-1913). Go R 4.2 mi to Old 18 Rd (SR-1924). Go L 2.7 mi to Ward's Gap Rd. Go R 1.4 mi to South Mountains Park Ave (SR-1904). Go R and drive 1.6 mi on this rough gravel road to the park gate. The park office and parking area are 2 mi further ahead. The entire route is posted with signs.

topography: The powerful effects of flowing water are evidenced in the rough, rugged shape of the mountains it has carved here. Many of the slopes are pitched at 60° or more as peaks and ridges rise abruptly from stream beds to elevations that near 3,000 ft. Benn's Knob, on the park's southern border, is the highest elevation at 2,894 ft, while Jacob's Fork descends to about 1,200 ft near the eastern edge of the park. **maps:** USGS Benn's Knob

starting out: The park office provides trail maps, information and camper registration for backcountry sites. Water and a pay phone are also here. A short walk down a wide, level trail brings you to a wooded picnic area with tables, grills and modern restrooms. Several signboards provide displays on park flora and fauna, and there's a large, plexiglass-enclosed 3-D model of the park. Horseback riding is a popular activity in the park. Approximately 30 mi of trails are open to horses.

Pets must be kept on a leash. Alcohol is not permitted.

activities: Hiking, Mountain Biking, Fishing, Camping.

hiking: A network of more than 40 mi of hiking trails follows narrow footpaths and disused forest roads to extend into all corners of the park. All park trails are open to hikers, though many are shared by equestrians and mountain bikers. Individual trails range in length from 0.5 to 5.6 mi, but are laid out in a manner that fosters connecting trails into longer loops. A loop around the park perimeter, for example, can be made by following 6 different trails for a total distance of 20 mi. The trails make possible exploration of all aspects of park topography and ecology. Because of the rugged terrain, hiking on most trails is moderate to strenuous; aside from creek beds, there are few level areas in the park. All trails are accessed from the main parking area. Trails are blazed, and signs along the way point to major features, such as campsites and natural landmarks, but the trails themselves are not signed. Some trails are improved, with footbridges at stream crossings and benches for much-needed rest stops, but many are not. Streams must often be rock-hopped or waded. Water is readily available on most trails.

mountain biking: A 14 mi series of trails, forming a loop in the park's S section, is open to mountain bikers. The route follows old forest roads that mostly have a surface of hard-packed dirt, with 2.5 mi of pavement. The route incorporates the park's high and low points; riding is strenuous. The trailhead is at the main parking area adjacent to the park office. Trails are signed and blazed. Water is available, but only along the northern portions of the route. The trails are also used by hikers and equestrians.

fishing: There are approx 14 mi of designated Public Mountain Trout Waters in the park. This includes Nettle Branch, Shinny Creek, and the portion of Jacob Fork River that is within park boundaries. All waters are classified as Wild Trout, except for the 2 mi stretch of Jacob Fork from the mouth of Shinny Creek (a footbridge marks the boundary) to the eastern park boundary, which is classified as Delayed Harvest. Fishing is mostly by wading—only Shinny Creek is followed by trails for a considerable distance. All 3 creeks, however, are crossed by one or more trails. The creeks are all small to medium, with mild to average gradients and good cover. Dense thickets of rhododendron and mountain laurel are prominent and overhang the streams in many places, making casting with a fly rod difficult.

camping: Campers have several options for overnight stays in the park. A primitive family campground off the park road beside Jacob Fork River has car-accessible sites. Each site has a fire ring and picnic table and there are several pit toilets present. Firewood may be purchased from a ranger. Sites are $5/night.

14 primitive backcountry sites are divided into 4 main groups (High Shoal Falls, 1–4; Shinny Creek, 5–8; Fox Trail, 9–11; Sawtooth Trail, 12–14). These areas are located 1.5–5 mi from the park office and can be reached by foot or mountain bike. Each is in a grassy meadow that once served for wildlife management. All are near water. Sites have a picnic table, fire ring and firewood. The fee is $5/night. Some of these sites are open to organized groups at a rate of $1/night/person. In addition, there's an equestrian backcountry site located about 5 mi from the horse loading area. Camping outside of these sites is not allowed in the park.

Tuttle Educational State Forest

The 175-acre Tuttle Educational State Forest is managed for preservation and education. Opened to the public in 1977, it encompasses lands that were deeded to the state by Lelia Tuttle, a schoolteacher and missionary in China. The forest is located in the foothills of the Blue Ridge Mountains, and features plant communities typical of the region. Several local buildings of historical significance have been relocated to the forest so that they can be seen by the public. Among these is the Old Lingle Schoolhouse, built in 1867. Although backcountry activities in the state forest are limited to short hikes, it affords the opportunity to study the ecology of the western Piedmont in a natural setting. The forest is open from the Tuesday before Arbor Day to the Friday before Thanksgiving.

Lenoir (NE) is the closest town.

contact: Chief Ranger, Tuttle Educational State Forest, Route 6, Box 417, Lenoir, NC 28645; 704/757-5608.

getting there: From NC-18 just NE of the Caldwell/Burke county line (6 mi SW of Lenoir), turn N onto Playmore Beach Rd (SR-1331). Go 1 mi to the gated forest entrance, R.

topography: A pine/hardwood forest—maturing again after previous logging—covers terrain that rolls in gentle hills cut by small drainage creeks. **maps:** USGS Morganton N.

starting out: You can pick up a map of the forest at the office just inside the main gate. Restrooms and water are located beside the picnic area. The forest is open Tu–F 9 am–5 pm, Sa, Su 11 am–8 pm, closed Mondays. You can use the trails even when the forest is closed; just park outside the gate (don't block it) and walk in.

Facilities in the forest include a large picnic shelter with a dozen tables and 2 fireplaces, additional tables and grills spread out in a large wooded area, a volleyball court and a forestry center. The shelter can be reserved after Jan 1 and is often booked months in advance.

Pets must be on a leash. Bikes and horses are prohibited.

activities: Hiking, Camping.

hiking: The forest has 3.5 mi of hiking trails. A 0.6-mi *Talking Tree Trail* features a number of stations where trees describe themselves on recorded audio tapes to musical accompaniment. A *Forest Demonstration Trail* features exhibits on forest ecology, management and logging practices. All trails are easy to hike. Trailheads are signed and trails are blazed. Footbridges cross streams and wetland areas.

camping: A group camping area with 3 sites is located in the forest. Each site has a fire ring and makeshift log seats. A cold-water shower, hand water pump and pit toilets are in the area. No fee is charged to use the campground.

Mount Jefferson State Park

Mount Jefferson State Park covers 489 acres of the upper slopes and summit of Mt Jefferson, located in Ashe County between the towns of Jefferson (N) and West Jefferson (W). The park preserves a virgin forest of great botanical diversity and provides visitors with spectacular vistas that include mountains in three states. It was opened in 1956 thanks to the efforts of local citizens. Due to the large variety and rarity of some of the mountain's flora, the area was declared a National Natural Landmark by the National Park Service in 1975. Of particular interest is the forest of chestnut and red oak, with an understory dominated by dense thickets of Catawba rhododendron and mountain laurel. The park has been established for day-use only, with picnicking, hiking and scenic viewing the principal activities. It's open year round.

Jefferson (N) is the closest town.

contact: Superintendent, Mount Jefferson State Park, P.O. Box 48, Jefferson, NC 28640; 910/246-9653.

getting there: From Jefferson, take US-221 S 2.3 mi from its jct with NC-88. Turn L onto Mount Jefferson State Park Rd (SR-1152) at the large brown state park sign. The park gate is 1.5 mi ahead.

topography: Densely forested mountainsides rise steeply to a horseshoe-shaped summit ridgeline with rocky outcrops and a peak of 4,683 ft. The park boundary extends only about 600 ft down the mountain. **maps:** USGS Jefferson.

starting out: A park map and brochure can be picked up at the park office, located to the L just past the park gate. Information about regularly scheduled nature programs is available as well. Restrooms and drinking water are located near the summit picnic area. Picnic tables and grills are scattered along the gravel summit road beneath oak and chestnut trees. The views are superb.

Pets must be kept on a leash. Alcohol is prohibited in the park.

activities: Hiking.

hiking: There are 2 short hiking trails in the park. The moderate 0.3-mi *Summit Trail* follows a gravel road uphill to the mountain summit. The views are unobstructed except for a communications tower on the mountaintop. The best views are from Luther Rock, a large outcrop of black volcanic rock at the end of the easy 1.1-mi *Rhododendron Trail.* From there, 270° views reveal a patchwork of farms, pasture land and small towns in the valleys below. To the NE is the New River, believed to be the oldest river in the western hemisphere. The *Rhododendron Trail* is also a self-guided nature trail; an interpretive pamphlet with descriptions of the mountain's botanical, geological and geographic features can be purchased for 50¢ from a newspaper machine at the summit parking area.

New River State Park

New River State Park consists of 3 separate tracts of land spaced at regular intervals along 26.5 mi of the New River in Ashe and Alleghany Counties. The park was created when Congress and the Department of the Interior designated the segment of the river between Dog Creek near Jefferson and the Virginia state line as a Wild and Scenic River. The 3 parcels of land have been developed primarily as primitive camping areas for canoeists floating the river. Each of the areas is relatively small, with a combined land area of 1,196 acres. Rising just east of Boone, the river flows 410 miles before emptying into the Kanawha River in West Virginia. It's believed to be second only to the Nile in age among the earth's rivers. Geologists estimate that it's been flowing along its present course for hundreds of millions of years, predating the Blue Ridge Mountains which now surround it. The park is open year round.

Jefferson (W) is the closest town.

contact: Superintendent, New River State Park, P.O. Box 48, Jefferson, NC 28640; 910/982-2587.

getting there: To get to the put-in and park headquarters, from NC-88 E of Jefferson turn N at the red brick Wagoner Baptist Church onto Wagoner Rd (SR-1590). A sign marks the turn from the W, but not the E. Go 1 mi to the park gate. Other river access points are at several of bridges and at the US-221 park access.

topography: The countryside which surrounds the river as it flows along a twisting course S to N consists of wooded hillsides, rolling meadows and the occasional pasture or plowed field. Smaller mountain streams feed the river from E and W. The river is between 30 and 60 ft wide and descends along a mild gradient.
maps: USGS Jefferson, Laurel Springs, Mouth of Wilson.

starting out: Most park facilities are located at the Wagoner Rd Access. A park brochure and river map are available at the park office. Information is also available about local guides and outfitters and park-sponsored events, such as guided river trips and nature hikes. Restrooms, water fountain, pay phone, and vending machines are all on the premises. There's also a small riverside picnic area with tables and grills.

Pets must be leashed. Alcohol is not allowed in the park.

activities: Canoeing, Camping, Fishing, Hiking.

canoeing: The park has been designed to facilitate either single- or multi-day canoe expeditions. There are 2 put-ins on state park land: one at river mi 26; another at mi 17. A number of additional accesses are possible at any of the bridges that cross the river. The water on the 26.5 mi Wild and Scenic portion of the New River is relatively flat, making it ideal for novice canoeists or those wishing a leisurely outing. Only an occasional mild rapid is encountered; a couple are rated class II. The river varies in width from about 30 to 60 ft. Highest water levels occur in May and June; lowest levels are in August and September. The river is runnable year-round. Portages are necessary at mi 18 and 7. For canoeists wanting to travel more of the river than the Wild and Scenic portion, you can put in at the Piney Creek bridge just E of Boone and float all the way into VA, a distance of 90 mi.

camping: A primitive camping area is located at each of the park's 3 major sections. From S to N they are: Wagoner Rd Access (river mi 26); US-221 Access (mi 17); and Alleghany County Access (mi 2). The first 2 can be reached by road or river, the last is only accessible by boat. The areas are ideally spaced for a weekend river trip. All sites are primitive—each has only a grill and picnic table. Pit toilets and water are centrally located. There are 9 sites at Wagoner Access, 5 at US-221, and 8 at Alleghany County. Sites cost $5/night.

fishing: The New River offers some of the best smallmouth bass fishing in the state. Redeye bass are also present, and downstream of the US-221 bridge the river has been stocked with the elusive muskellunge, the largest freshwater game fish in NC. For the most part, the river must be fished from a boat or by wading. Most of the land alongside the river is private, and the public lands have only very limited space on the banks clear enough for casting. The river is shallow, and there are enough access points to make wading a good option. The New River's attractiveness adds to the enjoyment of fishing it.

hiking: There's a half-mi nature trail in the main park tract. The easy loop trail follows a footpath through a hardwood forest and through the riparian zone at river's edge. 19 interpretive stations along the route describe the local ecology. The trailhead is near the picnic area.

W. Kerr Scott Reservoir

The W. Kerr Scott Reservoir was created in 1962 when a dam of the same name was built across the Yadkin River, inundating 1,475 acres of land. The resultant lakeshore has been developed to serve outdoor recreational pursuits. There are developed campgrounds, boat ramps, swimming and picnic areas, and hiking trails. The reservoir occupies a narrow channel with a 55-mile shoreline; rec areas occupy a substantial portion of the north and south shores. The best views of the lake and surrounding terrain are from the dam, which, like the lake, is named for William Kerr Scott, a former Governor and US Senator from North Carolina. The reservoir and rec areas are best suited to weekend water-based activities, as opportunities for backcountry travel are limited.

Wilkesboro (E) is the closest town.

contact: Resource Manager, W Kerr Scott Reservoir Management Center, P.O. Box 182, Wilkesboro, NC 28697; 910/921-3390.

getting there: From NC-421, take the NC-268 exit in the city of Wilkesboro. Turn W onto NC-268 and go 3.1 mi to a large sign for the dam and reservoir. Turn R and go 0.4 mi to the visitor's center, L. Most of the individual rec areas are located along a 6-mi stretch of NC-268 W of the dam and visitor's center. Roadside signs indicate the appropriate turns. Mileages, E to W are: 1.3 mi Berry Mtn Park; 2.1 mi Bandit's Roost; 3.9 mi Boomer Rd; 4 mi Blood Creek Overlook; 4.4 mi Warrior Creek Park; 5.8 mi Marley's Ford Rd (SR-1137).

topography: Reservoir elevation is 1,030 ft. Western Piedmont foothills covered by a forest of pines and hardwoods comprise the majority of the terrain that surrounds the reservoir. **maps:** USGS Boomer, Wilkesboro, Purlear, Moravian Falls.

starting out: Maps and brochures of the reservoir and rec areas are available at the visitors center, which also features exhibits on local history and ecology. Restrooms, a water fountain and vending machines are inside. Hours are M–F 8 am to 4 pm. A $2 day-use fee is charged at Bandits Roost Park and Warrior Creek Park. Facilities for picnicking are located at numerous locations around the reservoir. There are 4 swimming areas at the reservoir.

Alcohol is prohibited at reservoir parks.

activities: Camping, Canoeing/Kayaking, Fishing, Hiking.

camping: Campers at the reservoir have a choice of 3 different developed car campgrounds—Bandits Roost Park, Warrior Creek Park and Wilkes County Reservoir Park. In addition to these there are facilities for primitive car camping at Marley's Ford Park.

Bandits Roost has a 106-site full-service campground that is popular with RVers. The large campground is divided into 2 main areas on a pair of wooded peninsulas that jut out into the lake. Some sites are on the lakeshore, others are set back from the reservoir in wooded areas. Privacy varies with location, but is generally only average. An exception is the 9 sites that are for tents only. These sites are well spaced from each other and from the rest of the campground. All sites have a picnic table, grill and lantern post. Modern restroom/shower facilities (hot water) and pit toilets are located in the campground. Sites cost $8/night, $12 for a site with hookup. There's also a nice group camping area with similar facilities and a picnic shelter. These sites cost $35/night. The campground includes a small unsupervised swimming beach and a boat ramp. The campground is open Apr 1–Oct 31. It's very busy on weekends, and fills up during the peak season.

Warrior Creek Park has 88 sites in four main loops that cover a very large area on the reservoir's S shore. The campground has 2 additional loops that have been closed in recent years due to funding cuts. Sites are generally large and well-spaced in a scenic wooded area. Many of the sites are arranged in pairs, with plenty of space between other sites. Each site has a picnic table, 2 grills and a lantern post. Restroom/shower facilities (hot water) and pit toilets are located at various locations in the campground. Fees are the same as at Bandit's Roost. In addition to the individual sites, there are 3 group camping areas. One has 4 sites, one has 8 sites, one has 10. Each group area includes a picnic shelter with tables and grill, water fountain, and pit toilets. The sites cost $35/night. Group sites can be reserved up to a month in advance. The campground is often busy, but sites are usually available on weekends. It's open from Apr 20 to Sep 30.

Wilkes Co Reservoir Park is a predominantly day-use park on the N shore of the reservoir that includes a small campground. The sites are large and well-spaced on a wooded hillside overlooking the lake. Each site has a picnic table and grill. Pit toilets are centrally located. Sites cost $3/night. Other facilities include a boat ramp and picnic shelters. To get there from NC-421 turn L onto North Recreation Rd (SR-1145) and go 1.5 mi to the park entrance. Camping is available from Apr–Oct. The park is open year-round except Jan & Feb.

A 23-site primitive car campground is located at Marley's Ford Park. The sites are spread out along a gravel road in a wooded area near the SW corner of the reservoir. Sites are large and afford plenty of privacy. Each site has a picnic table. Pit toilets are in the area. Sites are free. 270° degree views of the lake can be seen from adjacent Mountain View Park. To get to the campground from NC-268, turn R onto Marley's Ford Rd (SR-1137) and go 0.9 mi. Turn R onto a gravel road and go up a hill 0.2 mi to the entrance, L.

canoeing/kayaking: Although W. Kerr Scott Reservoir is used primarily by bass boats and motor boats, the lake is well suited to canoes and kayaks. Boat traffic is generally fairly light, and the reservoir's forested shoreline creates a scenic setting for paddling. Boat ramps are located at most of the rec areas, including Bandit's Roost, Keowee Park, Wilkes Co Park and the dam site park behind the visitors center.

On the other side of the dam is a put-in for the Yadkin River Canoe Trail, a 165-mi stretch of the river between the reservoir and the Pee Dee River. The river is generally well-suited to novice paddlers, with mostly flat water and some class II rapids. It flows E and W through the western and central Piedmont, passing agricultural lands, forested upland and population centers. The canoe trail is well-suited for multi day expeditions. Shorter trips are possible by using the numerous access points at bridges and parks along the route. The next access point is 5.5 mi downstream from the put-in at Memorial Park in N Wilkesboro. For a map and brochure of the trail, contact the Yadkin River Trail Association, Inc, 280 S Liberty St, Winston-Salem, NC 27101; 910/722-9346.

fishing: The W. Kerr Scott Reservoir is known for its bass fishing. The lake supports populations of largemouth, Bodie and smallmouth bass. Fishing is best done from a boat, though there are fishing piers at Blood Creek Overlook and Keowee Park.

hiking: The primary hiking opportunity in the area is the Warrior Creek segment of the 313-mi *Overmountain Victory Trail*. The National Historic Trail is a non-continuous auto and foot trail that passes through 4 states, celebrating the route of the patriot militia who defeated British forces at King's Mtn on Oct 7, 1780. The segment in Warrior Creek Park is 4 mi long. Access to the trail is in the park. If the park is closed, park at a small pull-off just outside the gate and walk through the park following signs to the trailhead. If the park is open, you can drive to a parking lot at the trailhead, which is signed. The trail is not blazed, but its route is marked with the revolutionary soldier trail icon and easy to locate. It's improved with footbridges and steps. Hiking is easy.

The *Lakeside Nature Trail* is an easy 0.3-mi interpretive loop that begins at the visitor center. The trail is exceptionally well designed, with improvements that include footbridges and steps. Interpretive stations describe such flora and fauna as birds of prey, mammals and waterfowl.

Rendezvous Mountain State Forest

Rendezvous Mountain Educational State Forest covers 147 acres of hardwood forest in the foothills of the Blue Ridge Mountains. As its name suggests, the primary purpose of the forest is educational: school groups frequently visit the forest, and there are several facilities designed to demonstrate forest ecology and management techniques. Although there really aren't any opportunities for backcountry travel, a pair of short hiking trails offers the chance to acquaint yourself with many of the species of deciduous trees that cover most of the western half of the state. An old cabin built by the Civilian Conservation Corps is another attraction, as is the view from the fire tower on top of the eponymous mountain. The forest is open from the third Wednesday in March to the day after Thanksgiving.

Wilkesboro (SE) is the closest town.

contact: Rendezvous Mountain Educational State Forest, Route 1, Box 50-B, Purlear, NC 28665; 910/667-5072.

getting there: From Wilkesboro, take US-421 W to the jct with NC-16. Turn R onto NC-16 and go 2.9 mi to Boone Trail (Old US-421). Turn L and go 2.8 mi to Purlear Rd (SR-1346). Turn R and go 0.8 mi to a jct. Continue straight onto Shingle Gap Rd (SR-1346) and go 1 mi to Rendezvous Mountain Rd (SR-1348). Go 1.3 mi up the gravel road to the gated entrance.

topography: The forest is situated near the bottom of the E slope of the Blue Ridge. The terrain is fairly rugged, with steep ravines and mountain slopes, particularly on the N and S faces. Forest cover is predominantly deciduous. Elevation on top of the mtn is 2,450 ft. **maps:** USGS Purlear.

starting out: The forest is open T–F 9 am to 5 pm and weekends 11 am to 8 pm. Forest maps and brochures are available at the main office. Facilities (restrooms, water) are located at the lower parking lot beside the picnic area. The picnic area includes a stone and timber shelter with 2 fireplaces, as well as additional tables and grills isolated in small clearings in the rhododendron understory. The shelter can be reserved through the forest office.

activities: Hiking.

hiking: There are 2 short hiking trails in the forest. A quarter-mi *Logging History Demonstration Trail* features several stations where implements of logging from the past and present, such as saws, axes, a bump cart and a saw mill, are on display. The half-mi *Talking Tree Trail* includes short, recorded profiles of many of the hardwoods that make up the deciduous forest that covers the mountain slopes. Both trails are well-designed and follow a wide, crushed-gravel path. Hiking is easy. Signed trailheads are at the main parking lots.

Doughton Park
Blue Ridge Parkway

Doughton Park covers approximately 6,000 acres of mountainous terrain in Alleghany and Wilkes Counties. The park is located 20 miles south of the Virginia state line on the Blue Ridge Parkway. High grassy meadows, steep forested ridgelines and cool mountain creeks are the area's most prominent natural features. The park is named for Robert Lee Doughton, a U.S. Representative who served from 1911–1953 and an original advocate for the construction of the parkway. Park facilities, which include a campground, rustic lodge, cafe, gas station, and picnic area, are all located along the parkway, which forms the park's north and west borders. Significant cultural attractions include Brinegar Cabin, a well-preserved 19th century homestead, and the cabin of Martin and Janie Caudill, visible in a small forest clearing from several hiking trails. The park is open all year (except when winter storms close

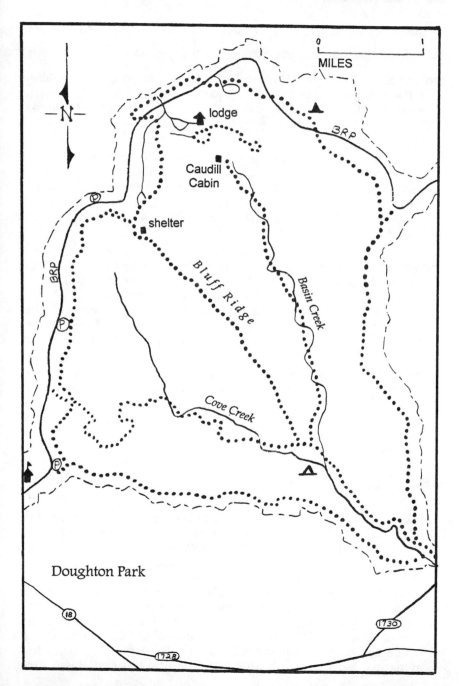

the parkway), although most facilities are closed from November to May.

contact: Superintendent, Blue Ridge Parkway, 400 BB & T Building, 1 Pack Square, Asheville, NC 28801; 704/298-0398 or District Ranger Office, Route 1, Box 263, Laurel Springs, NC 28644; 910/372-8568.

getting there: Access to the park is on the BRP between mp 238.5 and 244.7. Another access leads to the *Grassy Gap Trail* in the park's SE corner. To get there from the BRP exit at mp 248 and take NC-18 S 6.2 mi to Longbottom Rd (SR-1728). Turn L and go 4 mi to SR-1730. Turn L and go 3 mi to a parking area at the trailhead.

topography: The V-shaped park is defined by three main ridges, Cedar, Bluff, and Flat Rock, which descend more than 2,000 ft to valleys carved by Basin and Cove Creeks. At the N and W edges of the park, the Parkway winds through high meadows around Bluff Mountain (3,720 ft). In the park's SE corner, Basin Creek descends to an elevation of only 1,425 ft. **maps:** USGS Whitehead.

starting out: The gas station at mp 241 is the central source for park information. Trail maps, campground info and brochures on park wildlife are all available there, as are restrooms, water, pay phones, a cafeteria and convenience store. The Bluffs lodge and picnic area are across the BRP.

Pets must be kept on a leash.

activities: Hiking, Camping, Fishing.

hiking: A network of almost 32 mi of hiking trails provides access to all regions of the park. Trails range in length from the popular 1-mi *Fodder Stack Trail* to 7.5-mi *Bluff Mountain Trail*, with loops of up to 17 mi possible by combining trails. There's a great variety of trails, from an easy well-graded fire road to a strenuous, primitive, 2.8-mi trail that follows a ridge with an elevation change of more than 2,000 ft. The trails reflect the region's topography well; each ridgeline and creek is followed by a trail. Trailheads are spread along the BRP, with the exception of the *Basin Creek Trail*, which can only be reached via other trails. Signboards with trail maps are located at Alligator Back (mp 242.3) and Basin Cove

(244.7) Overlooks. Trails are signed, but blazes are irregular. Rock-hopping or wading is necessary on *Basin Creek Trail*.

camping: The developed campground at BRP mp 239.5 has 107 tent and trailer sites. A smaller, 20-site RV area is across the road. None of the sites has hookups. Each tent site has a tent pad, picnic table, grill (firewood is sold at the gas station) and lantern post. Sites are scattered in wooded areas and around a grassy hillside with an unsightly water tower on its top. There are restrooms and water spigots, but no showers. The campground is open from about May 1 to Oct 31, depending on the weather.

A 6-site backcountry camping area is located near the jct of *Basin Creek Trail, Bluff Ridge Trail,* and Grassy Gap Fire Rd. The sites are spread out in a large clearing at the confluence of Basin Creek and Cove Creek. The shortest route (1.5 mi) is to hike the Grassy Gap Fire Rd from the SE park access, described above. Camping at the sites is free, but a permit must be obtained in advance from the district ranger office. On busy summer weekends, it's a good idea to call a day or two before you plan on camping to check on availability of sites. The campsites are unimproved. Fires are permitted, but only dead, downed wood can be gathered. Backcountry camping outside of the designated sites is prohibited.

fishing: Basin Creek and Cove Creek together offer more than 5 mi of high quality trout fishing. Brook trout predominate, with some rainbows in the lower portions of the river. The BRP classifies these waters as "special"; fishing must be done on a fly rod using only an artificial fly tied on a single hook. Trails run beside both creeks, providing easy access. Both creeks are small, rarely widening to more than 10 ft across. The gradients are moderate to steep. Fishing pressure is moderate to heavy.

Stone Mountain State Park

At 13,447 acres, Stone Mountain is the largest state park in North Carolina. The park is located in Wilkes and Alleghany Counties south of the Blue Ridge Parkway, which passes along its northern boundary. The Thurmond-Chatham Game Land (W) forms another portion of the park's boundary. Stone Mountain, a massive exposed granite dome that's a geological rarity in this part of the country, is the park's centerpiece. The park was established to protect the mountain in 1969, on land donated to the state by the North Carolina Granite Corporation. Of historical interest is the Garden Creek Baptist Church, which exists more or less unchanged from when it was established in 1897 and continues to offer services in the spring and summer. Because of the park's many attractions, it's often crowded on weekends during the peak season, though a hike into the backcountry of only a couple miles is still likely to result in solitude. The park is open year round, with services limited in winter.

Wilkesboro (S) is the closest town.

contact: Superintendent, Stone Mountain State Park, Star Route 1, Box 17, Roaring Gap, NC 28668; 910/957-8185.

getting there: From US-21, turn W onto Traphill Rd (SR-1002) 10.5 mi S of the BRP. A small brown sign (easy to miss) marks the turn. Go 4.5 mi and turn R onto the John P. Frank Parkway. The park gate is 2.4 mi ahead.

topography: The S portion of the park is hemmed in by E Prong Roaring River, Stone Mountain Creek and Stone Mountain Rd and is dominated by the sheer SW face of Stone Mtn, which rises 600 ft from its base to a height of 2,305 ft. Wolf Rock and Cedar rock are lesser, geologically similar structures to the W and SW. The larger, northern section of the park is characterized by heavily forested ridgelines and streams that run NW-SE from the Blue Ridge. The park's highest elevation, 3,762 ft, is found here; low point, at the S edge of the park on East Prong Roaring River, is 1,270 ft. **maps:** USGS Glade Valley.

starting out: You can pick up a map or get park information at the main office. Inside there are exhibits on local wildlife and culture, including an old moonshine still. Restrooms, a pay phone and water are also at the site, as is information about rock climbing on Stone Mountain.

Pets must be leashed. Alcohol is not permitted in the park.

activities: Hiking, Fishing, Camping.

hiking: There are more than 20 mi of hiking trails in the park, covering a variety of terrain that includes isolated creek-carved valleys, exposed granite mountains (with outstanding views), and scenic waterfalls. The most heavily trafficked trails are in the southern portion of the park, on and around Stone Mtn. These total about 9 mi, and can be connected to form loops of varying length. A parking lot and road spur W of Stone Mtn provide access to all trailheads. Trail length varies from a 0.5-mi nature trail with interpretive stations at the base of Stone Mtn, to 3.3 mi *Stone Mountain Loop Trail.* All trailheads are signed; blazes occur, but are irregular. Treadways include dirt forest roads, narrow, rocky footpaths, and exposed granite, which can be slippery. Hiking on some trails is strenuous; most are moderate. Most stream crossings are unimproved.

Trails in the large N section of the park are all fairly similar. Each begins at a trailhead on Stone Mountain Rd (the road is gravel beyond the Stone Mtn parking lot and is usually closed to autos in winter) and follows a creek NW along abandoned forest roads and narrow footpaths to the vicinity of the BRP (some trails go all the way). Small parking areas are available at the trailheads. Hiking on most trails is easy, with some moderate segments as they ascend the Blue Ridge. Except for the *Widow's Creek Trail,* signing and blazing are very irregular. Stream crossings, with one or two exceptions, are unimproved. These trails receive less use than those around Stone Mountain and seem to be used mostly by fishermen or campers using the backcountry sites along Widow's Creek.

fishing: Stone Mtn SP is located at the E edge of trout habitat in NC. 8 creeks provide more than 17 mi of fishable trout waters in the park. E Prong Roaring River, the largest of these, is a medium-size stream that follows a mild gradient through the center of the park for about 3 mi. The park road runs beside it, providing easy access. In addition to anglers, sunbathers and swimmers use the river. It continues outside the park for another 6 mi. E Prong Roaring River is Hatchery Supported. Stone Mtn Creek offers similar conditions along a 2-mi stretch. It too is accessible from the main park road. Wild Trout regulations apply. Harris Creek, Garden Creek, Widow's Creek and Big Sandy Creek all offer more remote fishing in the park's extensive backcountry. These are small creeks that follow a moderate to steep gradient. Cover is frequently tight, making fly casting a challenge. The creeks each offer about 3–5 mi of fishable water. Access is via hiking trail and wading. Harris Creek is Catch & Release/Artificial Lures Only; the others are Wild Trout water.

The park also includes 2 rivers that are reserved for fly

fishermen wanting to hone their technique. For a small fee, each angler is assigned a stretch of water. Only fly rods and barbless flies can be used, and all fish must be returned to the creeks.

camping: Campers have a choice of a developed car campground or primitive backcountry sites. The 37-site car campground is laid out in 2 large loops in a wooded area. Adjacent clearings are popular feeding grounds for park wildlife, particularly white-tailed deer. Each campsite has a picnic table, grill and tent pad. Shower/restroom facilities (hot water) are centrally located. The fee is $9/night. The campground is open year-round, with water off from Nov–Mar.

6 backcountry sites are spread out along Widow's Creek. The widely-spaced sites are unimproved, though fire rings from previous campers are present. Getting to the sites requires hiking 1–3 mi along the *Widow's Creek Trail* and a spur trail. The sites cost $5/night. No more than 4 campers can occupy a site.

The park also has facilities for group camping. 2 group sites are located in different parts of the park. Each site has picnic tables and a fireplace. Pit toilets are nearby. The fee is $1/person with a $5 minimum.

Cumberland Knob Recreation Area

Blue Ridge Parkway

Cumberland Knob is a 2,000-acre day-use rec area that features several picnic areas and several mi of hiking trails. It's located at the western edge of Surry County, one mile south of the Virginia state line on the Blue Ridge Parkway. Completed in 1936 by the depression-era Civilian Conservation Corps, this was the first rec area on the Blue Ridge Parkway, as well as the site where construction on the parkway began. It is commonly held that it was named for William Augustus, the Duke of Cumberland and son of King George III. The area is open 8 am to 9 pm between May 1 and Oct 31.

Mt Airy (E) and Galax, VA (N) are the closest towns.

contact: Superintendent, Blue Ridge Parkway, 400 BB & T Building, 1 Pack Square, Asheville, NC 28801; 704/298-0398.

getting there: Cumberland Knob is located on the BRP at mp 217.5, 1 mi S of the VA-NC border. NC-18 and NC-89 both cross the BRP a little N of the rec area.

topography: Terrain in the SE corner of the rec area rolls gently up to Cumberland Knob (2,885 ft). N and W it drops sharply more than 800 ft to Gully Creek, a small, cascading stream that flows through a lush ravine at the rec area's lowest elevations. **maps:** USGS Cumberland Knob.

activities: Hiking.

starting out: Trail maps and brochures for Cumberland Knob and other BRP rec areas are available at the visitors center. A good selection of nature and guide books is sold here, as are postcards and other mementos. Restrooms, water and a pay phone are on the premises. Picnicking is the most popular activity at Cumberland Knob. Tables and grills are scattered throughout a wooded area beside the parking lot and at the edge of a large sports field with a volleyball net.

Pets must be kept on a leash.

hiking: There are 2 short hiking trails. The moderate 2.5-mi *Gully Creek Trail* forms a rough loop along the area's boundary. Another trail ambles 0.5 mi along a mild incline to a rustic stone and wood shelter on Cumberland Knob, the area's highest point. Both trails begin at signs near the visitor center and follow clearly defined footpaths.

The Piedmont

Piedmont Region Key Map

1. Crowder's Mountain SP
2. McDowell Park & Nature Preserve
3. Latta Plantation Park
4. Duke Power SP
5. Cane Creek Park
6. Pilot Mountain SP
7. Hanging Rock SP
8. Piedmont Environmental Center
9. Pee Dee NWR
10. Morrow Mountain SP
11. Uwharrie NF
12. Weymouth Woods Sandhills
    Nature Preserve
13. Greensboro Watershed Park

14. Hagan-Stone Park
15. Cedarock Park
16. Raven Rock SP
17. Jordan Lake SRA
18. Harris Lake
19. Eno River SP
20. West Point on the Eno Park
21. Duke Forest
22. William B. Umstead SP
23. Falls Lake SRA
24. Clemmons Educational SF
25. Kerr Lake SRA
26. Medoc Mountain SP

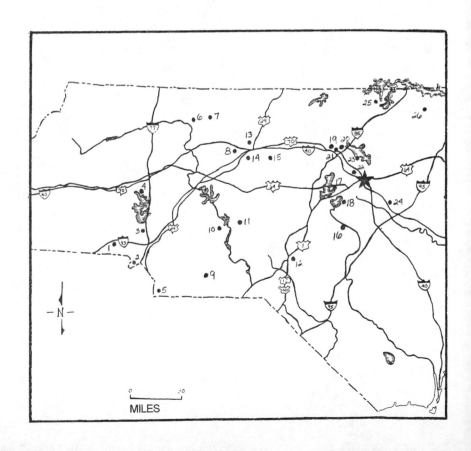

MILES

Introduction

The rolling countryside of the Piedmont begins at the fall line east of Raleigh and stretches west to the bottom of the Blue Ridge escarpment, where the mountain province begins. The Piedmont is large, accounting for nearly half of North Carolina's total area. Although elevations gradually increase from east to west, the geography of most of the region is similar: gently rolling hills of red clay that have been shaped by hundreds of millions of years of geologic and atmospheric forces. Rocky outcrops and granite and quartzite monadnocks are found at a small number of locations across the region. At one time in its distant past the Piedmont was home to active volcanoes and lofty mountains; at another, it was under a vast sea. Today, elevations are between 150 and 1,000 feet, with heights to twice that in some of the western foothills, befitting the name Piedmont, which means literally foothill.

More than any other part of the state, the Piedmont has been altered by human settlement. The great deciduous forest that once blanketed the rolling hills is almost completely gone, cleared to accommodate farming and the rapid expansion of towns and cities. None of the large rivers that flow through the region's center, draining the gentle hills and in some cases extending all the way into the mountains, remains free flowing. The Yadkin, Catawba, Pee Dee, Haw, Neuse, Cape Fear and Roanoke have all been dammed. The dams were built to provide flood control and electric power for the Piedmont's burgeoning population. More than half of the state's residents live here, a majority of them in the arc of cities that includes Charlotte, Winston-Salem, Greensboro, Durham and Raleigh.

Today, the remnant deciduous forest is relegated to small pockets in parks, along river floodplains and along the shores of the large lakes created by dams. Most of these areas had previously been cleared as well; the forests there now are second- or third-growth. In many places the forests are still in the early stages of succession, when pines are the predominant species and the large hardwoods such as oaks, maples and poplars have only just begun to establish a presence.

The largest mammal that inhabits these woodlands is the white-tailed deer. Its story in North Carolina is one of the successes of wildlife conservation. By the turn of this century deer populations had dwindled to approximately 10,000; current numbers exceed 800,000, close to the number biologists estimate to be its natural limit. Other species encountered are the raccoon, beaver and opossum. The black bear's range, which includes both the coastal plain and the mountains, does not extend into the Piedmont.

The Piedmont's climate is temperate. Winters are mild, with typically a handful of snowstorms and temperatures below freezing only for about 2 months out of the year. Summers are hot and humid, with temperatures often above 90°. Spring and fall are cool and pleasant; these are the best times of year for outdoor activity. Late spring and early summer are characterized by frequent late-afternoon storms. Although they rarely last more than an hour or two, these storms can include torrential downpours and frequent lightening strikes.

Opportunities for backcountry travel and outdoor pursuits on the Piedmont are influenced by the same factors that have so radically altered the land. Large tracts of undeveloped land are few. State parks and county parks account for the majority of the region's parkland. These are usually centered around a unique natural feature, such as Pilot Mountain or Stone Mountain, a small body of water, or have simply been carved out of surrounding development to serve as a natural oasis. Most are relatively small, with sizes that range from about 500 to 6,000 acres.

On the Piedmont, the largest undeveloped areas are water—the rivers and large lakes that were created when the rivers were dammed. Jordan Lake, Falls Lake and Kerr Lake are all managed with outdoor recreation as a major focus. Yet for lovers of backcountry solitude, the lakes require a compromise. All are heavily used by recreational boaters and anglers fishing from bass boats. The rivers offer paddlers a more serene environment. Despite the dams, many have long stretches suitable to multi-day trips. The dams have eliminated many of the rapids; flat water is common and whitewater, when encountered, is typically low grade. Several of these rivers are described in the following pages. All are open to use by canoeists and kayakers, with access points at bridge crossings and WRC boat ramps. Because all of the rivers pass through private property, paddlers should respect the rights of the landowners.

The Piedmont challenges the backcountry traveller to make the most out of limited resources. Although the natural areas of the region may be more suitable to a day-hike than a week-long backpacking trip, the lakes, rivers and woodlands all offer a variety of opportunities for exploration and recreation.

rowder's Mountain State Park

2,586-acre Crowder's Mountain State Park preserves one of the unique geological features of the western Piedmont: a pair of quartzite monadnocks that tower more than 800 feet above the rolling countryside that surrounds them. The hard core of rock has withstood millions of years of weathering, while the once lofty peaks that shared their heights have disappeared under the persistent forces of erosion. Crowder's Mountain, with sheer vertical walls up to 150 feet in height, is the more visually spectacular of the two peaks. Hiking trails lead to both peaks, where there are excellent views of the western Piedmont. The park is located in Gaston County.

Kings Mountain (NW) and Gastonia (NE) are the closest cities.

contact: Superintendent, Crowder's Mountain State Park, Route 1, Box 159, Kings Mountain, NC 28086; 704/853-5375.

getting there: From I-85, take exit 13 (Edgewood Rd). Turn S onto Edgewood Rd (SR-1307) and go 0.7 mi to US-74W. Turn R and go 1.9 mi to Sparrow Springs Rd (SR-1125). Turn L and go 2.6 mi to a fork in the road. Bear R and drive 0.5 mi to the park entrance, R.

topography: Crowder's Mountain and King's Pinnacle—geologically classified as kyanite-quartzite monadnocks—dominate the geography of the surrounding piedmont plateau. The mountainsides are steep and rocky, with peaks that reach 1,625 ft and 1,705 ft respectively. Deciduous trees comprise most of the forest cover. **maps:** USGS Kings Mountain.

starting out: Maps, brochures and backcountry campsite registration are all located in the park office. While there, check out the small wildlife exhibits, which include a live copperhead and timber rattlesnake. A pay phone is outside the office. 2 picnic areas are located along the park road. Each has a large shelter, as well as additional tables and grills. Restrooms and water fountains are nearby. Rock climbing is one of the most popular activities in the park. Areas open to climbing are restricted, and King's Pinnacle is closed to climbing. Check with the park office for additional information.

Alcohol is not permitted in the Park. Pets must be kept on a leash. The lake is closed to swimming.

activities: Hiking, Camping, Canoeing, Fishing.

hiking: 8 trails cover a distance of 15 mi, most of them between and on the 2 mountains, which are about 4 mi apart. Although some backtracking is necessary, the trails have been laid out to allow for long loops that take in the park's highlights, including outstanding views from the summits. Hiking along most of the trails is moderate, with rocky treadways and some steep, strenuous inclines on the pinnacle trails. Trails are all clearly defined, blazed and easy to follow. Trailheads are signed at the park office and picnic areas. Trail improvements include rock and railroad tie steps. There's a short nature trail with interpretive stations behind the picnic areas.

camping: A 10-site primitive camping area is located off the *Pinnacle Trail* about 1 mi from the park office. Sites are spread out over a large forested area on the NE side of King's Pinnacle. The sites are far from one another, insuring privacy. Each site has a tent pad, grill and trash can. There are 2 pit toilets in the area and water is available from a hand pump. Sites cost $5/night. The hike to reach them is moderate.

A short distance away is a primitive group camping area with 6 sites. The area is in a small forest clearing, with little space between the sites. Each site includes a grill, trash can and improvised log seats. Firewood is also provided. A pit toilet and water pump are close by. The fee is $1/person with a $5 minimum.

Campers using either area must register at the park office before selecting a site.

canoeing: A small (9 acres) artificial lake is located near the park entrance. The park rents canoes from Jun to Labor Day. Rental rates are $2.50/hr for the first 2 hrs, $1/hr for each additional hour. Private boats are not permitted on the lake.

fishing: The lake supports populations of bass and bluegill. You can fish from a rented canoe, or cast from the banks. A hiking trail circles the lake, providing easy access.

McDowell Park and Nature Preserve

Situated on the eastern shore of Lake Wylie, McDowell Park covers 956 acres of upland hardwood forest on mildly hilly terrain drained by several small creeks. The park was opened in 1976; it was Mecklenburg County's first nature preserve. Recreational opportunities in the mostly day-use park are oriented to both water and land. Lake Wylie covers more than 12,400 acres and has a 325-mi shoreline. Fishing and recreational boating are both popular on the lake. On land, there are hiking trails, picnic areas, and a full-service campground. The park is open year round; hours are November to February, 7 am to dark; March to October, 5:30 am to dark.

Charlotte (NE) is the closest city.

contact: Park Ranger, McDowell Park, 15222 York Rd, Charlotte, NC 28278; 704/588-5224.

getting there: From I-77 in Charlotte, take exit 6 and turn onto NC-49 S. Drive 10.4 mi to a large sign with a hiker icon and the park entrance, R.

topography: Elevation on the lake is 569 ft. A hardwood forest covers most of the rugged terrain that rises from the lake on park land. Elevations in the park reach 700 ft. **maps:** USGS Lake Wylie (SC).

starting out: Admission to the park is free, except on weekends and holidays from Mar to Nov, when there's a $2/vehicle fee for county residents, $4 for all others. The park's nature center is a good place to begin a visit; you can pick up a trail map, get information on activities at McDowell or other nearby parks and preserves, or just check out the exhibits in the small nature museum. Restrooms are there also. Nature Center hours are M–F 8 am–5 pm, Sa 9 am–5 pm, & Su 1–5 pm. Restrooms are also located at the picnic area and marina, where there's a pay phone too. Numerous facilities exist at McDowell Park for picnicking. A large octagonal deck that perches on the lakeshore near the boat rental dock has picnic tables and benches. Also located on the lakeshore are 17 individual picnic decks, each with its own table and grill. A large open air shelter is also in the area. Restrooms are located nearby.

Alcohol is prohibited in the park. Pets must be kept on a leash. Swimming is not allowed.

activities: Hiking, Camping, Canoeing/Kayaking, Fishing.

hiking: A small network of 9 trails covers 7 mi of lakeshore and hardwood upland forest. Hiking on the carefully designed and maintained trails is easy to moderate. Since most of the trails are less than a mile long, they're most suitable for short, casual hikes. Longer loops are possible by combining trails. Signed trailheads are grouped at the nature center, marina and picnic area. Trails are not blazed, but are easy to follow, with clearly defined treadways. Improvements include steps and footbridges. There's a 0.3-mi handicapped accessible trail with picnic tables beside a scenic stream.

camping: There's a large, 82-site campground with sites to accommodate almost every type of camping. The breakdown is this: 12 RV sites, 31 car sites, 30 primitive sites, 6 full service sites (2 of these are handicapped accessible), and 2 group primitive sites. Although the campground is located amidst a pleasant hardwood forest, the sites are bunched closely together, creating a sense of crowding. Another negative is that there's only one rest-room/shower facility (hot water). Each of the sites has a table and grill, except for primitive sites, which have a fire ring instead of a grill. The full-service sites come with a tent, cots, stoves and other camping gear. Water spigots are located throughout the campground. Primitive sites require a short walk from a common parking area. Overnight fees are as follows (county residents/non-county residents): Drive-in and RV sites: $12/18; primitive sites: $6/9; fully equipped sites: $25/35. Reservations are accepted for the full-service sites; call 803/831-2285. There's a pay phone and info center near the entrance. The campground is open year-round, weekends only Dec–Feb.

canoeing/kayaking: Although the whine and wakes of power boats are a nearly constant presence on Lake Wylie, the location of McDowell Park on an out-of-the-way cove offers paddlers some relatively quiet water. The park rents canoes at the following rates: $4/half-hr, $6/hr; $16/half-day, $27/day. Paddleboat rentals are available as well. Rentals are seasonal. Much of the lakeshore near the park is developed.

fishing: Lake Wylie is one of the premier fishing reservoirs on the Piedmont. The primary sport fish is largemouth bass, with striped bass also present. Crappie and bluegill are also regularly taken, and there's a large population of channel catfish. There are several fishing piers in the park; a fee of $1/day is charged, or you can buy a season pass for $20. Of course fishing from a boat is the most popular method, as it affords access to the whole lake.

Latta Plantation Park

Latta Plantation is a 2,247-acre multi-use park situated on the eastern shore of Mountain Island Lake, an artificial impoundment on the Catawba River. The park is named for Federal-style Latta Place, built circa 1800. The plantation compound is open to visitors. Also located within the park is the Carolina Raptor Center, which features more than a dozen different species of raptors in outdoor habitats. The center carries out a number of objectives, among them conservation, rescue and rehabilitation, and education. It's open Tu–Su, 10 am to 5 pm. Admission is $2. Another popular attraction with visitors is the Equestrian Center, which offers trail rides, lessons and hayrides. The center is open daily 9 am–5 pm. The park also features an extensive network of trails that wind through forested uplands on the shores of Mountain Island Lake. The lake itself is scenic and quiet. The park is run by Mecklenburg County Park and Recreation Dept. It's Open M–F 9am to dark; weekends 7am to dark.

Huntersville (NE) and Charlotte (SE) are the closest cities.

contact: Latta Plantation Park, 5225 Sample Rd, Huntersville, NC 28078; 704/875-1391

getting there: From I-77 6 mi N of Charlotte, take exit 18 and turn S onto Vance Rd. Go 1.7 mi to Mt Holly-Huntersville Rd. Turn L and go 1.2 mi to Beattie's Ford Rd. Turn R and go 1.5 mi to Sample Rd. Turn L and go 0.9 mi to the Park gate.

topography: Lake elevation is 648 ft. The gently rolling hillsides on the lake's shore are forested with pines and hardwoods. Elevations in the park do not exceed 750 ft. **maps:** USGS Mountain Island Lake.

starting out: Park information and maps are available at the Ranger Interpretive Center just inside the park gate. The center is open M–F 8 am–5 pm; Sa 9 am–5 pm and Su 1-5 pm. Restrooms, a water fountain and vending machine are located outside. A large picnic area with numerous tables and grills, 2 shelters, restrooms, a concession area with vending machines and a pay phone is located at the end of the park road. A popular park activity is horseback riding. There are organized rides as well as lessons for individuals or groups.

Alcohol is not allowed in the park. Pets must be kept on a leash. Swimming is not permitted in the lake.

activities: Hiking, Fishing, Canoeing/Kayaking.

hiking: A small network of hiking and horse trails covers about 10 mi. All areas of the park are accessible via the trails, including an Audubon bird sanctuary. Hiking on the trails is easy. Most trailheads are clearly signed; trails are not blazed, but heavy use makes them easy to follow. Improvements include footbridges and steps. *Buzzard Rock Trail* leads to an overlook with scenic views of the lake. The 0.6-mi *Educational Forest Trail* features interpretive stations along the route that describe forest succession and management and highlight area tree species. The trail is closed to horses.

fishing: Mountain Island Lake provides opportunities for fishing from land or a boat. Bank fishing is possible at many locations in the park; the clearing beside the canoe launch is one popular spot. There's also a small fishing pier near the picnic area. To get out on the water, you can either bring your own canoe or rent one from the park. A fishing day pass costs $1; season passes are available for $20. Game species are largemouth and striped bass and bluegill. Catfish are also regularly caught.

canoeing/kayaking: Mountain Island Lake is an impoundment on the Catawba River between Lake Norman (N) and Lake Wylie (S). Although power boats are permitted on the lake, in practice the 2 larger lakes receive the large majority of bass boats and pleasure boats. That leaves Mountain Island a relatively quiet body of water, well suited to a day of paddling. The lake is narrow and thin, and covers a distance of about 10 mi. Although parts of the shoreline are developed, the lake is generally scenic. A canoe launch is located in the park. If you don't bring your own boat, you can rent one from the park between Good Friday and Oct 31. Rates are $4/half-hr, $6/hr, $16/half-day, $27/day. Paddleboats and Jon boats are also available.

Duke Power State Park

Duke Power State Park occupies a part of the northeast corner of the largest man-made lake in North Carolina, 32,510-acre Lake Norman. The park itself covers 1,458 acres of upland pine/hardwood forest and 13 of the lake's 520 miles of shoreline. Prior to the construction of Cowans Ford Dam across the Catawba River in the early '60s, most of the land now submerged and on the lakeshore was agricultural. Although a large portion of that lakeshore is now developed, some of the agricultural land is gradually returning to a natural, forested state. The state park is one such area, with a young forest of pine and hardwoods beginning to reclaim the land. Recreation in the park is centered on the lake, and includes water-based activities such as swimming, fishing and boating, as well as hiking and camping.

Troutman (NE) is the closest town.

contact: Park Superintendent, Duke Power State Park, Route 2, Box 224M, Troutman, NC 28166; 704/528-6350.

getting there: From the intersection of NC-115 and Wagner St in Troutman, take Wagner St (it becomes Perth St [SR-1303]) 1.6 mi to State Park Rd (SR-1330). Turn R and go 2.1 mi to the entrance gate.

topography: Lake elevation is 760 ft. Park terrain is rolling countryside typical of the Piedmont. Forest cover is hardwoods and pines. **maps:** USGS Troutman.

starting out: Park maps and brochures are available at the visitors center. Restrooms and water are at several locations in the park. The busiest part of the park is the swimming area, where there's a supervised beach on the 33-acre lake. The area is open Jun 1 to Labor Day, 10 am–6 pm. There's a $2 fee; $1 for kids 12 and under. Facilities there include a bathhouse, 2 picnic shelters with tables and grills, restrooms and vending machines. Additional tables and grills are located in a wooded area adjacent to the lake.

Park regulations prohibit the use of alcohol. Pets are not allowed in the swimming area and must be leashed elsewhere in the park.

activities: Canoeing/Kayaking, Fishing, Hiking, Camping.

canoeing/kayaking: Lake Norman is popular with owners of many different types of watercraft, including bass boats, speed boats trailing waterskiers, jet-skis and sailboats. With the vast dimensions of the lake and the often heavy traffic, a canoeist or kayaker can begin to feel rather overwhelmed. If you avoid peak-season weekends, however, the lake's 32,500 acres and 520-mi shoreline will seem less daunting. Scenery on the lake is mixed, with considerable development (including a nuclear power plant), but also with many forested areas. Because of the lake's size, paddlers should be prepared for open water conditions. There's a boat ramp in the park, as well as dozens of other put-in around the lake.

Another option—for canoeists at least—is the 33-acre park lake. The lake is closed to private boats, but the park rents canoes from Jun 1 through Labor Day between 10 am and 6 pm. Rates are $2.50/hr for the first 2 hours, $1/hr for each additional hour.

fishing: Lake Norman is one of the most popular fishing destinations in the Piedmont. Largemouth and striped bass, channel catfish, yellow perch, black crappie and bluegill are the major species of game fish. Most anglers fish from a boat, though it's also possible to cast from the shoreline in the park.

hiking: 2 trails cover more than 7 mi. Hiking on the trails is easy to moderate. Both trails are blazed and easy to follow. Improvements include footbridges over wet areas. Trailheads are located near the group camping area, with several other access points on park roads. Scenery along the trails is the lake and pine/hardwood forest. Trail use is moderate.

camping: A 33-site car campground is located in a long loop at the end of the park road. The sites are large and well-spaced in a wooded setting, with considerable privacy. Each site has a picnic table and grill. A restroom/shower building (hot water) is centrally located. Sites cost $9/night. Firewood can be purchased for $2/bundle. The campground is open Mar 15–Nov 30.

In addition to the family campground there are 2 group campsites. The sites are primitive, with only fire rings and picnic tables. Cars are left in a central parking area and campers hike about 200 yds to either of the 2 sites. Restrooms and water are located near the parking area. The fee is $1/person/night, with a minimum of $5. The group campground is open from mid-Apr to mid-Nov.

Cane Creek Park

Cane Creek Park is a 1,050 acre county park with a 350-acre trophy bass lake as its centerpiece. The park is located in the southwest corner of Union County near the South Carolina state line. Although a popular outdoor destination among locals, it isn't very well known outside of the immediate vicinity. Aside from bass fishing, which is a major attraction, the park includes a vast array of activities and facilities, including a swimming beach; picnic area with shelters, tables and grills; volley ball court; baseball field; a network of trails open to hikers, bikers and horses; 3 camping facilities; a basketball court and a miniature golf course. Despite the high density of activities, the park does have some quiet corners where it's possible to steal away into the woods or sit by the lakeshore and birdwatch.

Waxhaw (NW) and Monroe (NE) are the closest towns.

contact: Park Superintendent, Cane Creek Park, 5213 Harkey Rd, Waxhaw, NC 28173; 704/843-3919.

getting there: From NC-75 at the E edge of the village of Waxhaw, take Old Providence Rd S 1.8 mi. Turn R onto Providence Rd and go 3.2 mi to the jct with NC-200. Continue on Providence Rd 1.7 mi to Harkey Rd. Turn L and go 1 mi to the park entrance, R. To reach the park campground, instead of turning onto Harkey Rd, continue on Providence Rd 1.1 mi to Cane Creek Rd. Turn L and go 1.7 mi to the campground entrance.

topography: Normal lake elevation is 549 ft. The surrounding terrain is gently rolling hillside covered with a relatively young pine and hardwood forest. Elevations in the park do not exceed 630 ft. **maps:** USGS Unity (SC).

starting out: An entrance fee of $2/vehicle is charged (campers excepted). All visitors must register at the operations center, located just inside the park entrance. You can pick up a trail map and brochure there. Restrooms are located beside the operations center, near the swimming beach and at the end of the park road.

A snack bar and pay phone are also located near the swimming beach.

Waterskiing is permitted on the lake on weekdays only. Boaters must register before using the lake. Pets must be kept on a leash, and are not allowed on the beach.

activities: Hiking, Canoeing/Kayaking, Fishing, Mountain Biking, Camping.

hiking: A network of 15 mi of hiking trails covers all sectors of the park, including lakeshore, upland forest, campground and day-use beach area. 12 mi are multi-use, open to horses and mountain bikes too. Trails are well-defined and easy to locate and follow. Trailheads are signed with hiker icons, but not named. Trails are blazed with bars of different colors. Hiking on the trails is easy. Trail use is moderate to heavy.

canoeing/kayaking: Cane Creek Lake is small (350 acres) and popular. In addition to canoes and kayaks, bass boats are a major presence, and water-skiing is allowed on weekdays. The lake is fully contained within the park; there's one boat ramp inside the park. A $2.50 launch fee is charged. If you don't bring your own boat, you can rent a canoe from the park. Rates are $4/hr or $20/day. Although hardly a wilderness setting, the lakeshore is attractive, with park facilities comprising the only development.

fishing: With a 350-acre trophy bass lake, fishing may be the most popular activity in the park. There are places along the shore to fish from, or you can fish from a boat. A valid NC license is required, as is a $1/day park fishing permit. The daily creel limit for bass is 5, with an 18" minimum. Other species caught in the lake are crappie, bluegill and catfish.

mountain biking: 12 mi of trails are open to mountain bikes. Trails are single track with difficulties that include poor drainage, rocky stretches and small creek crossings. Aside from those, riding is easy. Trails are also used by hikers and horses.

camping: An 89-site car campground is located on the S shore of the lake. Many of the sites are located right on the water with excellent views. Most sites are very closely spaced and offer little privacy, as the campground is in an area that has been largely cleared of vegetation. Each site has a picnic table and grill. 2 restroom/shower facilities with hot water are centrally located. Other amenities include a picnic shelter with tables and grills, a boat ramp and a beach. There's also a camp store, with vending machines, ice machine and pay phone located outside. Sites cost $13/night for Union Co residents, $14/night for others Mar–Oct; $1 less Nov–Feb. The campground fills up on summer weekends. It's open year-round.

Backcountry camping is allowed in a designated area on a rise above the lake. There are no individual sites, although there are several picnic tables and trash cans spread out across a wide area. The sites offer good privacy. Cars are parked in a clearing beneath a power line. A short trail (less than 50 yds) leads to the sites. Sites cost $2/night.

There's also a group camping area with 10 sites in an attractive lakeside setting. Each of the sites is about an acre is size and includes a fire ring and picnic tables. Cars are left in a central parking lot and campers walk a short distance to the sites. A bathhouse is centrally located. Sites cost $2/person with a $10/night minimum. A picnic shelter is in the area. The group camping area is open Mar 1–Oct 31.

Pilot Mountain State Park

Pilot Mountain takes its name from the Saura Indian word *Jomeokee*, meaning great guide or pilot. The name is apt, for the mountain dominates the local landscape, and can be seen from miles away in all directions as it rises magisterially from the surrounding Piedmont plateau. Geologically classified as a quartzite monadnock, the hard rock of the mountain has withstood the millions of years of weathering and erosion that have reduced many of the other former peaks of the Sauratown Mountain range to rolling countryside. Along with the rocky bluffs of Hanging Rock State Park to the east (visible from overlooks on the summit), Pilot Mountain is the easternmost extension of the state's mountainous region. Since 1968 it has been the centerpiece of a park that today covers 3,703 acres in two main parts. The Mountain section (N) and River section (S) are connected by a narrow, 5.5-mile corridor of land open to hikers and horseback riders. A scenic 2-mile stretch of the Yadkin River runs through the southern section.

The park lies roughly halfway between Winston-Salem (SE) and Mount Airy (NW).

contact: Superintendent, Pilot Mountain State Park, Route 1 Box 21, Pinnacle, NC 27611; 910/325-2355.

getting there: There are 3 access points to the park. To get to the main entrance take US-52 29 mi N of Winston-Salem and follow signs 0.5 mi to the park gate. • To get to the N part of the Yadkin River section, from US-52 take the Pinnacle exit (first exit S of the Park). Go 1.5 mi W on Perch Rd to Stony Ridge Rd (SR-2048). Turn R and go 2.8 mi to Shoals Rd (SR-2067). Turn L and go 1.4 mi to Caudel Rd (SR-2070). Turn L and go 2 mi to Hauser Rd (SR-2072). Turn R and go 0.9 mi to the green park sign (0.2 mi ahead is parking for the S terminus of the *Corridor Trail*). Turn L and drive 1.3 mi on a gravel road with 3 stream fordings to a parking loop. The entire route is marked with brown *Yadkin Islands Park* signs. • To reach the S half of the river section, from NC-67 in the community of East Bend take Old NC-67 E to Fairground Rd. Turn R and go 0.5 mi to Shady Grove Church Rd. Bear R and go 0.5 mi to Old Shoals Rd (SR-1546). Turn R and go 2.5 mi to the parking area.

topography: In the main section of the park, Pilot Mtn rises 1,400 ft from the valley floor to an elevation of 2,420 ft. It's capped by the sheer, 200-ft cliff face of Big Pinnacle. The terrain levels out at the lower elevations of the mtn and in the S section of the park, which straddles the Yadkin River. There are 2 large islands in the river on park land. Low point in the park is 750 ft. **maps:** USGS Pinnacle, Siloam.

starting out: A park map and brochure is available at the park office. Notices of park-sponsored events (such as wildlife study and nature hikes) are posted on an information board outside the office. Restrooms, a water-fountain and a pay phone are there also. The park road goes almost to the summit of Pilot Mtn, where short hiking trails lead to scenic overlooks. This area is frequently crowded.

Rock climbing on Big Pinnacle is prohibited. No alcohol is allowed in the park. Pets must be kept on a leash.

activities: Hiking, Camping, Canoeing/Kayaking, Fishing.

hiking: There are 18 mi of hiking and bridle (10 mi are hikers only) trails in the park. Trails range in length from the very short and frequently crowded trails that lead from the summit parking lot to scenic overlooks of Big Pinnacle and the surrounding countryside to a 10-mi hike along three trails from the Little Pinnacle summit to the Yadkin River. All trails in the N section of the park are accessible from the summit parking area, except the *Grassy Ridge Trail*, which begins at the park office parking area. The 5.5-mi *Corridor Trail* can be reached by hiking to the end of the *Grassy Ridge Trail* or *Mountain Trail*, or from a separate parking area at each end. Access to the shorter trails of the S section of the park is at the parking area, described above. All park trails are signed and blazed. Hiking ranges from easy to strenuous; the long mountainside trails are the most arduous.

camping: There's a 49-site car campground in the park's main section. Each site has a tent pad, picnic table and grill. The campground is located in a heavily wooded area on the mountainside. Each of the sites is large and affords ample privacy. 2 restroom/shower facilities with hot water are centrally located. The fee is $9/night. Water spigots can be found beside the campground road. Firewood is available for purchase. The campground is open Mar 15 to Nov 30.

In the River Section of the park, there's a group campsite ($1/person/night; $5 minimum) with drinking water, pit toilets, picnic tables and fire circles. When the river is high, flooding can be a problem at this site; call ahead to check on water levels. Reservations are required.

2 primitive sites are located on the largest of the river islands. These sites are used by canoeists running the river. No facilities are provided.

canoeing/kayaking: The 2-mi section of the Yadkin River that flows through the state park is one of the most scenic on the Yadkin River Canoe Trail, a 165-mi stretch of the river between the W. Kerr Scott Reservoir and the Pee Dee River. This portion of the river is wide (about 300 ft across) and relatively shallow. The put-in is in the park's SW corner on Old Shoals Rd (SR-1546). The closest access upstream from the park is located on Rockford Rd (SR-2221) 11.6 mi away. Downstream, nearby accesses are the Donnaha Access on NC-67 (6 mi) and the Old US-421 Park Access (12.5 mi). Hazards along this stretch of the river include boulders, rock cliffs, and islands. Canoe camping sites in the park are located on the largest island (see above). A canoe trail map and brochure is available from the Yadkin River Trail Association, 280 S Liberty St, Winston-Salem, NC 27101; 910/722-9346.

fishing: The shallow waters of the Yadkin River support sunfish, crappie, and catfish. Fishing in the park is possible either by wading or from a canoe. Dense thickets of water beeches and other vegetation make casting from the banks a near impossibility. The river is accessible by hiking trails that run for about a mile on each bank. Parking on either side is less than a quarter-mi from the river.

Hanging Rock State Park

Located in the Sauratown Mountains, eastern outliers of the Blue Ridge Mountains, Hanging Rock State Park is a 6,340-acre mountain environment set near the middle of the Piedmont. Although peaks in the park only reach modest elevations, they seem to tower over the flat tableland and rolling countryside that stretches for miles below in all directions. Numerous cliffside overlooks, unusual rock formations, scenic waterfalls and proximity to Winston-Salem combine to make this one of the most popular state parks. The best times to visit are spring, when the rhododendron and mountain laurel blooms, and fall, when foliage is at its most colorful. The park is still recovering from the severe ice storm that struck on March 2, 1994. Called the "most devastating natural occurrence in the history of the park," the storm resulted in the closing of the park for 3 months and the loss of more than 300,000 trees.

Danbury (SE) is the closest town.

contact: Superintendent, Hanging Rock State Park, P.O. Box 186, Danbury, NC 27016; 910/593-8480.

getting there: From Danbury, take NC-8/89 W 2 mi to Hanging Rock Rd (SR-1001) Turn R and go 1.6 mi to the park gate and entrance. The parking lot for lower cascades waterfall and hiking trail is 0.8 mi from the park gate on Hall Rd (SR-2012).

topography: The mountains in the park, particularly near the S and W borders, rise dramatically on 400-ft sheer cliffs from the Piedmont plateau. Elevations in the park are between 700 ft and 2,579 ft. Many of the ridges and peaks at upper elevations are exposed rock. **maps:** USGS Hanging Rock.

starting out: You can pick up a map and brochure at the park office. A pay phone is there as well. Restrooms are located at the bathhouse and at 2 picnic areas next to the main parking lots. In summer, a portion of the park lake is set aside as a supervised swimming area. The lake has a sandy beach and a diving platform. The large stone and timber bathhouse there is a National Historic Landmark. Swimming facilities are open Jun 1 through Labor Day, M 11 am–6 pm, Tu–Su 10 am–6 pm. A small fee is charged. 2 large picnic areas are located at opposite ends of the parking lots. Both have tables, grills and shelters with fireplaces. These can be reserved for a fee. Restrooms are nearby. Rock climbing is permitted on Cook's Wall and Moore's Wall.

Park regulations forbid the use of alcohol. Pets must be kept on a leash. Rock climbing is prohibited outside designated areas.

activities: Hiking, Camping, Canoeing, Fishing.

hiking: There are almost 20 mi of hiking trails in the park, ranging from short, easy nature trails to a 4-mi strenuous mountain ascent. Hiking on most trails, however, is moderate. The network of trails has been smartly laid out to provide access to all of the park's scenic and natural highlights, such as overlooks, waterfalls, and striking geologic formations. Some trails, such as *Hanging Rock Trail* and the E side of *Moore's Wall Loop Trail*, receive very heavy use. Expect crowds during peak seasons. With a couple of exceptions, all trailheads are located beside the two main parking lots. The trailheads are signed and the trails are generally easy to follow, with blazes or signs indicating the routes. Improvements include benches and footbridges.

camping: There's a large, double loop 73-site car campground that fills up early on summer and fall weekends. It's located in a heavily wooded area near the lake. Most sites are fairly well spaced, with about average privacy. Each site has a picnic table, grill and tent pad. There are 2 centrally located restroom/shower facilities with hot water. Water spigots are also located throughout the area. The campground is open year round. The fee is $9/night Mar 15 to Dec 1; $4.50/night the rest of the year.

Another camping area, located near the main entrance, is reserved for organized groups. There are 8 sites in a wooded area beside a large grassy meadow used for sports and games. Facilities include 2 picnic tables and a fire ring at each site and 2 pit toilets and a water source common to the area. The sites are large, with plenty of room to spread out. The fee is $1/person/night with a $5 minimum. Reservations are required.

Another, less rugged, option is to rent one of the fully equipped vacation cabins. Each cabin has 2 bedrooms, a kitchen and a living room. Cabins sleep 6. The fees are as follows: $250/wk from Jun to Labor Day, $270/wk with swimming privileges; $55/night from Mar to May with a 2 night minimum.

canoeing: You can paddle around the park's 12-acre lake, but you'll have to rent a canoe from the park; private boats are not allowed. The rental fee is $2.50/hr for the first 2 hrs, $1/hr for each add'l hr.

Another option is the Dan River Canoe Trail, a portion of which passes through the N extremity of the park. The river enters NC from VA in the NW corner of Stokes Co, near the community of Jessups Mill. From there, it continues E for about 100 mi before reentering VA NE of Eden in Rockingham Co. Conditions on the river near Hanging Rock SP are generally class I, but can jump to class II when the water is up. The river can be run year-round, except during dry periods. There's a boat launch in the park on SR-1482. To get there, go out the main park entrance, take the 2nd L onto Piedmont Springs Rd (SR-1489). At the end of the road go L onto NC-8/89. Take the first L onto SR-1482 and go to the launch area at the end of the road. Other boat access points are located at frequent intervals along the river.

fishing: The park lake is home to smallmouth bass and bream. You can fish from the banks or a boat. Smallmouth bass and catfish are caught in the Dan River. The river is accessible from a separate parking area outside the main park entrance on SR-1482. See above for directions.

Piedmont Environmental Center

Located on 376 acres on the western shore of High Point Lake between High Point and Greensboro, the Piedmont Environmental Center is a natural oasis amidst an ever-encroaching urban sprawl. The preserve is divided into two contiguous sections, north and south. The dual mission of the Center is to preserve a natural environment suited to outdoor recreation and to provide environmental education to children and adults. Nature programs are regularly scheduled, and last year 20,000 schoolchildren made use of the preserve's educational facilities. Field trips outside the preserve are also sponsored. The preserve is open year-round from dawn to dusk.

The preserve is in the NE corner of High Point. Greensboro (NE) is less than 10 mi away.

contact: Piedmont Environmental Center, 1220 Penny Rd, High Point, NC 27265; 910/883-8531.

getting there: From I-40, get off at exit 214 (Wendover Ave). Turn SW onto W Wendover Ave and go 4.6 mi to Penny Rd. Turn L and go 2.1 mi to the Center entrance, L.

topography: Preserve terrain is typical of the Piedmont—gently rolling hills covered with a forest of loblolly pines and hardwoods such as oak, cedar, poplar and dogwood. Elevations are between 757 ft on the lake and 850 ft. **maps:** USGS Guilford.

starting out: Information and trail maps are available in the Environmental Center building. Restrooms, a water fountain, pay phone and vending machines are also here. A nature store sells guidebooks, educational materials and environment-related souvenirs. The building is open M–Sa 8:30 am–5 pm. Behind the building, there's a small picnic area with 4 tables and a grill.

Center rules require that pets be kept on a leash. Fishing within the PEC is prohibited. Camping or campfires are not allowed.

activities: Hiking, Mountain Biking.

hiking: 9 easy trails cover a total distance of almost 9 mi. Most trails are less than a mile long, though the longest trail is 4.5 mi, with longer loops possible. In addition to the center trails, roughly half of the 6.5-mi Bicentennial Greenway is on preserve property. A very short trail constructed by the Youth Conservation Corps features interpretive plaques that describe the local ecology. Access to all trails is beside the main building. Trails are well-maintained, blazed with colored bars and easy to follow. Improvements include benches, footbridges (including a floating bridge) and graded steep sections. The *Lakeshore Trail* features a small wildlife blind and scenic views of the lake. Trails in the S half of the preserve get much heavier use than those in the N half.

mountain biking: The 6.5-mi Bicentennial Greenway begins just S of the Piedmont Envitonmental Center and travels 3 mi through forest and along the lakeshore from one end of the preserve to the other. The 10-ft-wide greenway is partially paved, with the rest of its surface made up of crushed stone. Pedalling is easy to moderate. Footbridges—bikes must be dismounted—cross several streams that feed the lake. The route is marked by posts with red and white dots.

Pee Dee National Wildlife Refuge

The Pee Dee National Wildlife Refuge covers 8,443 acres of upland, river bottom hardwood forest, and farmland in Anson and Richmond Counties. The Pee Dee River flows through the northern part of the refuge. Established in 1965, the refuge is managed for the protection of wildlife—particularly migrating and endangered bird species—and to allow visitors to experience these species and their habitat in a relatively undisturbed environment. All wildlife found in the central piedmont is represented in the refuge. Mammals you might catch a glimpse of include raccoons, mink, beaver, muskrat, eastern cotton-tail rabbit and white-tailed deer. Farming, timber harvest, water manipulation and prescribed burning are all management techniques used to optimize the preservation of wildlife habitat. The refuge is open year-round from dawn to dusk. Winter months are best for waterfowl viewing.
    Wadesboro (S) is the closest town.

contact: Refuge Manager, Pee Dee National Wildlife Refuge, Route 1, Box 92, Wadesboro, NC 28170; 704/694-4424.

getting there: The refuge office is located on US-52 6 mi N of Wadesboro.

topography: The refuge is relatively flat, with a large portion of it situated on the broad floodplain of Brown Creek. Elevations on the creek are around 200 ft. **maps:** USGS Ansonville.

starting out: A refuge map, wildlife checklist and hunting permit are all available in the main office, open M–F from 8 am to 4:30 pm. If the office is closed, the same items are available at the large display board outside. Visitation to the refuge is very light. Camping is prohibited. Pets are not allowed on the refuge.

activities: Hiking, Mountain Biking.

hiking: Wildlife Drive is a 2.2-mi vehicle or hiking loop that begins at the refuge office and offers excellent opportunities for viewing refuge habitats and wildlife, particularly wading birds. Information boards along the route describe birds of prey, a managed impoundment that is flooded in the fall, wild plants, wading birds, bottomland hardwoods and upland management. Other roads in the refuge are not as well marked. Short foot trails begin at parking areas on the refuge roads. One quarter-mi trail leads to a viewing blind. Hiking throughout the refuge is easy.

mountain biking: There are about 10 mi of dirt and gravel roads in the refuge that can be used as bike tracks. The roads are generally wide and level, with few hills. The best places to start out are at the main office or at the check station on SR-1634. Not all roads are connected. Keep in mind that the refuge is a quiet place intended to provide a stable environment for wildlife.

Morrow Mountain State Park

Located in Stanly County west of the Pee Dee River, 4,693-acre Morrow Mountain State Park is named for the highest peak in the Uwharrie Mountains. Compared to the Blue Ridge Mountains to the west, the Uwharries are an unassuming chain, with a summit that reaches only 936 ft. Once, when these ancient mountains were volcanic islands in a vast inland sea, they reached much greater elevations. Millions of years of weathering, however, have eroded all but the hardest volcanic rocks—basalt and rhyolite. Despite their small size, the Uwharries offer a beautiful mountain environment—summit views can be particularly arresting. On the ground, the park is home to many species of birds, reptiles, amphibians and small mammals. White-tailed deer are commonly seen. In April and May, the mountains put on a brilliant display of color when dogwood and mountain laurel bloom. The park is open

year-round.
Albemarle (W) is the closest town.

contact: Superintendent, Morrow Mountain State Park, Route 5, Box 430, Albemarle, NC 28001; 704/982-4402.

getting there: From US-52, go E onto US-24/27/73. At 1.7 mi continue on NC-740 N. Drive 3.6 mi to Morrow Mtn Rd (SR-1798). Take a R and go 3.2 mi to the park entrance.

topography: Despite their diminished size, the Uwharrie Mountains are characterized by rocky, and sometimes rugged and steep, terrain. Morrow Mtn, the highest peak in the park, is 936 ft. Low point, on the Pee Dee River, is about 280 ft. **maps:** USGS Badin, Morrow Mtn.

starting out: Park maps and brochures can be picked up at the park office. A number of park "pets" are housed in the building, including 3 species of snakes and a snapping turtle. A pay phone is located outside the office. A museum with exhibits on local natural and cultural history is located nearby in a separate building. A road leads to the summit of Morrow Mtn. Restrooms are located there and, in season, at the bathhouse and boathouse, where refreshments can also be bought. A swimming pool and bathhouse are operated from Jun 1 to Labor Day, 10 am to 5:45 pm. There's a small fee for the use of these facilities. There are 2 picnic areas in the park. One is in a beautiful setting at the summit of Morrow Mtn. A large shelter contains a fireplace and picnic tables, with a dozen more tables and grills scattered on the broad summit. Water fountains and restrooms are nearby. The other picnic area, also with shelter, tables, and grills, is located beside the swimming area and bathhouse. Use of all shelters is free, unless advance reservations are requested.

Park regulations do not permit alcohol. Pets must be kept on a leash.

activities: Hiking, Camping, Canoeing/Kayaking, Fishing.

hiking: The park's trails offer an opportunity to examine the volcanic rock formations of the Uwharrie Mountains, enjoy scenic vistas of rivers and countryside and perhaps encounter some of the region's wildlife. Hikers have their choice of more than 31 mi of trails; of these, roughly half are bridle trails, open to both hikers and equestrians. 9 hiking trails range from easy 0.5-mi nature trail loops to moderate to strenuous 3- and 4-mi climbs that pass over the park's 4 main summits. The bridle trail is a single loop that follows closely much of the park's border. All park trails are easy to locate and follow. Hiking trails are blazed with yellow dots, bridle trails with red dots. Trailheads are clearly signed and are found in 3 locations: at the horse trailer parking lot, the boathouse and the bathhouse. Where necessary, trails are improved with footbridges.

camping: There are 3 separate camping facilities in the park—a tent and RV campground, a primitive group campground, and a backcountry camping area.

The 106-site car campground is laid out in 3 loops on a wooded hillside. Each loop has a shower/restroom facility with hot water. Sites are fairly large, though the sparse tree cover means you'll have limited privacy. Each site includes a picnic table and fire ring. The fee is $9/night. Firewood can be bought in the park. The campground is open year-round, with water turned on Mar 15–Dec 15. Pit toilets are available in winter.

The 4-site backcountry camping area is reached by an easy 1.7-mi hike. The sites are in a remote area, and are spaced far apart from each other. The only facility in the area is a pit toilet. All supplies, including water, must be packed in. Fires are not allowed. A primitive camping permit, available at the park office, is necessary before heading out.

A 6-site camping area is available for organized groups. The sites, which are side-by-side, are located on a loop gravel road that begins near the boathouse parking lot. Each site contains picnic tables and a fire ring. There are pit toilets and water spigots centrally located. Sites cost $1/night/person, with a $5 minimum. Reservations are required, with at least one month's advance notice recommended.

For a less self-sufficient overnight, you can rent 1 of 6 vacation cabins that are available between Apr 1 and Nov 1. Each cabin has 2 bedrooms, a living room and a kitchen. Each can accommodate 6 people. In summer, cabins must be rented by the week, while in spring and fall they can be rented by the night, with a 2-night minimum. Applications, accepted for the year after Jan 1, must be made on a form supplied by the park. Pets are not allowed in the cabins.

canoeing/kayaking: The wide, slow-moving waters of the Yadkin and Pee Dee Rivers and Lake Tillery that front the park are ideal for leisurely paddling. These bodies of water form the park's 5-mi E border. The 2 rivers, which flow N to S, are actually 1; the name changes at the jct with the Uwharrie River. This jct also marks the end of the Yadkin River Trail, a 165-mi canoe trail that begins near the W Kerr Scott Reservoir. Badin Lake is only several miles N of the park, but Badin Dam and Falls Dam must be portaged to reach it. Inside the park, boats can be launched from the boat ramp located at the end of the park road. If you don't bring your own boat, you can rent a canoe from the park between Jun 1 and Labor Day between the hours of 10 am and 5:30 pm. The fee is $2.50/hr for the first 2 hrs and $1/hr for each additional hr. All park-owned boats must be off the water by 5:45 pm.

fishing: The easiest way to get to the fish in the Pee Dee River and Lake Tillery is to put a boat on the water at the park boat ramp. The other possibility is to cast from the trails that run beside the river. Approx 1 mi of the river is accessible in this manner. The trails begin at the boathouse parking lot. Primary species of game fish are largemouth, striped and white bass, crappie, bluegill and perch.

Uwharrie National Forest

The Uwharrie National Forest occupies almost 50,000 acres in a patchwork of holdings that spread out across 3 counties—Montgomery, Randolph and Davidson. The Birkhead Mountains Wilderness, established in 1984, covers 4,790 acres at the National Forest's northern end. The Uwharrie region is dominated by forested rolling hills and the Yadkin and Pee Dee, a pair of large rivers (they're actually 1 river with 2 names) which flow south along the western boundary of the National Forest and are separated by Badin Lake. The rolling hills that dominate the local terrain are actually mountains, or, more correctly, the remnant core of ancient mountains. Geologically, their significance is as the mountains that are most likely the oldest (dating back more than 550 million years) on the North American continent. The foundation of volcanic rock which remains—hyolite and andesite—has been exposed by the millennia of weathering that have worn down and carried away the rest of the mountains. Of more recent historical interest is the fact that the Uwharries were the site of the first gold rush in the United States. Gold was first found near the Uwharrie River in 1799; it was mined into this century, though early dreams of quick wealth and the ensuing rush panned out pretty quickly.

Troy (E) and Albemarle (W) are the closest cities. Asheboro (NE) is closest to the Birkhead Mtn Wilderness.

contact: District Ranger, US Forest Service, Route 3, Box 470, Troy, NC 27371; 910/576-6391.

getting there: US-220 provides the primary access from the E; NC-24/27 cuts across the S half of the NF, and NC-49 runs along the N boundary. The ranger station is located on NC-24/27 2 mi E of Troy and 5 mi W of Biscoe.

topography: Rolling hills characteristic of the Piedmont and the small creeks that drain them are the major features of the terrain of Uwharrie NF. The Yadkin/Pee Dee River is the region's major waterway. Elevations on the NF do not exceed 1,000 ft. **maps:** see below under separate listings.

starting out: You can buy NF and USGS-FS topo maps at the ranger station. Hours are M–F 7:30 am–4:30 pm; Sa (May to Nov only) 10 am–3 pm. If the office is closed, an information board outside displays a map of the NF and provides several brochures. Signboards that display the NF map can also be found at the major trailheads and camping areas.

activities: Hiking, Camping, Canoeing/Kayaking, Fishing.

hiking: There are nearly 50 mi of hiking trails on the NF. Trails are concentrated in 2 areas: along the *Uwharrie Trail* and in the Birkhead Wilderness.

camping: Numerous opportunities exist for camping on the Uwharrie NF. These include a developed car campground, 5 primitive campgrounds with vehicle access, a group campground and backcountry camping almost anywhere on the NF.

canoeing/kayaking: Paddlers have their choice of Badin Lake or the Uwharrie River. Overnight trips are possible on both, with water-

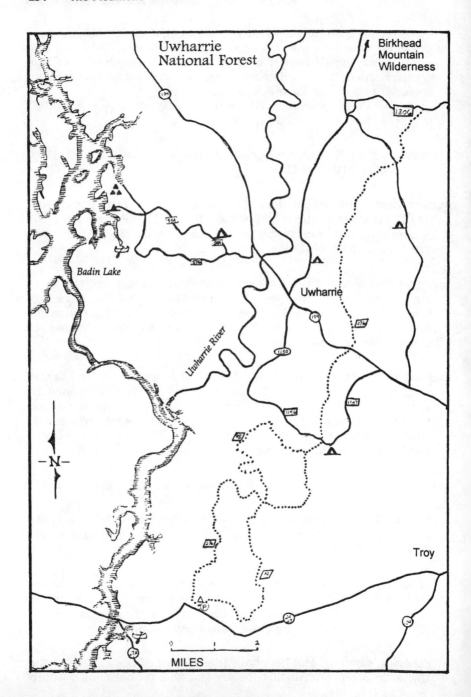

side primitive camping allowed on NF lands.

fishing: Most fishing activity is on Badin Lake, which can get pretty busy during the summer season. Bass tournaments are held on the lake from spring to fall. A more remote option is the Uwharrie River, accessible to waders and small boats.

Badin Lake Area

Although located at the western edge of the National Forest, Badin Lake is the center of recreation in the area. The 5,350 acre lake draws crowds of boaters, anglers and swimmers on warm spring and summer weekends. Created when the Badin Dam was built on the Yadkin River, the lake occupies a floodplain that stretches out in two main branches and is dotted with numerous small islands. The lake's eastern shore is the most heavily developed area on the National Forest, with several campgrounds, a boat ramp, picnic and swimming area, and a network of ORV trails. Despite its popularity, opportunities do exist to escape the crowds, both on land and on the water.

Badin (S) is the closest town.

getting there: From the community of Uwharrie, take NC-109 NW 1.6 mi to FR-1153. Turn L and go 0.4 mi to FR-576. Turn R and follow FS signs roughly 4 mi to either the campground or boat launch.

topography: Elevation on Badin Lake is about 300 ft. The E shore rises on gentle slopes forested with pines and hardwoods. **maps:** USGS-FS Badin, New London.

starting out: There's a picnic area at the Cove Boat Ramp on FR-597B that includes about a dozen picnic tables and grills in a large clearing beside the lake. Vault toilets are also here. With ORV trails, 2 campgrounds, and lake activities, this is typically the busiest part of the NF.

activities: Camping, Canoeing/Kayaking, Fishing, Hiking.

camping: Campers have their choice of 3 different campgrounds in the area. Substantial improvements to the area will be made in the next few years. A new campground will be completed by early

1996 and there are plans to pave some of the forest roads.

A 37-site car campground is in the general vicinity of the lake. Sites are bunched closely together in 2 loops. Each of the small sites has a picnic table and grill. The campground is in a wooded area not far from the Cove Boat Ramp and picnic area. Vault toilets and water are centrally located. Sites cost $5/night. The campground is open all year.

Nearby is the Uwharrie Group Camp. It features 3 sites, each of which can accommodate 15-20 people. Each site has picnic tables, grills, water pump and tent pads, with centrally located vault toilets. The fee is $10/night. Reservations, which can be made at the RS, are required. Also open year-round.

For slightly more primitive camping, there's the 8-site Uwharrie Hunt Camp. The camp is in an open rectangular clearing with sites spaced fairly close together. Each one comes with a picnic table, grill, tent pad and lantern post. Vault toilets and water are also at the camp. It's located at the jct of FR-1153 and FR-576 on the way to Badin Lake. Vehicles are parked in a single adjacent lot. There's no fee to camp.

Backcountry camping is allowed throughout the NF; best sites in this area are along the lakeshore.

canoeing/kayaking: Although Badin Lake can get pretty crowded with powerboats on warm weekends, the lake's 2 main branches and numerous coves are popular with paddlers too, particularly canoeists. The lake has a scenic shore covered with hardwoods and pines. There's also the chance of seeing bald eagles, which live on the lake. There are some good undesignated backcountry campsites along the lakeshore. Put-in is at the Cove Boat Ramp. There's also a WRC launch site on SR-1158.

fishing: Fishing is extremely popular on Badin Lake. There's ample opportunity to bank fish, either at the Cove picnic area or along 3 mi of the *Badin Lake Trail*. Most anglers, however, fish from a boat. The lake supports populations of many Piedmont game fish, including largemouth, white and striped bass, crappie, white perch and catfish. Bass tournaments are held at the lake on weekends during the warm months.

hiking: *Badin Lake Trail* (#94) is an easy 3-mi trail that follows the lake's E shore. The trailhead is at the Cove Boat Ramp. The trail is irregularly blazed but easy to follow, as the path is well-worn from use. Another access is at the Badin Lake Campground.

Uwharrie Trail Area

The *Uwharrie Trail* follows a north–south direction for 20 miles east of the Uwharrie River. It roughly parallels the river's course, but at a distance of several miles. The river forms the western boundary of this area, cutting it off from the major ridges of the Uwharrie Mountains. The forest that covers the gentle hillsides and narrow valleys are covered with a second-growth deciduous/pine forest that is slowly recovering from the poor land management practices of the earlier part of this century and last. Most of the land in this area is still in private hands; NF lands form a checkerboard corridor along either side of the trail.

Troy (E) and Albemarle (W) are the closest cities.

getting there: To reach the S trailheads for the *Uwharrie Trail* and *Dutchman's Creek Trail* take NC-24/27 11.7 mi W from the RS. The parking area is R. Additional trailheads for the *Uwharrie Trail* are on NC-109 5.8 mi NW of downtown Troy, and on SR-1306 1.7 mi E of Ophir and SR-1303.

topography: Elevations along the trail reach 732 ft on Dennis Mtn. The mild rolling terrain is blanketed with pine/hardwood forest. **maps:** USGS-FS Morrow Mtn, Lovejoy, Badin, Eleazer, Troy.

starting out: This mid-section portion of the NF receives the majority of hiking and backcountry camping activity. Facilities include pit toilets at the several campgrounds, but water is scarce. NC-109 cuts the area in half, with the small community of Uwharrie providing minimal services.

activities: Hiking, Camping, Canoeing/Kayaking, Fishing.

hiking: Nearly 30 mi of hiking trails wind through the mountains and hollows E of Badin Lake. This central section of the NF features its longest trail—the 20.5 mi *Uwharrie Trail* (#276), a National Recreation Trail. Along its N–S route several shorter trails branch off, forming connections to primitive camping areas. One other long trail, the 10-mi *Dutchman's Creek Trail* (#98), is also in the area. It begins at the same trailhead as the *Uwharrie Trail* and crosses it twice, making loops of various lengths possible. At the E edge of the NF, *Denson's Creek Trail* (#97) begins behind the RS. It's a 2.5-mi loop trail with interpretive posts and signs identifying tree and plant species. These trails are all somewhat similar, in that hiking is easy to moderate and they follow well-travelled dirt footpaths through the mixed forest of pines and deciduous trees that blanket the mountains. The trails are blazed, and improvements include footbridges and benches. Trailheads are signed.

camping: Backcountry camping is permitted throughout the NF, except where posted. In addition, there are 4 primitive camping areas in the general vicinity of the *Uwharrie Trail*. These primitive campgrounds are listed from S to N along the trail.

Wood Run Camp is located in a small field off of FR-517, a closed FS road that can be used as an alternate hiking trail. The area can be reached by hiking 2 mi on the road or on the *Uwharrie Trail* from its S trailhead on NC-24/27. The campsite has no facilities.

West Morris Mtn Hunt Camp is a recently constructed campground with 14 sites arranged around a gravel road that forms a loop through a mixed pine and hardwood forest. Each site has a picnic table, grill, tent pad and lantern post. 2 vault toilets are centrally located. The *Uwharrie Trail* can be reached via a 2-mi spur trail. If all 14 sites of the new campground are occupied, campers can still use a handful of sites which are in an adjacent area that was the former campground. These sites are more primitive, lacking any improvements. To reach either site, take Ophir Rd (SR-1303) 1.1 mi N of its jct with NC-109 in the community of Uwharrie. Turn R at a crossroads onto an unmarked gravel road.

Yates Place Camp is in a large grassy meadow in a forest clearing near the *Uwharrie Trail*. The only facility is a pit toilet. To get there by vehicle, take NC-109 2.9 mi SE from Uwharrie to FR-1147. Turn R and go 1.8 mi to rugged, gravel FR-1146. The camp is 0.6 mi ahead.

East Morris Mtn Camp is an undeveloped primitive camping area. There are half a dozen single-site clearings on either side of a rough dirt road that leads to a half-acre clearing. Privacy is minimal, unless none of the sites is occupied. There are no facilities. To get there take NC-109 4 mi from downtown Troy. Turn R onto Tower Rd (SR-1134) and go 3.9 mi to an unsigned dirt road L. Sites are along the short road.

canoeing/kayaking: The Uwharrie River heads up N of the NF near High Point and flows S through its central section E of the Uwharrie Mtns before emptying into Lake Tillery on the Pee Dee River. The scenic 35-mi stretch below NC-49 is suitable for running in spring and fall. The narrow, winding river contains class I-II water, with many flat stretches. There's one dam that must be portaged. The bridge on NC-49 above the NF is the most popular put-in; it's a 2-day trip from there to the river's mouth, with camping permitted along the river on NF land. Other put-ins are located along the state and forest roads that cross the river in the NF. The take-out is across lake Tillery at Morrow Mountain SP, or 6 mi S on the lake at the boat ramp on NC-24/27.

fishing: As an alternative to Badin Lake, the Uwharrie River is less crowded and more scenic. Fishing is from a small boat or by wading. Species caught include striped, white and largemouth bass, with a small population of smallmouth bass. Bluegill, pickerel and catfish are also present.

Birkhead Mountain Wilderness

The Birkhead Mountain Wilderness is a remote region of rolling hills and small creeks. Formerly settled and farmed, the area is now being allowed to slowly regenerate itself to a pristine natural state. The wilderness covers 4,790 acres of upland forest in the northern corner of the National Forest. The Birkhead Mountains take their name from the man who owned and farmed much of this land at the turn of the century. Evidence of settlement—crumbling chimneys, foundations and abandoned cabins—can still be seen in the Birkheads.

Asheboro (NE) is the closest city.

getting there: From the community of Uhwarrie on NC-109, turn N onto Ophir Rd (SR-1303) across from the fire station. Go 8 mi to Lassiter Mill Rd (SR-1107). Turn R and go 4.9 mi to a FS sign and gravel FR-6532. Turn R and go 0.8 mi on the narrow, single-track road to the trailhead and parking area.

topography: Elevations in the wilderness are between 950 ft on Cedar Rock Mountain and 450 ft along Robbins Branch. **maps:** FS Birkhead Mountain Wilderness; USGS-FS Eleazer, Farmer.

starting out: The Birkheads have only recently been designated as a wilderness area. The area is slowly recovering from decades of abusive logging practices, but scars from the recent past remain abundant. The FS prints a good topo map and guide to the wilderness ($3). It's available at the RS.

activities: Hiking, Camping.

hiking: 3 trails wind through 10 mi of upland hardwood forest in the wilderness. The trails are similar in character, and are all easy to moderate to hike. Trails are irregularly blazed or not at all in many places, though trail jcts are signed. Trails are relatively easy to follow, though it's still a good idea to carry a topo map and compass. All 3 trails can be reached from the single trailhead above.

camping: There are no developed camping facilities in the wilderness. Backcountry camping is allowed throughout the area.

Weymouth Woods Sandhills Nature Preserve

The first officially designated state-owned natural area, Weymouth Woods was created in 1963 to protect from logging a longleaf pine forest, donated to the state by its owner's widow. The 676-acre preserve is oriented toward observation and study, with hiking the only recreation activity available. Plant communities found in the preserve range from dense hardwood swamps of bald cypress, black gum and abundant mosses and ferns to sandy uplands of longleaf pine and turkey oak. 260 species of birds, including the endangered red-cockaded woodpecker, and animal species such as the red fox, long-tailed weasel, white-tail deer and tree frog, all dwell in the preserve. The preserve is open year-round. Hours are as follows: Apr to Oct: M–Sa 9 am to 7 pm; Nov–Mar: 9 am to 6 pm; Su, Noon to 5 pm year-round.

Southern Pines (NW) is the closest town.

contact: Superintendent, Weymouth Woods Sandhills Nature Preserve, 400 North Fort Bragg Rd, Southern Pines, NC 28387; 910/692-2167.

getting there: From US-1 in Southern Pines turn E onto Saunders Blvd (SR-2053). Go 1.3 mi and turn L onto Bethesda Rd (SR-2074). At 0.3 mi Bethesda Rd becomes Fort Bragg Rd. The nature preserve entrance is L at 1.7 mi.

topography: The sandhills region is relatively flat compared to surrounding parts of the Piedmont. An elevation difference of about 50 ft on the preserve encompasses environments that range from swamp bottom to sandy upland. **maps:** USGS Niagara.

starting out: An interpretive center is located just inside the preserve entrance. In addition to maps and brochures, there are some interesting exhibits on local flora and fauna. Next door is a museum, with more elaborate exhibits, including dioramas of a black-water pond and underground animal habitats, and a 10-minute audio-visual program on the night-time sounds and activities of nocturnal forest dwellers. Restrooms, water fountains and a pay phone are on the premises.

Camping is not permitted on the preserve. Pets must be kept on a leash. No alcohol is allowed.

activities: Hiking.

hiking: A 4-mi network of easy hiking trails provides access to all corners of the preserve, allowing close-up examination of the various habitats present. Trails are wide and well-maintained, with level, sandy surfaces. Improvements include boardwalks and footbridges across swampy areas and streams, benches for rest stops, and a viewing shelter on the boardwalk that passes through the swamp along *Pine Island Trail*. Trails are signed and blazed at regular intervals. Trailheads are at the interpretive center.

Greensboro Watershed Park

The Greensboro Watershed, from which the city gets its water supply, is formed by Lake Brandt, Lake Townsend, Lake Jeanette and Lake Higgins, plus the streams which connect them. The lakes are located about 5 miles north of the city. They're administered by the Greensboro Parks and Recreation Dept for boating and fishing; hiking trails have been constructed and are maintained through the cooperation of the city and private sponsors. The Wilderness Center, Sierra Club, Audubon Society, and Cycles De Oro all sponsor trails. The main park office, which provides information about recreation on and around all of the lakes, is located at the Lake Brandt Marina. Park hours are 7 am to dusk.

Greensboro (S) is the closest town.

contact: Lake Brandt Marina, 5945 Lake Brandt Rd, Greensboro, NC 27455; 910/545-5333.

getting there: Take Lawndale Dr (it becomes Lake Brandt Rd) 5.5 mi N from its jct with US-220 in N Greensboro. The entrance to the marina and the *Lake Brandt Trail* trailhead is L.

topography: Elevation on Lake Brandt is 745 ft. The surrounding lands are typical of the central Piedmont, with mildly hilly terrain cut by small drainages. Elevation gains do not exceed 100 ft. **maps:** USGS Lake Brandt, Summerfield.

starting out: A brochure with trail map and descriptions is available at the marina. It's worth picking up if you're planning on hiking or mountain biking. Also at the office are canoe rentals. Restrooms, water fountain, pay phone and vending machines are there too.

Wading and swimming in the lakes are prohibited, as are water- and jet-skiers. No alcohol is permitted in the park.

activities: Canoeing/Kayaking, Fishing, Hiking, Mountain Biking.

canoeing/kayaking: Fishing from boats is the main activity at the watershed lakes. Although most of the boats are motorized, canoeing and kayaking are fairly popular too. Canoes can be rented at Lake Brandt Marina ($7.50/3 hrs, less for city residents with I.D card). They rent sailboats and rowboats too. You can bring your own boat, but there's a boat launch fee ($6, slightly less for city residents). Despite the popularity of the lake and its urban location, it is reasonably quiet, even on weekends. There are plenty of coves that can be explored without too much distraction or competition from the motor boats. Each lake has its own boat ramp.

fishing: Most people who come to the lakes come to fish. The lakes hold largemouth and hybrid bass, catfish, crappie and bluegill. Fishing is allowed only from boats; no bank casting is permitted.

hiking: 9 trails in the watershed parks cover a total distance of nearly 28 mi. Trails range in length from 0.5 to 5.2 mi, with 3 mi about average. A 10-mi loop around Lake Brandt known as the *Lake Brandt Trail* is made up of 3 connected trails. All other trails must be backtracked. All park trails are signed and blazed and are generally easy to hike, following level terrain with only a small number of short, steep inclines in gulleys. The trails all pass through mixed forest of pine and hardwood on the shores of the lakes and Reedy Creek, which connects them. Occasional sandy stretches of shoreline make good resting places. Trailheads are scattered around the lakes; the highest concentration is beside Lake Brandt Marina, where there are 4.

mountain biking: The 3.7-mi *Reedy Fork Trail* is a single-track dirt trail open to mountain bikes. It passes through low-lying forest on the N bank of Reedy Creek. The trail is signed and blazed. Biking along the trail is easy. The trailhead is 0.3 mi N of the marina on Lake Brandt Rd, next to a small parking area. The trail ends on Church Rd, which forms another trailhead. Mountain biking is not permitted on any of the other park trails.

Hagan-Stone Park

Hagan-Stone is a 409-acre park owned and operated by the City of Greensboro. Located about 5 miles south of the city, it occupies land formerly used for agriculture. Today, about half the park is forested, with the remainder covered by 4 lakes and grassy meadows used for recreational facilities such as picnic grounds, softball fields, and a campground. Several buildings of historical significance—a tobacco curing barn and turn-of-the-century schoolhouse—are also located in the park. White-tailed deer and numerous small mammals inhabit the local woodlands. The park is active in efforts to restore the area's diminished eastern bluebird population; about 40 nesting boxes are scattered throughout park lands. Hagan-Stone is open year-round, from 8:30 am to sunset.

Greensboro (N) is the closest city.

contact: Superintendent, Hagan-Stone Park, 5920 Hagan-Stone Park Rd, Pleasant Garden, NC 27313; 910/674-0472.

getting there: From I-85, take exit 126. Turn onto US-421 S and go 6.7 mi to Hagan-Stone Park Rd. Turn R and go 2.3 mi to the park entrance, R.

topography: Rolling hills characteristize the park's terrain. Approximately half of the park is forested with pines and hardwoods. The other half has been cleared. **maps:** USGS Climax.

starting out: The park office, located near the entrance, doesn't keep regular hours. You can get a trail map and brochure from one of the rangers patrolling the park. Restrooms and water fountains are located at several locations around the park, as are vending machines. Picnic facilities are scattered throughout the park. They include 6 large shelters, as well as additional tables and grills. Each of the shelters can accommodate 60 to 150 people; they must be reserved (910/373-2173) and a fee is charged. There are also 2 softball fields in the park.

Pets are allowed, but must be kept on a leash. Alcohol is prohibited.

activities: Hiking, Camping, Fishing, Mountain Biking, Canoeing.

hiking: There are 8 mi of trails in the park; the longest is a 4-mi loop that follows the park's perimeter. The trails are all easy to hike, and generally follow wide, well-worn paths. Trails are not blazed, but are easy to follow. They are improved with footbridges across creeks. Trailheads—most of which are located at the Trail Center, a redwood structure with exhibits on local flora and fauna located near the park entrance—are signed.

camping: The developed campground is divided into 2 sections: 16 tent sites ($8/night) are spread out in a heavily wooded area, while an open meadow contains 69 closely-spaced trailer/RV sites with hookups ($10/night). All sites include a picnic table and grill. 2 bathhouses with hot water are conveniently located. Water spigots are located throughout the campground. Vending machines are also in the area. The campground gets busy on weekends from Apr to Oct. It's open year-round.

Separated from the main campground by an open field are 2 group campsites in a wooded area. Each site has several picnic table, a grill and fire ring. The walk to the main campground and bathhouse is a short one. Sites cost $2/person/night.

fishing: The 4 park lakes, ranging in size from 2 to 23 acres, are all open to fishing. Bank fishing is permitted on all 4, and boats (pedal boats, row boats, and canoes) can be rented for use on the largest lake. Species taken from the lakes are largemouth bass, channel catfish and bream.

mountain biking: Park trails are open to mountain bikes between Apr and Sep. The wide, well-maintained trails have a smooth, level surface well-suited to bikes. Trails are generally easy to bike. In addition to those in the main part of the park, there are another 2-3 mi of trails on park property located on the other side of Hagan-Stone Park Rd. These trails were developed by a local bike club, and do not show up on the park map. Ask a ranger for directions.

canoeing: The park rents canoes (as well as row boats and pedal boats) at the marina on the largest lake. Rentals are limited to weekends and holidays between Apr and Sep. The fee is $3/hr. Private boats are not allowed on the lake.

Cedarock Park

Cedarock is a 414-acre park operated by Alamance County. With hiking, bridle and biking trails, primitive camping, a frisbee golf course, picnic shelters, volleyball and basketball court, and several historical buildings, there's something for everyone there. Cedarock takes its name from the cedars found in the park and the rock outcroppings that overlook Rock Creek, which meanders slowly through the middle of the park. The creek once provided the power to turn millwheels; evidence of this former local economy is still present in the park. Most of the park is covered with a mixed pine/hardwood forest, which provides a habitat for white-tailed deer, raccoons, squirrels, opossum and wild turkey. Cedarock Park is open year-round from sunrise to sunset.
     Burlington (N) is the closest city.

contact: Alamance County Recreation–Cedarock Park, 217 College St, Graham, NC 27253; 910/570-6760

getting there: From I-85, take exit 145. Turn S onto NC-49 and go 5.8 to Friendship-Patterson Mill Rd (SR-1130). Turn L and go 0.2 mi to the park sign. Turn L onto Cedarock Park Rd (SR-2409) and go 0.6 mi to the park gate.

topography: Slow-moving Rock Creek meanders through gently rolling forested countryside characteristic of the central Piedmont. **maps:** USGS Snow Camp.

starting out: All facilities are located along the park road. You can pick up a trail map and brochure at the park office. Restrooms can be found at picnic shelter #2 and up the road a short distance from the park office. Picnic facilities include 3 shelters with tables and grills, as well as additional tables and grills located at various locations around the park. Picnic shelters must be reserved in advance (910/570-6760). Horseback riding is permitted on the bridle trail that loops around the park's border. A frisbee golf course occupies a large section of the park. There are also a volleyball court, basketball hoops and horseshoe pits.

Alcohol is not allowed in the park.

activities: Hiking, Fishing, Mountain Biking, Camping.

hiking: 6 short hiking trails cover a distance of just over 2 mi. In addition to these, there's a 1.25-mi fitness trail, a 1-mi mountain bike trail, and a 5-mi bridle trail that skirts the park's perimeter. A short ecology trail has 32 stations identifying local flora and fauna. The trails are well-maintained, blazed with color coded posts, and easy to follow. Improvements include benches, footbridges, and graded steep sections. Trailheads are located beside picnic shelter #3, where there's a large signboard with a park map and trail information.

fishing: Anglers have 2 options—a small fishing pond or Rock Creek, which is accessible via hiking trails at several points. The pond supports largemouth bass and bluegill; channel catfish are stocked. Fishing at the pond is from the banks. The creek can be fished from its banks or by wading.

mountain biking: A 1-mi single-track mountain bike trail begins beside picnic shelter #3, where the hiking trails also start. The black-blazed dirt trail is well-maintained and easy to follow, but provides some challenging terrain. Mountain bikes are not allowed on the hiking trails.

camping: There are a number of primitive camping sites that can be reached via the hiking trails. Sites are unimproved and without facilities, with only fire rings left behind by previous campers. A hike of about a half-mi is required to reach the sites, which are located in wooded areas and in a large clearing. A permit, available at the park office, is required. You can register by calling 910/570-6759.

Raven Rock State Park

2,847-acre Raven Rock State Park is situated along 4 miles of the Cape Fear River in Harnett County. The river divides the park into 2 separate sections; most park facilities are located in the larger southern portion. The name of the park comes from the massive crystalline rock—once the nesting site of ravens—which rises 150 feet above the river along a mile-long stretch of its south bank. Just upstream an important ferry crossing on the road from Raleigh to Fayetteville was once located. Remnants of one of the locks and dams—constructed to facilitate river travel and destroyed by a hurricane in 1859—can be seen from several of the park's trails. On land, the forests which were previously harvested for timber are now being allowed to proceed through the stages of succession to full maturity. The park is used primarily for day hikes, nature study and as a stopover for canoeists navigating the Cape Fear River. It's open year-round.

Sanford (W) and Lillington (E) are the closest towns.

contact: Superintendent, Raven Rock State Park, Route 3, Box 1005, Lillington, NC 27546; 910/893-4888

getting there: From US-421, take Raven Rock Rd (SR-1314) N 3 mi through fields of wheat and tobacco to its end at the park entrance. The turn onto Raven Rock Rd, which is marked by brown state park signs, is 6.4 m W of US-401 in Lillington and 17.8 m E of US-15-501 in Sanford.

topography: The 2 sections of the park—split by the river—are geographically distinct. The S section has the more rugged terrain, with the sheer face of Raven Rock rising 150 ft from the river and the upland watershed carved into ravines and ridges by several small creeks. Terrain in the N section rises more gently from a broad, low lying flood plain. The highest elevation in the park is

360 ft. The low point, where the river leaves the park, is about 110 ft. **maps:** USGS Mamers.

starting out: The park office just beyond the entrance is a good place to begin a visit to the park, and a necessity if you are camping. There's a registration board out front where campers must sign in for the night. Park maps are available here, as are brochures that provide information on the area's history and wildlife. Just down the road at the main parking area are a pay phone, restrooms and concession stand.

Rock climbing and swimming are prohibited. No alcoholic beverages are permitted in the park. Pets are allowed, but must be kept on a leash.

activities: Hiking, Camping, Canoeing/Kayaking, Fishing.

hiking: The park's 13 mi of hiking trails are all located in the S section. Distances range from the 0.5-mi *American Beech Trail*, a self-guiding nature trail, to 5-mi *Campbell Creek Loop*. Longer loops of more than 10 mi are possible by combining trails. All of the trails are accessible from the main parking lot and it's possible to hike all of them without returning to your starting point. The trails follow a combination of forest roadbeds and footpaths. All are well-maintained and easy to follow. All are signed at their trailheads and most are blazed with yellow or blue dots. Only the *Campbell Creek Loop* is of moderate difficulty; all other trails are easy, though some climbing of stairs or stepped paths is required. In addition to the hiking trails, there are 7 mi of bridle trails open to hikers. These are located in the N section of the park across the Cape Fear River. Access is on River Rd (SR-1481).

camping: Camping is available at 3 separate areas, none of which are accessible by car. 5 backcountry campsites are located on the *Campbell Creek Loop*, about a 2.5-mi hike from the parking area. Each site has a tent pad and stone fire ring (dead wood may be gathered for fuel). There's a single pit toilet. The fee is $5/night.

A backcountry group campsite ($1/person/night, $5 minimum) is located at the end of *Little Creek Trail*, 2.2 mi from the parking area. There are pit toilets and fire rings. The site accommodates up to 200 campers. Reservations are recommended for this site.

Canoeists or kayakers paddling the Cape Fear River can stop over for the night at any of 6 campsites on the river's S bank, 1.7 mi from the main parking lot via *Little Creek Trail*. Sites cost

$5/night. There are metal fire grills at each site and a single pit toilet. A buoy in the river marks the camping area. Paddlers are encouraged to contact the park office prior to their trip to reserve sites, as well as to check current river levels. If cars are to be left in the park overnight, they must be registered.

canoeing/kayaking: Although canoeing and kayaking are popular on the Cape Fear River and the park provides riverside campsites for canoeists, there is no put-in site within the park. Upstream, the nearest river access is at the bridge on NC-42, 9 mi above the park. This stretch of river is flat, until Buckhorn Dam, which must be portaged. Below the dam, the river varies between long flat stretches and several short class II-III rapids. 6 mi downstream from the canoe camping area in the park, the next put-in/take-out is the WRC access off SR-2016. This entire section of the river is runable year-round. Novice paddlers will want to avoid it during high water, however. The 15-mi stretch of the river from put-in to take-out, with an overnight camp in the park, is an ideal distance for a weekend trip.

fishing: Fishing in the park is limited due to the dense vegetation that crowds much of the riverbank and makes access to the river impossible in most places. Nevertheless, there are a few spots where fisherman can cast for the largemouth and spotted bass, catfish, bluegill and sunfish that inhabit the river. Try the mouth of Campbell Creek or the rocks at the Fish Traps. Boaters will of course have an easier time getting a line in the water. Wading is not a possibility, due to the size and depth of the river.

Jordan Lake State Recreation Area

Jordan Lake State Recreation Area covers a total of 46,768 acres in Orange, Chatham and Wake counties. The area of the lake itself is 13,900 acres at a water level of 216 feet, the top of its conservation pool; at 240 feet, the top of flood control, its area more than doubles. On shore, the State Recreation Area is made up of 8 separate rec areas with a total land area of 5,534 acres. The lake lies on a N-S axis south of Chapel Hill and Durham and west of Raleigh. It was created by the construction of B. Everett Jordan Dam in 1974, along the courses of the Haw and New Hope Rivers, as a means of flood control. Fishing and boating are the main recreational activities on the lake, though with more than 1,000 campsites in 5 rec areas, overnight camping has become a major attraction too. Naturalists are drawn to the area by the bald eagles which nest along its shores. Management of the lake and rec area is divided among the NC Division of Parks and Recreation, the Wildlife Resources Commission, and the Corps of Engineers. All areas listed below are operated by the Division of Parks and Recreation.

Durham (N) and Raleigh (E) are the closest cities.

contact: Superintendent, Jordan Lake State Recreation Area, Route 2, Box 159, Apex, NC 27502; 919/362-0586.

getting there: Primary access to the lake is via US-64, which runs E–W and crosses the lake near its middle. The main SRA office is on the lake's E shore on US-64 1 mi W of its jct with SR-1008 (Beaver Creek Rd) in Wilsonville.

topography: The terrain surrounding the lake is primarily gently rolling countryside characteristic of the eastern Piedmont. Normal lake elevation is about 200 ft. **maps:** USGS Green Level, Farrington, Merry Oaks, New Hill, SW Durham, Chapel Hill.

starting out: A map and brochure of the lake and rec areas is available at the main office and at each of the rec areas. Photocopied maps of individual rec areas showing basic features and giving additional information on the back are available at the fee shacks at the entry to each area. A $3 entrance fee (valid for the day at all areas) is required upon entry daily between Memorial Day and Labor Day and on weekends in Mar, Apr and Sep.

activities: Fishing, Camping, Canoeing/Kayaking, Hiking.

canoeing/kayaking: Boating is one of the most popular activities on Jordan Lake. Happily for the canoeist or kayaker, a large percentage of the boat traffic is sailboats, windsurfers and other non-motorized craft. With 150 miles of coastline, there's ample opportunity to explore the quiet waters of secluded coves and inlets. Many parts of the lake are surprisingly unvisited, even during busy weekends. This is particularly true of the northern parts of the lake, where there's only one boat access. The lake is scenic, with most of the shoreline forested with pines and hardwoods.

fishing: Jordan Lake is one of several highly regarded bass lakes in the Piedmont. Fishing is popular from both boat and shore. Principal game species are largemouth and white bass, crappie and catfish. The fishing has reportedly improved noticeably after a slump in the late '80s.

camping: With the recent construction of additional facilities, Jordan Lake now has more than 1,000 campsites in 5 different rec areas. Options for the camper include primitive walk-in sites, developed car campgrounds and group sites. Reservations are only allowed for stays of 7 days or longer; otherwise, campsites are available on a first-come basis. Campgrounds open 2 weeks before Easter and close around the middle of Nov. One campground (it changes each year) remains open all year.

hiking: Short hiking trails can be found in 3 of the rec areas. Currently, there are only about 5 miles of trails.

Wildlife Observation Deck

Jordan Lake is currently the home to 2 nesting pairs of bald eagles, and during the summer, more eagles are found on the lake than anywhere else in the eastern United States. The Wildlife Resources Commission maintains an observation area off NC-751 on the eastern shore of the lake. A half-mile hike from the parking area along an easy trail is necessary to reach the viewing area. There's a display and information board along the way and a separate short nature loop trail. Other species of birds are frequently seen as well.

Durham (N) is the closest city.

getting there: The parking area is located off NC-751 5 mi S of I-40 (exit 274) and 4.5 mi N of US-64. A brown Wildlife Resources Commission sign marks the parking area entrance.

activities: Hiking.

hiking: The attraction at this area is the possibility of seeing bald eagles and beautiful lake views. The hike to reach the viewing platform is an easy half-mi walk along a wide dirt road.

New Hope Overlook Rec Area

Completed in the spring of 1994, this 871-acre tract is located on the southeastern shore of the lake, not far above the dam. It has boat ramps, primitive campsites and a hiking trail. There are restrooms and a pay phone. Swimming is not allowed. The rec area is open all year.

Moncure (S) is the nearest town.

getting there: From Pea Ridge Rd (SR-1972; mislabelled on SRA maps), turn W onto WH Jones Rd, which ends at the entrance gate 0.3 mi ahead.

activities: Camping, Canoeing/Kayaking, Hiking.

camping: There are 24 primitive walk-in only campsites divided into 2 groups in an attractive forested area beside the lake. Each of the 2 main areas has its own toilet facility. Campsites have a picnic table, grill and lantern post. Cars must be left at a large parking area, from which campers hike to the campsites, a distance of not more than a quarter-mile. Sites cost $5/night. Firewood can be purchased from the rangers, but cannot be gathered or cut.

canoeing/kayaking: There are 6 boat ramps at the rec area from which a canoe or kayak can be launched. Although the campsites are only a short distance from the lake, canoe camping is not possible.

hiking: There's a single easy hiking trail about 1.5 mi in length. The trailhead is just behind the restrooms at the entrance to the boat launch parking area. The trail passes through a pine/hardwood forest above the lakeshore.

Vista Point Rec Area

Located on the west bank of the lake, Vista Point is developed for both day-use and camping. A picnic shelter, sailing beach and hiking trail are all found on the 400-acre tract. For overnight stays, there are 2 group camping areas. A swimming beach in the rec area is for the use of campers only. The area is open year-round.

Pittsboro (W) is the closest town.

getting there: From Griffin Crossroads on US-64, go S on N Pea Ridge Rd (SR-1700) 3 mi until it dead ends at the rec area entrance.

activities: Camping, Canoeing/Kayaking, Hiking, Fishing.

camping: 2 separate group campsites are located at Vista Point; one for tents only, and the other for RVs. Swimming at the rec area is allowed only by campers. Firewood may not be gathered, but can be purchased from the park.

5 tent-only sites are located in a semi-cleared area beside the lake. The sites are close to one another, and a communal atmosphere pervades. Getting to the sites requires a short hike from the parking area. Groups must have at least 7 people. Each site has picnic tables and grills. The fee is $35/night. Reservations are required.

The RV group camping area has 50 spaces; groups must occupy at least 5. Sites cost $14/night.

canoeing/kayaking: There's a boat ramp which can be used for launching canoes and kayaks (and other types of craft), as well as a sailing beach. Paddlers seeking solitude will want to head SW from the put-in to the corner of the lake where the Haw River drains into it.

hiking: An easy 1.5-mi hiking trail circles the rec area. It's signed, blazed with red dots and follows a clearly defined treadway through pockets of level hardwood and pine forest and along the beach. The trailhead is behind picnic shelter #7.

fishing: Fishing is possible from several places on the waterfront. If you're fishing from a boat, you can launch it from one of the boat ramps in the rec area.

Ebenezer Church Rec Area

Ebenezer Church is a popular day-use area with a beach, picnic shelters hiking trails and a large boat access area. The boat ramps are open 24 hrs a day. Either of the 2 picnic shelters can be reserved in advance. Restrooms, change rooms and pay phones are all located at the rec area. The area is open year-round.

Apex (E) is the closest town.

getting there: Ebenezer Church is located on Beaver Creek Rd (SR-1008) 2 m S of the jct with US-64 at Wilsonville.

activities: Hiking, Fishing, Canoeing/Kayaking.

hiking: There are 2 trails in the Ebenezer Rec Area. Both are signed and blazed with red diamonds. The *Old Oak Trail* is an easy 0.9-mi loop that passes through a forest of pine, oak, maple and dogwood. The trailhead is at a signboard near the parking lot at picnic shelter #8. The *Ebenezer Church Trail*, also 0.9 mi and easy to hike, passes by the site where Ebenezer Church stood until it was destroyed by vandals. The trailhead is at the SE end of the beach parking lot.

fishing: Although neither trail passes along the lakefront, fishing is possible from a number of locations within the Rec Area. Try hiking down to the water from behind either of the picnic areas.

canoeing/kayaking: The boat ramps receive heavy use from motor boats during peak periods, making the area a poor put-in. If you do decide to launch from here, paddling E will lead you to some isolated coves at the lake's E edge.

Seaforth Rec Area

Seaforth is a popular day-use area open from April to November. It covers about 600 acres on the west shore of the lake. The main attraction is a swimming beach; other facilities include boat ramps, a separate canoe/kayak launch area, a picnic shelter with tables and grill, and a hiking trail. There are restrooms, change rooms and pay phones.

Pittsboro (W) is the closest town.

getting there: Seaforth is located on US-64 1 m W of the SRA office, just past the bridge.

activities: Hiking, Canoeing/Kayaking, Fishing

hiking: There's an easy 1.5-mi hiking trail that begins at the W edge of the parking lot. The trail is blazed with white bars and follows a well-travelled path through forest stands past several small ponds. Several display boards with information about local wildlife are found along the route.

canoeing/kayaking: A boat access area for canoes and kayaks is located near the S end of the parking lot. Seaforth is located near the busy mid-section of the lake. Weekend paddlers should expect lots of company on the water.

fishing: Fishing is possible from many points along the shoreline of the narrow isthmus on which Seaforth is situated. Boat fishermen can put in at one of the ramps.

Parker's Creek Rec Area

Located off US-64 directly across from Seaforth day-use area on the lake's western shore, Parker's Creek is a 256-site car campground that also includes picnicking facilities with shelters, tables and grills, a small beach and boat ramps (for use by campers only). The rec area covers approximately 1,000 acres. It is open year-round.

Pittsboro (W) is the closest town.

getting there: The access road is off US-64 2 m W of Wilsonville and the jct with Beaver Creek Rd (SR-1008).

activities: Camping, Canoeing/Kayaking, Fishing.

camping: The developed car campground is arranged in 5 loops, with most sites closely spaced in a large wooded area. There are sites with full hook-up ($14/night) and sites with no hook-up ($9/night). Boats can be moored at sites near the water. Each site has a picnic table and grill. Hot-water showers and comfort stations are conveniently located. The campground is open from 2 weeks before Easter to mid-Nov. Firewood can be purchased from rangers; it cannot be gathered or cut.

Poplar Point Campground

Poplar Point is the largest developed campground on Jordan Lake. It has 362 sites with hookups ($14/night) and 216 sites without ($9/night). Sites are arranged in a series of loops and double loops, with many sites on the lakeshore. Each site includes a picnic table and grill. Sites are closely spaced, though the loops are spread out over a wide area, helping make the campground seem less enormous than it really is. Each loop has its own comfort station with showers and restrooms. In addition to the camping facilities, there's a swimming beach, boat ramps and pay phones. Poplar Point is located on the eastern shore of the lake just south of Wilsonville. It's open from 2 weeks before Easter to mid-Nov.

Apex (E) is the closest town.

getting there: The entrance is on Beaver Creek Rd (SR 1008) 0.7 mi S of its jct with US-64 at Wilsonville.

activities: Camping, Canoeing/Kayaking, Fishing.

Crosswinds Campground

Located just N of Wilsonville, Crosswinds Campground has 201 campsites laid out in 3 different lakeside areas. 47 of the sites are tent-only sites with no hook-up ($9/night); 154 can accommodate tents or RVs and have full hook-up ($14/night). Each site has a picnic table and grill. Restroom/shower facilities (hot water) are located at the center of each area. Crosswinds also has boat ramps and a swimming beach. The rec area is open from 2 weeks before Easter to mid-Nov.

Apex (E) is the closest town.

getting there: The entrance is on Beaver Creek Rd (SR 1008) 0.2 mi N of its jct with US-64.

activities: Camping, Canoeing/Kayaking, Fishing.

Harris Lake

Man-made 4,100-acre Harris Lake, whose shape resembles the footprint of a four-toed bird, was created when a dam was built across Buckhorn Creek. The lake's primary purpose is to supply a Carolina Power & Light nuclear reactor with water. The utility company has opened the lake and some of the surrounding land to the public for recreational uses, including boating, fishing and hunting. Approximately 5,000 acres of land have been designated as game lands, and an additional 2,600 acres have been set aside as a wildlife refuge.

The closest town is Apex (NE).

contact: Harris Visitors Center, Route 1, Box 327, New Hill, NC 27562; 919/362-3261 or 800/443-8395.

getting there: From US-1 5.8 mi S of NC-55, take the New Hill Exit. Turn S onto New Hill-Holleman Rd (SR-1127). The Harris Visitor Center is 1.4 mi ahead on the R.

topography: Rolling Piedmont forested with loblolly pines and hardwood species such as white oak and red cedar surrounds most of the lake. Elevations are between 220 and 300 ft. **maps:** A free topo map of the lake and surrounding area is available at the visitors center.

starting out: A box outside the Harris Visitors Center contains topo maps of the lake and surrounding land. Inside you'll find displays on the power plant, additional information about the lake, restrooms, a water fountain and a pay phone. Outside, there's a picnic area with 8 tables in a grove of hardwoods beside the visitors center. The visitors center is open M–F, 9 am to 4 pm, closed holidays.

activities: Hiking, Fishing, Canoeing/Kayaking.

hiking: There's a single hiking trail at Harris Lake. The *White Oak Nature Trail* is a self-guiding trail with numerous plaques identifying plant and tree species typical of the Piedmont. The trail has 2 loops, one 0.5 mi in length, the other 1 mi. Both are well-defined and -maintained and easy to hike. Posts with red or yellow dots mark the routes. Improvements include benches, boardwalks, footbridges, wildlife viewing platforms and a bird blind. The trailhead is beside the visitors center. You can pick up a trail map inside, but won't get lost without one.

fishing: Largemouth bass, black crappie, bluegill and catfish are the primary game fish taken from the lake. Fishing is done from a boat; there's no easy bank access. See below for the location of the boat ramp.

canoeing/kayaking: Despite its size and configuration, which have produced numerous small coves, there are a number of drawbacks to paddling on the lake. Competition from bass boats and other motorboats, a view dominated by a nuclear reactor and rather bland scenery all detract from the pristine natural setting usually sought by canoeists and kayakers. At least the boat ramp is located on game lands, which run the length of that particular part of the lake. This is probably the best area of the lake for exploring the coastline. To get to the boat ramp from the visitors center, go S on New Hill-Holleman Rd (SR-1127) 2.5 mi to gravel Bartley Holleman Rd (SR-1130). Take a R and drive 1.8 mi to the WRC boating access sign. The boat ramp is 0.2 mi ahead.

Eno River State Park

Eno River State Park covers 2,282 acres of land divided into 4 separate sections (Fews Ford, Cabe Lands, Cole Mill and Pump Station) that straddle 11 miles of the Eno River as it meanders along a twisting course through the low hill country of Orange and Durham counties. The river, which begins in the tobacco fields west of Hillsborough and empties into Falls Lake 33 miles downstream, once provided power to 30 mills, 12 of which were located within present park boundaries. 3 of the park's 4 sections are named for families that built and operated the mills in the 17th and 18th centuries. The patriarch of one of these clans, John Cabe, had nine daughters, all of whom reportedly married millers. Ruins of stone dams and old mill sites still seen along the trails and river are visible traces of these early homesteads. The river itself gets its name from one of the Indian tribes that once populated the area. The park is open year-round.

Chapel Hill (S), Durham (SE) and Hillsborough (W) are all within a short driving distance of the park.

contact: Superintendent, Eno River State Park, Route 2, Box 436-C, Durham, NC 27705; 919/383-1686.

getting there: From I-85, take exit 170 onto US-70W. Go 0.2 mi to the brown state park sign; turn R onto Pleasant Green Rd (SR-1567). Drive 2.2 mi, then turn L onto Cole Mill Rd (SR-1569). The park gate is 1 mi ahead. Access points to other parts of the park are on Howe St, Rivermont Rd, and at the junction of Umstead Rd (SR-1449) and Cole Mill Rd (SR-1401).

topography: Rocky ridges of wooded upland drop down to the narrow channel of the river bottom. Highest elevation in the park is 700 ft; low point, where the river leaves the park, is 300 ft. **maps:** USGS Durham NW, Hillsborough.

starting out: The park office just past the entrance to the Fews Ford sector on Cole Mill Rd is a good place to stop for information before heading out onto the river or hiking trails. Pick up a park map and pamphlets on the flora and fauna found in the park. Facilities here include a staffed information center, rest rooms, water fountain and a display case outside that contains maps and information about regulations and park-sponsored events (such as clinics on fly-fishing and birding). Inside the office there's a photo history and exhibit of the region's early settlers and the mills they built. Other activities that are popular in the park are horseback riding and picnicking. Horses are restricted to the power-line easements in Fews Ford. The park has three picnic areas with tables and grills; two in Fews Ford and one in Cole Mill. All are near road accesses.

Alcohol is prohibited. Pets must be kept on a leash.

activities: Hiking, Camping, Fishing, Canoeing/Kayaking.

hiking: The park's 20 mi of hiking trails vary in length from the 0.4-mi *Eno Trace Nature Trail* to the 4-mi *Cox Mountain Trail*. All are well-maintained, blazed with a red dot, and have treadways that are generally smooth and unobstructed. Hiking is easy to moderate; the least strenuous trails follow the river. There are also many miles of unofficial trails, including 2 that follow the river all the way to West Point on the Eno Park. Most trailheads are located at the park office and at the Fews Ford and Cole Mill parking areas.

camping: Camping facilities in the park are very limited, with only 1 group site and 5 backcountry sites, both in Fews Ford. Reservations are required in advance for all sites. The group campsite ($1.00/person/night, 20 people max.) has a pit toilet and fire ring, but firewood must be packed in, as it cannot be gathered from the park. The 5 backcountry campsites ($5.00/night), though at a single location, are nicely secluded from one another on a forest hillside. A single pit toilet is shared by the sites. Fires are prohibited. Water must be packed in for both areas. Getting to the sites requires a hike of not more than a mile.

fishing: The Eno River is a popular fishing spot with local anglers. Among the 56 species of fish that have been observed, a handful of game fish are found. The Roanoke bass (redeye) is native; other species are the largemouth bass, chain pickerel, redhorse sucker and crappie. Many of the hiking trails follow the river, making casting from the banks possible, though difficult in many places due to trees and other plants. By Piedmont standards, the Eno is a small river—about 20-30 ft across in most places. The river is shallow enough for wading.

canoeing/kayaking: The Eno River flows through the park for 11 mi. By paddling standards the river is small, often narrowing to less than 20 ft across. There are 3 canoe put-ins on park land: the first parking lot after the ranger station in Fews Ford; a signed access driveway 0.3 mi from US-70 on Pleasant Green Rd; and at the Cole Mill access. Other put-ins upstream from the park are in Hillsborough and at the US-70 bridge 2 mi E of Hillsborough and 5 m W of the park. The river flows S and E. Fall, winter, and spring are the best seasons for canoeing the river; the water guage should measure between 1 and 3 ft for conditions on the river to be suitable. A recent rainfall is often necessary to bring the water to up those levels. A water level above 3 ft is considered dangerous, while low water can be a problem during dry spells. When the water is up, rapids are class II & III. A single portage (very easy) must be made at Pleasant Green Dam. The last take-out before the river empties into Falls Lake is at the Old Oxford Hwy (SR-1004) bridge, 5 mi downstream from the eastern edge of the park.

West Point on the Eno Park

Laid out on the site of the original West Point Mill community (1778-1942), this busy 371-acre Durham city park offers a combination of historical exhibits and recreational activities. Opened in 1972, the park is operated jointly by the Friends of West Point and the City of Durham. It flanks the Eno River for 1.5 miles between Guess Rd and Roxboro Rd in north Durham, adjacent to Eno River State Park (W). The grassy meadows near the park's entrance are a popular family picnicking spot, and on warm weekends the lower stretch of the river is lined with fisherman. The park frequently sponsors special events, including monthly after-dark hikes ($3) and river trips under the light of the full moon ($12, children $6; call for reservations). An amphitheatre on the north side of the river is the stage for spring and summer concerts. A separate entrance is 0.5 miles north on Roxboro Rd. The park is home to the annual Festival for the Eno, held over the July 4th weekend. The park is open daily 8 am to sunset.

getting there: From I-85, take exit 176 or 177 N. From 177, go 4 mi N on Roxboro Rd (US-501). The park entrance is L at the intersection with Seven Oaks Rd. There's a traffic light and a small brown park sign. From exit 176, go N on Duke St 2.3 mi to where it merges with Roxboro Rd. Continue ahead 0.9 mi to the park entrance, L.

contact: Park Coordinator, West Point on the Eno Park, 5101 N Roxboro Rd, Durham, NC 27704; 919/471-1623.

topography: Wooded hillsides, grassy meadows, and granite bluffs rise from both banks of the Eno. Elevations in the park are between 270 and 450 ft. The river drops about 50 ft from one end of the park to the other. **maps:** USGS Durham NW.

starting out: Pick up a park map and calendar of events at the park office—located in the back of the Greek revival McCown-Mangum house (circa 1850)—before heading out to explore the grounds. The building's interior, renovated and furnished with period pieces, is open weekends only from 1 to 5 pm, as are a restored mill, blacksmith shop, tobacco barn and photographic museum. The last displays the early 20th century photographs and equipment of Hugh Mangum, as well as rotating exhibits by contemporary photographers.

Overnight camping and fires are not permitted. Alcohol is not allowed in the park. Pets must be kept on leashes.

activities: Hiking, Fishing, Canoeing/Kayaking.

hiking: The 3 short trails on the S side of the river which are shown on the park map total 1.2 mi. All are well-maintained, with treadways that are wide and packed hard from heavy use. 2 are blazed, the short (0.1-mi) *Sennett Hole Trail* is not. Trails are easy to moderate to hike. In addition to those, there are approximately 5 mi of unofficial, unmaintained trails, including 2 that follow the river from one end of the park to the other, one on each bank. The trail on the S bank is considerably more difficult than the others, requiring scrambling over rocky bluffs, locating obscure portions of the trail, and crawling through a thicket of downed trees. Either riverside trail can be used as a connector with the Eno River SP across Guess Rd.

fishing: The crosswalk beside the mill and the portion of the stream immediately below it are popular fishing spots with local bait fisherman. For more solitude, hike to the western reaches of the park. The foliage on both sides of the river upstream is dense, making casting from the banks impossible in most places. Wading is OK in some stretches of the river, but frequent deep pools pose a problem. Also, the slow-moving water is very clear, making even slight underwater disturbances detectable by wary fish. The best bet is probably to cast from a canoe. Species taken include the native Roanoke bass, largemouth bass, crappie and catfish.

canoeing/kayaking: A canoe or kayak can be launched at Guess Rd on the park's W border and paddled 1.5 mi to the dam near the E end of the park. Another possibility is from inside the park just above the dam near Roxboro Rd—the river can be navigated upstream to Sennett's Hole. Whitewater in the park is infrequent and low grade. The river channel is broader and flatter here than in the adjacent Eno River SP. For a city park, much of it is remarkably quiet and isolated. Bring a fly rod and lunch and take your time. Fish and turtles are frequently seen in the river's clear water.

Duke Forest

7,700-acre Duke Forest is a private nature preserve owned by Duke University. Forest holdings are spread out in 6 main divisions (Durham, Korstian, Blackwood, Eno, Hillsborough and Haw River) and two smaller tracts (Dailey and Dodson's Crossroads). The large majority of the forest, including Korstian and Durham, (the two largest segments and those most frequently used for recreation), is in Orange and Durham counties, W of downtown Durham and N of Chapel Hill. The forest was established in the 1920s, when the newly formed Duke University purchased 4,700 acres of adjacent farmland and forest. They were placed under the management of Dr. Clarence Korstian in 1931; in 1938 he became the first dean of the university's School of Forestry. Although Duke Forest today serves primarily as a living laboratory in which Duke faculty and students conduct research, it is also a sylvan retreat used for recreation and exploration by residents of Chapel Hill, Durham and the surrounding communities.

getting there: Access to all divisions is at chained gates numbered 1-38. Primary access to the Durham segment is on NC-751. 12 ingresses (1-12) are spaced fairly evenly along the highway between US-70 and US-15/501, with several more S of the overpass. A small parking area is in front of each gate. For the Korstian segment, there are 2 access points on Mt. Sinai Rd (21 & 23) and 3 on Whitfield Rd (24–26). The forest office is in the new LSRC building on Science Dr behind the Physics building.

contact: Duke Forest Resource Manager, A-116 Levine Science Research Center (LSRC), Duke University, Durham, NC 27708 or write to Office of Duke Forest, P.O. Box 90332, Durham, NC 27708-0332; 919/613-8013.

topography: The terrain of the various tracts is similar: gently rolling hills forested with mixed hardwood/pine forests in various stages of succession. **maps:** USGS Durham NW, Hillsborough, Chapel Hill.

starting out: If you're not familiar with Duke Forest, you'll want a map to find the trailheads and navigate the trails. A brochure and 3 large scale maps can be purchased for a small fee from the Duke

Forest office at the above address. The maps are good guides to the roads, trails and forest cover. The forest gets a lot of use from students, who use the wide paths for walking, jogging and mountain biking.

activities: Mountain Biking, Hiking, Fishing.

mountain biking: Duke Forest is probably the most popular mountain biking spot in the Triangle. Riding is along generally well-maintained gravel and dirt fire roads. Most trails are relatively short, though it's possible to work out some longer rides by stringing together a couple of the longer roads. Be aware that many joggers, hikers and walkers use these roads too. Mountain bikes are not permitted on single-track trails.

hiking: A loose network of more than 30 mi of trails covers most sections of the forest. Trails follow gravel and dirt fire roads, as well as some single-track footpaths. Generally the trails are short, though in the largest segments of the forest connections and loops are possible. Traffic on most trails is heavy, due to their popularity for walking, jogging, mountain biking and nature study. Hiking is easy.

fishing: New Hope Creek is open to fishing. The small creek can be waded or fished from the banks on sections where trails run alongside it. Mostly what you'll catch is pan fish, though some bass are present as well.

William B. Umstead State Park

William B. Umstead State Park covers 5,337 acres of pine and hardwood forest upland in the southeastern corner of the triangle formed by Raleigh, Durham and Chapel Hill. The first parcel of park land (5,000 acres) was purchased in 1934 and developed as a project of the depression era Civilian Conservation Corps; the park opened officially in 1937. In 1943, ownership of the land was transferred from the federal government to North Carolina for a fee of one dollar. Technically, the park is divided into two sections—Crabtree Creek (N) and Reedy Creek (S)—though their lands are contiguous. The division is a vestige of the South's segregationist past: in 1950, 1,234 acres were laid aside for black citizens and designated as Reedy Creek State Park. The two parks became one in 1966. With facilities for hiking, picnicking, camping and water-sports, this sizable park today serves as a natural oasis in the midst of an increasingly metropolitan area.

Raleigh (SE) and Durham (NW) are the closest cities. The park is bordered by Raleigh-Durham International Airport (RDU) to the west.

contact: Superintendent, William B. Umstead State Park, Route 8, Box 130, Raleigh, NC 27612; 919/787-3033.

getting there: Access to the Reedy Creek division is at exit 287 on I-40. The entrance to the Crabtree Creek division is on US-70 about 4 mi W of the Raleigh Beltline (US-1). Look for the large brown park signs 1,000 ft from the entrance.

topography: Gently rolling forested uplands are cut by Crabtree Creek, Sycamore Creek and the streams and rills which feed them. Forest cover is a mixture of hardwood and pines. **maps:** USGS Raleigh W, Cary, SE Durham.

starting out: Park maps can be picked up at either of 2 park offices or at an unstaffed information center just inside the Crabtree Creek section. Restrooms, drinking fountains and telephones can be found at the park offices and picnic areas. 2 large picnic areas with tables and grills are located near the main parking lots. The park also has three shelters for group picnics—2 in Crabtree Creek and 1 in Reedy Creek. Reservations are recommended.

Alcohol is prohibited. Pets must be kept on a leash.

activities: Hiking, Mountain Biking, Canoeing, Fishing, Camping.

hiking: Approximately 21 mi of hiking trails fan outward from trailheads at each of the 2 main parking areas. Trails vary in length from short, self-guided nature trails to the 6.5-mi *Sycamore Trail*, with longer treks made possible by connecting 2 or more trails. Although hiking and bridle/mountain bike trails cross between the Crabtree Creek and Reedy Creek sections, cars must leave the park to get from one section to the other. Hiking trails are generally easy, with treadways well-established and blazed with dots of varying color keyed to the park map. There are footbridges at all stream crossings and oversized trailmaps posted at regular intervals mark your progress. Off-trail hiking is favored by the mild terrain and a forest understory that is not particularly dense. This might be an ideal place to bring a topo map and compass and practice your orienteering skills. In addition to the officially maintained trails, there are numerous unmarked spurs. Bridle trails and park roads are open to hikers also, doubling the trail mileage. In the Reedy Creek section, the *Loblolly Trail* becomes the Richland Creek Greenway at the park border, continuing 3 mi to Carter-Finley Stadium on the NCSU campus in Raleigh.

mountain biking: The park lists 17 mi of bridle trails, though their heaviest use nowadays is from mountain bikers rather than equestrians. Most of the trails are actually dirt and gravel roads, with only the occasional single-track. The trails make for easy to moderate biking. Stone bridges add a scenic touch. Park roads not designated as bridle paths are open to bikers as well; hiking trails are not. Access to the bridle trails is on Ebenezer Church Rd (off US-70 a little E of the park entrance) and Reedy Creek Park Rd (accessible from I-40 exit 287).

canoeing: Canoeing is popular on the man-made 55-acre Big Lake, which lies along Sycamore Creek in the Crabtree Creek section of the park. Canoes can be rented at lakeside for $2.50/hr for the first 2 hrs and $1 for each additional hr. Canoes are available daily during summer and on weekends in spring and fall. Private boats are not allowed on the lake.

fishing: Fishing is permitted on the 3 park lakes—Big Lake, Reedy Creek Lake and Sycamore Lake. Big Lake can be fished from a rowboat or canoe (rented from the park) or from its banks; the other 2 lakes must be fished from their banks. Species commonly taken are largemouth bass, bluegill, crappie and sunfish. The streams that connect the lakes are open to fishing as well.

camping: The park offers a number of camping options. There's a car campground with 28 sites open Th–Su between Mar 15 and Dec 15. Each site includes a picnic table and grill. A shower/restroom facility with hot water is centrally located. Sites are $9/night.

Organized groups have a choice of 6 different locations. There are 2 primitive campgrounds reserved for groups. One is a tent camp that can accommodate 24 campers. Facilities include pit toilets and drinking water. The other option is the Maple Hill

Lodge, which can house about 20 people. The lodge has a fireplace, drinking water, and pit toilets. The fee for both these areas is $5/night or 50¢/person, whichever is greater. Reservations are required for both areas.

In addition to the above, there are four group camps that consist of a mess hall, dining area, cabins and washhouses. These camps are available from Apr 1 to Oct 31. The camps are rented on a weekly basis in the summer, and daily during spring and fall. Groups using these camps have swimming privileges in Sycamore and Reedy Creek Lakes. Call for prices and reservations.

Falls Lake State Recreation Area

Man-made Falls Lake was created in 1981 when the Army Corps of Engineers built a dam across the Neuse River north of Raleigh to assist in flood control. The long, serpentine lake that resulted covers 12,000 acres along a 22-mi course between the dam and the Eno River. The lake and approximately 26,000 acres of surrounding land have been designated as part of the Falls Lake State Recreation Area, which is managed cooperatively by the North Carolina Division of Parks and Recreation, the Wildlife Resources Commission and the Army Corps of Engineers. With its central location on the eastern side of the Triangle, Falls Lake is one of the busiest recreational lakes in the Piedmont, particularly during spring, summer and fall weekends. Facilities for boating, swimming, camping, picnicking and fishing are located at a number of rec areas on the lake's shore. All rec areas are open year-round, with the same hours as the state parks.

Raleigh (S) and Durham (W) are the closest cities.

contact: Falls Lake State Recreation Area, 13304 Creedmoor Rd, Wake Forest, NC 27587; 919/676-1027.

getting there: Primary access to the lake and rec areas is on NC-98, which parallels the lake's S shore. The main office is located on US-50 1.7 mi N of the jct with NC-98 and just S of the bridge that crosses the lake. Directions to individual rec areas are given below.

topography: The land surrounding the lake is typical of the Piedmont: gently rolling hills are blanketed with a second-growth forest of pines and hardwoods. **maps:** USGS NE Durham, Creedmoor, Bayleaf, Wake Forest.

starting out: A $3 entrance fee is charged at each of the rec areas daily from Memorial Day to Labor Day and on weekends in Apr, May and Sep. This fee is transferable among all rec areas. Maps and brochures—of the lake and of each rec area—are available at the main office or at the entrances to the various rec areas. Restrooms, pay phones and water fountains are located at the main office and at each of the rec areas. Ample opportunities exist at the lake for water sports such as swimming, windsurfing, and waterskiing. Both Rolling View and Beaverdam have swimming areas, as does Sandling Beach, located off NC-50 across from Beaverdam. On land, there are facilities for picnicking at all of the rec areas.

Alcohol is prohibited. Pets are not allowed in swimming areas; elsewhere they must be kept on a leash. Swimming is not allowed outside of designated areas.

activities: Canoeing/Kayaking, Fishing, Camping, Hiking.

canoeing/kayaking: Falls Lake receives as much boat traffic as any lake in the area. Although motorboats predominate, the elongated shape of the lake and the many fingers that stretch out from its main course create numerous sheltered coves where paddlers can escape the often crowded main channel. The portion of the lake above Beaver Dam is closed to motorboats, and is therefore popular with canoeists. There are more than half a dozen boat ramps on the lake.

fishing: Outstanding fishing is what draws most people onto the water at Falls Lake. The lake is actively managed to maintain healthy levels of game fish and the food that supports them. A program of regular stocking supplements the natural population. Principal catches are largemouth bass, bluegill, catfish and crappie. Although most fisherman use a boat, there are a number of piers and places along the shore at Falls Lake from which fishing from land is possible.

camping: Compared to the other Piedmont recreational lakes, camping facilities at Falls Lake are limited, though recent and planned future construction is helping to remedy the situation. There are currently 3 camping facilities on the lake. Rolling View

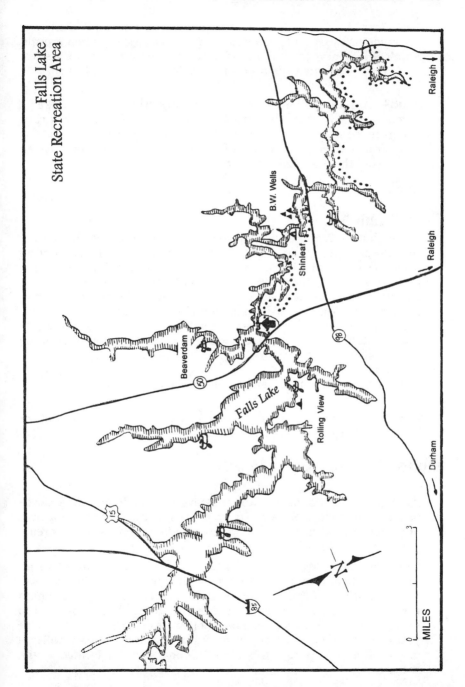

Falls Lake
State Recreation Area

Rec Area has a 117-site developed campground that can accommodate tent and trailer campers as well as organized groups. Shinleaf is a new tents-only primitive campground with 90 sites. B.W. Wells—also new—is a group camping area with 14 sites.

hiking: Although there's only one hiking trail at Falls Lake, it covers a considerable amount of ground. The *Falls Lake Trail* runs along the southern perimeter of the lake for almost 20 miles. The trail and a narrow corridor of land on either side have been designated the Falls Lake Trail SP.

Beaverdam Rec Area

Beaverdam SRA is a developed day-use area on the north shore of the lake near its geographic center. This part of the lake is cut off from the main lake by a dam and is closed to motorboats; as a result the atmosphere here is more laid back and serene than at the other rec areas. Facilities include picnic shelters, a boat ramp, a swimming beach and fishing piers. The 9 picnic shelters with tables and grills can be reserved for the day for $35 (8 tables) or $50 (12 tables). There's also a common use (no groups allowed) picnic shelter. The swimming beach is relatively small, but popular.

Creedmoor (N) and Durham (W) are the closest towns.

getting there: The rec area entrance is located on NC-50 2 mi N of the bridge that crosses Falls Lake.

activities: Fishing, Canoeing/Kayaking.

fishing: Most of the fishing above Beaverdam is done from a canoe or flat boats with motors of 10 hp or less. If you don't have a boat or prefer to cast from land, there are two fishing piers in the area.

canoeing/kayaking: Since this part of the lake is closed to all motorized boats (except flat boats with motors of 10 hp or less), most paddlers at Falls Lake tend to congregate here. Although there isn't a whole lot of room to stretch out in, the crowds tend to be relatively small, even on busy holiday weekends. If you decide you need more open water, an easy portage over the dam will put you on the main part of the lake. The boat ramp is located at the rec area.

Falls Lake Trail State Park

A part of the *Mountains-to-Sea Trail*, the *Falls Lake Trail* currently covers 20 of a proposed 24 miles between the Falls Lake Dam and the entrance to the main office on NC-50 just S of the lake. The State Park designation refers to a 200-foot wide corridor of land on either side of the trail. this narrow strip of land is distinguished from the adjacent game lands, which are administered by the NC Wildlife Resources Commission and on which hunting is permitted. Signs are posted at all trail accesses advising hikers of the potential danger during hunting season (Sep–Feb). Wearing at least one article of blaze orange clothing while on the trail during this period is recommended.

Raleigh (S) and Durham (W) are the closest cities.

getting there: The trail is divided into 10 sections, 8 of which have been completed. Each of these sections has 2 access points, one at each end. The endpoints of the trail are on NC-50 just S of the bridge that crosses the lake (park on the shoulder) and below the dam on Falls of the Neuse Rd, where there's a parking lot.

activities: Hiking, Camping.

hiking: The trail is clearly marked at each access and generally easy to follow. It's blazed with the white dot of the *MST*. The trail runs close by the lake shore, which is frequently in view, for most of its route. Terrain rises gently along the ravines and gullies formed by the lake's drainage, making for easy hiking. The treadway is well-defined and foot bridges cross all sizeable streams. In some of the western portions, the trail follows old forest roads. Despite the many access points and high quality of the trail, it is not very heavily used. You can pick up a map of the trail from the main SRA office on NC-50.

camping: With the recent construction of the primitive campground at Shinleaf, camping facilities are now available along the trail. Located on the E half of the trail, Shinleaf has 89 sites for tent camping. The sites are spread out in several loops in a very large wooded area, maximizing privacy. Each site has a picnic table, lantern post, and grill. There's a pit toilet and water spigot for every 10 sites. Non-hikers can park in a central parking lot and walk 100 yds to a half-mi to the sites. A modern restroom/shower facility is located at the parking lot.

Rolling View Rec Area

Covering approximately 800 acres, Rolling View is the largest rec area on Falls Lake. It's also the most intensely developed. Facilities at the site include a marina, full-service campground, boat ramps, a swimming beach and picnic shelters. With Sandling Beach Rec Area located on the opposite shore, this is often one of the busiest areas of the lake.

Durham (W) is the closest city.

getting there: From NC-98, go NE on Baptist Rd 4.1 mi to the rec area entrance.

activities: Camping, Canoeing/Kayaking, Fishing.

camping: Rolling View is the primary developed campground at Falls Lake. 117 campsites are laid out in 3 loops near the lakeshore. 82 of the sites have water and hookup (14$/night), 35 do not ($9/night). Each site has a picnic table and grill. Comfort stations with hot-water showers are centrally located.

Rolling View also has 4 group campsites ($35/night) which can accommodate up to 25 people each. Group sites have picnic tables and fire rings. Shower/restroom facilities are also in the area. Reservations are required for groups sites.

canoeing/kayaking: Rolling View is located near the geographic center of the lake. As this area sees the heaviest use by motorboats, it's less than ideal for paddlers. If you want to give it a try anyway, there's a boat ramp at the end of the rec area road.

fishing: Anglers at Rolling View have their choice of 2 piers from which to fish. It's also possible to find an open spot along the shore. The more typical method, however, is to put a boat on the water at one of the boat ramps.

Shinleaf Rec Area

Shinleaf is a primitive campground recently constructed on the lake's south shore. The campground has been designed to accommodate backpackers hiking the *Falls Lake Trail.* More sedentary campers can park their cars at the large central parking area and walk a short distance to one of the sites.

Raleigh (S) and Durham (W) are the closest cities.

getting there: From NC-98, turn N onto New Light Rd (SR-1907) and go 0.6 mi to the entrance, R.

camping: Campers who like backcountry settings will find Shinleaf the most amenable campground on the lake. The 89 sites are spread over a vast area blanketed with a young forest of pines and hardwoods. You have the option of arriving at the campground on the *Falls Lake Trail* or by automobile. The sites are widely spaced (many are not even in view of each other) and have a picnic table, lantern post and grill. A pit toilet and water spigot are available for roughly every 10 sites. If you park in the central parking area, sites are located up to a half-mi away. The campground is open year-round.

B.W. Wells Group Camping Area

B.W. Wells is a new, attractively landscaped rec area reserved for the use of large groups. Facilities include a developed group campground and boat ramps. It's located on the lake's north shore, roughly opposite Shinleaf. Swimming at the rec area is not permitted.

Raleigh (S) and Durham (W) are the closest cities.

getting there: From NC-98, turn N onto Stoney Hill Rd (SR-1917) and go 1.1 mi to Bud Morris Rd (SR-1918) and turn L. Go 0.3 mi to gravel Bent Rd (SR-1919) and turn L. Go 0.8 mi to the gated entrance to the campground.

activities: Camping, Canoeing/Kayaking, Fishing.

camping: Each of the 14 group campsites at B.W. Wells can accommodate 25–35 people. The sites are located in large clearings amidst pines and hardwoods on attractive hillsides that overlook the lake. Sites are generally well-spaced, permitting a high level of privacy. Each site has approx 5 picnic tables, 10 benches, 3 large elevated grills, a water spigot and 3 lantern posts. 2 large washhouses with toilets and showers (hot water) are centrally located. Sites cost $35/night. Reservations are required.

The campground typically fills on weekends in spring and fall. It's open year-round.

canoeing/kayaking: The boat ramp located in the campground is for the use of campers only. Although located near the lake's center, this area is generally less crowded than that around the large developed rec areas to the W.

fishing: Anglers can cast from the shore or launch a boat from the ramp. Because the campground is only open to campers, crowds are not really a problem.

Clemmons Educational State Forest

Clemmons Educational State Forest occupies a 307-acre tract of land between Raleigh and Clayton. The primary purpose of the forest is educational; there are exhibits on Piedmont ecology as well as forest management techniques. The forest's short trails are intended to acquaint the visitor with the various aspects of forestry. Other educational aids are numerous information boards, several amphitheaters and a forestry exhibit center. The forest's small size make it well suited to day visits. The forest is open from mid-March to mid-November.

Raleigh (NW) and Clayton (E) are the closest towns.

contact: Clemmons Educational State Forest, 2411 Old U.S. 70 West, Clayton, NC 27520; 919/553-5651.

getting there: From the W From the E, take US-70 1 mi W of Clayton to Shotwell Rd (SR-1553). Turn R and go 0.8 mi to Old US-70 (SR-1004). Turn L and go 0.8 mi to the entrance, R.

topography: Gently rolling terrain is cut by a couple of small creeks. The hillsides are covered with pines and deciduous trees. Elevations are between 200 and 350 ft. **maps:** USGS Clayton.

starting out: The forest is open Tu–F 9 am to 5 pm and weekends 11 am to 8 pm. A forest map and brochure can be picked up at the forest office. Facilities (restrooms, water) are located at the picnic area. A large picnic area includes about 2 dozen tables with grills. There's also a large double-sided shelter with 2 fireplaces.

Reservations are required for the shelter.
Alcohol is not permitted. Pets must be kept on a leash.

activities: Hiking.

hiking: 3 trails cover about 3 mi of forest terrain. A half-mi *Talking Tree Trail* features recorded descriptions of some of the trees that make up the pine/deciduous forest. A shorter *Forest Geology Trail* is based on the same idea, with rocks describing themselves. A third trail features stations where forest management and harvesting techniques are demonstrated. Trails follow well-designed, crushed gravel paths and dirt single-tracks. Improvements include steps and footbridges. The trails are blazed and easy to follow. Trailheads are located at the main parking area.

Kerr Lake State Recreation Area

One of the largest lakes on the Piedmont, Kerr Lake covers approximately 50,000 acres and has a shoreline of 850 miles in North Carolina and Virginia. The man-made lake was created in 1953 when the Roanoke River was dammed to assist in flood control and to provide hydoelectric power. Another result was the creation of one of the largest, most popular outdoor recreation areas in the state. Kerr Lake SRA consists of 9 separate rec areas spread out over 3,000 acres of land. Facilities at the rec areas include developed campgrounds, picnic areas and boat ramps. The lake sees heavy recreational use, with boating and bass fishing the most popular activities. Several of the rec areas are open year-round, others close during the winter months.

Henderson (S) is the closest town.

contact: Superintendent, Kerr Lake State Recreation Area, Route 3, Box 800, Henderson, NC 27536; 919/438-7791.

getting there: Access to the rec areas on the E side of the lake is from I-85; NC-39 runs up the W side of the lake and provides access from there. The Kerr Lake SRA main office is located on Glass House Rd (SR-1372) at Satterwhite Point. See individual listings below for directions to each rec area.

topography: Gently rolling Piedmont terrain covered with second-growth forests of pines and hardwoods predominates on the shores of the lake. **maps:** USGS Townsville, Middleburg, John H. Kerr Dam, Tungsten.

starting out: The NC half of the lake is oriented in a N–S direction, with SRAs on both the W and E sides. Maps of the lake and individual rec areas are available at the main office at Satterwhite Point and at each of the rec areas. Hours at the main office are M–F, 8 am to 5 pm. Kerr Lake is a popular outdoor recreation area in spring and summer. Fortunately the lake is large enough so that it rarely seems crowded. Keep in mind that the rec areas aren't designed with backcountry travel in mind.

You can fish on the lake with either a NC or VA fishing license. Alcohol is prohibited at all SRAs. Pets must be kept on a leash, and are not allowed in swimming areas.

activities: Camping, Canoeing/Kayaking, Fishing, Hiking.

camping: There are more than 850 developed campsites on Kerr Lake. Each of the rec areas described below has facilities for camping. At all rec areas, sites cost $9/night for tents or trailers; $14/night for sites with hookups.

canoeing/kayaking: Despite the presence of all kinds of watercraft, and its status as one of the major recreational lakes in the state, Kerr Lake is not a bad choice for lake paddling. The lake is so big, and has so many narrow coves and inlets, that it's possible to escape the bass boats and water-skiers, at least for a while. Boat ramps are located at all of the SRAs described below. Paddling conditions are similar near all of the rec areas.

fishing: Kerr Lake is one of the most highly regarded lakes for largemouth and striped bass fishing in NC. Tournaments are held here regularly during the spring and summer months. Other game fish frequently caught are catfish, sunfish and crappie. In general, the best times for fishing are spring and fall. Although most fishing is done from boats, most of the campgrounds have shorelines with at least some portions suitable for casting. A NC or VA fishing license is valid on the lake.

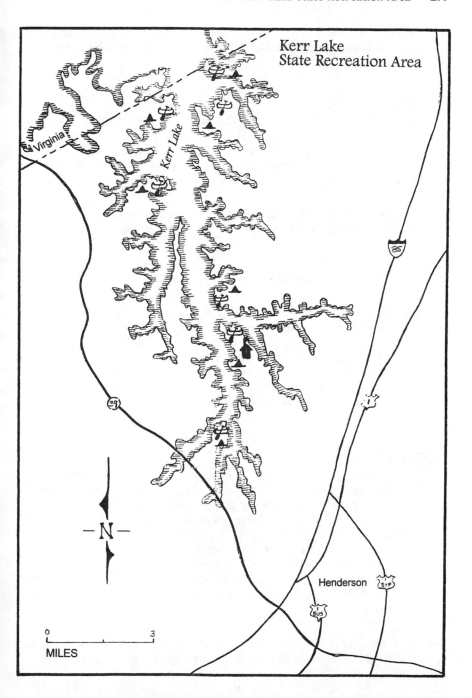

hiking: Hiking opportunities at Kerr Lake are limited. There are short trails at Satterwhite Point, County Line, and Bullocksville.

Nutbush Bridge

Located at the southern end of the lake, Nutbush Bridge is a large developed campground and rec area that covers 363 acres. In addition to the camping facilities, there are 2 boat launches and a picnic area with a shelter, tables, and grills. There's also a pay phone at the site. Open year-round.

getting there: From I-85, take exit 214. Turn NW onto NC-39 and go 4.5 mi to Nutbush Rd (SR-1308). Turn R and proceed 1.3 mi to the rec area.

activities: Camping, Canoeing/Kayaking, Fishing.

camping: 109 campsites are laid out in 4 widely spaced loops. Within each of the loops, the sites are tightly spaced, minimizing privacy. Each site has a picnic table. About half of the sites are on the lake. Fishing or launching a canoe or kayak is possible from these sites. 59 sites, occupying 2 of the loops, have hookups for RVs. There are 3 centrally located hot water shower/restroom facilities with additional pit toilets nearby.

Satterwhite Point

Satterwhite Point covers 282 acres at the southern end of the lake. Facilities here include a developed campground, a boat ramp, 2 short hiking trails, swimming beach and picnic grounds. Inside the campground, there are numerous places from which to launch a canoe or fish from the bank. 3 picnic shelters with tables and grills are spread out along the lakeshore. There's a pay phone at the campground. A separate swimming beach in the area is operated by the Henderson-Vance Rec & Parks Dept. Hours are M–Sa Noon to 6 pm; Sun 1 pm to 6 pm. Satterwhite Point is open year-round.

getting there: From I-85, take exit 217 and turn N onto Satterwhite Pt Rd (SR-1319). Proceed 5.7 mi to the rec area.

activities: Camping, Canoeing/Kayaking, Fishing.

camping: The J.C. Cooper Camp Area has 123 sites, 24 of which have RV hookups. The sites are closely spaced in a lightly wooded area along the lake shore. Each site has a picnic table. There are 2 shower/restroom facilities with hot water. Water spigots are located throughout the campground.

A separate group camping area is located down the road a bit from the main campground. The area has a shower/restroom facility with hot water and picnic tables on the lakeshore.

Hibernia

Hibernia is a 446-acre rec area on the western side of the lake. There are facilities for camping, picnicking and launching boats. A large picnic area with shelters, tables and grills is located on the lakeshore. Fishing is possible from many locations on the shore. A pay phone is beside the ranger station. Hibernia is open year-round.

getting there: From I-85, take exit 214. Turn NW onto NC-39 and go 12.9 mi to Hibernia Rd (SR-1347). Turn R and go 2 mi the rec area entrance.

activities: Camping, Canoeing/Kayaking, Fishing.

camping: There are 150 sites (30 with hookups) arranged in 3 distinct areas. The sites are closely spaced, with most of them fronting the lake. Each site has a picnic table and grill. There are 2 shower/restroom facilities with hot water, with several additional pit toilets.

Henderson Point

Located on the western lakeshore just below the Virginia State line, Henderson Point is a 329-acre rec area. In addition to a developed campground, there's a swimming area closed to all boat traffic, 4 boat ramps and picnic facilities that include 3 shelters with tables and grills. A pay phone is located at the ranger station. Henderson Point is open from May to Oct.

getting there: From I-85, take exit 214. Turn NW onto NC-39 and go 13.8 mi to Rock Spring Church Rd (SR-1356) and bear R. Go 2.9 mi to Reverend Henderson Rd (SR-1359). Turn R and proceed 1.4 mi to the rec area entrance.

activities: Camping, Canoeing/Kayaking, Fishing.

camping: There are 79 sites at the campground, 24 with hookups for RVs. The sites are arranged in 2 large loops, with almost all of the sites located on the lake. A restroom/shower building is located at each loop.

Bullocksville

Bullocksville sits on 455 acres on the eastern shore of the lake across from Satterwhite Point. Facilities in this park-like setting include a developed campground, boat ramp, 2 picnic shelters with tables and grills, a baseball diamond, concession stand and community building. There's a short, easy hiking trail called the *Old Still Trail* in the park. It's blazed with white dots and begins near the ranger station. A pay phone is there as well. There are numerous places in the park where it's possible to fish from the banks. Bullocksville is open from May to Oct.

getting there: From I-85, take exit 223 and turn NW onto Manson Rd (SR-1237). Go 2.3 mi to a crossroads in Drewry. Continue straight onto Bullocksville Park Rd (SR-1366). The rec area is 3.1 mi down the road.

activities: Camping, Canoeing/Kayaking, Fishing, Hiking.

camping: The developed campground has 69 sites, none with hookups. Each site has a picnic table. The sites, most of which are quite large, are spread out along the lakeshore and in a wooded area. There's a centrally located shower house (no hot water) and a couple of pit toilets.

County Line

As its name suggests, County Line Park straddles the border between 2 counties—Vance and Warren. It's located on the eastern side of the lake, across from Henderson Point. Facilities include a campground, boat ramp, small picnic shelter with tables and a grill and a hiking trail. The easy, 0.4-mi trail begins beside the ranger station. It's blazed with red dots. There are limited areas from which to fish on the banks. A pay phone can be found at the campground. The rec area is open from May to Oct.

getting there: From I-85, take exit 223 and turn NW onto Manson Rd (SR-1237). Go 2.3 mi to a crossroads in Drewry. Go R onto SR-1369 and drive 3 mi to Buchanan Rd (SR-1202). Turn L and go 0.7 mi to County Line Rd (SR-1361). Turn R and go 1.2 mi to County Line Park Rd (SR-1360). Turn R and proceed 0.2 mi to the park entrance.

activities: Camping, Canoeing/Kayaking, Fishing, Hiking.

camping: The campground has 84 sites (11 with hookups) spread out along a wide area on the lake. Many of the sites are arranged in small groups, which offer more privacy than the sites at most of the other rec areas. The sites are large, and each has a picnic table and fire ring. There's a centrally located hot water shower/restroom facility, with additional pit toilets nearby.

Kimball Point

Kimball Point is situated on a long, narrow spit of land on the eastern shore of the lake that almost reaches into Virginia. The site only occupies 93 acres. Most of that is taken up by a campground, but there are also 2 picnic shelters with tables and grills, a boat ramp, and a sandy stretch of shoreline suitable for swimming. There's ample room to fish from shore. The views from the area are superb. There's a pay phone at the ranger station. Kimball Point is open from May to Oct.

getting there: From I-85, take exit 223 and turn NW onto Manson Rd (SR-1237). Go 2.3 mi to a crossroads in Drewry. Turn R onto SR-1369 and go 5.2 mi to Kimball Pt Rd (SR-1204). Turn L and proceed 1.3 mi to the rec area entrance.

activities: Camping, Canoeing/Kayaking, Fishing.

> **camping:** 91 campsites are spread out across most of the rec area. Most sites are fairly large; almost all are on the lake. A handful of the sites are located in a grassy, treeless meadow. Each site has a picnic table and grill. There are 2 shower/restroom facilities with hot water.

Medoc Mountain State Park

Medoc Mountain takes its unlikely name from a province in the wine-growing region of Bordeaux in France. Sidney Weller, the man credited with developing the American System of winemaking and a former owner of the land in the park, named the mountain. In the early 1970s, the mountain and surrounding land were chosen as the site for a state park, and in 1975 the 2,287-acre park was opened to the public. It is located at the eastern edge of the Piedmont in the northwest corner of Halifax County. Its proximity to the fall line and the start of the coastal plain is apparent in the gentle rise and fall of the terrain and the slow, flat water of the park's creeks. Even Medoc Mtn, located near the park's center, defies its name: although it's the highest point in the region, it rises only 325 feet above sea level. Lacking spectacular vistas or unusual geology, the park offers visitors instead the opportunity to slow down and look near rather than far, to explore up-close eastern Piedmont ecology, to relax for a day in the woods. After years of cultivation for grapes and various other crops, the forests which today cover the park are gradually returning to a pristine state, though the process is still in its early stages. The park is open year-round.

Henderson (W), Roanoke Rapids (NE), and Rocky Mount (S) are the closest cities.

contact: Superintendent, Medoc Mountain State Park, PO Box 400, Hollister, NC 27844; 919/445-2280.

getting there: The park office is located on Medoc Mountain Rd (SR-1002). From I-95, get off at exit 160 and go W on NC-561 to NC-4/48. Turn L and go 2.2 mi to the jct with SR-1002. Turn R and go 0.9 mi to the park office.

topography: Park terrain is more or less level except for the ridge that rises to Medoc Mountain (325 ft), the highest point in the park. Several drainages which feed the Tar River meander through the park's interior. **maps:** USGS Aurelian Springs, Hollister, Essex.

starting out: Stop off at the park office to pick up a park map and brochure before heading out into the backcountry. Related information is available there as well, and park staff are happy to answer questions. Water, restrooms and a pay phone are on site. A large meadow and shelter are reserved for picnicking. Numerous tables and grills are spread across the grassy meadow and the shelter has a fireplace, water fountain and restrooms. The shelter can be used free of charge unless advance reservations are requested.

Pets must be kept on a leash. Alcohol is prohibited.

activities: Hiking, Camping, Fishing, Canoeing.

hiking: 8 mi of hiking trails provide access to forests, creeks, bluffs and the peak of Medoc Mtn. Trails are relatively short, with lengths that vary from three-quarters of a mi to 3 mi, and are concentrated in the S half of the park. All are well-maintained and easy to hike, with wide, level treadways. Improvements include footbridges across creeks, benches for rest stops and rock steps where soil erosion is a potential problem. Trailheads are signed, and the trails themselves are blazed, though irregularly. The easy, 3-mi *Summit Loop Trail* goes to the top of Medoc Mtn, while 3 trails run alongside Little Fishing Creek. The trailhead to the *Summit Loop Trail* is located behind the park office; all other trails begin behind the picnic shelter at the access off Medoc State Park Rd (SR-1322).

camping: 6 campsites are located in a wooded area off the park road that leads to the picnic shelter and trailheads. Campers must leave their cars in a central parking lot, but the walk to the sites is very short—less than 50 yds. The sites are grouped close together, which minimizes privacy. Each site has a tent pad, grill and picnic table. A water fountain and a modern restroom and shower facility (water off Dec 1–Mar 15) are all located at the parking lot. Sites cost $9/night. Plans are currently underway to bring the total number of campsites to 40, including some with RV hookups.

fishing: Bluegill, redbreast sunfish, Roanoke and largemouth bass and chain pickerel are all found in the slow, shallow waters of Little Fishing Creek. Hiking trails follow the creek for most of its length, offering anglers easy access. There are many points along the banks from which to cast a spinning outfit, though the vegetation is not so sparse that fly-fishermen will be able to cast clear of overhanging trees. Wading, or fishing from the rocky ledges that create several of the creek's riffles, is a good option. Another possibility is to fish from a canoe. The slow water makes it relatively easy to cast and keep a canoe under control at the same time. The river averages about 50 ft across.

canoeing: Perhaps the best way to experience the park is from a canoe as it meanders along the 2.5-mi stretch of the Little Fishing Creek that runs through the heart of the park's S half. The water is slow along the entire course, with only a handful of riffles, making it perfect for novice canoeists or those looking for a lazy float downstream. Water levels are best during the fall; low water during dry spells may necessitate a portage or two. The put-in is at the bridge on Medoc State Park Rd (SR-1322) 0.9 mi from its jct with Medoc Mtn Rd (SR-1002). Take-out is on SR-1002, about 1 mi from the park office. A map and brochure of the canoe trail, produced by Boy Scout Troop 40, is available at the park office.

The Coast

Coastal Region Key Map

1. Lumber River SP
2. Jones Lake SP
3. Bladen Lakes SF
4. Singletary Lake SP
5. Lake Waccamaw SP
6. The Green Swamp
7. Zeke's Island ERR
8. Fort Fisher SRA
9. Carolina Beach SP
10. Masonboro Island ERR
11. Cliffs of the Neuse SP
12. Hammocks Beach SP
13. Croatan NF
14. Theodore Roosevelt SNA
15. Fort Macon SP
16. Rachel Carson ERR
17. Cape Lookout NS
18. Cedar Island NWR
19. Goose Creek SP
20. Roanoke River NWR
21. Merchants Millpond SP
22. Pocosin Lakes NWR
23. Pettigrew SP
24. Swan Quarter NWR
25. Mattamuskeet NWR
26. Alligator River NWR
27. Cape Hatteras NS
28. Pea Island NWR
29. Jockey's Ridge SP
30. Nags Head Woods Preserve
31. Currituck Banks
32. Mackay Island NWR

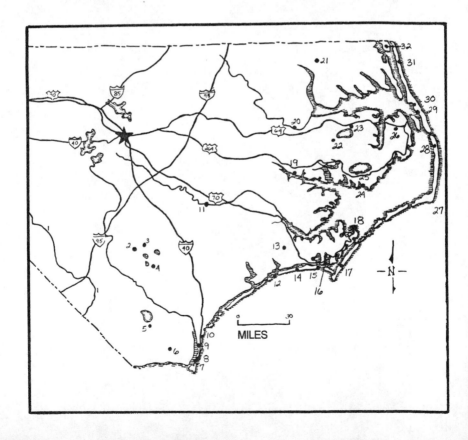

Introduction

North Carolina's coastal region is a large, varied region of barrier islands, shallow sounds and tidal estuaries, swamp forests, peat bogs, blackwater rivers and pine forest. It extends from the Outer Banks to the eastern edge of the Piedmont at the fall line east of Raleigh, encompassing roughly half of the state's total area. Much of the inland area has been cleared for farming, with hogs, tobacco and cotton the major products. Wilmington is the region's largest city, although much of the coast has been developed to accommodate a heavy tourist trade.

The topography of the coastal plain and barrier islands has been shaped over the millennia by the forces of wind, sea and weather. At various times in prehistory the entire region has been submerged beneath the ocean. The dynamism of the past continues into the present. Particularly on the Outer Banks, where the shape and location of the land is part of an unending process of alteration, driven by the implacable power of wind and water.

The Outer Banks stretch the entire length of the state, a distance of 320 miles. Formed when the sea levels rose after the last ice age, these fragile barrier islands are less than a mile across in most places. All share certain physical characteristics. On the ocean side a wide, white sand beach slopes upward to a system of dunes anchored by sea grasses. These dunes provide the shelter necessary for shrub thickets and, in some places, maritime forests, to take root. The inland edge of the islands fronts one of three major sounds—Currituck, Albemarle and Pamlico. Saltwater and brackish marshes are found here, as are tidal flats. The islands include some of the longest pristine stretches of beach on the East Coast as well as some of the most developed.

The species of flora and fauna that inhabit the Outer Banks have adapted to the harsh environment. Vegetation is limited to sea grasses and shrub thickets, with pockets of maritime forest where sufficient shelter from wind and sea spray exists. Species include wax myrtle, yaupon and live oak. The best-known mammals on the islands are the wild horses that live on Shackleford Banks, Currituck Banks and the Rachel Carson Estuarine Reserve. The horses are descended from those owned by settlers of various periods, who left them behind when they relocated to the mainland. Other mammals that live on the islands include raccoons, mice and rabbits. The islands also provide an important habitat for loggerhead sea turtles, who come ashore to lay their eggs during full phases of the moon in summer. The islands' most visible residents are birds, due in large part to their sheer numbers. Hundreds of species, including shore birds, marine birds, raptors and waterfowl, have been recorded on the islands. Some of these species are permanent residents; many more pass through during annual migrations, as the North Carolina coast is located on the Atlantic Flyway.

Across the sounds is the mainland. The coastal plain extends west approximately 200 miles. No less than the barrier islands, this region is defined by water. Through it flow the state's great coastal rivers: the Chowan, Roanoke, Pamlico, Neuse and Cape Fear. These rivers drain the low-lying habitats of the coastal plain, which do not rise to more than 150 feet above sea level. Where the rivers empty into the sounds, fresh water mixes with salt water from the ocean, producing estuaries, aquatic habitats essential to the early stages of many forms of marine life. Near their mouths—and often for several dozen miles upstream—these rivers are tidal, supporting both freshwater and saltwater species. The rivers at this point are also large, with most several miles wide.

The coastal plain is also home to a series of natural lakes known as Carolina bay lakes. These lakes are something of a mystery, as their exact origin is not known. They are most abundant in the state's southeast corner. All share certain characteristics: an oval shape; northwest-southeast orientation; clear, shallow water; a peat and sand bottom; and a sandy shoreline at the southeast end. The lakes are not fed by rivers, but are maintained by rainwater. Lake Waccamaw is the largest.

On land, the major habitats of the coastal plain are cypress swamps, bottomland hardwood forests, upland pine forests,and a type of bog known as pocosin, an Algonquin Indian word meaning "swamp on a hill."

Cypress swamps are found at the lowest elevations—in river floodplains or other natural wetland areas. The swamps are characterized by baldcypresses and the thin veils of Spanish moss that hang from their limbs. They provide habitat for many animal and bird species, among them egrets, herons, river otters, snakes, alligators and white-tailed deer. At one time, a much larger percentage of the coastal plain was covered by cypress swamp and other wetlands than at present. Draining for agriculture and settlement has reduced the area significantly.

The bottomland hardwood forest shares many features with the cypress swamp. They are found along the edges of rivers, thriving in the moist soils of the rivers' floodplains. Characteristic tree species are the baldcypress and water tupelo. Animal species that inhabit the forests are often the same as those in the cypress swamp. The largest tract of bottomland hardwood forest in North

Carolina is along the Roanoke River. In another large forest tract—Alligator River National Wildlife Refuge—the previously eradicated red wolf has been reintroduced.

One unique type of wetland found in the coastal region is the pocosin. These dense shrub thickets grow up on beds of peat associated with Carolina bays, elliptical depressions that dot the coastal plain. The bays get their name from the major plant species of the pocosin: loblolly bay, redbay and sweetbay. These nearly impenetrable plant communities provide a rich habitat for all kinds of wildlife. The black bear is encountered, as are numerous species of poisonous snakes. An extensive system of pocosins exists at Croatan National Forest, where they have been designated wilderness areas.

On higher land, the sandy soil of the coastal plain supports pine forests. Numerous species of pines, among them loblolly, longleaf, Virginia, shortleaf, pond and slash, dominate these forests, though species of hardwoods such as live oak also flourish. Animal species include white-tailed deer, raccoons, the American alligator, and cottonmouth snake. Among bird species, the endangered red-cockaded woodpecker makes its home in the tall trunks of loblolly pines.

Befitting the dominance of water in the coastal region, many of the opportunities for outdoor recreation and travel are centered around one or more bodies of water. On the ocean, sounds, lakes and rivers anglers revel in a diversity of sport fishing conditions that may be unmatched in the nation. These same waters offer canoeists and kayakers a chance to explore a wealth of coastal habitats, including some of the largest undeveloped tracts of waterfront land on the East Coast. Major public holdings are the two national seashores, Croatan National Forest, and 10 national wildlife refuges, managed primarily to preserve wildlife habitat. State parks and the estuarine research reserves preserve smaller tracts of land.

The climate on the coast is temperate to sub-tropical. Summer temperatures frequently reach 90°, while days with freezing temperatures are limited to a couple of months in winter. Although the climate is usually pleasant, the weather can be unpredictable and violent. Tropical storms and hurricanes pound the coast from summer through fall. The damage caused by the severest of these storms is measured in the millions of dollars. In winter, the winds change direction, and nor'easters begin to blow down the coast. Spring and fall are the most pleasant times to visit; summer is peak tourist season at the beaches.

Lumber River State Park

The Lumber River is a narrow, slow-moving, black-water coastal river that begins as Downing Creek on the border of Hoke and Scotland Counties and ends in South Carolina where it joins the Pee Dee before emptying into the Atlantic Ocean. In 1989, the 115-mi stretch of the river in North Carolina was designated a State Park and a Natural and Scenic River. It had already been designated a state and national canoe trail. The river is of rare and exceptional beauty, meandering through bottomland forest and hardwood swamp dominated by baldcypress and water tupelo. The river's floodplain is broadest, and the swampland most extensive, between Lumberton and the NC/SC state line. Wildlife along the river is abundant and regularly seen: white-tailed deer, river otters, turtles, snakes, ducks, cormorants, and warblers are all present in numbers. In addition to the river, the state park has acquired 2,100 acres south of Lumberton. There are plans to build park facilities on these lands.

Maxton, Pembroke, Lumberton, and Fair Bluff are all located near the river.

contact: Park Superintendent, Lumber River State Park, PO Box 10, Orrum, NC 28369; 910/628-9844.

getting there: The following put-ins are listed from the beginning of the state park downstream. Above Lumberton, put-ins are at Turnpike Rd (SR-1412), US-401 and numerous other bridge crossings; Below Lumberton, put-ins are at NC-72, Phillips Rd (SR-2121), US-74, the SP office on Princess Anne Rd (SR-2225), and NC-904 in Fair Bluff.

topography: Flat hardwood swamp and bottomland forest with occasional bluffs that rise 10-50 ft from the river's edge. **maps:** USGS Pinebluff, Silver Hill, Wagram, Wakulla, Maxton, Pembroke, McDonald, SW Lumberton, SE Lumberton, Evergreen, Fairbluff.

starting out: It's a good idea to use the relevant USGS topo quads as navigational aids. The river follows a twisting, tortuous course, with numerous intersecting sloughs, ditches and feeder streams. Unless you know the river, wrong turns are inevitable without a large-scale map. Also be sure to bring as much water as you'll need while on the river. Facilities are at towns along the river and at the small SP office, located atop a high bluff at Princess Anne. A small picnic area, port-o-san, and water pump are on the grounds.

activities: Canoeing, Fishing, Camping.

canoeing: The Lumber is a slow-moving, black-water river for its entire length. Paddling is easy and the only challenges the canoeist needs to worry about are the low-hanging and downed trees that present frequent obstacles along many stretches of the river. Park personnel try to keep the river as clear as possible; call the park office to check current conditions. The river can be paddled in either direction, though the current is swift enough that downstream travel is considerably easier. One of the best things about canoeing the Lumber is the minimal boat traffic. The river is too narrow and tight in most places to permit anything but small craft. Although the river offers canoeists one of the most scenic, serene and pleasant trips in the state, the large majority of river traffic is fishermen. They're usually encountered within a mile or 2 of a landing or bridge crossing, plying the river in small, one- or two-man skiffs with low-horsepower outboards. The river is most isolated, and the swamp most extensive, on the segment between Lumberton and the NC/SC state line.

fishing: Fish are abundant in the Lumber, and are often seen breaking the river's smooth, black surface. The river supports a population of largemouth bass, though smaller species such as yellow perch, redbreast and bluegill occur in greater numbers. Catfish are a popular catch with local fishermen. Fishing is done from a boat or from the banks at one of the river landings.

camping: Wilderness camping is permitted along the length of the river. In practical terms, however, the dense swamp forest that grows along the river's shallow flood plain makes camping impossible in most places. Fortunately, landings are not so infrequent that paddlers will be left without a place to make camp. Signs of previously used campsites are evident at most landings. Avoid camping at any of the few landings that are on private property. The state park has plans to develop a primitive camping area at Piney Island Landing.

Bladen Lakes State Forest

Covering 32,237 acres of sandy forest, swamp and bay in the Carolina bays area of Bladen County, Bladen Lakes is the largest state forest in North Carolina. Its primary uses are as a commercial enterprise producing timber products such as pine straw, fence posts, and charcoal, and as an area of research in the fields of forest management, botany and zoology. Three species of pine (longleaf, loblolly, and slash) make up the majority of tree species planted in the forest. In cooperation with the North Carolina Natural Heritage Program, the state forest maintains the 4,773-acre Carolina Bays Natural Area and the 22-acre Turkey Oak Natural Area, both of which provide habitat to endangered species such as the venus fly trap, red-cockaded woodpecker, and the pine barrens tree frog. Although not intended primarily as an area for backcountry recreation, the miles of forest roads that lace the forest make ideal foot- and bikepaths.

Elizabethtown (S), just across the river, is the closest town.

contact: Forest Supervisor, Bladen Lakes State Forest, Route 2, Box 942, Elizabethtown, NC 28337; 910/588-4964.

getting there: The SF office is at the intersection of NC-242 and Sweet Home Church Rd (SR-1511), 0.6 mi N of the entrance to Jones Lake State Park and 4 mi N of Elizabethtown on NC-242.

topography: The geography of Bladen Lakes is dominated by several Carolina bays and surrounding sandy uplands of predominantly pine forest. Pocosins occupy low-lying depressions. **maps:** USGS Elizabethtown N, White Lake, Garland, Ammon.

starting out: Accesses to the campground and trails are along Sweet Home Church Rd (SR-1511). You can pick up a forest map and brochure at the SF office, open weekdays. The forest receives few visitors. A pit toilet and water are located along the auto-accessible *Smith Swamp Trail.*

activities: Hiking, Camping.

hiking: There's only one officially designated hiking trail in the SF, though any of the 140 mi of sandy forest roads can be used by hikers wanting to explore the area. *Smith Swamp Trail* is a dirt and sand auto trail located 0.3 mi from the park office on Sweet Home Church Rd (SR-1511). The trail is open to autos M–F 9 to 5, Sa 11 to 5, closed Su. Hikers and bikers can use it any time. A couple of interesting exhibits are found along the trail. The first, at 0.2 mi, is dedicated to naval stores, and consists of a number of stations which reproduce aspects of the production of turpentine and tar from timber, an industry that was once important to the region. To reach the second exhibit, take a fork in the road L at 0.4 mi onto Flynn Expressway. At 0.7 mi is an exhibit that illustrates the use of various types of timber for making rail posts and the harvesting of pine needles. A water fountain and pit toilets are here. Across the road is the outstanding *Turnbull Creek Trail*, a well-designed 0.5-mi nature trail with interpretive posts that explain the local forest ecology and habitat. Another 0.4 mi up the road, beside a grassy landing strip, is an exhibit which consists of a prop plane, helicopter, and lookout tower.

camping: A seldom-used primitive campground with picnic tables and a fire ring is located in a scenic forest clearing. The campground has no clearly marked sites, but the half dozen picnic tables are scattered over a large area with plenty of level spots to pitch a tent. To get there, take Sweet Home Church Rd (SR-1511) 3.7 mi from the park office to the Camp Chamblee sign. The campground is 0.8 mi to the R on *Neil Suggs Trail*, a dirt road.

Jones Lake State Park

Jones Lake State Park covers 1,669 acres of Carolina bay forest that surrounds Jones Lake (224 acres) and Salters Lake (315 acres), two prime examples of the Carolina bay lake. Of more than 500,000 Carolina bays—elliptical depressions of uncertain origin—only a handful still contain water. Jones Lake and Salters Lake, like the other bay lakes, share certain features: a NW-SE orientation; clear, shallow water; a bottom of sand and peat; a sandy shore at the SE end; and the characteristic elliptical shape. The bays are so named for the loblolly bay, red bay and sweet bay that dominate the dense band of vegetation that grows along their perimeters. All park facilities are located at Jones Lake; Salters Lake is inaccessible to park visitors. The park is open year round, although many facilities are closed in winter.

Elizabethtown (SE) is the nearest town.

contact: Superintendent, Jones Lake State Park, Route 2 Box 945, Elizabethtown, NC 28337; 910/588-4550.

getting there: From Elizabethtown, go 1 mi N on NC-41/242/US-701 to the jct with NC-53. Continue N on NC-242 for 2.6 mi to the park entrance, L.

topography: The park land surrounding Jones Lake and Salters Lake is tabletop flat, never rising more than several feet above the waterline. With a maximum depth of only 8.7 ft, Jones Lake is one of the shallowest of the Carolina bay lakes. **maps:** Elizabeth Town N, Dublin.

starting out: A park map & brochure can be picked up at the SP office. Most park facilities are located at the large picnic area beside the swimming beach. There's a bathhouse there with changing rooms, showers, drinking fountains, vending machines and a pay phone. Picnic facilities include several dozen tables and grills, as well as a large shelter that is free unless reserved in advance. A nearby interpretive center offers displays on local wildlife with occasional nature talks. Swimming is the most popular activity at Jones Lake. A long white sand beach leads to a small roped off area of the lake which is supervised by lifeguards.

Pets are not allowed in the swimming area; they are permitted elsewhere in the park if leashed. No alcohol is permitted in the park.

activities: Canoeing, Fishing, Hiking, Camping.

canoeing: A canoe is probably the best way to explore the clear water and Carolina bay ecology of Jones Lake. The lake has a shoreline of 2.2 mi. There's a boat launch at the W end of the swimming beach. If you don't have your own canoe, you can rent one from the park. Rates are $2.50/hr for the first 2 hrs and $1/hr for each additional hr. Boats must be off the lake by 6 pm. Motorboats are allowed on the lake, but are rare. Larger, commercially developed White Lake, 8 mi down the road, gets most of that traffic.

fishing: Due to the high acidity levels found in the Carolina bay lakes, the number of fish species which inhabit them is limited.

Yellow perch is the principal catch at Jones Lake; chain pickerel, catfish, chub suckers and blue-spotted sunfish are also present. Fishing is best done from a boat, though there are some places along the bank from which a line can be cast.

hiking: There are 2 hiking trails in the park. *Lake Trail* is an easy, 3-mi loop around the lake that offers the chance to explore the environment of a Carolina bay. The trail is signed and follows a well-maintained path. Although footbridges provide dry stream crossings, the treadway, which is often only a foot or two above water level, is boggy, and there are frequent moist, mushy areas. A handful of short side trails lead to scenic overlooks of the lake. Trailheads are located at the edge of the picnic area and at the campground. The other trail is an easy, 1-mi self-guided nature trail, with interpretive posts that explain some of the features of a Carolina bay. The trailhead is located at the N end of the picnic area.

camping: A 20-site campground is located in a large wooded area about a quarter-mi from the lake. The sites are well-spaced and shaded by stands of pines and bays. Each site has a picnic table and grill. The *Lake Trail* passes beside the campground. There's a centrally located shower/restroom facility with hot water. The fee is $9/night.

Singletary Lake State Park

Reserved primarily for the use of groups, Singletary Lake State Park is one of three parks that encompasses a Carolina bay lake. Located in Bladen County, the park includes 649 acres of bay forest around the 572-acre lake. The local flora and fauna are typical of a Carolina bay: loblolly bay, red bay, sweet bay and Atlantic white cedar mingle with smaller shrubs in a dense band of vegetation that almost completely surrounds the lake. This wetland habitat is known as a peat bog, or pocosin, an Algonquian word meaning "swamp on a hill." The water of the lake is crystal clear and shallow, with a maximum depth of just under 12 ft. The origin of the Carolina bays, of which there are an estimated 500,000, remains a mystery. What is known is that they are shrinking: while most once held water, today only a handful still do. It's probable that like most of the others, Singletary Lake will one day dry out and become overgrown with swamp vegetation. The park is open year-round.

Elizabethtown (NW) is the nearest town.

contact: Superintendent, Singletary Lake State Park, 6707 NC-53 E, Kelly, NC 28448; 910/669-2928.

getting there: The park entrance is located on NC-53, 5 mi SE from the town of White Lake.

topography: Flat, low-lying habitat typical of a Carolina bay. Elevations surrounding the lake do not exceed more than several ft above water level. The lake reaches a depth of not more than 12 ft.
maps: USGS Singletary Lake.

starting out: The park is geared toward large organized groups. When one or both of the group camps are occupied, the park is closed to the rest of the public. If you're coming on your own, call in advance to see if the park is open. A key to the gate, which is always locked, can be picked up at the park office. A park map and brochure are available there as well. Swimming is only permitted for group campers. There isn't really any beach or sandy shoreline in the park, but a 500-ft pier provides easy access to the lake. Supervision must be provided by group leaders.

Pets must be kept and a leash and are prohibited from swimming areas. Alcohol is not allowed in the park.

activities: Camping, Canoeing/Kayaking, Fishing, Hiking.

camping: There are 2 large developed group campsites in the park, each consisting of cabins, mess hall and restrooms facilities. The camps are only open to groups of 20 or more from a verifiable organization. Camp Ipecac has a capacity of 88, and is open from Apr 1 to Oct 31. Camp Loblolly Bay is open year-round and can accommodate up to 48 campers. Both camps feature large campfire rings, volleyball courts and basketball baskets. Each camp rents for $390/wk, $95/day. A mess hall can be rented by itself for $75/day or the cabins can be rented for $40/ day or $1/person, whichever is greater. Reservations—accepted for the year after Jan 1—are required.

canoeing/kayaking: Like the other Carolina Bay Lakes, Singletary Lake is ideal for exploration by canoe or kayak. The lake is open to motorized boats (motors must be 10 hp or less), though you're not likely to encounter other boats of any kind on the lake. The 572-acre lake has a shoreline of almost 4 mi. In addition to bay shrubs, pine, and Atlantic white cedar, ancient cypress trees line the shore. A boat launch area is located near the group camps. The park has purchased a fleet of canoes and has plans to make them available for rent.

fishing: As in the other Carolina bay lakes, only a limited number of species of fish are able to survive the high acidity level at Singletary Lake. Yellow Perch is the principle game fish. Fishing is probably best done from a boat, though wading and casting from the pier are both possibilities.

hiking: *Singletary Lake Trail*, the park's only hiking trail, is an easy 1-mi trail that passes alongside the SE edge of the lake and through bay forest. There are several outlooks along the trail from which to view the ancient cypress trees draped with Spanish moss that grow in the shallow waters near the lake's edge. The trail begins near the pier between the two group camps.

Lake Waccamaw State Park

The largest of the Carolina bay lakes, Lake Waccamaw covers almost 9,000 acres amid the Green Swamp in Columbus County. The lake exhibits features that are characteristic of all bay lakes: an oval shape with a NW-SE orientation; clear, shallow waters; a bed of peat and sand; and a dense bog forest known as a pocosin around its perimeter. Unlike the other bay lakes, however, the water of Lake Waccamaw is not highly acidic. The lakewater's neutral pH, caused by a large limestone outcrop, has resulted in a greater variety of marine life than in any of the other area lakes. A number of species of fish and mollusk that inhabit the lake are found nowhere else in the world. Lake Waccamaw State Park, with a land area of 1,732 acres, occupies a relatively small segment of the lake's SE shore. It's one of the least developed parks in the state, with only primitive camping facilities and a short nature trail. Nevertheless, the natural beauty of the lake and surrounding area, as well as the diversity of habitats, make it one of the most

enjoyable to visit. The park is open year-round.
The town of Lake Waccamaw is located on the N shore.

contact: Superintendent, Lake Waccamaw State Park, Route 1, Box 147, Lake Waccamaw, NC 28450; 910/646-4748.

getting there: From the town of Lake Waccamaw, go E on NC-214 to the edge of town. Turn R onto Jefferson Rd (SR-1757). Go 1.3 mi to SR-1947 and turn L. The park entrance is 2.6 mi ahead on the L.

topography: Park geography is dominated by the lake, a transition zone of fresh-water marsh, shrub thickets and sandy uplands covered with a pine/hardwood forest. The terrain is level. **maps:** USGS Lake Waccamaw W, Lake Waccamaw E.

starting out: Although plans are underway to build a visitors center, for now the only facility in the park is a small building that houses modern restrooms, a water fountain and pay phone. Several signboards nearby point out some of the natural highlights of the park, and you can pick up a trail guide with a very basic park map at the nature trail trailhead. A long boardwalk and dock with a sunshelter lead out onto the lake. There's a beautiful area for picnicking with tables and grills spread out beneath longleaf pines and oaks draped with Spanish moss. The cool, clear waters of the lake make it ideal for swimming. There's no beach in the park, but short ladders lead from the dock into knee-deep water. If you're wading or swimming, be sure to keep an eye out for cottonmouths.

Food and drinks are not allowed on the dock and boats may not be tied to it. Pets must be kept on a leash. Alcohol is prohibited.

activities: Camping, Hiking, Canoeing/Kayaking, Fishing.

camping: There are 3 walk-in primitive group campsites in the park. Each is located in a sandy clearing amidst pine savanna a short distance from the lake. Sites, which vary in size, all include picnic tables, a fire pit and grills. A pit toilet is near each site. Supplies must be packed in. The fee for all sites is $1/person/night with a $5 minimum.

hiking: There's one short hiking trail in the park. The easy, 0.8 mi *Sand Ridge Nature Trail* is a self-guided nature trail loop with interpretive posts along its route. The guide to the trail can be picked up at the trailhead, which is beside the picnic area. Spanish moss, reindeer lichen, and sweet bay are some of the more interesting examples of area flora highlighted on the trail. The trail is well-designed and -maintained, with a level, sandy surface.

canoeing/kayaking: With its clear, shallow waters, and a coastline of almost 15 mi lined with sea grasses and pocosin plant species, Lake Waccamaw is ideally explored from a canoe. Although there is no boat launch in the park, the WRC maintains 2 boat ramps on the lake. One is close to the park on SR-1947, 0.6 mi W of the park entrance. The other is on the lake's W shore. If you want to go beyond the lake, you can paddle or drive to the Waccamaw River, which begins at the lake's S end. The dark, languid river passes through the Green Swamp, a preserve of exceptional biological diversity. You can follow the river all the way to the WRC boat ramp at NC-904, a distance of 42 mi.

fishing: Due to its neutral pH, Lake Waccamaw is the only one of the Carolina bay lakes that supports a wide range of fish species. In addition to the yellow perch, sunfish, and catfish typical of the bay lakes, Lake Waccamaw contains largemouth bass and bluegill. Fishing is possible from the dock, a boat or by wading in the lake's shallow waters.

The Green Swamp

The Green Swamp Preserve covers 15,722 acres of pocosin, white cedar swamp, and pine savanna in Brunswick County. It is owned and managed for the preservation of natural habitats and wildlife by the Nature Conservancy. Among the rarities that inhabit the preserve are the Venus' flytrap—found only in this region of the United States—and a dozen other species of carnivorous plants, four species of pitcher plant, the American alligator, eastern diamondback rattlesnake, and the red-cockaded woodpecker, which inhabits the tall trunks of the loblolly and longleaf pines that cover much of the preserve. The Green Swamp has been registered a National Natural Landmark, one of eight in North Carolina. The Preserve is open year-round.

Middle River (S) is the closest town.

contact: North Carolina Nature Conservancy, Southeast Coastal Plain Office, 313 N Front St, Suite A, Wilmington, NC 28401; 910/762-6277.

getting there: A small sandy parking area at the S edge of a pond is located on the E side of NC-211 5.8 mi N of its jct with US-17 in Supply and 18.2 mi S of NC-214 near Lake Waccamaw. Slow down as you approach the vicinity, as the turnoff is easy to miss.

topography: The preserve is more or less flat, with most of the land covered by dense pocosins. Pine savanna, cedar swamp and pine plantations occupy the remainder. **maps:** USGS Supply.

starting out: There are no facilities on the preserve, which is not really managed for backcountry travel. A signboard at the parking lot provides some basic information and lists restrictions. The preserve is used by hunters in fall and winter. If you visit during that period, be sure to wear at least one article of blaze orange clothing.

activities: Hiking.

hiking: An easy 1.5-mi hiking trail that passes through pocosins and across grassy pine savanna begins at the parking area. The trail, which is unsigned and unblazed, begins on a wide, sandy forest road that soon narrows to a footpath. A long narrow boardwalk has been built across the wettest pocosin area. There's no water supply along the trail. The trail is rarely used.

Zeke's Island Estuarine Research Reserve

Located near the mouth of the Cape Fear River, Zeke's Island Estuarine Research Reserve comprises a narrow barrier spit and 3 main islands: Zeke's Island (42 acres), North Island (138 acres), and No Name Island (3 acres). Salt marshes and tidal flats form most of the islands and surrounding habitat here, with smaller areas of sand beach, dunes, shrub thicket, and maritime forest. The total area of the reserve is approximately 1,160 acres. A long jetty known as "The Rocks" separates the islands from the Cape Fear River, which runs directly behind them before emptying into the Atlantic Ocean. The shallow, protected waters of the reserve are ecologically important as a spawning ground for fish, mollusks, crustaceans and other marine life. Bottlenose dolphins and humpback and pygmy sperm whales are sometimes seen in the area. Shorebirds are abundant. The reserve is open year-round.

Kure Beach (N) is the closest town.

contact: Reserve Coordinator, Center for Marine Science Research, Zeke's Island National Estuarine Research Reserve, 7205 Wrightsville Avenue, Wilmington, NC 28403; 919/256-3721; or Division of Coastal Management, PO Box 27687, Raleigh, NC 27611; 919/733-2293.

getting there: The 3 main islands of the reserve can be reached only by boat or on foot. From the end of US-421 at Federal Point, either hike approx 1 mi across the jetty known as "The Rocks," or launch a kayak or canoe from the WRC boat ramp or the small beach beside it. Access to the barrier spit portion of the reserve is on a sand road (4WD only) that begins in Fort Fisher SRA.

topography: The estuarine environment of the reserve is characterized by tidal flats and salt marshes with smaller areas of elevated sand dunes, shrub thicket and maritime forest. North Island has the most extensive beach-dune-forest complex, while No Name Island is entirely salt marsh and tidal flat. **maps:** USGS Kure Beach.

starting out: The reserve is used primarily for scientific research and conservation; the 3 islands and barrier spit are completely undeveloped. The only on-site information source is a roadside sign near the WRC boat ramp at the end of US-421. The barrier spit portion of the reserve—popular with fishermen and 4WD enthusiasts—receives the most traffic by far. Camping is not permitted on the reserve.

activities: Kayaking/Canoeing, Fishing, Hiking.

kayaking/canoeing: A kayak or canoe is ideal for navigating the narrow channels and tidal flats that surround the reserve's small islands and form its fragile estuarine ecosystem. From the put-in at the WRC boat ramp, the paddle across the Basin is less than a mile. The Basin is relatively enclosed, alleviating some of the usual open water conditions, though stiff winds are often preva-

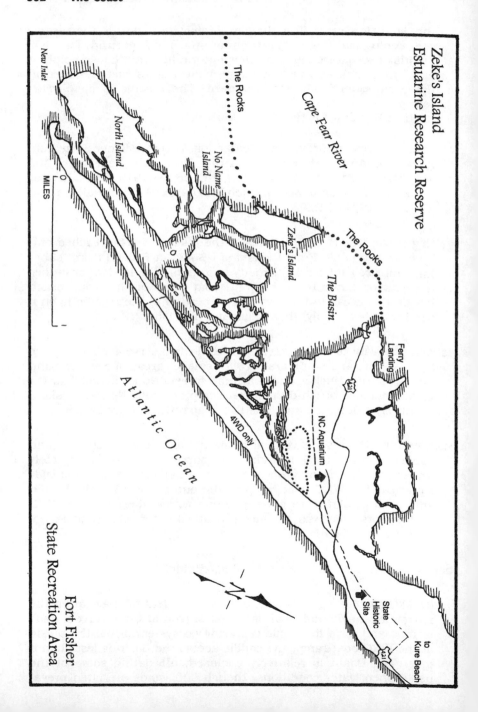

Zeke's Island
Estuarine Research Reserve

lent. On nice days, expect to share the water with windsurfers. Beach landings are possible on Zeke's Island, North Island, and the barrier spit. For a longer trip, continue S past the reserve to Smith Island, where you can either paddle the enclosed waters of Buzzard Bay or head out to the ocean and follow the 5-mi beach to the point at Cape Fear on Bald Head Island.

fishing: The waters around the islands of Zeke's Island ERR provide excellent fishing. Species caught include spot, founder, virginia mullet, black drum, and bluefish. From shore, the best fishing is probably in the surf off the barrier spit near New Inlet. There are also sand beaches on Zeke's Island and North Island, though the latter can only be reached by boat.

hiking: The main hiking opportunities on Zeke's Island are along the beach and on a short, unmarked trail on the E side of the island, or on the jetty which runs along the entire length of the W side of the island. Hikers walking along the jetty do so at their own risk, and should be wary of slippery conditions caused by sea spray and high tide. The jetty is interrupted by an excellent white sand beach on the W side of Zeke's Island, which forms a natural barrier. Hikers should check tide schedules before setting out, as large portions of the beaches and jetty become submerged at high tide.

Fort Fisher State Recreation Area

Fort Fisher State Recreation Area is a popular day-use area that combines a State Historic Site, a branch of the North Carolina Aquarium, and seaside recreation. The site occupies 287 acres of beach, dunes, salt marsh and maritime forest between the Cape Fear River and Atlantic Ocean north of New Inlet. Despite the presence of the recreational and educational facilities, Fort Fisher is one of the last underdeveloped tracts of land on Pleasure Island. The lagoon know as "The Basin," which forms part of the south boundary of Fort Fisher, was created by a 3.3-mi jetty built by the US Army Corps of Engineers shortly after the Civil War. The estuary which has resulted is an important breeding and nurturing area for various fish and shellfish, as well as the shorebirds that prey on them. The rec area is most popular with sunbathers, swimmers and fishermen. The SRA is open year-round, though facilities are limited during the winter.

Kure Beach (N) is the closest town.

contact: Superintendent, Fort Fisher State Recreation Area, c/o Carolina Beach State Park, P.O. Box 475, Carolina Beach, NC 28428; 910/458-8206 (office), 910/458-8207 (marina).

getting there: From Wilmington, drive S on US-421 18.8 mi to Fort Fisher. The fort is 5.5 mi S of Carolina Beach State Park. • From Southport, take the 30-minute Southport-Fort Fisher ferry. Cost is $3/car. The ferry departs every 50 minutes during summer.

topography: Fort Fisher SRA consists of several different coastal environments, including sand beach and dunes, tidal flats, salt marshes and maritime forest. **maps:** USGS Kure Beach.

starting out: A Fort Fisher SRA map and brochure can be picked up at Carolina Beach SP. Most recreational facilities are located adjacent to the main parking lot off US-421. Restrooms, changing rooms, and a snack bar—open from June to Labor Day—are located on the boardwalk that crosses the sand dunes to the beach. There's also an outdoor shower, a pay phone and water fountain. Additional facilities are at the fort and aquarium.

The NC Aquarium is located S of the beach and boardwalk. Hours are M–Sa 9 am to 5 pm, Su 1 to 5 pm. Admission is $3 for adults, $1 for children aged 6 to 17. There are a couple of exhibits at the State Historical Site: The Civil War museum hours are M–Sa 9 am to 5 pm, Su 1 to 5 pm. Admission is free. An underwater archaeology exhibit called "The Waves" is open M–F 9 am to 4:30 pm.

Windsurfing is popular on the ocean side of the jetty that begins at Federal Pt. Windsurfers launch their boards from the beach just beyond the WRC boat ramp. There's a supervised swimming area in the SRA at the end of the boardwalk near the main parking lot and snack stand. Expect crowds on summer weekends. The rest of the 3-mi beach is relatively deserted, even during peak season. Swimmers should beware of strong ocean currents.

4WD vehicles are not allowed on the beach after dark from Jun to Aug because of loggerhead turtle nesting activity. Alcohol is not permitted at the SRA. Pets must be kept on a leash.

activities: Kayaking/Canoeing, Fishing, Hiking.

kayaking/canoeing: paddlers have the option of the open ocean or the more sheltered waters of "The Basin." The best place to launch a boat from is the WRC boat ramp at the end of US-421 on Federal Point just past the ferry terminal. From there, the tidal flats and salt marshes at the edges of The Basin can be explored, as can the islands of Zeke's Island ERR. Another possibility is to put in on the ocean or basin side of the barrier spit by driving out on the 4WD road.

fishing: There are a number of good, popular fishing spots within the SRA. S of the supervised swimming area, the 3-mi stretch of sandy beach on the narrow spit is relatively isolated and accessible only by walking or 4WD vehicle. Bluefish, pompano, flounder, puppy drum, and Virginia mullet are all taken from the surf. Another spot popular with local anglers is "The Rocks," the long jetty that extends out from Federal Point. Fisherman have the option of casting into the salt water of the estuary or the fresh water of the Cape Fear River.

hiking: A nature trail begins and ends at the NC Aquarium parking lot. The trail is an easy 1.5-mi loop that passes through a dense maritime forest and out across grasslands and over salt marshes. Boardwalks are built over the wettest areas. The trail is signed at the trailhead and marked with blue posts along the route, though the posts are irregular and the route confused at times due to side trails. The trail is a good place to observe estuarine fauna, particularly the vast colonies of fiddler crabs that scurry ahead of your footsteps. Hermit bunker is a local landmark. Come prepared for fierce mosquitoes and sharp sea grasses; long pants are a good idea.

Carolina Beach State Park

Located on the banks of the Cape Fear River at the north end of Pleasure Island, Carolina Beach State Park covers 1,773 acres of brackish marsh, swamp forest, cypress pond, pine savanna and pocosin. Several natural features distinguish the park. One is the presence of the rare Venus' fly trap, found only within about a 75-mi radius of Wilmington. 4 other insectivorous plants also grow in the park. Another distinctive feature is the 60-ft high sand dune called Sugarloaf that rises from the shore of the river. As early as the first half of the eighteenth century it served as a navigational landmark for passing ships. Today the dune provides a scenic overlook of the Cape Fear River. Along the river and further inland the various coastal habitats that coexist in the park provide refuge and food to numerous bird species. The snowy egret, laughing gull, great blue heron and belted kingfisher are all seen regularly. The park is open year-round.

The resort town of Carolina Beach is adjacent to the park.

contact: Superintendent, Carolina Beach State Park, P.O. Box 475, Carolina Beach, NC 28428; 910/458-8206 (office), 910/458-8207 (marina).

getting there: From Wilmington, take US-421 S 13.3 mi to Dow Rd. Turn R and go 0.2 to the state park sign and entrance to the R.

topography: Low-lying plant communities typical of the coastal plain cover most park terrain. The park's SW corner is covered by a system of sand dunes that reach elevations of approx 50 ft. **maps:** USGS Carolina Beach.

starting out: Most park facilities are located at the marina at the end of the park road. Park maps and brochures can be picked up there, and restrooms, a water fountain, pay phone and vending and ice machines are on the premises. The marina sells a small selection of fishing tackle. A separate park office is located just inside the park gate. The park has a large picnic ground in a wooded area of oaks that includes tables, grills and modern restroom facilities.

Pets must be kept on a leash in the Park. No alcohol. Swimming is not permitted.

activities: Camping, Fishing, Canoeing/Kayaking, Hiking.

camping: There's a large campground located in a heavily wooded area with 83 sites for tents and trailers (no hookups). The sites, which cost $9/night, are well spaced and large. Each contains a picnic table and grill. There are 2 centrally located rest-room/shower facilities with hot water and drinking fountains. To register for a campsite, take a round green tag from the marker at the site you want to occupy. Bring the tag to the marina and pay for the site. The campground is open year-round.

There's also a primitive group camping area with 2 sites in an open area of pine savanna. The sites, each of which can accommodate up to 35 people, consist of 2 picnic benches and a fire ring. Pit toilets are nearby. The sites are located about a quarter-mi from the S end of the *Swamp Trail*. Water and other supplies must be packed in. The fee is $1/person/night with a $5 minimum. Reservations for the sites can be made in advance. Firewood can be purchased at the marina for $3.50/bundle.

fishing: There are a number of good places to fish from within the park. Just past the marina and boat ramp is a designated fishing area with benches for spectators, pine trees, a grassy area and a thin strip of sand at the water's edge. *Sugarloaf Trail* provides access to many open, sandy stretches on the river's edge. Principal species found in the river near the park are spot, flounder, sheepshead and striped bass. The marina sells live bait and other fishing tackle.

canoeing/kayaking: Canoes or kayaks can be launched from the boat ramp beside the marina. There's a launch fee of $3. Paddlers can explore the wide waters of the Cape Fear River, or head up the narrower, man-made Snow's Cut and out to the open, estuarine environment of Masonboro Sound. The park itself has a coastline of about 3 mi. Fort Fisher SRA and Zeke's Island ERR are about 6 mi downstream from the park.

hiking: 5 mi of hiking trails provide access to all of the various environments found in the park, including pine savannas, cypress ponds, pocosins, sandy beaches, and Sugarloaf, the 60-ft high sand dune that has been a navigational landmark for centuries and provides good views out over the river. A short nature trail loop offers the chance to see the Venus' fly trap in its natural habitat. All trails are well maintained, blazed with colored dots at regular intervals, and easy to hike. Trails are mostly soft sand and dirt, with boardwalks built over perennially wet areas. Information boards explain some of the park's more prominent natural features. Trailheads are signed, and are located at the marina and campground. *Fly Trap Trail* begins at the end of a signed access road.

Masonboro Island Estuarine Research Reserve

In an area that is becoming increasingly developed, Masonboro Island is one of the few barrier islands that remains in a pristine natural state. Located only several hundred yards offshore from the mainland near Wilmington, the island is a 5,097-acre preserve that consists of dunes, salt marshes and sandy beach. It's the largest undeveloped barrier island on the state's south coast. Although backcountry travel opportunities on the island are limited by its fragile environment, size and shape, visitors come to walk along the 9-mi sandy beach, to fish the abundant waters around the island, to watch for more than 250 species of birds or to study the island's ecology. Loggerhead turtles, peregrine falcons and brown pelicans are some of the more interesting wildlife encountered on the island. Because of its location on the most crowded stretch of North Carolina's coast, Masonboro Island is both an oasis and a prime destination for area visitors looking to get off the beaten path.

Wrightsville Beach (N) and Carolina Beach (S) are the closest towns.

contact: Masonboro Island National Estuarine Research Reserve, 7205 Wrightsville Avenue, Wilmington, NC 28403; 910/256-3721 or Division of Coastal Management, P.O. Box 27687, Raleigh, NC 27611; 919/733-2293.

getting there: The reserve can only be reached by boat. The easiest accesses are from Wrightsville Beach and Carolina Beach. From Wrightsville Beach, take US-76 to where it dead ends at a parking area and beach access. It's about a 100 yd walk through sand dunes to the edge of Masonboro Inlet. • From Carolina Beach, take Canal Dr to its end at the beach and fishing pier. 4WDs can drive on the beach, other vehicles must park along the road and walk about 200 yds to the ocean.

topography: Masonboro Island is a small barrier island. The ocean side is characterized by a sandy beach that rises into a complex of sand dunes. The sound side is salt marsh. Shrub thickets and tracts of maritime forest occupies a small part of the island. **maps:** USGS Wrightsville Beach, Carolina Beach.

starting out: There are no facilities on the island. Much of the island habitat is fragile and easily damaged. You'll have the least impact if you stick to the beach, forest and shrub thickets. Camping is not permitted on the island.

activities: Kayaking/Canoeing, Fishing.

kayaking/canoeing: Although the island cannot be reached by vehicle or on foot, it is easily accessible by boat from 3 directions. Carolina Beach Inlet (S) and Masonboro Inlet (N) provide the easiest and shortest water routes to the island. Paddling across either should take no more than 15 minutes. Landings are possible on the sandy beaches that stretch along the entire 8.4-mi length of the island. Although the island is completely undeveloped, the waters around it are a popular commercial and sport fishery. In other words, expect company while paddling. Adjacent Wrightsville Beach (N) and Carolina Beach (S) are both heavily developed tourist beaches.

fishing: Anglers have the option of surfcasting from the beach or of fishing from a boat offshore. Species caught include bluefish, black drum, mackerel, flounder and spot, among others.

Cliffs of the Neuse State Park

The cliffs for which the park are named rise more than 90 feet above a bend in the Neuse River. They're the centerpiece of the 751-acre park, which was created primarily to protect them and to permit public access. The Neuse is one of the major waterways of the coastal plain, beginning at the eastern end of Falls Lake and emptying into Pamlico Sound. The cliffs provide excellent views of a short segment of the river and surrounding floodplain. Because of its small size, the park is best suited to day visits. In addition to the cliffs, other attractions are a small lake, 2 campgrounds and a natural history museum with exhibits on the area's geologic history, fossil record, flora and fauna and Indian settlement. The park is open year-round.

Goldsboro (NW) is the closest town.

contact: Superintendent, Cliffs of the Neuse State Park, 345-A Park Entrance Rd, Seven Springs, NC 28578; 919/778-6234.

getting there: From US-70 approx 6 mi SE of Goldsboro, turn S onto NC-111. Go 8.4 mi to Park Entrance Rd (SR-1743). Turn L and go 0.3 mi to the park entrance.

topography: 98-ft cliffs overlooking the Neuse River are the park's geographical highlight. The rest of the park terrain rises and falls on gentle slopes. A pine/hardwood forest covers most of the park. **maps:** USGS Williams, Seven Springs.

starting out: You can pick up a park map at the SP office, where there's a pay phone as well. Other facilities are located at the lake (bathhouse, concession stand), picnic area (restrooms, water) and natural history museum (restrooms, water). There's a swimming beach at the 11-acre lake. Nearby is a large picnic area with several dozen tables and grills as well as a large shelter.

Alcohol is not permitted in the park. Pets must be kept on a leash. Rock climbing on the cliffs is prohibited.

activities: Hiking, Camping, Fishing.

hiking: 3 short trails follow the cliffs, the river and meander through the park's forested uplands. The trails are best suited to short strolls, as the total distance covered is not more than 2 mi. Signed trailheads are located at the parking lot near the cliffs and overlook. The trails follow wide, sandy treadways that are easy to follow. Improvements include steps and several footbridges. Hiking is easy.

camping: A 35-site car campground is situated in a wooded area. Sites are arranged in a single large loop with a restroom/shower facility (hot water) in the center. Sites are fairly large and provide adequate privacy. Each site has a picnic table and grill. The fee is $9/night. The campground is open Mar 15 to Nov 30. It fills occasionally on fall weekends.

A primitive group camping area features 4 sites with picnic tables set amidst a pine/hardwood forest. Privacy at the sites is average. A pit toilet and water supply are in the area. An easy half-mi hike is necessary to reach the sites. Sites cost $1/person/night with a $5 minimum. The campground is open all year.

fishing: The Neuse River provides habitat for largemouth bass, bluegill and catfish. There are a number of places along the bank from which it is possible to cast.

Hammocks Beach State Park

2 tracts of land comprise Hammocks Beach State Park—a 33-acre parcel on the mainland that includes the park office and ferry landing, and 892-acre Bear Island, one of a string of barrier islands separated from the mainland by salt marsh, tidal flat and the intracoastal waterway. With development on Bear Island limited to a bathhouse and some picnic tables, it is one of the natural treasures of the North Carolina coast. In fact, the National Park Service has designated it a National Natural Landmark. A 3.5-mile white sand beach fronts the Atlantic Ocean, wrapping around the island's east and west ends at Bogue Inlet and Bear Inlet, respectively. The protected waters of the sound side provide abundant food for crustaceans, young fish and birds. The island can only be reached by boat, and the number of visitors is restricted in order to help preserve the island's natural state. Loggerhead turtles are among the rarest of the wildlife that uses the island's resources; they make their nests there during full moons in the summer.

Swansboro (NE) is the closest town.

contact: Superintendent, Hammocks Beach State Park, 1572 Hammocks Beach Rd, Swansboro, NC 28584; 910/326-4881.

getting there: From Swansboro, take NC-24 W 1.9 mi to Hammocks Beach Rd (SR-1511). Turn L and go 2.4 mi to the Park entrance, R. From there, you can either launch a canoe or kayak or take the 25-min ferry, which costs $2 round-trip for adults and $1 for children. Between Memorial Day and Labor Day the ferry runs every half-hour on W–Su, every hour M & T. In May & Sep, it only runs on weekends. Ferry service stops when the island reaches capacity.

topography: Small barrier island with extensive dune system, shrub thickets, maritime forest and extensive salt marshes. The dunes reach heights of about 60 ft. **maps:** USGS Hubert, Swansboro.

starting out: You can pick up a park map and brochure at the main office. Facilities on the island are limited. A bathhouse has modern toilets and showers, which cost $2. It's open 10 am-5:30 pm. The building houses a concession stand as well that sells sodas and snacks. The most popular summertime activity on the island is swimming at the lifeguard-patrolled beach. Daytime crowds gather there, though by night they're gone and the island is deserted except for campers staying at one of 14 designated sites. 2 small picnic areas are sheltered among the dunes on either side of the bathhouse. One has 2 small shelters and a grill, the other has 3 small shelters and grills.

activities: Kayaking/Canoeing, Fishing, Camping, Hiking.

kayaking/canoeing: A scenic 2-mi canoe/kayak trail has been developed between the put-in near the park office and a landing on the NE side of Bear Island. A series of orange and white markers along the route serve as navigational aids. The island is perfectly sized for a day's circumnavigation. Longer trips are possible by heading down the coast to Masonboro Island, Fort Fisher Rec Area and Zeke's Island, or along the coast to the E to Bogue Banks and Shackleford Banks and Cape Lookout National Seashore. This latter option is best for multi-day trips, as camping is restricted at the areas to the S.

fishing: Fishing on the island is possible from the beach or from a boat. Main catches are bluefish, mullet, drum, flounder and sea trout.

camping: Bear Island features 14 primitive campsites and 3 group sites. The sites are located at the edge of the dunes and the beach. 10 sites are on a long stretch of oceanfront beach and are reached by hiking about a half-mile from the ferry landing; 4 other sites—2 at either end of the island—are designed to be reached by canoe or kayak. Sites are not visible to one another, making it seem almost like you have the island to yourself. Each site includes a picnic table. Water and restrooms are located at the bathhouse. Sites cost $5/night. They generally fill up on summer weekends.

There are also 3 primitive group sites, each with a capacity of 12. These sites are located not far from the bathhouse amidst the dunes. They are only open to organized groups. The fee is $1/person/night.

The island is closed to all camping during the full moon in Jun,

Jul and Aug so that loggerhead turtles will not be disturbed while nesting.

hiking: Although there are no designated hiking trails on the island, the wide, sandy beach is ideal for long walks.

Croatan National Forest

Established in 1936 by President Franklin Roosevelt, the Croatan is one of four National Forests in North Carolina. The only National Forest in the state that lies on the coastal plain, it covers 159,102 acres of estuary, pocosin and pine savanna in Jones, Carteret and Craven Counties. Along its perimeter and throughout its interior, the land of the Croatan is defined by water. 2 rivers and a sound— the Neuse River, White Oak River and Bogue Sound—form most of the boundary of the National Forest. 5 freshwater lakes and an extensive system of elevated bogs make water no less prominent or important on the interior of the Croatan. 31,221 acres of this wetland habitat have been set aside as 4 designated wilderness areas—Catfish Lake South (8,530 acres), Sheep Ridge (9,297 acres), Pone Pine (1,685 acres), and Pocosin (11,709 acres).

The Croatan is home to a large number of mammal, bird, and reptile species, as well as some rare and unusual plants. While you're more likely to see a white-tailed deer than any other mammal, black bear, mink, river otter and other small mammals are also found. The American alligator is the largest reptile that lives in the National Forest, though snakes and lizards are far more numerous and easily seen. Since it's located on the Atlantic Flyway, the Croatan makes a temporary home or rest stop for numerous migratory birds, ducks, and geese. Year-round residents include ospreys, egrets, herons, owls, and woodpeckers.

New Bern (N) and Morehead City (SE) are the closest cities outside the National Forest. The towns of Havelock, Newport, and Maysville are all located within National Forest boundaries.

contact: District Ranger, Croatan Ranger District, US Forest Service, 141 E Fisher Ave, New Bern, NC 28560; 919/638-5628.

getting there: Access to the NF is via US-70 from the N or E, US-17 from the W, and NC-24 from the S or W. The NF district office is located on E Fisher Ave (SR 1104) off US-70 10 mi S of New Bern.

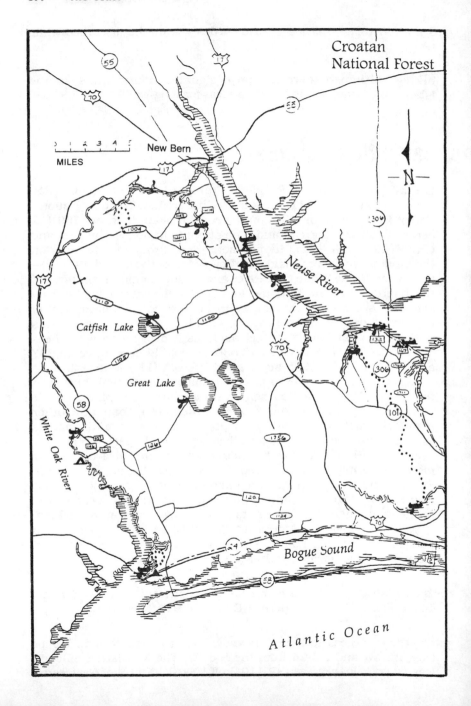

topography: Surrounded by tidal rivers and laced with blackwater creeks, the Croatan is a flat, low-lying, water-saturated environment. Much of the interior is covered with dense shrub thickets known as pocosins, a type of bog. Other plant communities include pine savannas and coastal forests. Elevations on the NF do not exceed 50 ft. **maps:** see below under individual listings.

starting out: The district office is a good place to check in before beginning a trip. You can pick up maps and brochures inside, where a small selection of nature and guide books are also for sale. The office is open M–F 8 am to 4:30 pm. If it's closed, you can buy Croatan NF maps ($3) from a vending machine outside the office. Hunting is a very popular activity on the Croatan during fall and winter months. If you're going into the backcountry, be sure to wear at least a one article of clothing that's blaze orange.

Poisonous snakes—among them the cottonmouth, eastern diamondback rattlesnake, copperhead, pigmy rattlesnake and canebrake rattlesnake—are abundant in many parts of the NF. Biting insects, particularly mosquitoes, are prevalent during warm-weather months.

activities: Camping, Canoeing/Kayaking, Fishing, Hiking, Mountain Biking.

camping: Croatan NF has 2 large developed campgrounds: Neuse River, with 24 sites, and Cedar Point, with 40. Both have undergone recent renovations, including the construction of new modern restroom/shower facilities. A fee is charged at both areas. Both are open from May 1 to Sep 30. Fishers Landing is a partially developed campground, particularly well-suited to groups. It has 9 walk-in sites, pit toilets and a fresh water supply. Wilderness camping is permitted on most NF land, but the dense vegetation of the pocosins that cover most of the interior makes finding a clearing large enough to pitch a tent a near impossibility. Catfish Lake, Great Lake and Long Point are 3 areas that have sufficiently large clearings to permit a number of campers. None of these areas has any facilities.

canoeing/kayaking: Bordered on all sides by bodies of water, and with an interior laced with small, meandering creeks and dotted by lakes, Croatan NF offers countless opportunities for paddlers to explore the waterways of the coastal backcountry. In all, there are more than 40 mi of streams and 4,300 acres of lakes within the

NF, with an additional 20 mi of river forming a part of the NF boundary. Remote blackwater streams, inland lakes, tidal marshes, and the Neuse River are all suitable for canoe or kayak. Each of the rec areas described below is located on a body of water; most have some form of boat launch.

fishing: Both freshwater and saltwater species are caught in the waters of the Croatan. Principal freshwater species are the largemouth bass, yellow perch, chain pickerel, bluegill, catfish and sunfish. Tidal marshes and the lower reaches of the Neuse River provide opportunities for saltwater fishing. Gigging for flounder is one unusual form of fishing that occurs in the estuarine waters of the NF. The interior lakes offer rather poor fishing, due to high levels of acidity.

hiking: Although the number of hiking trails on the NF is limited, those that do exist are among the most interesting in the coastal region. The *Neusiok Trail* ranges over 20 mi of the E portion of the NF between Pinecliff and Oyster Point. The *Cedar Point Tideland Trail* is a National Rec Trail located in the extreme SW corner of the NF at the Cedar Point Rec Area. It is an exceptionally well-designed trail, with long boardwalks that pass over tidal marshes and two elevated viewing blinds for wildlife observation. The *Island Creek Forest Walk* is a half-mi nature interpretive trail with observation posts and a companion brochure.

mountain biking: Although there are no officially designated biking trails on the NF, there are dozens of miles of unpaved road that criss-cross the Croatan's interior. Some of these roads are only suitable for 4-wheel drives, ATVs, or mountain bikes. If you do decide to bike the Croatan, be prepared for a number of hazards. Most of the primary forest roads, although unpaved, receive relatively heavy use, particularly during hunting season. When it's dry, trucks and jeeps leave a cloud of sand or dust in their wake. When it's wet, however, many of these dirt roads quickly become impassable bogs of mud and muck.

Neuse River Area

The Neuse River flows along the eastern boundary of the Croatan on its route to Pamlico Sound and the Atlantic Ocean. The large river is one of the busiest in North Carolina, with commercial ships, powerboats and sailboats all common. So much heavy use has made pollution a problem in recent years, though efforts are underway to reverse that trend. (A Keeper of the Neuse has been appointed to spearhead the effort.) The shoreline is heavily developed in the region, with New Bern only about 5 miles north of the National Forest. The Croatan occupies a 15-mi stretch of the river's southern shore, preserving a portion of the habitat of upland pine/hardwood forest, pine savanna and cypress swamp that once dominated the region. There are 5 National Forest rec areas located on or near the Neuse: Fishers Landing, Neuse River, Pinecliff, Cahooque Creek, and Siddie Fields. Opportunities for backcountry recreation are mostly on the river and several feeder creeks and on the *Neusiok Trail*, the longest trail on the Croatan National Forest.

New Bern (NW) and Havelock (S) are the closest cities.

getting there: Directions are to 5 rec areas on the river. They are listed heading downriver from NW to SE. To get to Fishers Landing, from US-70 just N of the Croatan RS (10 mi S of New Bern), turn E onto gravel FR-141. The road ends after 0.5 mi at the rec area parking lot. • To reach Neuse River Rec Area, from US-70 approx 11 mi S of New Bern, turn E at the NF Rec Area sign onto Flanner's Beach Rd (SR 1107). The campground entrance is 1.6 mi ahead, R. • To get to Cahooque Creek, from Havelock take NC-101 5 mi E to Cahooque Creek Rd (SR-1717). Turn L and go 3.4 mi (at 2 mi the pavement ends, bear L) to the end of the rd and parking area. • Pinecliff Rec Area is located off NC-101, 5.5 mi E of Havelock. From NC-101, turn L onto NC-306 at the rec area sign and go 3.3 mi to FR-132. Turn L and proceed 1.4 mi to the gated rec area entrance. • To get to Siddie Fields, from Havelock, take NC-101 E 7.5 mi and turn L onto SR-1711. Go 2 mi and turn L onto gravel Pine Cliff Rd (SR-1762). At 1 mi bear R at a jct. Go 0.5 mi to another jct and keep L. Proceed 1 mi to the end of the road and the rec area.

topography: The Croatan fronts the Neuse River not far from where it empties into Pamlico Sound. Along the shoreline a 20-ft bluff overlooks the river and a narrow white sand beach. A few cypress trees grow out at the river's edge, with a predominantly pine forest covering the upland. **maps:** USGS Havelock, Cherry Point, Upper Broad Creek.

starting out: Facilities are at Fishers Landing and at Neuse River and Pinecliff Rec Areas. Both rec areas have picnic grounds that overlook the river. At Neuse River, several dozen picnic tables and grills are scattered across a wide area shaded by a grove of hardwoods and pines. There are also water fountains and flush toilets. Pine Cliff is a day-use only area (8 am-8 pm) with a shelter, picnic tables and grills. Facilities include pit toilets and a hand water pump. Both areas have narrow, white sand beaches that are popular sunbathing and swimming spots. Swimming is unsupervised. Fishers Landing has a water fountain and pit toilets.

activities: Canoeing/Kayaking, Fishing, Camping, Hiking.

canoeing/kayaking: Paddlers have several options in the area. The Neuse River offers the opportunity to explore the scenic eastern shore of the Croatan from the water. The shore is lined with white sand beaches that form subtle arcs; cypress trees draped with Spanish moss grow out at the water's edge. The shoreline is about 15 mi long, though a third of that fronts the Cherry Point Naval Station. The Neuse is the largest body of water touching Croatan land—about 3 mi across in this area—so be prepared for open water conditions. Also be aware that this close to the sound the river is tidal. Check a tide chart before deciding which direction to paddle. Fishers Landing, Neuse River, Pinecliff and Siddie Fields all have access to the river, though you'll have to carry your boat at least a short distance. If you'd rather not, put in at Cahooque Creek and paddle the mile and a half out to the Neuse.

Another option is to put in at Cahooque Creek and explore the more intimate waters of this blackwater stream as it meanders out of the Croatan. This is best for a short trip, as the creek can only be paddled for several miles upstream. Hancock Creek is accessible from the same boat ramp. It flows for several miles between the NF and the Naval Station. Both creeks are popular with anglers.

fishing: Anglers have the option of fishing the Neuse or one of several smaller creeks that drain into it. At this point in its course, the Neuse is a tidal river, which means that the fishing is for both fresh- and saltwater species. Freshwater game fish caught include largemouth and striped bass, catfish, crappie, bluegill and, during the spring spawning season, American and hickory shad. Saltwater species include bluefish, red drum, spotted sea trout, grey trout, blue crabs and oysters. The sandy shoreline at any of the 5 rec area offers a good place from which to cast, though during peak season the beaches at Neuse River and Pinecliff can become crowded with sunbathers and swimmers. A canoe or kayak will allow more freedom to follow the fish on this very large river, which is about 3 mi across where it passes the Croatan.

Another freshwater fishing are the quiet waters of Cahooque and Hancock Creeks. Both creeks flow for several miles out of the Croatan's interior. The boat ramp at Cahooque Creek is a popular starting point for anglers. There's also a small dock here.

camping: Campers on this part of the NF have a number of options. the 25-site car campground at Neuse River Rec Area is one of two developed campgrounds on the Croatan. The sites are spread out along a loop drive in a level, sparsely wooded area set above the bluffs that overlook the Neuse River. The sites are large and fairly well spaced. Each one has a picnic table, grill and lantern post. The fee is $8/night. If you're planning on camping here for the weekend, arrive early Friday as the sites go pretty quickly. Sites that overlook the river are always taken first. The campground has been recently renovated. A new addition is a centrally located bathhouse facility, with modern toilets and hot showers. Water spigots are located at regular intervals. The campground is open from May 1 to Sep 30.

A 9-site primitive walk-in campground is located at Fishers Landing. The sites are situated in a scenic clearing that overlooks the river. Sites are spaced closely together, with barely any distinction made between them, making the area well suited to groups, not so well for those seeking solitude. Each site has a picnic table and grill. Pit toilets and a water fountain are the only facilities in the area. There's a central parking area about 50 yds away from the sites.

Siddie Fields offers camping even more primitive than Fisher's Landing. There's a small clearing that overlooks the river with room for perhaps 5 or 6 sites. There are no facilities in the area.

Finally, backcountry camping is available along the Neusiok Trail, which runs N–S between Pinecliff and Oyster Point on the Newport River. Be sure to bring enough water, as none is available along the trail.

hiking: The N terminus of the 20-mi *Neusiok Trail* is located at Pinecliff Rec Area. The easy trail winds southward through various habitats—sandy shoreline, riparian bottomland, pine/hardwood upland forest, cypress-palmetto swamp, and pocosin—before emerging at the salt marshes of the Newport River at Oyster Point. The trailhead is located near the picnic shelter. The trail is blazed with white bars, generally well-defined, and easy to follow. Although improvements include numerous boardwalks across wet areas, there remain several streams and swamps that must be waded. Late fall and winter are the best seasons to hike the trail, as insect and snake activity is at a minimum. If you're planning on hiking the entire trail, bring enough drinking water, as there are no water sources along the trail. Camping is permitted along the trail.

Note: If you're parking your car overnight at Pine Cliff, leave a note on the dash so that the NF staff know it is alright to lock the gates with your vehicle inside. During winter, when the rec area is closed, park outside the gate (don't block it).

Bogue Sound Area

Although NC-24 forms most of the actual southern boundary of the National Forest, Bogue Sound is the natural feature that defines the area. At either end of the sound 2 large rivers that drain much of the Croatan—the Newport and White Oak—reach their mouths. In the estuarine marshes located here ocean saltwater meets with the freshwater carried downstream by the rivers to create an aquatic habitat that supports a diversity of wildlife. Waterfowl can often be observed wading in the shallow waters, and it is here that crabs, oysters and numerous other marine lifeforms get their start. On shore, live oak and pine forests thrive on uplands high enough to have adequate drainage. Recreation is mostly water based, though there are 2 outstanding hiking trails in the vicinity.

getting there: To get to Oyster Point, from Mill Creek Rd (SR-1154) 0.2 mi W of the community of Mill Creek, turn S onto gravel FR-181 and go 1 mi to a fork in the road. Keep L and go 0.1 mi to a small parking area in the woods just beyond the cul de sac. • To reach Cedar Point, from NC-58 0.6 mi N of the jct with NC-24, turn W onto VFW Rd (SR-1114) and go 0.5 mi to FR-153-A. Turn L and go 0.8 mi to the rec area entrance.

topography: Estuarine rivers and salt marshes characterize this region of the Croatan. At their mouths at Bogue Sound, both the Newport and White Oak are large tidal rivers. Elevations are only a few ft above sea level. **maps:** USGS Swansboro, Core Creek, Newport.

starting out: Facilities are at Cedar Point, which is divided into a campground and day-use area (open 8 am–8 pm). There's a picnic ground with tables and grills here, as well as a pit toilet. Oyster Point, with no facilities, is used primarily as the S access to the *Neusiok Trail.*

activities: Kayaking/Canoeing, Camping, Hiking, Fishing.

canoeing/kayaking: Although this part of the Croatan is surrounded by water, much of it is not really suitable for an enjoyable paddling trip. The Newport River and the eastern end of Bogue Sound are both heavily developed, with industrialized Morehead City situated on a point between the 2. Newport River does offer some smaller attractive feeder creeks, including its own upper reaches, which extend into the heart of the Croatan. Access is at Oyster Point, where there's a primitive boat ramp. If the tide is out, you'll probably have to slosh through some muck to get to the water. At the other side of the sound is the mouth of the White Oak River, a less developed area. The river at his point is more than a mi across, with a tidal flow. If you put in at the boat ramp at Cedar Point, you have the choice of exploring the nearby estuarine marshes, paddling up the White Oak River, or heading out to the open water of Bogue Sound and the Atlantic Ocean. The White Oak River is a large tidal river as far upstream as the town of Stella (7 mi N), after which it narrows considerably and becomes more similar in character to the small, intimate dark-water creeks that penetrate the Croatan. Another 6 mi N of Stella, the river passes Haywood Landing and Long Point, where you can make camp. Paddling S from Cedar Point, navigating the numerous islands that crowd the mouth of the river will bring you to Bogue Inlet, a distance of not more than 4 mi. From there you can head E along Bogue Banks or turn W and soon land on Hammocks Beach SP. The boat ramp at Cedar Point is located at the end of the parking lot in the day-use area.

camping: Campers have their choice of a full service developed campground or primitive backcountry camping. Cedar Point features a 41-site car campground that is popular with families and the RV crowd. Sites are spread out over a large open area with minimal tree cover and little privacy. Each site has a picnic table, grill and lantern post. All sites have electrical hookups and cost $15/night. A new hot water restroom/shower facility is centrally located. Water spigots are situated throughout the campground.

It's open May 1–Sep 30.

Primitive camping is available at Oyster Point, where there are several small clearings near the trailhead/parking area amidst a forest of live oak. There are no facilities here and the area doesn't get much use. Camping is also permitted along the *Neusiok Trail*, whose S terminus is here. There's no water along the trail, so be sure to bring enough.

hiking: There are a pair of outstanding hiking trails in the area. The S terminus of the 20-mi *Neusiok Trail* is at Oyster Point. The trailhead is unsigned, but is easy to locate, as it's just behind the small parking area. Look for the blaze of white bars on trees as you walk N from the river. A full description of the trail is given under the Neuse River area (above). At the other end of the sound, the *Cedar Point Tideland Trail* is one of the real highlights of the NF. Designated a National Recreation Trail, it follows a loop that meanders for a mile and a half through tidal marshlands and upland forests beside the White Oak River. Long boardwalks, rest benches, and two elevated viewing blinds are all featured on this well-maintained trail. The trail is wide, level, and easy to follow. The signed trailhead is located adjacent to the parking lot and boat ramp. Pit toilets are also nearby.

fishing: The brackish water found at the mouths of the rivers that empty into Bogue Sound supports populations of both salt- and freshwater species of fish. These conditions exist along the entire stretch of the rivers that receive tidal flow. Freshwater species are largemouth bass, bluegill, white perch, crappie, and pickerel. Saltwater fish caught include red drum, seatrout, flounder and spot. Although some opportunities for bank fishing and wading exist, the primary means of pursuing fish is from a boat. The White Oak River is ideal for a combined paddling/fishing trip.

White Oak River

The White Oak River forms the western boundary of the National Forest. On its northern reaches, the river is a narrow, meandering, stream not unlike many of the smaller creeks that flow out of the Croatan's center. This part of the river possesses great natural beauty, with dense bottomland forest on the banks and abundant wildlife. When the river reaches the community of Stella, however, it widens considerably and gradually becomes a large tidal river similar to the Neuse and the Newport. There are 2 small rec areas on the river north of Stella: Long Point and Haywood Landing. The areas are about a 3-mile drive apart; both are described below.

getting there: To get to Haywood Landing, turn W off of NC-58 onto FR-120 2.6 mi N of the community of Kuhns and go 0.1 mi. Turn R onto dirt FR-157 and go 1.9 mi to FR-146. Turn R and go 0.3 mi to the boat ramp and dock. • To get to the camping area at Long Pt you can either take dirt FR-120 from NC-58 or, from Haywood Landing, take dirt FR-146 1.5 mi SE to FR-120 and turn R. The camping area and river are 1.2 mi ahead.

topography: The White Oak River has a tidal current where it flows past the Croatan NF. The riverbanks are covered with a dense bottomland forest. **maps:** USGS Stella, Swansboro, Hadnot Creek.

starting out: Facilities on the river are very limited. There are pit toilets at Haywood Landing and no facilities at all at Long Point.

activities: Canoeing/Kayaking, Fishing, Camping.

canoeing/kayaking: The stretch of river that flows between Maysville and Stella is probably the most beautiful and haunting on its entire course. As the river passes through dense swampland, trees and other vegetation crowd its banks and offer a haven for wildlife. The current is faster than on the smaller creeks found in the NF interior; paddling against it can be a chore. There's a boat ramp at Haywood Landing and a very small sandy clearing at Long Pt where you can get a canoe or kayak on the river. Haywood Landing is about 5 mi upstream from where the river widens and 7 mi downstream from the next river access at the bridge on US-17. This would be a good starting point for a 2 day trip that ended at Cedar Point or Hammocks Beach SP.

fishing: Fishing is for a mixture of salt- and freshwater species: Striped mullet, largemouth bass, chain pickerel, pumpkinseed, gar, spot and croaker are all caught from the river. Fishing is typically done from a boat; a small dock at Haywood Landing is another possibility.

camping: There's a small clearing suitable for primitive camping where FR-120 ends at Long Point. About 4 or 5 campers can camp there comfortably. There are no facilities.

The Central Croatan

The heart of the Croatan presents the traveller with something of a conundrum: it's easy to get to but just about impossible to see. A number of dirt and sand Forest Service roads criss-cross the Croatan's center, yet beyond the side of the road grow virtually impenetrable pocosins, a type of bog where moisture-loving evergreen shrubs and small trees thrive. Much of this habitat—more than 31,000 acres—has been designated as wilderness. Other features of this part of the National Forest include several bay lakes and a number of small, slow-moving creeks that serve as wildlife corridors.

Maysville (W) and New Bern (N) are the closest towns.

getting there: Directions are to Great Lake, Catfish Lake and Brice Creek. To reach Great Lake, from NC-58 in the community of Kuhns, Go N on SR-1100 0.7 mi to SR-1101 and turn R. After 0.7 mi the road becomes dirt and sand Great Lake Rd (FR-126). From there, it is another 5.9 mi to the lake and boat ramp. 4WD vehicles are recommended for this route, though it's passable in a car if it hasn't rained recently. • To get to Catfish Lake, begin in Maysville. Take NC-58 S 2.3 mi. Turn L onto SR-1105 which becomes gravel after 2.1 mi. At the county line the road becomes SR-1100. Go 1.8 mi and turn L onto FR-158. The boat launch and camping area are 1.3 mi ahead on the L. • To get to Brice Creek, from US-70 just across the Trent River S of New Bern, turn S onto Island Creek Rd (SR-1004) and go 3.3 mi to SR-1143. Turn L and go 1.5 mi to FR-121-A. Turn L and go 1.3 mi to the parking area and boat ramp.

topography: Pocosins, bay lakes, and narrow blackwater creeks characterize the low-lying wetlands of the central Croatan. Flooding is common during rainy spells. The entire area has poor drainage and elevations are less than 50 ft above sea level. **maps:** USGS Catfish Lake, Hadnot Creek, New Bern, Maysville.

starting out: Although access to even the remote parts of the central Croatan is not too difficult, there are no facilities, so bring whatever you need, particularly water. Hunters flood the area in fall and winter. If you're planning a visit during that time, be sure to wear blaze orange while in the backcounty.

activities: Canoeing/Kayaking, Camping, Fishing, Hiking, Mountain Biking.

canoeing/kayaking: Paddlers can choose between 2 lakes and 1 creek in the heart of the NF. The 2 lakes are Catfish Lake and Great Lake. Both are examples of Carolina bay lakes, shallow oval lakes of uncertain origin that sit on a thick bed of peat. The lakes are surrounded by pocosins, including several designated wilderness areas. 2,950-acre Great Lake is the larger of the 2; Catfish lake occupies 962 acres. One of the nicest things about canoeing or kayaking on either of these lakes is that you're likely to have it all to yourself, or almost. Because of the poor fishing, the lakes don't see much boat traffic. The water of the lakes is typically mirror-smooth, and the serenity is punctuated only by birdsong. Be sure to bring a compass; surrounded by pocosin, the shoreline has few distinguishing landmarks. Both lakes have primitive boat ramps.

The other paddling choice is Brice Creek, a narrow, scenic river that meanders slowly out of the middle of the Croatan and eventually empties into the Trent River. Cypress trees hanging veils of Spanish moss arch out over the dark waters of the river for most of its course. The river is fairly small—less than a hundred yards across—and slow moving; paddling in either direction should be no problem. The creek covers a distance of about 10 mi. If you're putting in at the boat ramp, most of the creek is to the S, upstream.

camping: There are no developed camping facilities in the central Croatan. In theory, primitive backcountry camping is permitted anywhere. In practice, however, the number of sites where there's enough room to make camp is quite limited. Catfish Lake has the largest clearing, one that's popular with hunters in winter. It's located next to the boat ramp. There's also a clearing at Great Lake, though it's a little smaller. To reach it, park in the lot at the end of the road and walk N along the ORV trail for about 50 ft until you see the clearing to the R. Neither lake has any facilities. There's another small clearing near the Brice Creek boat launch that is suitable for setting up camp. Construction of a pit toilet should be complete by 1996. All of these areas can be reached by vehicle.

fishing: Brice Creek offers the best fishing in the NF interior. The creek's dark waters are home to largemouth bass, black crappie and bluegill. On land, you can fish from the new fully accessible pier beside the boat ramp; otherwise you'll need a boat. Fishing on Catfish and Great Lakes is generally poor, due to their high level of acidity. Nevertheless, a number of species inhabit the lakes, yellow perch and black crappie among them. If you decide to give the lake a try, you'll need a boat; the dense pocosin that surrounds the lake makes access from the banks impossible.

hiking: Unless you're bushwhacking, hiking is on a single trail. The *Island Creek Forest Walk* is an easy half-mi nature trail that follows a creek through a forest with trees representative of bottomland swamp and upland pine/hardwood forest. 15 interpretive posts along the route identify trailside flora and geology. The trail is well-maintained, level and easy to follow. It's blazed with white dots and there's a footbridge at the only stream crossing. To reach the trailhead go 8.6 mi W of US-70 on Island Creek Rd (SR-1004).

mountain biking: Although there are no designated mountain bike trails on the NF, there are plenty of dirt roads and ORV trails. Despite the fact that all of these byways are virtually flat, riding them can be a real challenge. Sandy roadways turn to minor duststorms in the wake of passing vehicles during dry spells. If it's wet, the roads can quickly become impassable, tire-sucking muck. A bike may be the best way to get to the heart of the backcountry.

Theodore Roosevelt State Natural Area

The Roosevelt State Natural Area is a 265-acre preserve that encompasses parts of a maritime forest and salt marsh on Bogue Banks. It's located beside the Pine Knolls branch of the North Carolina Aquarium. Because of its small size, the natural area is best suited to nature study or to a short hike in conjunction with a visit to the aquarium. The preserve is open year-round.

Indian Beach (W) and Atlantic Beach (E) are the closest towns.

contact: Superintendent, Theodore Roosevelt State Natural Area, PO Box 127, Atlantic Beach, NC 28512; 919/726-3775.

getting there: From Atlantic Beach, take NC-58 (Salter Path Rd) 4.8 mi to a traffic light at Pine Knoll Blvd. Turn R and go 0.2 mi to Roosevelt Blvd. Turn L and go 0.2 mi to the State Natural Area and Aquarium entrance.

topography: A diversity of coastal habitats is found in the area, including maritime forest, swamp forest, salt marsh and dunes. **maps:** USGS Mansfield.

starting out: Facilities (restrooms, water, pay phones, vending machines) are in the adjacent NC Aquarium. The aquarium is open M–Sa 9 am to 5 pm and Su 1–5 pm. Admission is $3. You can call at 919/247-4003. The Roosevelt SNA is a nature preserve that is undeveloped except for the hiking trail.

activities: Hiking.

hiking: The *Alice G. Hoffman Nature Trail* begins at the Aquarium parking lot. The easy half-mi trail follows a well-worn path through the maritime forest and along the marshes. It's blazed with red dots and the trailhead is signed. 20 interpretive stations along the route briefly describe the ecology of coastal habitats. A self-guiding pamphlet is available inside the aquarium.

Fort Macon State Park

389-acre Fort Macon State Park combines the attractions of a state historical site with outdoor recreational activities associated with the coast and other coastal state parks. Fort Macon was built in 1826-34 on the eastern tip of Bogue Banks as a coastal defense. The fort was built with bricks in the shape of a pentagon. Its military function was abandoned in 1903 and in 1924 it was sold to the state for the sum of $1. 12 years later, Fort Macon State Park opened, only the second state park in the system. In addition to exploring the fort, which is open to the public, visitors come to swim in the ocean, fish from a jetty on Bogue Inlet, or walk along the white sand beach. With almost a million and a half visitors per year, Fort Macon is the busiest state park in North Carolina.

Atlantic City (W) is the closest town.

contact: Superintendent, Fort Macon State Park, P.O. Box 127, Atlantic Beach, NC 28512; 919/762-3775.

getting there: The state park is located at the end of NC-58, 2.2 mi E of the town of Atlantic Beach.

topography: Park terrain consists of a broad band of dunes oriented E–W that forms a natural barrier between the beach and ocean on one side and a narrow belt of maritime forest and a low-lying salt marsh on the other. The dunes reach a maximum height of 40 ft. **maps:** USGS Beaufort.

starting out: There are two main centers of activity in the park, a large wood and stone bathhouse with a long boardwalk that crosses the dunes and provides access to the oceanside beach, and Fort Macon. There are restrooms, water and a pay phone at both. The bathhouse also has a concession stand that is open seasonally. A picnic area with 7 shelters is located nearby among the sand dunes. There's a bookstore in the fort where you can pick up a park map and brochure. With no real backcountry, easy auto access and a popular tourist attraction, Fort Macon SP is frequently very crowded. Swimming is the most popular recreational activity in the park.

Alcohol is not allowed in the park. If you bring a dog, it must be kept on a leash.

activities: Fishing, Hiking, Kayaking/Canoeing.

fishing: Aside from visiting the fort and sunbathing, fishing is probably the most popular activity in the park. The main centers of activity are the beach and a long jetty that juts out into Beaufort Inlet. Another option is to fish from a boat, though don't expect to escape the crowds that way; the inlet is often crowded with fishing boats as well. The main catches in the surf and inlet include bluefish, mackerel, spot, flounder and seatrout.

hiking: There's one designated hiking trail in the park. The easy, half-mi *Elliot Coues Nature Trail* features plants such as red cedar, wax myrtle, virginia creeper, live oak and poison ivy as it passes through a small pocket of maritime forest before emerging onto some low sand dunes that overlook the sound. The well-maintained trail is blazed with a red dot. The trail begins near the entrance to the fort and ends on the beach next to the parking lot.

kayaking/canoeing: Paddling around Fort Macon is something of a mixed bag. On the one hand, there are miles of shoreline both ocean and sound—to explore along Bogue Banks and close proximity to Shackleford Banks and the Rachel Carson Estuarine Reserve, both of which are less than a mile away. On the other hand, these waters—particularly Beaufort Inlet—are frequently crowded with fishing boats and commercial vessels. Also, there's no overnight parking at Fort Macon, so any trip will have to begin and end on the same day. If you decide to give it a try, park at the fort and portage the 50 yds or so across the beach.

Rachel Carson Estuarine Research Reserve

Three main islands—Town Marsh, Carrot Island and Middle Marsh—and several lesser ones comprise the Rachel Carson component of the National Estuarine Research Reserve. The islands cover a total area of 2,675 acres, most of which is salt marsh. Other habitats present on the islands are shrub thicket, sand beach, and tidal flat. The reserve is located in the protected waters northeast of Beaufort Inlet between the mouths of the Newport and North Rivers. Most of the reserve is located just offshore from the community of Beaufort, and can easily be seen over the masts of sailboats and upper decks of fishing boats from the waterfront. Wild horses can be seen easily on the islands, which also provide an important habitat to less common wildlife, such as the peregrine falcon. More than 160 species of birds have been observed on the islands.

Beaufort (NW) is the closest town.

contact: Reserve Education Specialist, PO Box 1040, Beaufort, NC 28516; 919/728-2170

getting there: The only way to reach the islands is by boat. You can get a boat ride at the NC Maritime Museum or with any of a number of local private ferry concessions. Private ferries cost about $8 round-trip. Several leave from Front St in downtown Beaufort. If you have your own boat, you can put in at the public boat ramp at the E end of Front St, 2 mi from downtown. There's a large parking lot, as well as restrooms. The reserve is only about 100 yds across the narrow channel.

topography: The fragile islands of the Rachel Carson Reserve are dispersed over a wide area. There is little upland on the islands, which are mostly tidal flat and salt marsh. Bird Shoal has the most extensive sand beach. **maps:** USGS Beaufort, Harker's Island.

starting out: There are no facilities on any of the islands. Beaufort is a busy tourist destinations, with restaurants, hotels and shops. The islands of the reserve are day-use only; camping is not allowed.

activities: Kayaking/Canoeing, Hiking, Fishing.

kayaking/canoeing: A canoe or kayak is the best type of craft for exploring the shallow waters and fragile estuarine environment of these islands. A day is sufficient time to circle the islands and paddle in and out of the various channels that have helped form them. This is a very busy boating area, with both recreational and commercial vessels present in numbers. For longer paddling trips, head S and E to Cape Lookout National Seashore, which features more than 50 mi of undeveloped barrier islands. The NS is about 2 mi S from Carrot Island.

hiking: Although there are no designated trails on the reserve, several areas are suitable to hiking. The largest is the long stretch of beach on Bird Shoal. At low tide, you can walk across the tidal flats between islands.

fishing: With so much boat traffic, this is a less-than-ideal place to fish. Still, it can be done. Gigging for flounder is popular in the shallower waters. Other catches are spot, mullet and drum.

Cape Lookout National Seashore

Cape Lookout National Seashore consists of 3 long, narrow, low-lying barrier islands that are completely undeveloped except for a ghost town shipping village and the well-known landmark lighthouse with the black and white diamonds (closed to the public). The 3 islands—North Core Banks, South Core Banks, and Shackleford Banks—are together more than 55 mi long, rarely more than half a mile wide, and cover about 28,400 acres of beach, sand dune, shrub thicket, maritime forest and salt marsh.

Although the islands were settled in the 18th century and populated as recently as the 1960s, today they are uninhabited—except for wildlife and a herd of some 200 feral horses on Shackleford Banks. Unlike the better-known Cape Hatteras, Cape Lookout National Seashore is free of roads and a heavy tourist trade. No bridge connects any of the islands to the mainland; they can only be reached by private boat or toll ferry. One of the longest stretches of natural beach on the East Coast, its various habitats support literally hundreds of bird species, such as the brown pelican, laughing gull, common loon, herons and egrets; mammals such as the river otter, raccoons, and rabbits; and diamond-back terrapins and the endangered loggerhead turtle, which comes ashore to nest.

Beaufort (W) and Ocracoke (N) are the closest towns.

contact: Superintendent, Cape Lookout National Seashore, 131 Charles Street, Harker's Island, NC 28531; 919/728-2250.

getting there: The NS headquarters is located at the SE end of Harker's Island, 12 mi from Beaufort. Take US-70 N then E approx 9 mi out of Beaufort to Harker Island Rd (SR-1332). Go R at the brown NS sign and proceed 8.7 mi to the NS headquarters. Shackleford and Core Banks can only be reached by boat. Private ferries leave from Harker's Island, Beaufort, Davis, Atlantic, and Ocracoke and provide access to various points along Core Banks. round-trip rates very from about $12 for a person to $65-80 for a 4-wheel drive vehicle.

topography: Long, narrow barrier islands with tidal flats and salt marshes on the sound side and white sand beaches on the ocean front. The center of the islands are covered by dunes anchored by sea grasses, shrub thickets, and small tracts of maritime forest. **maps:** USGS Harker Island, Beaufort, Cape Lookout, Horsepen Point, Styron Bay, Wainwright Island, Portsmouth, Atlantic.

starting out: If you're approaching the NS from Beaufort or Harker's Island, the modern new headquarters building is worth a visit. In addition to a small selection of books for sale, museum-style exhibits on the history and natural features of the seashore's barrier islands and a 12-minute film, rangers can provide maps, brochures and information on local wind, weather and tide conditions. Restrooms, water fountains, and pay phones are on the premises. The headquarters is open year-round, 8 am–4:30 pm.

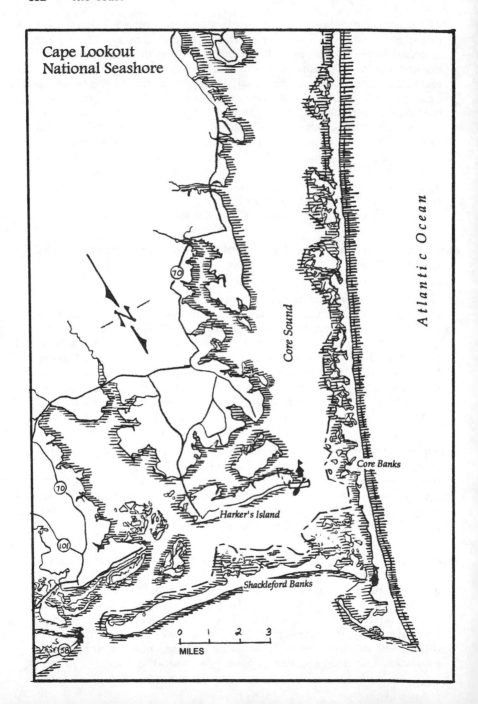

Cape Lookout
National Seashore

Atlantic Ocean

Core Sound

70

N

Core Banks

Harker's Island

70

101

Shackleford Banks

58

0 1 2 3
MILES

Another, smaller visitors center is located on Core Banks beside the lighthouse. The white brick building houses exhibits on local history and ecology. A small selection of books is for sale. There are restrooms in the building, but no water taps. There are a couple of water pumps nearby, but signs caution that they are not always reliable. In any case, you should bring your own water supply to the islands.

Picnic areas with shelters, tables and grills are located on Harker's Island, near the lighthouse on S Core Banks and on the W end of Shackleford Banks. Swimming is allowed in either the sound or the ocean, but there's no supervision. Officially, swimming is discouraged, due to the strong, unpredictable currents and riptides that are frequently present on the ocean side. If you do swim, be sure to have at least one other person with you.

Pets are not allowed on the NS.

activities: Kayaking/Canoeing, Camping, Fishing, Hiking.

kayaking/canoeing: With well over 100 mi of coast on the ocean and sounds, you could spend weeks kayaking up and down the islands of Cape Lookout NS. The close proximity of most of the seashore to the mainland, however, makes it easy to go out just for the day. Either way, a kayak is an ideal vessel for exploring close-up the shallow estuarine environment of Back and Core Sounds. Paddlers have their choice of 5 launch sites, all of them within 3 mi of the islands (most are within 1 or 2 mi). Put-ins are at Fort Macon SP, the boat ramp in Beaufort, NS headquarters, and at WRC boat ramps at Sealevel and Green Pt. Regardless of where you're starting out from, it's a good idea to check local conditions with the staff at the NS office on Harker's Island. Wind, weather, and tides can all affect your trip. Even on beautiful, sunny days the wind and tides should be taken into account. Another factor to keep in mind is that you'll be sharing the water with boats of all kinds. Although it's possible to paddle for hours without coming within earshot of a motor boat, certain areas—Beaufort Inlet, Bearden Inlet and Lighthouse Channel—are typically busy. If you're planning on camping, be aware that finding a suitable landing site on the sound side can be difficult, as sandy beaches are relatively scarce. A couple good areas are near the lighthouse and on Shackleford Banks. Of course if you're near an inlet, you can always paddle around to the ocean side.

camping: There are no developed campgrounds on Cape Lookout NS. Backcountry camping is permitted on all 3 islands, except where posted. Camping is not allowed within 100 ft of the lighthouse or a shade shelter, in Portsmouth Village, or near any of the concession cabins. There are restrooms (no showers) in the visitor center near the lighthouse and in the picnic area at the W end of Shackleford Banks. Other than those, there are no facilities within the NS. Plan on bringing all the water you'll need. Generally, the area around the lighthouse sees the most camping activity. Other parts of the seashore may be virtually empty. Bring extra long tent stakes to make sure your tent stays put in high winds. Campfires are allowed, but only below the high-tide line. Given the scarcity of driftwood on the beaches, a portable stove is a good idea. Mosquitoes—present May to Oct—are generally more prevalent on the sound side of the islands.

fishing: Between the protected waters of the sounds, the open surf of the Atlantic, and the transitional zones at the inlets, there's a wide variety of marine habitats to fish. Surfcasting, wading in the shallow flats of the sounds or fishing from a boat are the primary methods. Among the many species caught are striped bass, spotted sea trout, red drum, flounder, weakfish and bluefish.

hiking: Although there are no designated hiking trails, the 60 mi of beaches on the three islands are ideal for a short stroll or a multi-day expedition. Along the way, you're not likely to see anything permanent except beach, dunes, sea and sky. This is particularly true on Shackleford Banks, where the only structures of any kind are at a small picnic area on the W end of the 9-mi island. 4-wheel drive vehicles are allowed on N and S Core Banks; they're prohibited on Shackleford Banks. Wherever you're heading, be sure to bring sunscreen, a hat, long sleeved shirt and long pants, as there's almost no shade on the islands.

Cedar Island National Wildlife Refuge

Cedar Island National Wildlife Refuge covers 12,525 acres of black needlerush marsh and maritime forest off the edge of the mainland in Carteret County. With 80% of the refuge salt marsh, and no trails or developed facilities, the refuge is one of the hardest backcountry areas to visit in the state. Most visitors see the refuge from their cars, passing through incidentally on NC-12 on the way to or from the busy Cedar Island–Ocracoke ferry located at the island's northern edge. Nevertheless, with 270 species of birds sighted on the refuge, it's an excellent part of the coast for wildlife viewing. Among the bird species is an abundance of ducks, among them black ducks, bufflehead, red-breasted mergansers and redhead ducks.

Beaufort (SW) is the closest town.

contact: Cedar Island National Wildlife Refuge, c/o Mattamuskeet National Wildlife Refuge, Route 1, Box N-2, Swan Quarter, NC 27885; 919/926-4021.

getting there: NC-12 runs through the heart of the refuge. The only other access points to the refuge are the boat ramps described below. The refuge headquarters on Lola Rd has been closed due to budget cuts.

topography: Salt marsh and low-lying maritime forest comprise the vast majority of the refuge. Elevations are not more than 50 ft. **maps:** USGS Atlantic, North Bay.

starting out: The refuge is best seen from NC-12 in a vehicle or from a canoe or kayak. The aquatic habitats that comprise the refuge are not really suitable for backcountry travel. There are currently no facilities on the refuge. It's open only during daylight hours; camping is not permitted. Restrooms and water are at the Cedar Island–Ocracoke ferry terminal located at the end of NC-12.

activities: Canoeing/Kayaking, Fishing.

canoeing/kayaking: Paddling along Cedar Island's edges is probably the closest you'll come to actually experiencing the refuge. The refuge is surrounded by Core Sound (E), Pamlico Sound (N) and West Bay (W). These are generally quiet waters that receive relatively light boat traffic. 2 channels cut through the refuge, connecting West Bay and Core Sound. Cape Lookout NS is less than 4 mi E. There are 2 boat ramps on the refuge. One is at the end of Lola Rd, 2.4 mi from NC-12. The other is located on an unnamed side road off NC-12 at the S end of Thorofare Bay Bridge.

fishing: The waters surrounding the refuge support populations of the major saltwater species found along the NC coast, among them bluefish, flounder, drum, seatrout and tarpon. Fishing is from a boat.

Goose Creek State Park

Goose Creek State Park covers just under 1,600 acres of wetlands and wooded upland on the north shore of the Pamlico River. The natural habitats of the park are defined by the water that surrounds them on 3 sides. Moving inland from the Pamlico River and Goose, Flatty and Mallard Creeks, sandy coast, brackish marsh, southern bottomland hardwood swamp and upland pine forest are all represented within a relatively small area. Spanish moss adds to the drama of the park's environment, hanging in loose trellises from pines and baldcypresses, particularly along the river. The park is home or temporary resting place to a wide assortment of birds; depending on the season, you might encounter egrets, herons, swans, geese or ducks. The endangered red-cockaded woodpecker nests in the park's towering loblolly pines. White-tailed deer seem particularly abundant in the park, and rather accustomed to contact with people. Note: The Park is infested with ticks during warm-weather months. Mosquitoes are also abundant during this period.

Washington (W) and Bath (E) are the closest towns.

contact: Superintendent, Goose Creek State Park, Route 2, Box 372, Washington, NC 27889; 919/923-2191.

getting there: From US-264 10 mi E of Washington, turn S onto Camp Leach Rd (SR-1334). The park entrance is 2.3 mi ahead.

topography: The park's geography is typical of the eastern part of the coastal plain. Lower elevations are dominated by marsh and swampland, with a pine/hardwood forest covering elevations high enough to have adequate drainage. **maps:** USGS Blounts Bay.

starting out: Maps and brochures are available at the Park office, open M–F 8 am to 4:30 pm. At the site are restrooms, a pay phone, water fountain and display board with park map. There's another pay phone at the swimming beach and restrooms with water fountain nearby. There are also several picnicking areas in the park, all of them located near the large parking lots at the end of the park road. Each area has a large open-air shelter, as well as individual tables and grills. Pine and oak trees provide shade. Modern restrooms are nearby. Also in the area is a small white-sand swimming beach (open seasonally). Several picnic tables are close by, as is a pit toilet.

Alcohol is not allowed in the park. Pets must be kept on a leash.

activities: Hiking, Camping, Canoeing/Kayaking, Fishing.

hiking: 7 mi of hiking trails allow you to wander along the shoreline and through upland pine/hardwood forest, cypress swamp and brackish marshes. 2 observation platforms provide views of the river and creeks and their shorelines. The trails are all easy to locate and follow, with signs posted at trailheads. Boardwalks provide an elevated pathway through several wet areas. Don't miss the one that zigzags through the dark and gloomy bald cypress swamp along *Goose Creek Trail*. The boardwalk near the end of *Ragged Point Trail* crosses a densely vegetated marshland and leads to an observation platform with outstanding views of the river and marsh bog. Identifying markers along the way point out native plant and animal species. Trailheads are located near the campground and picnic areas.

camping: There's a large, 12-site campground located near the confluence of Goose and Fatty Creeks. The sites are located along a primitive dirt road that dead ends in the campground (large trucks and RVs are not allowed on the road—they can be left at a small parking area). Stands of pine provide shade. Each of the widely-spaced sites has a picnic table and grill. There are 2 very modern pit toilets (no showers) and a number of water spigots along the road. Sites cost $5/night. 3 trails pass through the campground, providing scenic views of the river and creeks. The canoe/kayak launch area is also in the campground.

canoeing/kayaking: Between the Pamlico River and Goose, Flatty and Mallard Creeks, there are more than a dozen miles of shoreline in the park to explore by canoe or kayak. Each of the creeks begins as a narrow stream that widens to a broad channel as it flows S and empties into the Pamlico River, which is about 3 mi across when it passes the park. The currents of these creeks and the river are slow enough to allow leisurely paddling up- or downstream.

Canoes and kayaks can be launched onto Goose Creek from a small landing in the park campground. A short portage from the parking area is necessary. Larger boats can be launched from the WRC boat ramp at Dinah's Landing, located on the W bank of Goose Creek at the end of Dinah Landing Rd. To get there from the park take Camp Leach Rd (SR-1334) 2 mi to Goose Creek Rd (SR-1332) and turn L. At the jct with Dinah Landing Rd—about 2 mi—turn L and proceed to the boat ramp.

fishing: Both salt- and freshwater fish are found in the tidal waters of the Pamlico River and its feeder creeks. Although there are places along the shore from which it is possible to cast, fishing from a boat is the best method. Freshwater species in the area include largemouth bass, bluegill and white and yellow perch. Among the many saltwater fish are American shad, seatrout, drum, bluefish and mullet.

Roanoke River National Wildlife Refuge

The Roanoke River National Wildlife Refuge is part of an ambitious project, involving government agencies, conservation groups and private industry, to protect the entire ecosystem of the lower Roanoke floodplain. The ecological importance of this region was made clear by a 1981 study that found that the 137-mile river floodplain contains the largest bottomland hardwood forest in the mid-Atlantic region. At present, more than 80,000 acres of the lower Roanoke are protected by the US Fish & Wildlife Service, The NC Wildlife Resources Commission, and a partnership between The Nature Conservancy and Georgia Pacific. The Roanoke River National Wildlife Refuge, which includes 33,000 acres along the north shore of the river in Bertie County, was established in 1989. These lands are being managed primarily to protect the habitat of wintering waterfowl and the abundance of other wildlife that inhabits the region. In addition to this conservation objective, recreational activities such as hunting, fishing and boating are permitted. The refuge is open year-round during daylight hours.

Williamston and Plymouth are both located on the river's S side.

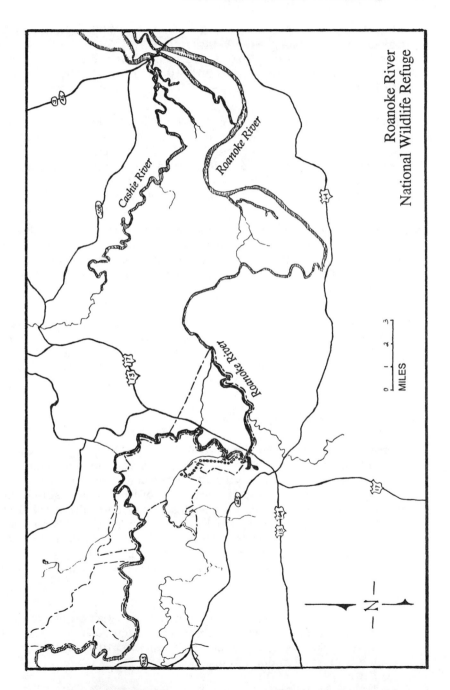

Roanoke River
National Wildlife Refuge

contact: Refuge Manager, Roanoke River National Wildlife Refuge, PO Box 430, Windsor, NC 27983; 919/794-5326. Additional information on the lower Roanoke River floodplain is available from the Nature Conservancy, Suite 201, 4011 University Dr, Durham, NC 27707; 919/403-8558.

getting there: Currently, most of the Refuge is only accessible by boat. There are 3 WRC ramps on the lower river. The busiest is located on the E side of the US-17 bridge near Williamston. Upriver from there a ramp is located in the small community of Hamilton. Downriver, there's a ramp at the bridge on NC-308, just before the river empties into Albemarle Sound.

topography: The Roanoke is a wide, slow-moving river. Dominant plant communities on the river's broad, shallow flood plain are cypress-gum swamp and hardwood bottomlands. **maps:** USGS Hamilton, Quitsna, Williamston, Jamesville, Windsor South, Plymouth West, Woodard, Westover.

starting out: The Roanoke River NWR is still in its infancy. Although there are tentative plans to construct a visitors center and public-use facilities, at present the refuge is entirely undeveloped. Information about visiting the refuge, including several basic maps, is available from the headquarters in Windsor.

activities: Canoeing/Kayaking, Fishing.

canoeing/kayaking: A canoe or kayak is the ideal vessel from which to explore the refuge. The river's slow current makes paddling almost effortless, and the quiet of a non-motorized boat will allow you to come in close contact with some of the refuge's abundant wildlife. Put-ins and take-outs are described above. From the first put-in at Hamilton to the mouth of the river is about 57 mi. The river becomes tidal on its last 15-20 mi. Paddlers wanting to take a tour of a week or more may want to continue E along Albemarle Sound to the Alligator River and the canoe/kayak trails of the Alligator River NWR.

fishing: Fishing is one of the most popular activities on the refuge. Primary game species in the river are largemouth and striped bass, American shad, white perch, channel catfish and crappie. Fishing is most often done from a boat.

Merchants Millpond State Park

Merchants Millpond State Park is one of the most varied and exotic natural environments in North Carolina. A southern cypress swamp, 760-acre millpond, and upland pine/hardwood forest are all found on the park's 2,918 acres. The park centerpiece is Merchant's Millpond, a freshwater impoundment whose dark waters are covered by duckweed and shaded by bald cypress and tupelo gum trees draped with Spanish moss and resurrection ferns. The play of light and shadow creates a moody, dramatic atmosphere unlike that anywhere else in the state. At the eastern end of the pond is Lassiter Swamp, where an "enchanted forest" of twisted, misshapen tupelo gum trees grows out of a soft, boggy bottom. Some of the trees in the swamp are more than 500 years old.

Gatesville (W) and Sunbury (E) are the closest towns.

contact: Superintendent, Merchants Millpond State Park, Route 1, Box 141-A, Gatesville, NC 27938; 919/357-1191.

getting there: The park entrance is located on US-158 between the towns of Easons Crossroads and Sunbury, 4.8 mi W of the jct with US-32. To get to the millpond and canoe launch area, from the main park entrance go W on US-158 0.3 mi. Turn L onto Millpond Rd (SR-1403) and drive 1.4 mi to the parking lot, L.

topography: A large pond, an extensive cypress-gum swamp, and forested upland comprise the geography of the park. The upland terrain is gently rolling hills, with elevation gains of less than 100 ft. **maps:** USGS Beckford.

starting out: Maps, brochures and other park information are available at either the park office or the canoe rental shack. Restrooms and a pay phone are also at both locations. Vending machines are located at the canoe launch. A small picnic area with tables and grills is there too. The park is infested with ticks, which are worst from Apr to mid-Oct.

Alcohol is not permitted in the Park. Pets must be leashed.

activities: Canoeing/Kayaking, Camping, Hiking, Fishing.

canoeing/kayaking: Canoeing is by far the most popular activity in the park. On busy weekends—spring and fall are busiest—dozens of paddlers ply the dark, heavily vegetated waters of the 760-acre millpond and swamp. Fortunately, you won't see many of them: cypress and tupelo gum trees grow in dense groves, carving the pond into maze-like channels and pockets. The boat ramp is at the Millpond Rd entrance. You can bring your own canoe or rent one from the park. Rental rates are $2.50/hr for the first 2 hrs, $1/hr for each additional hr, with a max of $10 for a full day or overnight. Merchants Millpond is the only state park with campsites that can only be reached by canoe (see below). Except for campers, all boats must be off the pond by one hour before park closing time.

camping: If you're planning on spending the night at Merchant's Millpond, you have 5 different camping facilities to choose from.

A 20-site tent & trailer campground is located in a wooded area beyond the park office. The sites are well-spaced, and each has a tent pad, picnic table and grill. A shower/restroom facility is located in the center of the loop drive. Sites cost $9/night. One of the hiking trails begins at the edge of the campground. The campground is open Mar 15 to Nov 30.

A youth group camping area with 2 sites is located 0.3 mi S of the canoe launching area on Millpond Rd. The sites occupy a large grassy meadow and adjacent wooded area. There are grills and picnic tables. Pit toilets and water (off Dec 1 to Mar 15) are also in the area. Sites can be reserved in advance. The fee is $1/person/night with a $5 minimum per site.

A 2.5-mi hike to the far end of the loop trail will bring you to a 5-site primitive backcountry campground perched above Lassiter Swamp. The sites are spaced far enough apart that you won't get to know your neighbors unless you want to. Each site has an iron grill. There's a single pit toilet in the area. Bring your own water, since there's no source near the campsites. Sites cost $5/night.

The primitive canoe camp is located in a wooded area beside the millpond about a mile from the canoe launch area. The route is marked by orange buoys. There are 6 campsites, each with its own grill. A pit toilet is centrally located. Water must be packed in, as there is no source in the area. Picnicking is not permitted in the area. Sites cost $5/night. If you're renting a canoe to camp here, $10 covers the rental for a 24-hour period. These sites are very popular, and can fill up early on busy weekends.

The group canoe camp has 3 sites. It's located about a half-mi beyond the primitive canoe camp. Each site has a grill, and there's a central pit toilet. Yellow buoys mark the route from the canoe launch area, which is about 1.5 mi away. Water is not available at the camp. Reservations are accepted for these sites. The fee is $1/person/night with a $5 minimum per site.

hiking: There are about 9 mi of hiking trails in the park. The main trail is an easy 6.7-mi loop which winds through the scenic hardwood/pine upland forest that rises above the millpond and swamp. The trail follows a ridge for part of its route with excellent views of the swamp. The trail is unnamed, but is often referred to as the *Millpond Loop Trail*. It's blazed with white dots and signed at the trailhead and at trail crossings. Improvements include one long boardwalk and footbridges and logs that cross wet areas. The trailhead is located just N of the bridge across Bennett's Creek on Millpond Rd. Park at the canoe rental area and walk about a quarter-mi up the road to a sign, R. There's also a new, 2-mi trail named the *Coleman Trail* that follows a wide, level forest break in a loop along the S edge of the millpond. This trail is also blazed with white dots. It begins and ends at the S end of the boat ramp parking lot.

fishing: Bennett's Creek and the millpond are home to a number of species of game fish, principally largemouth bass, black crappie, chain pickerel and bluegill. Although fishing from a boat offers the most freedom to follow the fish, casting from the banks near the bridge on Millpond Rd seems to be popular with regulars.

Pocosin Lakes National Wildlife Refuge

Pocosin Lakes National Wildlife Refuge is made up of a checkerboard of holdings that total 111,000 acres in Hyde, Tyrrell and Washington Counties. The refuge includes all or parts of 3 lakes—16,600-acre Phelps Lake, 2,800-acre Pungo Lake and 4,100-acre New Lake—with pocosin and bottomland hardwood forest accounting for most of the vegetation on land. The refuge functions primarily as a winter stopover for migratory birds and waterfowl. Pocosin Lakes has not been developed for visitation, though backcountry travel is possible for those willing to make the effort. One improvement is an observation tower on Pungo Lake, from which the thousands of geese, swans and ducks that winter there can be viewed. In all, 207 species of birds have been observed on the refuge.

Roper (NW), Creswell (N) and Columbia (NE) are the closest towns.

contact: Refuge Manager, Pocosin Lakes National Wildlife Refuge, Route 1, Box 195-B, Creswell, NC 27928; 919/797-4431.

getting there: A number of state roads criss-cross the dispersed holdings of the refuge. Access is from US-64, NC-45 and NC-94. To reach the refuge office, from US-64 in the community of Roper, take Newland Rd E 6.7 mi to Shore Dr. Turn R and drive 3 mi to the refuge office.

topography: The predominant plant communities on the refuge are low-lying pocosin and bottomland hardwood forest. The terrain is flat. **maps:** USGS Pungo Lake, New Lake NW, New Lake, Creswell SE, Fairfield NW, Scotia, Roper South, Frying Pan.

starting out: Aside from hunters in the fall, most visitors see Pocosin Lakes NWR from their cars. Exploring the refuge up close takes some initiative and effort, as there are no designated hiking trails. Refuge maps and a birding list are available at the office on Shore Dr. Hours are M–F 7:30 am–4 pm. When the office is closed, some maps are usually left outside the door. If you're going to be on the refuge during hunting season, blaze orange should be worn.

Camping and fires are not allowed.

activities: Mountain Biking, Hiking, Canoeing/Kayaking.

mountain biking: A mountain bike may be the best and most challenging way to see the refuge. The refuge is crossed by dozens of miles of gated dirt and grass roads, all of which are open to bikes. Bikers should be aware, however, that the roads are unimproved and not frequently used; even in the best of conditions they can be difficult to ride; after a wet spell, they can become impassable.

hiking: Although there are no designated hiking trails on the refuge, the numerous gated, primitive roads that cross it offer an opportunity to explore its fascinating habitats up close. Conditions are extremely primitive. There are no signs or blazes, and you'll

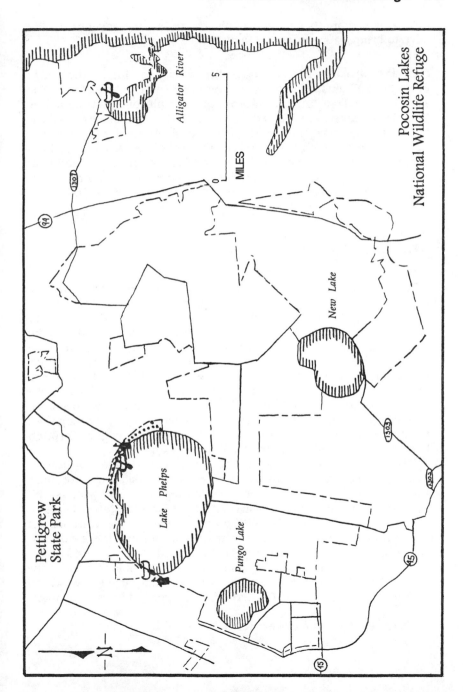

Pocosin Lakes
National Wildlife Refuge

Alligator River

MILES

New Lake

Pettigrew
State Park

Lake Phelps

Pungo Lake

N

not likely see another person while you're in the backcountry. Be sure to bring a topo map and compass.

canoeing/kayaking: The best opportunity for paddling on the refuge is on Lake Phelps. Refuge lands comprise the lake's S shore. The 16,600 acre lake is an outstanding example of a Carolina bay lake. Boat ramps are located on Shore Drive and on the lake's N shore in Pettigrew State Park (see below). Another option is the Alligator River, which is fronted by a parcel of refuge land on the N shore of an inlet known as the Frying Pan. From there, paddlers can leave the refuge and head out to the open waters of the Alligator River. A boat ramp is located at the end of SR-1307.

Pettigrew State Park

Pettigrew State Park occupies a long, narrow crescent along the north shore of Lake Phelps. Park land covers more than 1,100 acres of Cypress swamp and hardwood forest. 16,600-acre Lake Phelps is the second-largest natural lake in North Carolina. Like many other Carolina bay lakes in the region, its origin is a mystery. The lake is not fed by any river or stream, relying entirely on rain to maintain its water level. As a result, the lake water is crystal clear, with a sandy bottom easily visible on most of the lake. Maximum depth is only 9 ft. In winter, the lake becomes temporary home to migrating waterfowl such as the Canada goose, tundra swan, and numerous duck species. December through February are the best months for birdwatching.

History is also on display in the park. Approximately 30 Indian dugout canoes have been excavated from the lake. Most are more than 1,500 years old and one, estimated at 4,380 yrs, is the second oldest canoe ever unearthed in the United States. Of more recent historical interest is Somerset Place, the antebellum plantation of Josiah Collins, the man who drained the swamp in the eighteenth century and transformed it into productive farmland. The state historic site is located on park land west of the park office. Also nearby is the Pettigrew family cemetery, which includes the grave of Confederate general James Johnston Pettigrew.

Creswell (N) is the closest town.

contact: Superintendent, Pettigrew State Park, Route 1, Box 336, Creswell, NC 27928; 919/797-4475.

getting there: From US-64, turn S at the SP sign onto Sixth St. Go 0.3 mi and turn L onto Main St. Go 1.8 mi and turn R onto Thirty Foot Canal Rd (SR-1160). Go 5.6 mi and turn L onto Lakeshore Dr (SR-1166). The park entrance is immediately R.

topography: Park geography is dominated by the lake, bald cypress swamp and a narrow corridor of dense bottomland forest with several state champion trees. The lake has a maximum depth of 9 ft. **maps:** USGS Creswell, Roper South, New Lake NW.

starting out: Park maps and brochures are available at the SP office, open M–F from 8 am to 4:30 pm. Restrooms and a pay phone are there. A large picnic area, with shelter, tables, grills, and water fountain is located between the park office and boat ramp. A grove of bald cypresses provide shade. A small building beside the boat ramp houses displays on local wildlife and the dugout canoes that have recently been excavated from the lake.   Alcohol is not allowed in the park. Pets must be kept on a leash.

activities: Canoeing/Kayaking, Fishing, Camping, Hiking.

canoeing/kayaking: The shallow, crystal-clear waters of 16,600-acre Lake Phelps offer an unusual opportunity for canoeists and kayakers: to explore what's below the boat as easily as what's above it. The lake's 15-mi shoreline includes cypress swamp, fresh-water marsh and hardwood forest. A stiff wind often blows across the lake. You may want to call ahead to check local conditions before making a trip. The park boat ramp is located just beyond the park office. It's the only access to the lake, which helps keep boat traffic to a minimum. Watch for river otters on the muddy shore beside the ramp.

fishing: Most fishing on Lake Phelps must be done from a boat. Although there are a couple short piers beside the boat ramp from which you are allowed to cast, this is a busy area. Another popular spot is the new pier at the lake's W end. The lake is well known for its largemouth bass. Other species commonly caught are yellow perch, chain pickerel, catfish, and bluegill.

camping: There's a nice little 13-site campground just E of the park office. Although the campground is set back only a short distance from the lake, it's separated from the water by the impenetrable curtain of dense swamp and hardwood forest. About half of the sites are on the edge of this forest; these provide the most privacy. The others are scattered across a large grassy clearing. The limited number of sites and the towering trees and lush vegetation which surround them lend a feeling of isolation that's rare for state park car campgrounds. All sites are large, and each includes a picnic table and grill. A shower/restroom facility is centrally located. Sites cost $9/night. A portion of the hiking trail that runs beside the lake passes through the campground before leading to Somerset Place and the Bee Tree Overlook.

Also E of the park office, but further along the hiking trail (about 0.5 mi) is a youth group camp. This area, which can only be reached by foot, is set amidst looming cypresses and sweetgums. There are picnic tables, tent pads and a grill in the area. A water pump and pit toilet are also close by. All other supplies must be packed in. The fee is $1/person/night.

hiking: Starting from the park office, an unnamed carriage trail runs E and W for about 4 mi. As might be expected from its original purpose, the trail, which is now only open to hikers, is wide, level and easy to follow. It's signed in both directions at the main parking lot. If you head E you'll pass through a cypress-sweetgum forest that contains some of the largest specimens of tree species in the state. The trail also passes by historic Somerset Place and ends at a short boardwalk at Bee Tree Overlook. The view out over the lake is OK, but is partially obscured by two trees. A short spur leads from the main trail to the Pettigrew family cemetery. If you're heading W from the parking lot, the trail runs about 3 mi through a cypress-hardwood forest before ending at a long boardwalk that passes through an eerie cypress swamp and ends at Moccasin overlook. There's a small platform with benches that offers the best views of the lake in the park. This part of the park is particularly rewarding at sunset.

Swan Quarter National Wildlife Refuge

Swan Quarter National Wildlife Refuge occupies 15,500 acres of loblolly pine forest and salt marsh on the north shore of Pamlico

Sound. The refuge also includes 27,082 acres of open water on the sound. It has been left in an almost completely undeveloped state, and is being managed primarily for waterfowl habitat protection and conservation. Located on the Atlantic Flyway, Swan Quarter is visited by more than 200 species of birds. A lack of hiking trails or roads limits the opportunity for backcountry travel on the refuge, though the relatively quiet waters of the sound are ideal for kayaking, canoeing and fishing.

Swan Quarter (N) is the closest town.

contact: Swan Quarter National Wildlife Refuge, Route 1 Box N-2, Swan Quarter, NC 27855; 919/926-4021.

getting there: From the jct of US-64 and Main St in Swan Quarter, go 6 mi W on US-64 to a gravel Refuge access road, L. The 2-mi road ends at a parking area and fishing pier on Pamlico Sound.

topography: Refuge habitats are low-lying and aquatic. A relatively small area has drainage sufficient to allow the growth of forest species. **maps:** USGS Swan Quarter, Scranton, Great Island, Pamlico Point.

starting out: The refuge is more or less completely undeveloped; the only structure is a long fishing pier. There are no facilities on the refuge, nor is there a main office. Information about Swan Quarter is available at the Mattamuskeet NWR. Camping is not allowed on the refuge.

activities: Kayaking/Canoeing, Fishing.

kayaking/canoeing: Almost two-thirds of the refuge is open water on Pamlico Sound. There are dozens of miles of coastline and several islands to explore within the refuge. Paddlers should be comfortable with open water conditions before attempting the sometimes rough water of Pamlico Sound. Boat traffic in the vicinity of the refuge is generally very light. Although there's no official boat launch within the refuge, a kayak or canoe could be launched easily from beside the pier at the end of the refuge access road.

fishing: Anglers have the option of fishing from land or a boat. On land, there's a 1,000-ft pier at the end of the refuge access road that's popular with local fishermen. There's also some open space on the banks adjacent to the pier from which it's possible to cast. A canoe or kayak can be put in the water there as well. Species caught include gray trout, seatrout, mackerel and red drum

Mattamuskeet National Wildlife Refuge

With a surface area of 40,000 acres, Lake Mattamuskeet is the largest natural lake in North Carolina. Like most of the Carolina bay lakes, it's shallow—average depth is 2 feet—and has a bed of peat. The forces that created the lake are the subject of debate, with proposed causes including cataclysmic events such as a conflagration or meteor shower. In addition to the lake, the refuge encompasses 10,000 acres of marsh, forest and farmland in a narrow strip around its shoreline. It was established in 1934 as a waterfowl sanctuary, a role which is still the primary focus of refuge management. Every fall and winter, Lake Mattamuskeet becomes temporary home to tens of thousands of migrating ducks, geese, and swans. In all, more than 200 species of birds have been observed at the refuge, including the bald eagle, peregrine falcon and osprey. November to February are the best viewing months. Among mammals, the white-tailed deer is the most frequently seen. Other less welcome inhabitants are mosquitoes and cottonmouth snakes. The refuge is open year-round during daylight hours.

Engelhard (E) and Swan Quarter (SW) are the closest towns.

contact: Refuge Manager, Mattamuskeet National Wildlife Refuge, Route 1, Box N-2, Swan Quarter, NC 27885; 919/926-4021.

getting there: The primary access to the refuge is from US-94, which runs N and S on a thin embankment of land that bisects the lake. The refuge office and most facilities are located at the end of a 2-mi gravel road (E from US-94) at the S end of the lake.

topography: The knee-deep lake is surrounded by marsh, agricultural land, and bottomland forest. Elevations on this terrain rarely rise more than 10 ft above the lake. Drainage is naturally poor, but has been augmented by the construction of a series of canals. **maps:** USGS New Holland, Fairfield, Engelhard W, Middletown, Swanquarter, New Lake SE.

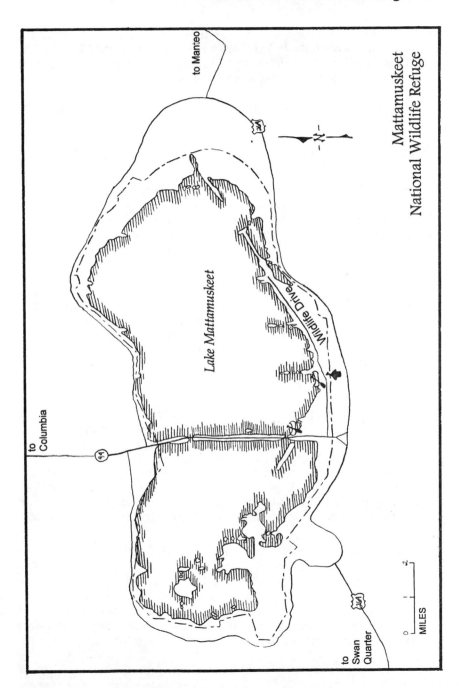

Mattamuskeet
National Wildlife Refuge

Lake Mattamuskeet

Wildlife Drive

to Manteo

to Columbia

to Swan Quarter

MILES

starting out: Refuge maps and brochures can be picked up at the NWR office, open M–F 7:30 am to 4 pm. Most visitors see the refuge from US 94, which bisects the lake. The road has very wide grassy shoulders, making it easy to park for wildlife viewing or fishing.

Camping on the refuge is not allowed, nor is swimming in the lake.

activities: Canoeing/Kayaking, Fishing, Hiking.

canoeing/kayaking: Lake Mattamuskeet covers about 40,000 acres with a shoreline of roughly 50 mi. The 16 mi long by 8 mi wide lake is effectively cut in half by the embankment on which NC-94 runs, although it's easy enough to move a canoe or kayak from one side of the lake to the other. With an average depth of only 2 ft, it's perfectly suited to the shallow draft of a canoe or kayak. During the fall and winter, paddlers can expect to share the lake with thousands of swans, geese, and ducks. Portions of the lake do freeze every so often in winter, though ice rarely lasts for long. The number of boats on the lake can often be counted on one hand. Boats can be launched from either of 2 ramps at the S end of the lake. One is near the refuge office and the old Mattamuskeet Lodge. The other is on US-94 immediately N of the refuge access road.

fishing: Largemouth and striped bass, catfish and bream are all found in the lake and adjacent canals. Fishing is permitted from Mar 1 to Nov 1. Fishing from a boat is probably the easiest method, although the wide grassy shoulders of US-94—from which bank fishing is permitted year-round—seems to be popular with locals. Bank fishing is not permitted from the refuge access road. Herring dipping is allowed between Mar 1 and May 15. Blue crab fishing is permitted from the water control structures year-round.

hiking: Although there are no designated hiking trails on the refuge, all dikes and roads are open to hikers year-round. The easiest option is 3.6-mi Wildlife Drive, which begins near the refuge office. Although the unpaved road is open to vehicles, it's sparsely enough travelled to make a good option for hiking. A short footpath at the end of the drive leads to an open marsh area with excellent views of the lake.

Alligator River National Wildlife Refuge

Covering 150,000 acres of swamp, marsh, pocosin and pine/hardwood forest, Alligator River is the largest national wildlife refuge in North Carolina. Surrounded by water on three sides, it's located on a broad peninsula in Dare and Hyde Counties between the Alligator River (W), Albemarle Sound (N) and Pamlico Sound (E). Established in 1984, the refuge acts as a preserve for significant wildlife resources, including migratory waterfowl, black bears, stands of Atlantic white cedar, and endangered species such as the American bald eagle, American alligator, and the red-cockaded woodpecker. The refuge has gained national attention in recent years for its successful reintroduction of the red wolf, begun in 1986. Efforts have also been undertaken to counter the effects of decades of commercial logging and agricultural draining by restoring portions of the refuge to their former state as natural wetland areas. Managed primarily for the protection of natural resources, the refuge remains largely undeveloped, ensuring a wilderness experience for those willing to make the effort.

Manteo (E) is the closest city.

contact: Refuge Manager, Alligator River National Wildlife Refuge, PO Box 1969, Manteo, NC 27954; 919/473-1131.

getting there: There are 2 primary accesses to the refuge, both located along US-64. An information kiosk and paved parking lot are located at the start of Milltail Rd, 4.4 mi from the jct of US-64 and US-264. Buffalo City Rd is 7.7 mi from the same jct, or 4.2 mi from the E end of the bridge across the Alligator River. The 2-mi gravel road runs S and ends at a parking area and boat launch.

topography: Alligator River is a low-lying environment that supports such water-dependent habitats as cypress swamp, pocosin and bottomland hardwood forest Drainage in the area is generally poor, though agricultural canals have disturbed the natural balance between wetland and drier upland. The terrain is flat. **maps:** USGS Buffalo City, East Lake SE, Engelhard NW, Engelhard NE, East Lake, Mann's Harbor, Wanchese, Stumpy Point.

starting out: Facilities in the refuge are very limited. There's no on-site office; the refuge is managed from Pea Island NWR. An information kiosk has recently been constructed next to the parking lot on Milltail Creek Rd. The best map of the refuge is the one inside the hunting regulations & permit brochure; you can get one by calling the refuge office. Hunting on the refuge is a popular activity in fall and winter. If you'll be there during those seasons, be sure to wear blaze orange. Aside from hunters, most visitors see the refuge from a boat; the ramp on Buffalo City Rd is the busiest area. Cottonmouth snakes are abundant on the refuge. The refuge is open year-round during daylight hours only; camping is not allowed.

activities: Canoeing/Kayaking, Fishing, Hiking, Mountain Biking.

canoeing/kayaking: Alligator River is the first wildlife refuge in the state to develop designated canoe/kayak trails. There are 4 of them, located on Milltail Creek, Sawyer Lake and adjacent feeder creeks and canals. Trails range in length from a 1.5-mi loop to a 5.5-mi one-way river trip. Since all of the trails begin at the Buffalo City Rd boat ramp, it's possible to connect 2 or more to form longer routes. The trails are blazed, with colored bands on white posts positioned at each trail beginning, end and at trail intersections. The 2 longest trails combine to cover almost 10 mi of Milltail Creek, a narrow, scenic, slow-moving body of dark water that widens considerably in its midsection to form Boat Bay. The creek empties into the Alligator River 4 mi W of the Buffalo City Rd boat ramp. Milltail Creek is also accessible from a small parking area and boat launch 6.6 from US-64 on Milltail Rd, a dirt and sand road best suited to 4-wheel drive vehicles. The other option for paddlers is of course the Alligator River, which is several miles across where it forms the W boundary of the refuge. Expect open water conditions on the river.

fishing: The freshwater rivers, lakes, and creeks of the refuge provide habitat for largemouth and striped bass, sunfish, crappie, perch and catfish. Access to these waters is primarily by boat. An exception is a small fishing pier that has recently been constructed behind the info kiosk on Milltail Creek Rd. The boat ramp at the end of Buffalo City Rd provides the easiest access to the refuge interior. Fishing in the canal that runs beside US-64 is also popular. You can pull off onto the wide grass shoulder of US-64 and cast from the bank or put a canoe on the water.

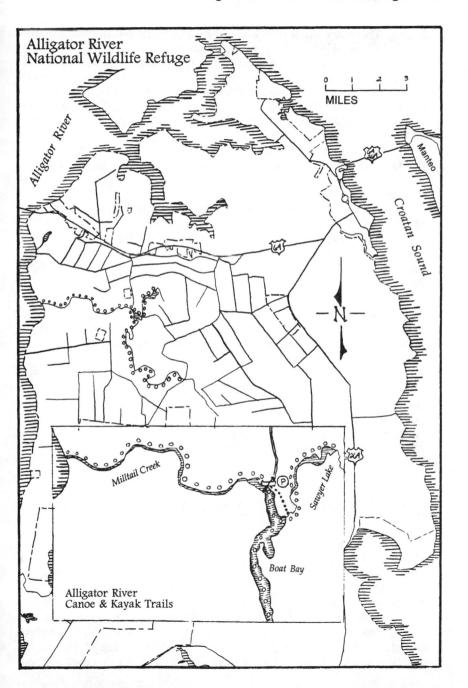

Alligator River
National Wildlife Refuge

MILES
0   1   2   3

Alligator River

Manteo

Croatan Sound

N

Milltail Creek

Sawyer Lake

Boat Bay

Alligator River
Canoe & Kayak Trails

hiking: There are currently 2 short hiking trails in the refuge. The *Sandy Ridge Wildlife Trail* is a 0.5-mi trail that is unsigned and unblazed, but nevertheless easy to locate and follow. The level trail begins across a footbridge at the Buffalo City Rd boat launch and follows a narrow canal that's a good place for wildlife viewing. Long boardwalks have been laid across wet areas. The *Creef Cut Wildlife Trail* is a half-mi trail that begins at the information kiosk at the jct of US-64 and Milltail Rd. The flat, paved trail runs along the edge of a cypress swamp. There are 2 boardwalks at the end of the trail. One is 50 ft and offers views of a soil management area, the other, which zigzags through a swampy area, is 250 ft and has a bench at its end.

In addition to these 2 short trails, there are literally hundreds of miles of rarely used dirt roads that criss-cross most areas of the refuge. The best access for cars is Buffalo City Rd or the first few miles of Milltail Rd. A topo map and compass are essential for navigating these primitive roads, which are unsigned and all look more or less the same.

mountain biking: 200 mi of primitive, unimproved roads that criss-cross the refuge are open to the public year-round. Most of these roads are suitable only to motor vehicles with 4-wheel drive; wet weather can make the roads impassable. Road surfaces are dirt and sand. All refuge roads are flat, making a mountain bike ideal for exploring a maximum amount of refuge terrain. Best places to park are at the new parking lot at the jct of US-64 and Milltail Rd or at the boat ramp on Buffalo City Rd. Bring a topo map and compass, as most roads are unsigned and difficult to distinguish. ATVs are prohibited on refuge lands.

Cape Hatteras National Seashore

Three main islands—Bodie, Hatteras and Ocracoke—comprise Cape Hatteras National Seashore. The islands are long and skinny; total length is 70 miles with an average width of about a mile. They are part of the long chain of barrier islands—collectively known as the Outer Banks—that form a natural buffer between the Atlantic Ocean and the North Carolina mainland. As such, the islands bear the brunt of the coast's often severe weather. On Cape Hatteras, the barrier islands reach the point furthest from the mainland, a circumstance that exacerbates their natural dynamism and instability. The islands are gradually migrating south and west; severe storms, such as the hurricanes and tropical storms that regularly strike, continually change the shape of the islands. This combination of shifting sands, extreme weather and rough seas gained for Cape Hatteras an infamous reputation among mariners of the past 4 centuries. Dubbed the "Graveyard of the Atlantic," the waters off Hatteras Island have been the site of more than 600 shipwrecks. Today the lighthouses that were built to warn ships of the dangerous shoals are popular tourist attractions and the beaches fill with sunbathers, swimmers and surfers.

North to South, towns adjacent to the national seashore lands are Rodanthe, Waves, Salvo, Avon, Buxton, Frisco, Hatteras and Ocracoke. These are all small communities, with limited services.

contact: Superintendent, Cape Hatteras National Seashore, Route 1, Box 675, Manteo, NC 27954; 919/473-2111

getting there: NC-12 runs down the spine of the Outer Banks and the NS. Ocracoke Island can only be reached by boat. NC DOT ferries connect the island to Hatteras Island and 2 points on the mainland, Swanquarter and Cedar Island.

topography: The NS occupies all or part of 3 barrier islands. The geography of these narrow strips of land is always changing, subject to the forces of sea and storms. Wide sandy beaches, sand dunes, maritime forest, shrub thicket, salt marsh and tidal flats comprise the major topographical features of the islands. **maps:** see below under separate listings.

starting out: Although development is much more severely restricted on the NS than along many other areas of the coast, Cape Hatteras remains one of the most popular tourist destinations in the state. During peak season, NC-12 can get pretty busy. The most popular activities are swimming and sunbathing and fishing. Information is available during the summer season at Whalebone Junction on the N edge of the NS, just S of the jct of NC-12 and US-64. Restrooms and pay phone are located on the site. Other facilities—including restaurants, hotels, mini marts and gas stations—are located in the communities on each of the islands. Sunscreen and insect repellent are essentials during the warm months.

activities: Camping, Kayaking/Canoeing, Fishing, Hiking.

camping: There are 4 developed car campgrounds on the NS: Oregon Inlet, Cape Point, Frisco and Ocracoke. Extra long tent stakes are recommended to secure tents in loose sand. Backcountry camping is not permitted anywhere on the NS.

kayaking/canoeing: The Outer Banks are beginning to be discovered by kayakers and canoeists as one of the premier destinations on the east coast. Paddlers have a choice of two very different environments: the shallow marshes and tidal flats of Pamlico Sound or the open water of the Atlantic Ocean. Beginners will find the sound a more forgiving place to paddle, though open water conditions such as strong winds and rough water are often encountered. There are put-ins on all 3 islands.

fishing: Cape Hatteras has long been regarded as one of the hot spots on the east coast for fishing. Surfcasters, inshore boat anglers and deep sea fishermen all come to Hatteras to try their luck. The marina on Bodie Island is the main center of activity. The major game species are bluefish, mackerel, red drum, flounder, spot, seatrout and pompano.

hiking: The primary hiking opportunity at Cape Hatteras is along the beach. In addition, each island has a short nature trail.

Bodie Island

Bodie Island is a good example of the forces that continually change the shape of the Outer Banks: it's no longer an island, but has joined with the land adjacent to the north. Nevertheless it's still referred to locally and on maps as Bodie (pronounced BOD-ee) Island. With several popular attractions bunched close together, the busy island offers less opportunity for solitude than Hatteras or Ocracoke. Tourists stop at Bodie Island Lighthouse, built in 1872, and now restored with a new visitors center and museum. The lighthouse itself is closed to visitors.

Manteo (NW) is the closest town

getting there: Bodie Island is the northernmost of the 3 islands that comprise the NS. Access is via US-64 from Roanoke Island and the mainland, and on NC-12, which runs the length of the island.

topography: More than 2 mi across in places, Bodie is the widest of the 3 islands. Oregon Inlet is now the northernmost inlet on the Outer Banks. Topography is typical of a barrier island. **maps:** USGS Roanoke Island NE, Oregon Inlet.

starting out: Most visitors enter the NS on Bodie Island. Facilities on the island are at Whalebone Jct (restrooms, water, pay phone) and the visitors center beside the lighthouse (restrooms, water, pay phone). The visitors center is only open seasonally, but access to the restrooms is year-round. A park map, brochure and other information are available at both locations. The busiest part of the NS—at least among fishermen—is undoubtedly the marina near Oregon Inlet. Dozens of sport fishing boats leave from there every morning and return with the day's catch late in the afternoon. Another popular spot is Coquina Beach, where the wreck of the Laura Barnes can be seen.

activities: Camping, Fishing, Kayaking/Canoeing, Hiking.

camping: Oregon Inlet is a 120-site car campground located on the ocean side of the island about a half-mi N of the bridge across Oregon Inlet. Sites are spread out among the dunes. Privacy is fairly minimal due to the lack of cover. Each site includes a picnic table and grill. Modern restrooms and cold-water showers are centrally located. Sites cost $12/night. The campground is open mid-Apr to Labor Day.

fishing: The ocean side of Oregon Inlet is generally regarded as one of the best fishing spots on the entire Outer Banks. It's also one of the most crowded, with a small fleet of 4Wds often seen on the strand NE or the bridge. Main catches are bluefish, mackerel, drum, spot, flounder, seatrout and pompano.

kayaking/canoeing: Because of the very heavy boat traffic that passes through and around Oregon Inlet, this is the least appealing part of the NS for paddling. If you're determined to give it a try anyway, you can put in on the ocean side at Coquina Beach or at Oregon Inlet, where 4WDs can go right to the water's edge. Paddlers should be aware that the currents in and around Oregon Inlet are swift and dangerous.

360 • The Coast

hiking: Hikers on Bodie Island have 2 options: hike the 8-mi stretch of sandy beach between Whalebone Jct and Oregon Inlet or explore the sound side on the 1.5-mi (round-trip) *Bodie Island Dike Trail*. The trail begins near the Bodie Island Lighthouse and passes through a loblolly pine forest and shrub thicket beside the marshes and ditches of Pamlico Sound. The treadway is grass and sand and is easy to follow. The trail is improved with benches. Interpretive guides are available at the trailhead. To reach it, follow the gated gravel road at the W end of the grounds about a quarter mi to the start of the trail, L. The trail ends on NC-12.

Hatteras Island

Hatteras Island is the largest of the 3 islands and comprises the large majority of the national seashore. The famous lighthouse with the diagonal black and white bands is the centerpiece of the island and one of the definitive landmarks of North Carolina. At 208 feet, it is also the tallest lighthouse in the United States. It was designed to warn ships of the treacherous waters around Diamond Shoals, an ever-shifting bank of underwater sand that has claimed hundreds of ships attempting safe passage. Opportunities for backcountry exploration on the island are excellent, with dozens of miles of virtually empty beach.

The small communities of Rodanthe, Waves, Salvo, Avon, Buxton, Frisco and Hatteras are all on the island.

getting there: From the N, the island is reached by driving on NC-12 across the bridge over Oregon Inlet. From the S, the only way to get to the island is to take the free 40-minute ferry from Ocracoke Island. The ferry runs every half-hour during peak season; every hour during off-season. Call 800/BY FERRY for more info.

topography: At almost 50 mi, Hatteras is the longest of the 3 islands that comprise the NS. Topography is typical of a barrier island, with beach, dunes, shrub thicket, salt marsh and maritime forest all represented. **maps:** USGS Pea Island, Rodanthe, Little Kinnakeet, Buxton, Cape Hatteras, Hatteras.

starting out: The busiest part of the island is the bend at Cape Hatteras. The famous lighthouse is there, and the 2 campgrounds on the island are nearby. There's also a visitors center and museum adjacent to the lighthouse, located in the former quarters of the

Assistant Keeper. Hours are 9 am–6 pm daily during peak season; 9 am–5 pm other times. Restrooms, water and a pay phone are on site. Swimming is popular at the lifeguard supervised beach at the cape. Ocean currents are very strong along the Outer Banks; swimming in unsupervised areas is not advised, and swimmers should never swim alone.

activities: Camping, Kayaking/Canoeing, Fishing, Hiking.

camping: There are 2 developed car campgrounds on Hatteras Island, Cape Point and Frisco. The campgrounds are located not far from each other and are similar in character. Both are located on the ocean side of the island, with most sites situated among the complex of sand dunes. Most sites are large, though privacy is reduced by the open nature of their setting. All sites have a picnic table and grill. Modern restrooms and cold-water showers are centrally located in both campgrounds. Cape Point has 202 sites, Frisco 127. Sites at both campgrounds cost $12/night. Cape Point and Frisco are open from Memorial Day to Labor Day, though opening dates have varied in recent years. There are also several private campgrounds on the island.

Camping outside designated campgrounds is not permitted.

kayaking/canoeing: Paddlers have their choice of the ocean or Pamlico Sound. Because backcountry camping is not permitted on the NS, only day-trips are possible. That means that you'll run out of time long before you run out of coast. You can put in on the ocean side by parking at one of many beach access areas and making a short portage. On the sound side, there's a boat ramp at Pea Island NWR at the N end of the island. There are also a couple other put-ins near Salvo and Buxton used primarily by windsurfers.

fishing: Surfcasting, pier fishing and boat fishing are all popular in the waters around Hatteras Island. If you're going to fish the ocean surf, use one of the many beach access points along NC-12. Fishing in Pamlico Sound is probably best done from a boat. Major sport fish caught here are bluefish, pompano, flounder, seatrout, spot and red drum.

hiking: The primary hiking opportunity on the island is along the seemingly endless sand beach. There are numerous access points along NC-12. Although parts of the beach get relatively crowded with sunbathers and swimmers in summer, many stretches remain more or less deserted. Be aware that most of the beach is open to 4WD vehicles.

Ocracoke Island

Seemingly isolated from the rest of the world by time and water, Ocracoke has a charm all its own. Without a bridge to connect it to Hatteras Island, Ocracoke receives far fewer visitors that other parts of the national seashore. Major attractions on the island are the peaceful village of Ocracoke, built on the natural harbor of Silver Lake, and the Ocracoke lighthouse. Constructed in 1823, it's the oldest operating lighthouse in North Carolina. A small herd of wild horses lives on the island; presently, they're protected in a large corral off NC-12. Backcountry travellers will enjoy the miles of empty beaches, the superb fishing, and canoeing or kayaking in the waters around the island

Ocracoke Village is located near the south end of the island.

getting there: The island can only be reached by boat. From Hatteras Island, a free ferry runs every half-hour (every hour during the off season) and takes about 40 min. From the mainland, ferries leave from Swan Quarter ($10/car) and Cedar Island ($10/car). Both trips take about 2.5 hours. Reservations are recommended during peak season, as the ferries fill early. Call 800/BY FERRY for info and reservations. Once on the island, NC-12 runs the entire length. Crowds, such as they are, gather in the village and on the supervised beach.

topography: Ocracoke Island lies on a NE–SW axis between Hatteras Island and N Core Banks, part of the Cape Lookout NS. A long sand beach, a complex of sand dunes, shrub thicket and salt marsh are the major geographical features of the island. **maps:** USGS Ocracoke, Howard Reef, Green Island, Portsmouth.

starting out: Facilities are at Ocracoke Village on the S end of the island. A visitors center is located beside the ferry terminals. Maps, brochures and other NS info are available here. The small building houses exhibits on local history and a small bookshop. Restrooms, pay phone and a water fountain are located outside.

activities: Camping, Kayaking/Canoeing, Fishing, Hiking.

camping: Ocracoke campground has 136 sites situated amidst the dunes on the ocean side of the island. Most of the sites are located in a large, level clearing. Privacy is minimal, though the sites are generally large. Each site has a picnic table and grill. Modern restrooms and cold-water showers are centrally located. The beach is a short walk away across the dunes. Sites cost $13/night. The campground is the only one in the NS that accepts reservations. Call 800/365-2267 for information. The campground is open mid-Apr to Labor Day (reservations accepted after Memorial Day). Ocracoke is typically the least crowded of the 4 campgrounds on Cape Hatteras NS.

kayaking/canoeing: The geography of Ocracoke Island is well suited to exploration by kayak or canoe. The put-in is at a boat ramp and large parking lot beside the ferry terminals at the S end of NC-12. From there, you have the option of paddling the intimate waters of Silver Bay or of heading out to more open water. The shallow waters of Pamlico Sound are a popular destination, as is abandoned Portsmouth Village on Cape Lookout NS, about 5 mi SW. If you're heading in that direction, be certain that you have the skills necessary to negotiate the dangerous currents of Ocracoke Inlet. Almost all boat traffic on the island begins at the harbor on Silver Lake. There are 2 kayak tour outfitters in Ocracoke Village.

fishing: Fishing conditions are similar to the other 2 islands, with both surfcasting and boat fishing popular. Species caught include bluefish, mackerel, seatrout, spot, drum and flounder. There are numerous beach accesses along NC-12; boats leave from Silver Lake.

hiking: The *Hammock Hills Nature Trail*, an easy 0.75-mi loop with interpretive plaques, begins across the road from the campground. Pine forest, shrub thicket, sand dunes and wetlands are all encountered on the trail. The trailhead is signed and the trail is easy to follow. Improvements include long boardwalks across wet areas and a viewing platform.

Hikers also use the miles of open beach, which are generally less crowded with swimmers and sunbathers than those on Hatteras and Bodie Islands.

Pea Island National Wildlife Refuge

Pea Island National Wildlife Refuge lies along 12 miles of Hatteras Island, one of the chain of barrier islands that form the Outer Banks. The refuge covers 5,915 acres of beach, barrier dunes, salt marshes, fresh and brackish water ponds, and tidal creeks and bays. The protected environment is ideal for migrating waterfowl, and the refuge was established in 1938 to provide them a safe haven on their annual flights north and south. 265 species of bird are regular visitors to the refuge, which is located midway on the Atlantic Flyway. Among these visitors are literally thousands of Canada and snow geese and tundra swans during peak migrations. In addition, the refuge's beaches provide summertime nesting sites for the endangered loggerhead turtle. The refuge is open year-round during daylight hours.

Rodanthe (S) and Nags Head (N) are the nearest towns. The Refuge is surrounded by Cape Hatteras National Seashore (N & S).

contact: Refuge Manager, Alligator River National Wildlife Refuge, P.O. Box 1969, Manteo, NC 27954; 919/473-1131 or Pea Island Office: 919/987-2394.

getting there: The refuge is located at the N end of Hatteras Island. NC-12 provides the only vehicle access.

topography: Salt marshes, white sand beaches, and barrier dunes are the major topographical features of the refuge. 2 fresh-water impoundments are located near the middle of the refuge. **maps:** USGS Pea Island, Oregon Inlet, Rodanthe.

starting out: Visitors center hours vary with the season, but during the summer and bird migration periods it's open daily 9 am–4 pm. Maps and other refuge info are available there, as are souvenirs and guide books. Restrooms are at the site. There's also a roadside kiosk with information panels 3.4 mi N of the visitor center. The refuge is particularly popular with birders. Swimming on the beach is also popular, though there's no lifeguard present. Swimmers should always swim in pairs and be aware of the dangers posed by strong littoral currents and riptides.

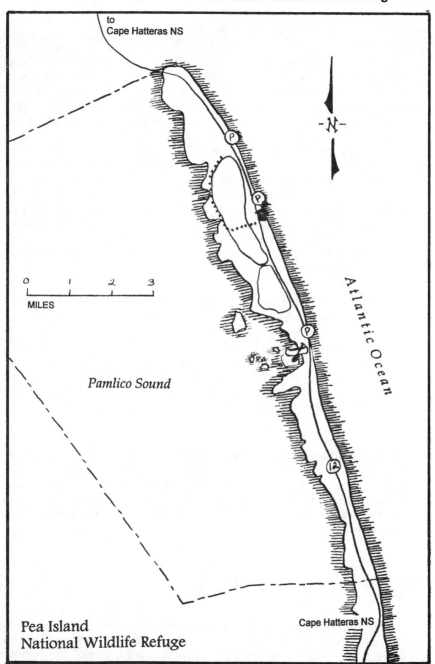

to
Cape Hatteras NS

-*N*-

Atlantic Ocean

0   1   2   3

MILES

Pamlico Sound

12

Cape Hatteras NS

Pea Island
National Wildlife Refuge

activities: Hiking, Fishing, Kayaking/Canoeing.

hiking: The *North Pond Interpretive Trail* is an easy 4.5-mi loop that begins and ends at the visitors center. The trail has been designed for waterfowl observation, and is probably the best trail in the state for that purpose. The trail circles North Pond; along its S side (a portion which is often hiked alone) there are benches, viewing platforms and fixed binocular stations to facilitate observation of the hundreds of ducks, geese, swans and other waterfowl that are often on the pond during seasonal migrations. The trail follows a short boardwalk, a sandy path, and then a service road. A second access to the trail is at the N end of the pond, 1.6 mi N of the visitor center. There's a small parking area and another elevated viewing platform there. Pets are not allowed on the trail. Although this is the only hiking trail in the refuge, the 12-mi stretch of beach, closed to motor vehicles, offers additional hiking opportunities.

fishing: The 12 mi of ocean shoreline on the refuge are a popular place for surf fishing. There are a number of paved parking pulloffs on the E side of NC-12. The N boundary of the refuge is Oregon Inlet, considered one of the best fishing spots in NC. Species taken from the surf include bluefish, spotted seatrout, flounder, sea mullet and drum. Pamlico Sound, on the W side of the Refuge, also offers excellent fishing. A boat is necessary to fish these waters. You can put in at the boat ramp on NC-12 3 mi S of the visitors center.

kayaking/canoeing: The shallow waters of Pamlico Sound on the W side of the refuge are ideally explored in a kayak or canoe. There's a boat ramp on the W side of NC-12 3 mi S of the refuge visitor station. The unsheltered waters of the sound are subject to strong winds and choppy water; call ahead of time to check prevailing conditions.

Jockey's Ridge State Park

Created in 1975 to protect the landmark dune that gives the park its name, Jockey's Ridge State Park covers 414 acres of barren sand dunes and shrub thicket on Bodie Island, one of the barrier islands that collectively form the Outer Banks. With a maximum height that varies from 110 to 140 ft, Jockey's Ridge is the highest sand dune in the eastern United States and a National Natural Landmark. Theories as to the formation of the dune and associated lesser dunes vary, but it's known that their height and ever-shifting shape are the result of competing coastal winds, which blow out of the northeast in winter and southwest in summer. The top of Jockey's Ridge offers spectacular 360° views of the Atlantic Ocean, Roanoke Sound and Bodie Island. Also apparent from that vantage is the extent to which Jockey's Ridge has become an oasis amid commercial development. The popularity of the Outer Banks with vacationers has made Jockey's Ridge one of the most heavily visited of all the state parks—expect crowds during peak season.

The Park is located in the town of Nags Head.

contact: Superintendent, Jockey's Ridge State Park, Box 592, Nags Head, NC; 919/441-7132.

getting there: From US-158 in Nags Head, turn W onto Carolista Dr at the state park sign.

topography: Rising to 140 ft, the dunes are the park's major geographical feature. Lower elevations are covered with shrub thickets. **maps:** USGS Manteo.

starting out: Park facilities are at either end of a large parking lot. At the S end are restrooms, along with a water fountain, vending machines, and sand rinse. At the N end are the park office and the Carolista Museum. Park maps and brochures are available at both. The museum features displays on park geography and wildlife; it's open Apr–Sep 9 am–8 pm and Oct–Mar 9 am–5 pm. One unusual park activity is hang-gliding; the dunes function as a take-off point. A special park permit is required for this activity. A secluded picnic area with 7 shelters isolated from the rest of the park by dense shrub thicket is near the main parking lot. Each shelter has 2 picnic tables and a grill.

Alcohol is not permitted in the park. Pets must be kept on a leash.

activities: Hiking.

hiking: The most popular hiking in the park is off trail, along the sides and tops of the massive dunes. Although almost all park terrain is open and accessible to visitors on foot, there's also a designated hiking trail. The *Tracks in the Sand Nature Trail* is an easy 1.5-mi loop that follows 14 interpretive posts across open sand, through shrub thicket to a narrow beach on Roanoke Sound. The accompanying guide, available at the first post, provides information about the plants and animals that live in the park. The trail begins and ends at the parking lot.

Nags Head Woods Preserve

Owned and managed by The Nature Conservancy, Nags Head Woods Preserve covers 1,100 acres of maritime forest, fresh-water wetlands, and sand dunes. It's located west of the main strip in Kill Devil Hills near Albemarle Sound. The forest of which the preserve is a part was designated a National Natural Landmark in 1974; it's one of the few intact mature maritime forests in the world. Typically, the harsh environment of a barrier island is too inhospitable to allow for the stability needed by tall hardwood species such as live oak, hickory and rosebay to develop and flourish. At Nags Head Woods, that stability is provided by a series of sand dunes that afford protection from ocean winds and sea spray. Some of the trees in the forest are as old as 500 years. Animal and bird species associated with swamp and maritime forests, such as river otters, white-tailed deer, cottonmouths, prothonotary warblers, herons and pileated woodpeckers also make their home in the preserve. It's open year-round.

The preserve is located within the towns of Kill Devil Hills and Nags Head.

contact: Nags Head Woods Preserve, 301 W Ocean Acres Dr, Kill Devil Hills, NC 27948; 919/441-2525.

getting there: From US-158 in Kill Devil Hills (1 mi S of Wright Brothers Monument), turn W onto Ocean Acres Dr. Go 1 mi (after 0.6 mi the road becomes gravel, then sand) to the visitors center, L.

topography: A fairly extensive system of dunes shelters much of the preserve from ocean winds. Habitats include an extensive maritime forest, small creeks and wetland depressions. **maps:** USGS Manteo.

starting out: Days on which the preserve is open to the public vary with the season. Hours are always 10 am–3 pm. Visitors should call ahead to check the current schedule of open days. Members of The Nature Conservancy may visit the preserve at any time. All visitors are requested to register at the office. There's a small store and information center, where you can pick up preserve maps and brochures. Restrooms are on the premises.

Pets are not allowed in the Preserve. Picnicking, camping, campfires, and fishing are also not permitted. No alcohol or smoking.

activities: Hiking.

hiking: There are 3 hiking trails in the preserve, covering a total distance of about 4 mi. Trails range in length from the quarter-mi *Center Trail*, a nature trail with interpretive posts, to the 2.5-mi *Sweetgum Swamp Trail*. A loop of 4 mi is possible by combining the two longer trails. All trails are easy to hike, though there are some short, steep sections that climb the preserve's sand dunes. Trails are blazed with colored triangular markers. Improvements include rustic footbridges, benches and stairs or steps where soil or sand erosion is a potential problem. Off-trail hiking is not permitted.

Currituck Banks

3 adjacent tracts of land—administered separately as a National Wildlife Refuge, an Estuarine Research Reserve and a Nature Conservancy Preserve—cover 2,807 acres of the barrier island north of the village of Corolla. Currituck Banks is part of a long barrier spit that was once several islands, though the inlets have been closed for more than 150 years. Today Currituck Banks extends north to Virginia and south to Oregon Inlet at Hatteras Island. One effect of this long natural barrier has been the transformation of Currituck Sound into a fresh-water estuary. Although the region south of Currituck Banks is in the midst of rapid development, the fragile habitats preserved in these holdings remain in an almost pristine state. That is due in part to the fact the NC-12, the only major road in the area, ends in Corolla. The 3 sites are managed primarily for preservation, with

opportunities for visiting limited by a lack of access and facilities. Corolla (S) is the closest town.

contact: Refuge Manager, Currituck National Wildlife Refuge, P.O. Box 39, Knott's Island, NC 27950; 919/429-3100.

getting there: NC-12 ends just N of the community of Corolla at the S boundary of the Estuarine Research Reserve. 4WD vehicles are permitted on the beach.

topography: The habitats typical of a barrier island are all found on Currituck Banks, including a wide sand beach, dunes, shrub thicket, brackish and freshwater marsh, tidal flat, and maritime forest. **maps:** USGS Corolla.

starting out: There are no facilities on Currituck Banks. None of the 3 parcels of land are managed for heavy visitor use; visitors should respect the fragile environments being protected and stay on the beach or in a boat.

Camping is not permitted. Pets must be leashed.

activities: Kayaking/Canoeing, Fishing, Hiking.

kayaking/canoeing: Probably the best way to get to and see Currituck Banks is in a kayak or canoe. Possible put-ins are on Mackay Island NWR and on the mainland at Goose Point, where there's a boat ramp. From either site, it's about a 5-mi paddle across Currituck Sound to the barrier island. Although the waters of the sound are shallow (average depth is 5 ft) and protected, paddlers should be prepared for winds and rough water.

fishing: Anglers have 2 fishing options on Currituck Banks. Surfcasters and boat fishermen on the Atlantic side can fish for the major saltwater species found along the Outer Banks: bluefish, seatrout, drum, flounder, spot and pompano. On the sound side, however, freshwater species such as largemouth bass, white perch, crappie, chain pickerel and channel catfish are the main catches. Fishing in the sound is from a boat.

hiking: Hiking on Currituck Banks is primarily along the beach. Some areas in which the piping plover is nesting are signed against disturbance. There are no designated trails in the area.

Mackay Island National Wildlife Refuge

Located in the extreme northeast corner of the state, Mackay Island National Wildlife Refuge was established to provide migratory and winter habitat for ducks, geese and swans. Its 8,000 acres, nearly a thousand of which are in Virginia, include brackish marsh, freshwater impoundments, forest and several small parcels of cropland. The refuge is surrounded on three sides by water, and its low-lying terrain is intersected by canals and ditches and dotted by small ponds. Wildlife management takes priority on the refuge; as a result much of it is closed to visitors during the winter months. Bird species that may be seen regularly include the greater snow goose, Canada goose, osprey, great blue heron and several species of egret. In all, 182 different species of bird have been observed. Mammals that live on the refuge include muskrat, river otters, deer and fox. The poisonous cottonmouth snake is abundant; visitors should take care, particularly during the warm months.

Knott's Island (E) is the closest town. Services are very limited in the town. Several private campgrounds are located on the perimeter of the refuge on NC-615.

contact: Refuge Manager, Mackay Island National Wildlife Refuge, PO Box 39, Knott's Island, NC 27950; 919/429-3100.

getting there: Mackay Island can be reached by driving from VA or by taking a free 40-min ferry (it runs about once every 2 hours) from Currituck on the NC mainland. The entrance to the refuge headquarters is on NC-615 1.1 mi S of the NC/VA state line. Turn S off of the highway and go 0.9 mi on the gravel refuge road which ends at the Joseph P. Knapp Visitor Contact Station. To get to the refuge's trails and boat launch, take NC-615 5.1 mi further S and turn R at the refuge sign.

topography: Land and sea intermingle on the refuge, often without clear division between the two. Salt marshes are interspersed with canals, ditches, ponds and impoundments. Uplands are covered with pines and hardwoods. **maps:** USGS Knott's Island, Barco.

starting out: Refuge information, including brochures and maps, can be picked up at either the visitor center (open 8 am–4 pm) or at an

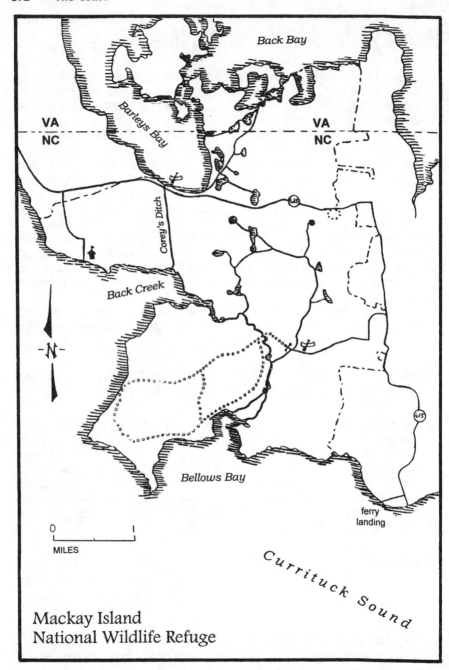

Back Bay

Barleys Bay

VA
NC

VA
NC

Corey's Ditch

Back Creek

-N-

Bellows Bay

0

MILES

ferry
landing

Currituck Sound

Mackay Island
National Wildlife Refuge

information board at the beginning of Mackay Island Rd. Facilities (restrooms, water) are at the visitors center. Parts of the refuge close during winter to protect waterfowl habitat.

Pets must be kept on a leash. Fires and camping are prohibited.

activities: Hiking, Canoeing/Kayaking, Fishing, Mountain Biking.

hiking: 3 hiking trails cover a distance of about 7 mi. *Great Marsh Trail* is an easy 0.3-mi footpath that circles a marsh pond. It's used primarily by fishermen and birders. The trailhead is S of the refuge office on NC-615. Access to the other two trails, *Mackay Island Trail* and *Live Oak Point Trail*, both open from Mar 15 to Oct 15, is at the S entrance to the refuge. From the entrance, drive about 1 mi to a gate and small parking area; both trails begin here. The trails skirt 3 large pools on a refuge service road. They combine to form a loop of 6.5 mi, with a shorter loop of 4 mi possible. Water is not available along the trails.

canoeing/kayaking: Paddlers have the option of touring the open water of the refuge's perimeters or of navigating the narrow stillwater canals and ponds of its interior. The launching of boats within the refuge is permitted Mar 15—Oct 15 during daylight hours. Primary launch sites are along NC-615 and at a small boat launch on Mackay Island Rd near the start of the *Mackay Island Trail*. A canoe is ideal for exploring the miles of narrow canals and numerous ponds that meander through the refuge marshlands. A kayak is more suitable for the rougher open waters of the sound and bays which surround the refuge on 3 sides. Corey's Ditch, approx 1.5 mi long, connects Back Bay (N) and North Landing River (W), which feeds Currituck Sound (S). Back Creek connects the open waters of North Landing River and the Sound with the waterways of the refuge.

fishing: Species which inhabit the canals, bays, and impoundments of the refuge are largemouth bass, catfish, crappie, bream, bluegill, and sunfish. Fishing is permitted from Mar 15—Oct 15, except for Corey's Ditch, the pond at the *Great Marsh Trail*, and the canal on the N bank of NC-615, which are all open to fishing year-round. Bank fishing only is allowed on East Pool, Middle Pool, and West Pool, which are all served by the hiking and biking trails described above.

mountain biking: The *Mackay Island Trail* and *Live Oak Point Trail* are both open to bikes. The trails follow refuge service roads closed to motor vehicles. Total distance is 6.5 mi, with a shorter loop of 4 mi possible. The roads are level, with gravel and dirt surfaces. See above for directions to the trailheads.

Outfitters & Supply Stores

The following businesses sell gear or offer services for the outdoor activities covered in this book. Businesses are arranged geographically, by city, from west to east. Within a given city, listings are alphabetical. Fishing supply stores and bike stores have not been included; you'll find them in just about any town near a popular fishing or mountain biking area.

Key to some terms used below: camping=tents, backpacks, sleeping bags & clothes; paddling=canoes, kayaks & accessories; topos=USGS 7.5 minute topographic maps.

Almond

Rolling Thunder River Co—PO Box 88; 704/488-2030
M–F, Su 9 am–5 pm, Sa 9 am–6 pm
Sells: canoes; Rents: canoes; Trips· canoe; Vehicle shuttles

Bryson City

Nantahala Outdoor Center—13077 US-19W; 704/488-2175
M–Su 8 am–5 pm (open later in spring, summer & fall)
Sells: camping, paddling, mountain bikes, topos;
Trips: paddling, mountain biking

Sylva

Venture Out—4812 US-441S; 800/586-1464
M–Sa 10 am–6 pm, Su 12–4 pm
Sells: camping, topos; Rents: camping

Highlands

Highland Hiker—100 E Main St; 704/526-5298
M–Sa 9 am–5:30 pm, Su 12–4 pm (shorter hrs Jan–Mar)
Sells: camping, canoes, fly-fishing, mountain biking, topos
Rents: canoes; Trips: fly-fishing

Cashiers

Brookings—Route 70; 704/743-3768
M–Sa 10 am–5 pm, Su 1–5 pm
Sells: camping, fly-fishing, canoes; Trips: fly-fishing

Highland Hiker—US-64E & NC-107S; 704/743-1732
M–Sa 9 am–5:30 pm, Su 12–4 pm (shorter hrs Jan–Mar)
Sells: camping, canoes, fly-fishing, mountain biking, topos
Rents: canoes; Trips: mountain biking

Rosman

Headwaters Outfitters, Inc—US-64 & NC-215; 704/877-3106
M–Su 8 am–5 pm
Sells: paddling, fly-fishing, topos; Rents: canoes/kayaks
Trips: canoe; Vehicle Shuttles

Waynesville

Mast General Store—148 N Main St; 704/452-2101
M–Sa 10 am-6 pm, Su 1-6 pm
Sells: camping, fly-fishing

Pisgah Forest

Backcountry Outfitters—US-276 & US-64; 704/883-9453
M–Sa 9 am–9 pm
Sells: camping, paddling, mountain biking, topos; Rents: canoes,
mountain bikes; Trips: paddling, mountain biking.

Looking Glass Outfitters—33 New Hendersonville Hwy;
704/884-5854; M–Sa 9 am–5 pm, Su 1–5 pm
Sells: camping, topos

Naples

Diamond Brand Camping Center—US-25; 704/684-6262
M–Sa 9 am–6 pm
Sells: camping, paddling, topos; Rents: some camping

Arden

Zippy Boat Works—US-25A and Azalea Rd; 704/684-5107
M–F 10 am–5 pm, Sa 10 am–4 pm
Sells: canoes/kayaks; Rents: canoes/kayaks; Trips: canoes

Asheville

B.B. Barns, Inc—831 Fairview Rd; 704/274-7301
M–Sa 9 am–6 pm
Sells: some camping, topos

Black Dome Mountain Sports—140 Tunnel Rd; 800/678-2367
M–Sa 10 am–8 pm, Su 1–5 pm
Sells: camping, kayaks, topos; Rents: camping
Trips: hiking, paddling, mountain biking

The Compleat Naturalist—2 Biltmore Plaza; 704/274-5430
M–Sa 10 am–6 pm, Su 1–5 pm
Sells: partial camping, topos; Trips: hiking; Field Classes

Banner Elk

Edge of the World Outfitters—NC-184; 704/898-9550
M–Sa 9 am–10 pm, Su 1–10 pm
Sells: camping, kayaking; Trips: canoe

Valle Crucis

Mast General Store—NC-194; 704/963-6511
M–Sa 10 am–6 pm, Su 1–6 pm
Sells: camping, fly-fishing

Boone

Footsloggers—553 W King St; 704/262-5111
M–Sa 9:30 am–5:30 pm, Su 1–5 pm
Sells: camping

Mast General Store—630 W King St; 704/262-0000
M–Sa 10 am–6 pm, Su 1–6 pm
Sells: camping, fly-fishing

Jefferson

New River Outfitters—PO Box 433; 910/982-9192
M–Su 8:30 am–6 pm
Sells: canoeing, topos; Rents: some camping, canoes;
Trips: canoes; Vehicle Shuttles

Zaloo's Canoes—3874 NC-16S; 910/246-3066
M–F 9 am–5 pm, Weekends 8 am–6 pm—Apr 1 to Oct 31
Sells: used canoes; Rents: canoes; Trips: Canoes; Vehicle shuttles

Hickory

Berndt's—117 Government Ave SW; 704/322-1222
M–F 9 am–6 pm, Sa 9 am–5:30 pm
Sells: camping, canoeing, fly-fishing, topos

Outdoor Supply Co—3006 N Center St; 704/322-2297
M–Th, Sa 10 am–6 pm, F 10 am–8 pm
Sells: camping, paddling, topos; Rents: camping, canoes.

River Mountain Sports—906 US-321 Bypass; 704/323-1255
M–F 10 am–6 pm, Sa 10 am–5 pm
Sells: camping, kayaking

Shelby

J.N. Rich Inc Camping Outfitter—NC-74 Bypass; 704/482-9606
Tu–F 9 am–5 pm, Sa 9 am–4 pm
Sells: camping, paddling, mountain bikes, topos

Charlotte

Alanby Outfitting—Arboretum Shopping Ctr; 704/543-4415
M–Sa 10 am–9 pm, Su 12:30–6:30 pm
Sells: camping; Rents: camping

Alanby Outfitting—SouthPark Mall; 704/364-7311
M–Sa 10 am–9 pm, Su 12:30–6:30 pm
Sells: camping

Bicycles South & Backpacking—8914 Pineville-Matthews Rd;
704/542-6379. M–F 10 am–7 pm, Sa 9 am–5 pm
Sells: camping, mountain biking; Trips: hiking, mountain biking

Great Outdoor Provision Co—Park Rd Shopping Center;
704/523-1089. M–F 10 am–9 pm, Sa 10 am–6 pm, Su 1–6 pm
Sells: camping, paddling, fly-fishing; Rents: camping

Jesse Brown's Outdoors—4732 Sharon Rd; 704/556-0020
M–Sa 10 am–9 pm, Su 1–6 pm
Sells: camping, fly-fishing, topos; Trips: hiking, fly-fishing

Moe Levy's—8400-A Park Rd; 704/553-0717
M–F 10 am–8 pm, Sa 10 am–6 pm, Su 1–6 pm
Sells: camping, topos; Rents: camping

Cornelius

Outdoors Etc—20212 Knox Rd, Suite 1; 704/892-1848
M–F 10 am–8 pm, Sa 10 am–5 pm
Sells: camping, canoeing/kayaking, topos; Rents: camping

Granite Quarry

Rough Trails & Tall Tales—NC-52 & 106 N Salisbury;
704/279-6081. M–F 7:30 am–6:30 pm, Sa 8:30 am–2:30 pm
Sells: camping, fly-fishing

Lexington

Backlands Outpost—115 Green Needles Dr; 704/956-1329
M–F 9 am–6 pm, Sa 9 am–2 pm
Sells: camping

Winston-Salem

Army Navy Surplus Store—815 Waughtown St; 910/788-1464
M–F 10 am–5:30 pm, Sa 10 am–5 pm
Sells: camping

Great Outdoor Provision Co—Thruway Shopping Ctr;
910/727-0906. M–F 10 am–9 pm, Sa 10 am–6 pm, Su 1–6 pm
Sells: camping, paddling, fly-fishing

Hills & Trails—527 S Stratford Rd; 910/765-5623
M–F 10 am–8 pm, Sa 10 am–5 pm, Su 1–5 pm
Sells: camping, paddling, topos; Rents: camping, canoes/kayaks
Trips: hiking, paddling

Trivitte's Sporting Goods—420 R Jonestown Rd; 910/760-0188
M–F 9 am–6 pm, Sa 9 am–4 pm
Sells: camping, fly-fishing

Greensboro

Appalachian Outfitters—2447 Battleground Ave; 910/282-5108
M–F 10 am–9 pm, Sa 9:30 am–6 pm
Sells: camping, fly-fishing, topos;
Rents: camping; Trips: fly-fishing

Blue Ridge Mountain Sports—803-B Friendly Center Rd;
910/852-9196. M–F 10 am–9 pm, Sa 10 am–6 pm, Su 1–6 pm
Sells: camping, canoes, topos; Rents: camping

Pro Canoe & Kayak—1515 W Lee St; 910/294-3918
M–Sa 10 am–6 pm
Sells: camping, paddling; Rents: paddling

Sports Unlimited—6428 Burnt Poplar Rd; 910/668-1106
M–F 9:30 am–9:30 pm, Sa 9 am–9 pm, Su 11 am–6 pm
Sells: camping, canoeing, fly-fishing, mountain biking, topos

Fayetteville

Outdoor Specialty Sports—6207 Yadkin Rd; 910/868-1806
M–F 9 am–8 pm, Sa 9 am–6 pm
Sells: camping

Pittsboro

Blackwood Station Outfitters—5670 US-15-501 N; 919/542-7076
Tu–F 10 am–6 pm, Sa 9 am–5 pm
Sells: camping, canoes, fly-fishing; Trips: canoe

Carrboro/Chapel Hill

Townsend Bertram & Company—Carr Mill; 919/933-9712
M–F 10 am–7 pm, Sa 10 am–6 pm, Su 1–5pm
Sells: camping, topos; Rents: camping

Trail Shop—308 W. Franklin St; 919/929-7626
M–F 10 am–7 pm, Sa 10 am–6 pm, Su 1–5 pm
Sells: camping, topos; Rents: camping

Durham

Eno Traders—737 Ninth St; 919/286-4747
M–F 10 am–7 pm, Sa 10 am–6 pm, Su 12–5 pm
Sells: camping; Rents: camping

Great Outdoor Provision Co—Northgate Mall; 919/286-9201
M–F 10 am–9 pm, Sa 10 am–6 pm, Su 1–6 pm
Sells: camping, paddling, fly-fishing, topos

River Runners' Emporium—201 Albemarle St; 919/688-2001
M–F 10 am–8 pm, Sa 9 am–6 pm, Su 12 pm–6 pm
Sells: camping, paddling; Rents: camping, paddling

Lillington

Cape Fear Adventures—100 S Main St; 910/893-3594
M–F 8 am–8 pm, Sa 8 am–9 pm
Rents: canoes; Vehicle Shuttles

Cary

Great Outdoor Provision Co—1105 Walnut St; 919/380-0056
M–Sa 10 am–9:30 pm, Su 1–6 pm
Sells: camping, topos; Rents: camping

REI—255 Crossroads Blvd; 919/233-8444
M–F 10 am–9 pm, Sa 10 am–6 pm, Su 12–6 pm
Sells: camping, paddling, mountain biking, topos;
Rents: camping, paddling

Wilderness House—1249 Kildaire Farm Rd; 919/460-8151
M–F 10 am–7 pm, Sa 10 am–6 pm
Sells: camping; Rents: camping; Trips: hiking

Raleigh

Great Outdoor Provision Co—Cameron Village Shopping Ctr;
919/833-1741. M–F 10 am–9 pm, Sa 10 am–7 pm, Su 1–7 pm
Sells: camping, paddling, fly-fishing; Rents: camping, fly-fishing

Great Outdoor Provision Co—Crabtree Valley Mall; 919/781-1533
M–Sa 10 am–9:30 pm, Su 1–6pm
Sells: camping

Outback Trading Co—7407 Six Forks Rd; 919/847-1099
M–F 10 am–7 pm, Sa 10 am–6 pm
Sells: camping, fly-fishing; Rents: camping

Pro Canoe & Kayak—5710 Capital Blvd; 919/872-6999
M–Sa 10 am–6 pm
Sells: paddling; Rents: paddling

Sports Unlimited—8600 Glenwood Ave; 919/787-7720
M–F 9 am–9 pm, Sa 9 am–9 pm, Su 11 am–6 pm
Sells: camping, paddling, biking, fly-fishing

Wild Bill's Backpacking—1210 Ridge Rd; 919/828-3022
M–Sa 9 am–6 pm
Sells: camping; Rents: camping

Wilson

Adventure Bike & Trail—138 Parkwood Plaza; 919/243-6730
M–Sa 9 am–6 pm
Sells: camping, paddling, mountain bikes; Trips: canoe

Wilmington

Cape Fear Outfitters—1934-A Eastwood Rd; 910/256-1258
M–F 10 am–7 pm, Sa 10 am–6 pm, Su 1–6 pm
Sells: camping, paddling, topos;
Rents: camping, paddling, mountain bikes; Trips: paddling

Wrightsville Beach

Windsurfing & Sailing Center—275 Waynick Blvd;
910/256-9463. M–F 10 am–5 pm, Weekends 10 am–6 pm
Rents: kayaks; Trips: kayaks

Cedar Point

Waterway Marina Rentals—1023 Cedar Point Blvd;
919/393-8008. M–Su 7 am–6 pm
Sells: paddling; Rents: paddling; Vehicle Shuttles

Indian Beach

Island Rigs—1980 Salterpath Rd; 919/247-7787
M–Su 9:30 am–6 pm (summer only)
Sells: kayaks, clothing; Rents: kayaks; Vehicle Shuttles

Ocracoke

Ocracoke Adventures—NC-12; 919/928-7873
Hours vary
Sells & Rents: kayaks (open deck); Trips: kayak

Ride the Wind Surf Shop—NC-12; 919/928-6311
Hours vary
Sells & Rents: kayaks (open deck); Trips: kayak

Manteo

Outer Banks Outdoors—307 Queen Elizabeth Ave; 919/473-2357
M–Sa 10 am–8 pm; Su 10 am–6 pm
Sells: kayaking; Rents: kayaks, mountain bikes;
Trips: kayaking, mountain biking

Nags Head

Kitty Hawk Sports/Kayaks—NC-158, milepost 13; 800/948-0759
M–Su 9 am–9 pm (longer hrs in summer)
Sells: some camping, kayaking; Rents: kayaks;
Trips: paddling, mountain biking

Environmental Organizations

The organizations listed below are working to preserve the natural resources of North Carolina. They're divided here into three groups—local, state, and national & global. Most of the national organizations have local chapters which you're automatically enrolled in when you join.

Aside from names and addresses, I've included the number of members, annual dues, and publications. In some cases, this information was not readily available. Dues refers to the cost for a single adult to join. The letters after the publications indicate the frequency of publication. M=monthly, B=bi-monthly, Q=quarterly.

Local

Association for the Preservation of the Eno River Valley, Inc
4409 Guess Rd, Durham, NC 27712
Dues: $10/yr

Friends of the Blue Ridge Parkway
P.O. Box 341, Arden, NC 28704; 704/687-8722

Lumber River Basin Committee
P.O. Box 2185, Lumberton, NC 28358
Members: 45

North Carolina Coastal Federation
3609 Hwy 24 (Ocean), Newport, NC 28570; 919/393-8185
Members: 3,200; Dues: $15/yr
Publication: *Coastal Review* (Q)

Pamlico-Tar River Foundation
P.O. Box 1854, Washington, NC 27889; 919/946-7211
Members: 2,000; Dues: $15/yr
Publication: *Currents*

Piedmont Land Conservancy
P.O. Box 4025, Greensboro, NC 27404; 910/299-2651
Members: 200; Dues: $25-49/yr
Publication: *Newsline*

Save Our Rivers, Inc
P.O. Box 122, Franklin, NC 28734; 704/369-7877
Members: 75; Dues: $5/yr

The Southern Appalachian Highlands Conservancy
34 Wall St, Suite 802, Asheville, NC 28801-2710; 704/253-0095
Members: 1,600; Dues: $25/yr
Publication: *View from the Highland* (Q)

State

Friends of State Parks
4204 Randleman Rd, Greensboro, NC 27406
Dues: $7.50/yr
Publication: Newsletter (Q)

NC Environmental Defense Fund
128 E Hargett St, Ste 202, Raleigh, NC 27601; 919/821-7793
Members: 7,000; Dues: $10-20/yr
Publications: *EDF Letter, NCEDF Alert*

NC Wildlife Federation
P.O. Box 10626, Raleigh, NC 27605; 919/833-1923
Members: 44,000; Dues: $20/yr
Publication: *Friend of Wildlife*

National & Global

American Hiking Society
P.O. Box 20160, Washington, DC 20041-2160; 703/255-9304
Dues: $25/yr
Publication: *American Hiker* (Q)

American Whitewater Affiliation
P.O. Box 85, Phoenicia, NY 12464
Dues: $20/yr
Publication: *American Whitewater* (B)

Appalachian Trail Conference
P.O. Box 807, Harper's Ferry, WV 25425; 304/535-6331
Members: 24,000; Dues: $25/yr
Publication: *Appalachian Trailway News* (B)

Defenders of Wildlife
1101 Fourteenth St, NW, Suite 1400, Washington, DC 20077
Members: 100,000; Dues: $20/yr
Publications: *Defenders* (Q), *Wildlife Advocate* (Q)

Environmental Defense Fund
275 Park Ave S, New York, NY 10010; 212/505-2100
Members: 250,000; Dues: $20/yr
Publication: *EDF Letter* (M)

The Nature Conservancy
1815 N Lynn St, Arlington, VA 22209; 703/841-5300
Members: 725,000; Dues: $25/yr
Publication: *Nature Conservancy* (B)

National Audubon Society
700 Broadway, New York, NY 10003;
Members: 600,000; Dues: $35/yr
Publication: *Audubon* (B)

Rails-to-Trails Conservancy
1400 Sixteenth St, NW, Suite 300, Washington, DC 20036
Dues: $18/yr
Publication: *Trailblazer* (Q)

The Sierra Club
730 Polk St, San Francisco, CA 94109; 415/776-2211
Members: 550,000; Dues: $35/yr
Publication: *Sierra* (B)

Trout Unlimited
1500 Wilson Blvd, Ste 310, Arlington, VA 22209; 703/522-0200
Members: 70,000; Dues: $25/yr
Publication: *Trout* (Q)

The Wilderness Society
900 Seventeenth S, NW, Washington, DC 20006; 202/833-2300
Members: 300,000; Dues: $30/yr
Publication: *Wilderness* (Q)

Outings Clubs

Carolina Canoe Club
PO Box 12932
Raleigh, NC 27605
Membership: $15–20/yr

Carolina Mountain Club
PO Box 68
Asheville, NC 28802

Lumber River Canoe Club
PO Box 7493
Lumberton, NC 28358
Membership: $10/yr

Nantahala Hiking Club
31 Carl Slagle Road
Franklin, NC 28734

NC Bartram Trail Society
PO Box 144
Scaly Mountain, NC 28775
Membership: $7/yr

Piedmont Appalachian Trail Hikers
PO Box 4423
Greensboro, NC 27404-4423
Membership: $10/yr

Raleigh Ski and Outing Club
PO Box 10364
Raleigh, NC 27605
Membership: $35/yr

Western Carolina Paddlers
PO Box 8541
Asheville, NC 28814
Membership: $12/yr